LEFT OF HOLLYWOOD

Left of Hollywood

*Cinema, Modernism, and the
Emergence of U.S. Radical Film Culture*

CHRIS ROBÉ

UNIVERSITY OF TEXAS PRESS
Austin, Texas

Portions of Chapter Two were first published as "Eisenstein in America:
The *¡Que Viva México!* Debates and the Emergent Popular Front in
U.S. Film Theory and Criticism," *Velvet Light Trap* 54 (2004): 18–31.
Copyright © 2004 the University of Texas Press. All rights reserved.
Portions of Chapter Two were also first published as "Revolting Women:
The Role of Gender in Sergei Eisenstein's *Qué Viva México!* and U.S.
Depression-Era Left Film Criticism," *Jump Cut* 48 (2006). Reprinted
with the permission of the publisher. Chapter Four was first published
as "Taking Hollywood Back: The Historical Costume Drama, the
Biopic, and Popular Front U.S. Film Criticism," *Cinema Journal* 48, no. 2
(2009): 70–87. Copyright © 2009 the University of Texas Press. All
rights reserved.

Requests for permission to reproduce material from this work should be
sent to: Permissions, University of Texas Press, P.O. Box 7819, Austin,
TX 78713-7819, www.utexas.edu/utpress/about/bpermission.html

♾ The paper used in this book meets the minimum requirements of
ANSI/NISO Z39.48-1992 (R1997) (Permanence of Paper).

LIBRARY OF CONGRESS CATALOGING-IN-PUBLICATION DATA

Robé, Chris, 1972–
Left of Hollywood : cinema, modernism, and the emergence of U.S.
radical film culture / Chris Robé. — 1st ed.
    p.   cm.
Includes bibliographical references and index.
ISBN 978-0-292-73753-2
1. Motion pictures—Political aspects—United States—History—20th
century. 2. Motion pictures—Social aspects—United States—
History—20th century. 3. Motion picture industry—United States—
History—20th century. 4. Socialism and motion pictures—United
States. 5. Film criticism—United States—History—20th century.
6. Radicalism—United States—History—20th century. 7. Politics in
motion pictures. 8. Working class in motion pictures. I. Title.
PN1995.9.P6R63 2010
791.43′6581—dc22

                2010019017

Contents

Acknowledgments

As with any sustained creative endeavor, numerous people have influenced the shape and trajectory of this one. I would like to thank first of all the members of my dissertation committee—Alex Doty, Dawn Keetley, and Seth Moglen—who slogged through an avalanche of drafts, going far above and beyond the call of duty. Coming in a close second is the dissertation reading group—Lisa Vetere, John Lennon, Tony Bleach, Tracey Cummings, Harry Brown, and Bob Kilker—which at least had the buffer of cheap beer to endure a still-unfocused project.

Florida Atlantic University has provided an ideal environment in which to complete this project. Eric Freedman and Mike Budd are two of the best colleagues anyone could wish to work with; they shared valuable feedback that sharpened the material. Ryan Moore provoked many late-night discussions regarding the Frankfurt School, thereby assisting in theoretically orienting the manuscript and proving once again the value of Marxist thought in forging meaningful relationships. I would like to thank the graduate students of my Historiography and the Archeology of Film and Media Studies course, who further assisted in indirectly theorizing the project. A Scholarly and Creative Accomplishment Fellowship in the fall of 2007 provided needed course-release time to complete the manuscript.

Numerous people also vitally assisted in collecting archival materials. Ron Magliozzi and Charles Silver of the Film Studies Center in the Museum of Modern Art offered tremendous assistance in tracking down needed resources, often of their own initiative. Tom Brandon, although I never met him, was a pioneer and ceaseless archivist of 1930s Left film culture, supplying the foundations for many studies still to come. The librarians of the New York Public Library were incredibly helpful in tracking down esoteric periodicals. The interlibrary-loan staff of both Lehigh University and Florida Atlantic University diligently answered my numerous requests for "just one more" document.

I would like to thank the anonymous readers of *Cinema Journal* and the *Velvet Light Trap* who supplied vital revision comments regarding early drafts of some of the book's sections. Julia Lessage's precise and nuanced analysis of material from Chapter Two immensely improved its overall shape. Drake Stutesman has offered welcomed encouragement and support ever since first hearing about the project during the Society for Cinema and Media Studies Conference in 2007.

I would also like to thank my editor, Jim Burr, for his enthusiasm regarding the book and for making it a reality.

Bill Tremblay, poet of the West, profoundly affected my scholarship and life by being the first teacher to show me the importance of making my teaching and scholarship an expression of myself.

Finally, and most importantly, I want to thank my family for being so supportive of my work and life. My mother, Barbara Robé, has always symbolized independence, intelligence, and ceaseless curiosity, boldly exposing me to New York City and the arts at an early age. My uncles, Roy and Donald Kowalski, embody the explorer spirit that I have since incorporated into my life, research, and writing. My grandmother and grandfather, Stephanie and Walter Kowalski, represent the tenacity of those second-generation immigrants who, with grit and blind will, thrust themselves out of poverty and staked their claim to a better life, which America, after all, promised. It is upon this promise that this work has been founded.

LEFT OF HOLLYWOOD

Introduction

UNFINISHED PROMISES TO
AN ORPHANED TIME

The aim of the book is [to] gather for scholars and labor etc.
people, especially the young, in one place some basic facts and
areas of experience I am tentatively calling A Missing Chapter
in American Film History: Social and Political Films of the
1930s.

TOM BRANDON TO HIS EDITOR, JUNE 11, 1975

Deep within the archives of the Museum of Modern Art rests Tom
Brandon's incomplete manuscript of *A Missing Chapter in American
Film History: Social and Political Films of the 1930s.* Back in 1970, when
Brandon initiated the project, *A Missing Chapter* was to be the first book-
length study to chronicle the emergence of U.S. Left film criticism during
the 1920s, its developments throughout the 1930s, and its relation to radi-
cal and progressive Depression-era film groups like the Film and Photo
Leagues, NYKino, and Frontier Films.[1]

In many ways, Brandon was well positioned to write this history. Not
only had he meticulously collected thousands of Left film reviews, along
with related brochures, mimeographs, and paraphernalia, but he had also
served as a cameraman, producer, lecturer, and programmer for the New
York Film and Photo League (NYF&PL) during the white-hot years of the
Depression, 1930 to 1935.[2] During Brandon's tenure, the league represented the front lines of radical filmmaking in the United States, coun-
tering the reactionary subject matter and form of commercial newsreels
with its own montage-inflected documentaries that brilliantly illuminated
the flashes of social protest that were being ignited across the country but
banned from its mainstream screens. As the radicalism of the early decade
became tempered into the populism of its later half, Brandon established
his own distribution company, which specialized in foreign, documentary,
and orphan films. Through this company, he gained the rights to key Left
films of the 1930s.[3] Armed with both an intimate, firsthand knowledge
of the NYF&PL and a vast collection of primary sources concerning U.S.

Left film criticism and production, Brandon seemed the ideal candidate to finally recount this grossly neglected period of U.S. film history.

But once immersed in the project, Brandon felt the overwhelming vertigo that afflicts all historians who desire to erect unassailable certainties upon the always-shifting sands of conjecture that accompany archival work. The manuscript is littered with variable interpretations, often at odds with one another. On one page, Brandon writes that the goals of Frontier Films "never were fully realized."[4] Yet three pages later, he declares: "It is significant that despite financial hardships a group [Frontier Films] was not only able to make these films, but that each of them, with one exception, made a contribution in the sense that each had been made for a specific purpose and each, to a great degree, fulfilled that objective at the time it was produced."[5]

As nuances multiplied, history blurred, causing Brandon to seek outside assistance from friends who had participated in events. Yet their responses only further complicated matters by challenging the already shaky framework that Brandon had tentatively erected. Leo Hurwitz proved particularly problematic, caustically accusing the NYF&PL of being "narrow and sectarian" in its refusal to "back [his suggestion of] a full-time, professional type group to experiment etc. and broaden the filmmaking approaches and forms."[6] After several unsuccessful attempts to come to an understanding with Hurwitz, Brandon sent a general letter in September 1974 to surviving league members, asking for their clarification. Brandon implored: "Let us examine as dispassionately as we can and reconstruct the historical process of the reality we experienced and knew."[7]

Yet twelve years after its inception, Brandon's manuscript still foundered on the shoals of passion, selective memory, and archival shards, stubbornly refusing to coalesce into the coherent image of the past that each successive revision attempted to summon, a past that he intimately belonged to but never possessed. In 1982, as his health began to decline, Brandon reluctantly abandoned the project before dying the same year. *A Missing Chapter in American Film History* remains his unfinished promise to an orphaned time, a time that was shunned by the gatekeepers of official history and, even worse, eluded his own tender grasp, which simply wanted to set it down once and for all in the ledgers of history.

Brandon's manuscript serves as a painful testament to the moment when a historian must confront the realization that, in Fredric Jameson's words, "history is *not* a text, not a narrative, master or otherwise, but that, as an absent cause, it is inaccessible to us except in textual form, and that our approach to it and to the Real itself necessarily passes through its prior textualizations."[8] According to Jameson, only by reading texts relationally and allegorically, thereby opening them up "to multiple meanings, to successive rewritings and overwritings which are generated as so many levels and as so many supplementary interpretations," can one begin to construct, after the fact, the ways in which history or the Real itself haunts all cultural forms like an afterimage.[9] Mediation becomes a key concept in reunifying "the fragmentation and autonomization, the compartmentalization and specialization of the various regions of social life" into a totalizing passing glimpse that allows one to tentatively map the ineffable vectors of history and the Real.[10] "The fact that our boundaries are not exact and our categories are always subject to revision," warns Michael Denning, "should not lead us to give up the task."[11] It was precisely Brandon's unvanquishable belief in the exacting categories and impermeable boundaries preached by official historiography that undermined the completion of his project. The traditional methodology of dispassionate examination and historical certainty proved anathema to the counterhistory that Brandon wanted to resurrect.

Walter Benjamin, one of the most astute analysts of the cultural underground during the 1930s, warned against this very methodology when he advised researchers "to abandon the tranquil contemplative attitude toward the object in order to become conscious of the critical constellation in which precisely this fragment of the past finds itself in precisely the present."[12] For Benjamin, the past always weaves into the present, since its very transmission and survival depends upon the production and reception processes of the contemporary moment.[13] The researcher must be cognizant not only of how the present mediates our understanding of the past, but more specifically of how the ruling class deploys selective historical narratives to legitimize its rule.[14]

In opposition to the bourgeois historian who paves over the contingencies of history with a homogeneous, teleological narrative that exonerates the privileged at the expense of the dispossessed, the historical materialist instead seizes hold of those furtive moments in which narrative coherence ruptures under the multivalent pressures of conflicting interests and in which historical possibilities proliferate into tenuous, undecided futures. The historical materialist intercedes by producing "a [theoretical] configuration pregnant with tensions . . . in order to blast a specific era out of the homogeneous course of history—blasting a specific life out of the era or a specific work out of the lifework."[15] As a result, "to articulate the past historically does not mean to recognize it 'the way it really was.' It means to seize hold of a memory as it flashes up at a moment of danger."[16]

Tom Brandon, however, wanted to achieve both—presenting history as "it really was" while seizing hold of a memory of 1930s Left film culture that marked a moment of danger for Hollywood hegemony—without realizing how these mutually exclusive goals doomed his project's ultimate completion.

Despite Brandon's adherence to certain tenets of official history, he was not unaware of the ideological biases that guided traditional film history. He was well schooled in Marxism and ideological analysis. Although Brandon's Marxist perspective might have led at times to his overvalorization of its methodology, it nonetheless provided a useful framework for exposing traditional film history's bourgeois assumptions.

One of Brandon's most insightful critiques interrogates the limited archival sources that most film scholars relied upon when investigating Depression-era film criticism: "Most scholars and film students who concern themselves with criticism in this period have used as their sources 'major' publications and critics, assuming these are to be most properly reflective of the opinions of the day."[17] These scholars failed to recognize the ways in which both a critic's class background and the cultural mode of production inflect the type of criticism produced. Such scholarship naturalizes the bourgeois perspective as *the* one and only American perspective. The independent presses of the historical Left, African American, immigrant, and working-class communities remained unexplored. Specifically in regard to the 1930s, Brandon argues that film scholars' reliance upon such limited bourgeois sources missed "the stirrings of serious socio-aesthetic criticism" found within the film columns of various Left journals and periodicals, which offer a decidedly different picture of 1930s film culture.[18]

In essence, Brandon emphasizes the mediating function of the critic in interpreting culture. This, in many ways, anticipated cultural studies' focus upon the role of the intellectual. As Andrew Ross observes in *No Respect: Intellectuals and Popular Culture*:

> A history of popular culture cannot simply be a history of producers—artists, the culture industries, the impersonal narrative of technological "progress"—and/or a history of consumers—audiences, taste makers, subcultures. It must also be a history of intellectuals—in particular, those experts in culture whose traditional business is to define what is popular and what is legitimate, who patrol the ever shifting borders of popular and legitimate tastes, who supervise the passports, the temporary visas, the cultural identities, the threatening "alien" elements, and

the deportation orders, and who occasionally make their own adventurist forays across the border.[19]

The study of popular culture must also include an analysis of the critics who embed cultural texts within specific interpretative frameworks that guide audiences' reception. This reminds us that no cultural form or text has a necessary class allegiance on its own, but must be fought over by each succeeding generation of critics, intellectuals, and artists "to wrest tradition away from a conformism that is about to overpower it," as Walter Benjamin would have.[20]

The function of U.S. cultural critics took on a heightened importance during the Depression, when seismic socioeconomic transformations shattered the foundations of older belief systems. The onslaught of modernity had been transforming the United States from a producer-based to a consumer-based society since 1900, uprooting older notions of character, family, work, and leisure.[21] The Depression burst through the hallucinatory promises of laissez-faire capitalism as one-third of the U.S. workforce suddenly found itself thrust into a whirlwind of unemployment and a currency shortage. The future suddenly became uncertain as the verities of the past crumbled under the pressure of the present. Cultural critics became modern soothsayers, desperately scanning the horizon for any glimmer of hope, but more often prophesying the onslaught of further storms.

Film critics played a particularly important role in redefining cinema as it flickered dangerously across a liminal zone of cheap amusements and the avant-garde, depravity and reform, American and foreign influences—and the introduction of sound further burst open its possibilities.[22] As Haidee Wasson observes in *Museum Movies: The Museum of Modern Art and the Birth of Art Cinema*, "Throughout the 1920s and 1930s there was a widespread effort to classify, to differentiate, and to build distinct and authoritative frames through which film viewers would ideally enter in order to shape their encounter with films and their experience of cinema."[23] Although many scholars have documented the roles of groups like the Women's Christian Temperance Union, the Legion of Decency, and the Character Education Movement, as well as of institutions such as Columbia University, Harvard University, the New School for Social Research, and the Museum of Modern Art, in redefining cinema spectatorship throughout the 1920s and 1930s, relatively little work has addressed U.S. Left film theorists' and critics' important interventions.[24]

U.S. Left film critics in general wanted to transform their readers into critical spectators who could detect the bourgeois classist, racist, and nationalistic biases within mainstream and independent films while also searching for the utopian moments residing within mass culture and sparking from foreign and independent cinema. Their criticism encouraged readers to explore the ideological implications of both form and content, and the multifaceted ways in which cinema mediated viewers' understanding of history, politics, and the mundane events that defined their lives. Tom Brandon well summarizes U.S. Left film critics' socio-aesthetic outlook:

> To the writers in the Left press, film and their subjects—form and content—were inseparable. For all their concern with technique and the need to innovate, to improve, to bring film nearer to the ideal of what the medium of our time ought to be, they never lost sight of the place of film in society, its role as a force for reform and revolution—film was to be a weapon in changing the world. But, if it was to be such a weapon, they felt, it not only had to convey the collective life of human beings organized in society, but also had to be understood in the collective nature of its own creation.[25]

To transform the nature of film production and recalibrate the larger socioeconomic processes of society as a whole for the better, U.S. Left film critics realized that they first needed to critically intervene in redefining the nature of film spectatorship itself. This would free viewers from seeing the world in a rote, reactionary fashion by extending their visual parameters in progressive directions. Only by enlarging their field of vision could viewers act in substantively more progressive ways. To change the world, one must first see it differently, acting outside the perceptual limits that naturalize poverty, inequality, and injustice and dismiss collective action and utopian hopes as nothing more than pipe dreams.

In general, U.S. Left film theory and criticism anticipated the critical reading strategies deployed by *Cahiers du Cinema, Screen,* and *Jump Cut* during the 1960s and 1970s. Sylvia Harvey's description of *Cahiers* criticism could equally apply to 1930s Left film critics: "A living film culture could not grow simply out of the watching of movies, rather it would grow out of the *relationship* between the act of watching and a critical awareness of the techniques of the cinema. Film education would change the context in which the films were viewed, and make possible a more active role for the spectator: the role of challenging, analyzing and criticizing the spectacle, not simply consuming it."[26] Yet U.S. Left film theorists and critics were interested not only in altering reception practices, but also in harnessing these new modes of reception for mass mobilizations that could alter the functions of the cinematic apparatus and extend into critical interventions in state power and the vectors of capitalism.[27]

In "The Author as Producer," Walter Benjamin critically demarcates between simply supplying the cultural apparatus with material and transforming it in more-egalitarian directions. According to Benjamin, the cultural apparatus possesses manifold abilities to appropriate revolutionary material: "The bourgeois apparatus of production and publication can assimilate astonishing quantities of revolutionary themes, indeed, can propagate them without calling its own existence, and the existence of the class that owns it, seriously into question."[28] U.S. Left film theorists and critics were well aware of Hollywood's endless appropriation of revolutionary themes, as their critiques of films like *Queen Christina* (Mamoulian, 1933), *Viva Villa!* (Conway, 1934), and *Marie Antoinette* (Van Dyke, 1938) bear witness to. With this in mind, they used their columns to transform the cinematic apparatus in three primary ways: by stimulating readers to not only attend foreign and independent films, but also join amateur filmmaking societies, where they could take hold of the cinematic means of production themselves; by interviewing and reporting on sympathetic Left directors, actors, screenwriters, and producers within Hollywood in order to court progressive filmmaking within the studios; and by encouraging readers to join audience groups so that they could use their collective power to demand more-progressive films from the studios and to boycott their more reactionary fare.

U.S. Left film critics hoped also to catalyze mass mobilization in other areas. As Chapter Three demonstrates, they formed interracial alliances between blacks and whites in order to combat lynching and discriminatory racial practices. Furthermore, they organized both within and outside Hollywood against fascism, war profiteering, and antiunion practices. Tom Brandon explains how Left film criticism "meant support for the Spanish Republic; struggle against the non-intervention strangle-hold of U.S. policy and all their supporters: big business, the Catholic Church, isolationists, the Hearst press and right-wingers in all sections. Film criticism had political impact."[29]

A focus on U.S. Left film theory and criticism not only draws needed attention to its critical interventions in redefining film spectatorship and production, but also significantly revises our conception of Hollywood during the 1930s. By studying it, we learn of another Hollywood, one that mainstream film reviews, fan magazines, and studio marketing ignored — one that could have potentially addressed issues of social justice through innovative film styles, caused viewers to reenvision their world in less alienating ways, and promoted international solidarity for a more humane and just future.

A NEW HOLLYWOOD

A study of U.S. Left film theory and criticism moves us away from the decontextualized accounts that typically define 1930s Hollywood, perhaps best exemplified by David Bordwell, Janet Staiger, and Kristin Thompson's *Classical Hollywood Cinema: Film Style and Mode of Production to 1960,* a text that has been routinely attacked by feminist and historical-materialist film scholars since its appearance in 1985. Although it remains a central work in providing an overview of classical Hollywood's technological, aesthetic, and production transformations, it both ignores the contentious internal studio politics of the 1930s and 1940s, and effaces the sociopolitical processes that helped shape Hollywood's practices. According to Miriam Hansen, *Classical Hollywood Cinema* "brackets the history of reception and film culture, along with the cinema's interrelations with American culture at large."[30] Hollywood is thus treated as an entity unto itself, one that freely arranges its labor, products, and styles as it deems appropriate. Although the authors occasionally make vague historical references to internal and external pressures, they assume that competing historical forces were always incorporated into Hollywood's production system rather than significantly challenging its structure.

For example, when remarking on studio unionization in the 1930s, Staiger writes, "In many instances, unions battled less against the owners and more against competing unions for jurisdiction of work functions. These struggles resulted in very distinctly drawn job boundaries."[31] This claim, however, overlooks the fact that much of this infighting was between company-controlled unions and independent unions—no minor distinction. Painters, carpenters, and plumbers fought against the mob-led International Alliance of Theatrical Stage Employees (IATSE), which extorted money from studio moguls while promising a no-strike pledge. The Screen Writers Guild fought for democratic representation and screen credit against the elitist Screen Playwrights, who were allied with the studio bosses. The studios fought tooth and nail against such independent unions, since their formal recognition, and the resulting collective bargaining, would have dramatically curbed moguls' abuses of power and forced them to cede some control of the cultural mode of production back to screenwriters. What seems a minor issue in historical hindsight was of utmost importance at the time. Contrary to Staiger's general dismissal of unionization as simply a solidification of job boundaries, it yielded innumerable alterations to production, distribution, and exhibition practices. Even when such challenges failed to achieve their specific aims, they nonetheless forced studios to alter their practices for better or worse. To ignore these struggles is to ignore the contingency of history.[32]

Additionally, as Miriam Hansen notes, we cannot adequately understand the appeal of mass culture "unless we take seriously the promises of mass consumption, and the dreams of a mass culture often in excess of and conflict with the regime of production that spawned that mass culture."[33] U.S. Left film theory and criticism provides a starting point from which to begin mapping some of the dreams that Hansen mentions.

Contrary to popular assumptions about U.S. Left film critics of the 1930s, they did not regard Hollywood as simply a monolithic entity to rally against. Although it is undeniably true that much of early U.S. Left film theory and criticism was critical of Hollywood, it did not simply view the studios as innately corrupt institutions. Instead, Left film critics viewed those who controlled Hollywood as being largely allied with capitalist interests. But if some historically momentous event allowed progressive collective pressure to be effectively applied, perhaps the cultural mode of production could be disrupted and reconfigured in more-liberating directions. For many on the Left, the Depression signified that historic event.

Hollywood was at its most unstable after the stock market crash, especially during the early 1930s. A third of theaters were closed. Admission prices fell. Severe financial troubles plagued most of the studios by 1933. Four out of eight were in financial disorder: Paramount was bankrupt; RKO and Universal were in receivership; and Fox was under serious reorganization, only to be taken over by Twentieth-Century two years later.[34] Because the Depression struck exactly when Hollywood was investing in costly sound technology, many studios were encumbered with Wall Street loans that had been used to finance their investments and stave off bankruptcy and receivership. Although some historians have argued that Wall Street's intervention in Hollywood at this time further regimented filmmaking, bankers possessed no coherent economic plan—other than admonitions to economize—to impose on the studios.[35] Wall Street lacked sufficient practical knowledge to offer realistic suggestions for reducing production costs.[36]

An unlikely source that well chronicles some of the historic changes that took place within the managerial structure of the studio system in the 1930s is F. Scott Fitzgerald's unfinished novel *The Last Tycoon* (1941).

Rather than seeing such changes as simply enforcing greater regimentation, Fitzgerald's text conjures the 1930s as an uncertain moment of transition between two phases of Hollywood.[37]

The Last Tycoon chronicles the exploits of Monroe Stahr, a character loosely based on the young genius producer Irving Thalberg, who worked for MGM. Fitzgerald takes pains to present Stahr as a transitional figure supplanting the pioneers who founded Hollywood but preceding the newer generation of producers, who viewed its products as nothing more than commodities. Both artistically savvy and ruthlessly materialistic, Stahr leads an intense and ambiguous existence within Hollywood, one that cannot help but be brief, since he is a man located in what are to become two mutually exclusive worlds. As a result, Stahr is deeply conflicted about his role. Fitzgerald has Stahr reflect, "The system was a shame, he admitted—gross, commercial, to be deplored. He had originated it—a fact that he did not mention."[38] Responsible for creating an increasingly standardized and profit-centered system, Stahr is unable, like later producers, to take pride in his ruthless business acumen. In subtle ways, he psychologically distances himself from the system he created. For example, he occasionally produces pictures that he knows will lose money. Stahr explains his reasoning to some of the studio's personnel, "For two years we played safe. It's time we made a picture that'll lose some money. Write it off as good will—this'll bring in new customers . . . We have a certain duty to the public, as Pat Brady [the studio's head] has said at Academy dinners."[39] Stahr justifies the unprofitable picture by claiming that it will generate new customers and benefit the public good. But one also wonders whether Stahr creates financially unsuccessful pictures in order to prove to both others and himself that profit is not his only motive, that aesthetics and the public good still remain symbolically, even if not practically, important.

Although Fitzgerald never mentions what type of money-losing picture Stahr desires to make, many progressive filmmakers and critics during the 1930s were arguing in similar terms for the creation of social-problem, historical, and biographical films. Director William Dieterle, linked to the Communist Party and known for making political biopics, argued in a 1940 issue of *Liberty* that he did not believe that progressive pictures ever lost money, and even if they did, they at least created a superior Hollywood product and appealed to an audience that otherwise never attended Hollywood films.[40]

Furthermore, he adds, "It is also undeniable that the progressive films have gained for the industry as a whole more world-wide and favorable journalistic comment than any other faculty."[41] One sees here how progressive filmmakers and critics could have indirectly benefited from a studio system that contained producers who resembled Monroe Stahr. Unable to come to terms with their profit-driven business acumen, these producers could have provided a creative outlet for progressive filmmakers. Appealing to these producers' desire for superior Hollywood products, Left filmmakers could have created films that were both politically progressive and appealing to a niche audience untapped by more conventional pictures.

Walter Wanger symbolized for Left film critics the producer most receptive to controversial and progressive material. With a showman's knack for enticing various studios to fund his semi-independent ventures, Wanger produced some of the decade's most controversial and political films, including *Washington Merry-Go-Round* (1932), *The Bitter Tea of General Yen* (1932), *Gabriel Over the White House* (1933), *The President Vanishes* (1934), *You Only Live Once* (1937), *Blockade* (1938), and *The Long Voyage Home* (1940). As Matthew Bernstein has shown, Wanger wanted "to educate popular taste, but also to persuade cultural snobs to accept the level of popular taste that prevailed."[42] He felt that film was the perfect medium to reconcile highbrow and lowbrow culture by elevating Hollywood films with ideas and experimental techniques while reminding intellectuals that progressive content could entertain as well as generate thought.[43]

Wanger pursued the production of films "that . . . had nothing financially to gain . . . but the prestige of innovating . . . political subject matter."[44] For example, despite warnings by the Motion Picture Producers and Distributors of America (MPPDA) about the controversial political content in *Gabriel Over the White House,* which advocates a presidential dictatorship, he finished production undeterred and subsequently defended its content. Even after the 1934 Production Code took effect, Wanger produced a controversial political film concerning the Spanish Civil War, *Blockade.* Vehement protests by conservative groups were lodged against the film. It was accused of being Red propaganda despite the removal of all specific political references. Yet Wanger defended the film, not for its implied political stance, but because it represented an initial step toward creating more explicitly political Hollywood films: "It is not *Blockade* reactionaries are fighting against but against the fact that, if *Blockade* is a success, a flood of stronger and stronger films will appear and the films will not only talk but say something. The plan is to frighten the distributor, exhibitor, and producer from attempting films that may say something."[45] Because of Wanger's defense of film as a social force, he became a favorite of U.S. Left film critics by the mid-1930s. As Matthew Bernstein observes,

"No producer in the industry . . . [was] as openly concerned with using movies as a social force."[46]

Another Hollywood producer who served as an ally for progressives was Darryl Zanuck. When Zanuck became head producer at Warner Bros. in 1930, his desire for contemporary topics soon became apparent. According to Thomas Schatz, Zanuck held significant control over the production of Warners' films during the early 1930s because the studio still operated under a central-producer system.[47] Unable to afford assistant producers to assist Zanuck, the studio charged him with personally overseeing most productions. He pushed to make such films as *Little Caesar* (1931), *Public Enemy* (1931), *Five Star Final* (1931), *I Am a Fugitive from a Chain Gang* (1932), and *Gold Diggers of 1933* (1933). As Schatz explains, "Zanuck valued those filmmakers—writers and technicians as well as directors—who could take a news headline or magazine piece, a recent novel or Broadway hit, and transpose it to the screen quickly enough to exploit its social currency."[48] And even when people like Harry Warner and the censors offered wholehearted resistance to a film like *I Am a Fugitive*, he pushed for its production because he believed it would nonetheless appeal to Depression-era audiences.[49]

After Zanuck's departure in 1933, producer Hal Wallis and supervisor Henry Blanke continued his interest in pursuing socially conscious films. They were responsible for some of the most acclaimed biopics of the mid to late 1930s: *The Story of Louis Pasteur* (1936), *The Life of Emile Zola* (1937), and *Juarez* (1939). In a sociological study of Hollywood published in 1941, Leo Rosten reported that most screenwriters considered Warners the best studio because of its receptivity to dramatizing socially relevant themes: "The preference of movie writers for Warner Brothers' pictures, many of them indicated in their answers, rests upon the fact that Warner Brothers 'are not afraid to do films on current political topics' . . . The unsaccharine realism and substance of Warners' general output elicits more respect from writers than florid spectacles with star-studded casts produced by other studios."[50]

Furthermore, Warners took the strongest political stance against the growing threat of fascism. It was the first studio to discontinue doing business with Nazi Germany, to reject newsreels glorifying Hitler, and to excise pro-Nazi material from news shorts.[51] Rosten praised Hollywood's antifascist stance, claiming, "It will be to Hollywood's credit that it fought the Silver Shirts, the German-American Bund, and the revived Ku Klux Klan at a time when few realized their ultimate menace."[52]

But it wasn't simply that some producers showed interest in controversial, contemporary topics that offered U.S. Left film theorists and critics hope that Hollywood might be more receptive to progressive films. More importantly, these theorists and critics advocated and chronicled a host of other transformations occurring inside and outside the studios, making Hollywood more sympathetic to Left ideas in general. Although producers like Wanger and Zanuck might not have been averse to progressive filmmaking, U.S. Left film theorists and critics were well aware that collective pressure would need to be placed upon the studios if more such films were to be made.

One of the most significant internal factors that liberalized Hollywood was the change in composition of the film community in the early to mid-1930s. A large influx of progressively minded German émigrés had escaped from Nazi Germany and come to Hollywood, and a significant number of the liberal New York literati had relocated to Hollywood, since it provided the best opportunity to be involved in a medium that might translate their political and artistic ideas to a wider audience.[53] Many of the writers, directors, and actors from New York had been affiliated with the Left before arriving at the studios. Screenwriter John Bright had contacts with the anarchist movement. John Howard Lawson, Clifford Odets, John Garfield, and Elia Kazan came from the Group Theatre. Others, like Paul Jarrico, Maurice Rapf, James Cagney, and Paul Muni, grew up in working-class environments that made them sympathetic to Left causes. Furthermore, many of these actors, screenwriters, and directors knew writers from radical publications like the *New Masses* and the *Daily Worker*, as well as members of the independent and avant-garde East Coast film communities; together, these diverse groups established an informal social network among themselves.[54]

Because of the growing number of Left film workers in Hollywood, the film community became increasingly politicized throughout the decade. Perhaps the most significant cause of this politicization was the community's growing awareness of the threat of fascism, exemplified by the flood of émigrés from Nazi Germany. The rise of antifascist sentiment within the film community, according to Tom Brandon, "changed the complexion of Hollywood for the better . . . and gave many people in the Left cause for hope. Part of this was the increased activism and awareness of those most prominent in Hollywood, the stars of the screen."[55] The Spanish Civil War further galvanized the progressive Hollywood community. In 1937, the Motion Picture Artists Committee for Loyalist Spain was founded. In

1938, the Motion Picture Democratic Committee was formed. But most important was the creation of the Hollywood Anti-Nazi League (HANL) in 1936.

The HANL was initiated by two German refugees: Prince Hubertus Löwenstein and Otto Katz.[56] Katz, who had close connections with the Hollywood community, involved such figures as Charlie Chaplin, Fritz Lang, Clark Gable, David Selznick, and Greta Garbo with the organization. As Neal Gabler points out in *An Empire of Their Own: How the Jews Invented Hollywood,* although the HANL's primary task was to fight fascism, it also centralized many of Hollywood's Left activities.[57] The league "sponsored two weekly radio programs, published its own bi-weekly tabloid, *Hollywood Now,* and generated a number of subcommittees to address and educate specific constituencies—women, youth, labor, race, religion, professions."[58] Saverio Giovacchini adds that the HANL used the antifascist struggle to unify various social rituals, like parties and social gatherings, in Hollywood: "In many cases, the organization politicized the traditional hangouts of the Hollywood New Yorkers and the salons of the refugees."[59] Furthermore, the group desired to produce creative works with antifascist messages. Perhaps slightly overstating the case, Giovacchini claims that the "HANL strove to reconcile what up until that time had been considered opposites: anti-Nazi struggle and Hollywood."[60] The HANL was, in any event, one of the central forces that brought the antifascist struggle to the forefront of Hollywood's films.[61]

Contemporary film critics often remarked on the growing politicization of Hollywood. Margaret Thorp, a professor at Yale who wrote a book on Hollywood in 1939, observed that antifascism might have been the main cause for such politicization: "It may have been the Spanish War, which caused eager partisanship for the anti-Fascist cause. Stars gave benefit parties; screen writers spoke at meetings; directors raised money for ambulances. Their interest spread from the oppressed in Europe to the oppressed in California. They worked for Tom Mooney. They helped the Salinas strikers."[62] Similarly, Joseph North noticed how the awareness of fascism abroad made the Hollywood community more aware of domestic oppression: "Hollywood could stand and look into the camp at Dachau. It happened in Germany. Could it happen here? Hollywood artists remembered the Scottsboro case; it wasn't fascism but something like it, they thought. A group of them had banded together to try to free the obviously framed Negro boys."[63]

Another unifying internal political force was the formation of the Screen Actors Guild (SAG) and the Screen Writers Guild (SWG) in 1933.

SAG was affiliated with the American Federation of Labor in 1934 and recognized by producers in May 1937, after the threat of a strike.[64] The SWG went through a greater struggle during its fight with the elitist, studio-controlled union, Screen Playwrights. Although the SWG won recognition by the National Labor Relations Board in 1938, it was not until 1942 that the producers signed an agreement with it.[65] As Larry Ceplair and Steven Englund have observed, the fight over unionization "showed where the real conflict in Hollywood lay—not over money, but over the control of movie making."[66]

According to Michael Denning, these unionization efforts were a central part of the Hollywood Popular Front, since they radicalized many screenwriters, artists, and musicians who worked for the studios.[67] Because of management's harsh reaction to the guilds' formation, many creative personnel who had once sympathized with management no longer did so. For example, screenwriter Maurice Rapf recounts a speech made by Irving Thalberg on May 1, 1936, in the MGM commissary. Thalberg demanded that the SWG not vote to amalgamate with the Author's League the following day, since such a merger would undercut Hollywood's and the screenwriters' autonomy. Rapf recalls, "It was a tough speech . . . People who had known him and worked with him and thought he was a nice guy saw him so tough and so hard that we were absolutely shocked."[68] Writers rebelled against Thalberg's and other producers' reactionary stances by flocking to the SWG and voting for amalgamation. Joseph North saw the fight for the guilds as a valuable educational experience. He claimed that the struggle succeeded "in smashing the illusion of the Motion Picture Academy as a pro-labor quantity."[69] As writers and actors joined together to fight for their rights, they were creating a base that enabled other Left organizations to push Hollywood in progressive directions.

A major external factor that U.S. Left film theorists and critics cited for destabilizing Hollywood was the stock market crash of 1929. Initially, the crash seemed as if it would bulwark Hollywood's conservatism. There was a fear of Wall Street gaining control of the industry because of the money it provided to bail out many of the studios. Lewis Jacobs writes in *The Rise of the American Film,* "A new fight . . . began as the Morgan and Rockefeller interests went after the sound-film business with a firm determination to control it."[70] The critic Joseph North quoted a *Wall Street Journal* article that purported to represent the New York financial community's conservative stance toward film production: "You have seen the last for many a long day of these gallant gallopings toward the goal of artistry . . . Definitely no more flirtings with the 3 or 4 percent of the movie going population who cry aloud for 'better pictures.' No, sir. From now on we're as practical as all get-out, with an eye on the box-office and to hades with art for art's sake."[71] Although the *Journal* was explicitly referring to art films, North understood that such a rejection implied a renunciation of all politically progressive films, since they also appealed to a minority audience and did not often translate into large box-office returns.

Despite Wall Street's attitude, North and other critics realized that countervailing forces allowed Hollywood to ignore the bankers' socioeconomic mandates. One was the rise of U.S. independent and avant-garde productions and the growing exhibition of foreign films. As Jan-Christopher Horak has demonstrated, the Little Cinema movement dramatically expanded in the U.S. during the mid to late 1920s. It "provided both an exhibition outlet for the avant-garde and European art films and an alternative to the commercial cinema chains dominated by the major Hollywood studios."[72] Audiences, at least urban ones, had access to a wider variety of films than ever before. These films offered exciting challenges to Hollywood's hegemony. Robert Forsythe, a *New Masses* critic, wrote in 1934, "As a general proposition I should say that one Soviet picture to every six from Hollywood would be necessary to maintain sanity" and prevent oneself from completely falling sway to the allure of Hollywood spectacle.[73] According to Forsythe, Soviet films' reliance upon montage exposed U.S. audiences to the ideological and aesthetic limits of typical Hollywood fare. Independent, avant-garde, and foreign films provided viewers with a wider understanding of film aesthetics and content; therefore, they provided a check on standard Hollywood fare by revealing its socio-aesthetic limits while fostering demand for more-sophisticated film alternatives.

Independent, avant-garde, and foreign films assisted not only in developing spectators' critical responses, but also in extending the range of filmic possibilities within Hollywood itself. Joseph North writes: "Independent movies have pointed the way: pioneers like Joris Ivens, in his Spanish and Chinese films, Paul Strand's Mexican work, Herbert Kline's Czechoslovakian documentary. Add to that the entrance of the government on the scene—Pare Lorentz's *The River* and *The Plow That Broke the Plains*—splendid jobs—and you see what is prodding the Hollywood moguls."[74] Many Left film critics felt that Eisenstein's *¡Que Viva México!* (1932) prodded MGM's decision to film *Viva Villa!* (1934) in the same location, that the epic cinematography of the Dust Bowl seen in Pare Lorentz's *The Plow That Broke the Plains* (1936) influenced Gregg Toland's cinematography for *The Grapes of Wrath* (1940), and that the popularity of Joris Ivens's documentary on the Spanish Civil War, *The Spanish Earth*

(1937), led Walter Wanger to produce his own film on the same subject, *Blockade*, starring Henry Fonda.[75]

NEW AUDIENCES

U.S. Left film critics' desire to foster critical spectatorship and to collectively mobilize a demand for progressive films was centered on several audience organizations that had been formed by the mid-1930s. In many ways, the Left was emulating its conservative counterparts like the Legion of Decency, which had effectively pressured Hollywood during the early 1930s to create the Breen Office and to rigorously enforce the Production Code.[76] To combat such pressure groups' reactionary influence upon commercial film production, the Left established its own audience organizations, hoping to sway studios in the other direction.

The New Film Alliance (NFA), one of the first such groups, also attempted to mass-distribute independent, avant-garde, and foreign films. Founded in September 1935 by members of NYKino, the Film and Photo League, and others, it proposed a series of ambitious goals. As William Alexander notes, "Modeling itself on the new theater movement, the organization intended to coordinate independent film producers throughout the country, to provide sponsorship, distribution, et cetera, to build a strong audience organization, and to present a lecture series, screenings of nondistributed classics, and a magazine."[77] The NFA counted among its members progressive screenwriters Albert Maltz, John Howard Lawson, and Clifford Odets, but it lasted for only eight or nine months.[78] Its main successes included the creation of a lecture series, the screening of progressive films at the New School for Social Research, and the compiling of a film library for progressive groups' use.[79] Although the NFA was influential only on the East Coast, many of its members helped organize powerful national audience organizations shortly thereafter.

Probably the most effective audience organization was the Associated Film Audiences (AFA), created in March 1937. Its membership was drawn from groups like the Federal Council of Churches of Christ, the National Council for the Prevention of War, and the Workers Alliance and included Hollywood insiders like Fritz Lang, Walter Wanger, Dudley Nichols, and Fredric March.[80] The group defined itself in the following way: "Associated Film Audiences represents the interests of church, social, racial, labor, and educational and youth groups. Its purpose is to give Hollywood every encouragement to produce films that give a true and socially useful portrayal of the contemporary scene; to encourage production of films that will better the understanding between racial and religious groups; and to encourage the production of anti-war films. Conversely, it is opposed to any film portraying militarist, anti-labor, or reactionary attitudes in a favorable light."[81] According to Tom Brandon, the AFA's most important activity was to organize audience groups in New York, Los Angeles, and Washington, D.C., in order to pressure exhibitors to show progressive films and ban reactionary ones.[82] The AFA conducted radio broadcasts, lectures, film screenings, and discussions, and published two newsletters, *Film Survey* in New York and *Film News* in Los Angeles.[83]

The newsletters contained information about social and political activities, such as unionization in Hollywood, pending legislation regarding the studios, criticism of the Hays Office and the Legion of Decency, and reports on film and politics in other countries.[84] But Brandon believes that the group's most valuable endeavor "was its evaluation of films and recommendations for possible films to boycott or support."[85] Each month new films were evaluated by AFA's participating organizations for their social and political content. Some of the questions asked were:

1. Does it [the film] portray the contemporary social scene?
    a. Does it give a false impression of any strata of society? Living conditions? Working conditions?
4. Are there any references to religious, racial, national groups? Or their members? Direct? Indirect?
    a. Name the groups portrayed.
    b. Does the comic relief tend to caricature race? Religion? Nationality? Individual?[86]

Surprisingly, many producers, in their desire for support and viewers, announced their willingness to cooperate with the AFA by sending it their scripts well before production.[87] As Howard Dietz of MGM stated, "We do not care what their political views may be if they can help us put people in line at box offices."[88]

Brandon notes how the AFA drew particular attention to Warner Bros. pictures in the hopes of spurring Warners to make more progressive films in the future. One way the AFA supported films was by "buying blocks of tickets to the film and selling them to labor unions and other groups, advertising the films for free, and urging audience organizations locally to mobilize for the films."[89] By 1939, AFA was confident that mainstream screens were changing for the better "and that audience organizations were an important factor in shaping this process."[90]

Even Will Hays, the censorship czar who had been proclaiming Hollywood films to be "pure entertainment" for the past seventeen years, had to admit in 1939 that film possessed a social function: "The past year had been notable for the rising tide of discussions as to the social function of the screen . . . The increasing number of pictures produced by the industry which treat honestly and dramatically many current themes proves that there is nothing incompatible between the best interests of the box office and the kind of entertainment that raises the level of audience appreciation."[91] Margaret Thorp assessed Hays's turnabout as "an official recognition of a force which had at last grown too strong to be ignored . . . More and more intelligent comment on the film is being written and read, more and more people are going to the movies not just to relax or to pass the time but for the same reasons that take them to the theater."[92] Audiences were making clear to the industry and its observers that they wanted smarter, more progressive films.

Because of the gradual strengthening of Left film communities within and outside Hollywood, and because of the disastrous effects of the Depression on Hollywood's profits, many Left film theorists and critics who once held the belief that the studio system was unwaveringly conservative had to reevaluate their positions. Clifford Howard, a critic for the journal *Close Up,* believed in 1931 that although "culture, art, and genius have been lured in abundance to the cinema capital," it has "for the most part . . . [been] rebuffed and denied."[93] Yet a mere year later, he stated, "Hollywood today is more nearly in tune with the normal honesties of life than it has been since the days when Jesse Lasky and Sam Goldwyn made pictures in a barn and ate their lunches from paper bags . . . It will not be the first time in human experience that stress and disaster have served as an ultimate good."[94] Lewis Jacobs, a film critic for the journal *Experimental Cinema,* recounted how Dalton Trumbo wrote in the *Hollywood Spectator,* "'All hail collapse.'"[95] Trumbo "voiced the general opinion that the public and the industry were being purged by the depression and would emerge intellectually, socially, and economically improved."[96] Or as Frank Daugherty stated more bluntly in 1932, Hollywood had one of two choices: "to develop itself intelligently, and within its limitations to seek full expression — or to die."[97] Either Hollywood had to live up to its potential by creating films that intelligent audiences wanted to see, or it would collapse under its own weight as audiences rejected formulaic films that seemed to have no relation to contemporary life.[98]

As the decade progressed, U.S. Left film critics took note of the positive changes occurring within the studios. Many encouraged their readers to become involved with local audience groups and amateur film societies in order to continue influencing Hollywood films in progressive directions. In 1939, Joseph North saw the battle over Hollywood as one between Wall Street and Main Street: "Wall wants retrenchment—scuttles socially intelligent pictures. Main—since 1931—wants better pictures, something corresponding to the bewildering realities of our time."[99] Main Street always trumps Wall Street, according to North's and others' analyses, since it represents the majority opinion, which Wall Street must heed if it wants to keep its coffers full.

Although one can debate the amount of influence the Left had upon Hollywood, the studios increasingly became the focus of U.S. Left film theorists and critics as the decade progressed—not least because Hollywood represented a site of democratization where audiences could influence the kind of pictures produced and where the techniques of independent, avant-garde, and foreign films could converge to create a superior product, one that appealed to both intellect and emotions. As Margaret Thorp noted in 1939, "The movie seems to be quite as capable of proceeding on two levels as the Elizabethan tragedy: poetry and psychology for the gentleman's galleries, and action and blood for the pit."[100] Yet many U.S. Left film critics would add that the "gentlemen" also want as much action and blood as the "pit," and that the "pit" wants as much psychology and poetry as the "gentlemen."

Film was an ideal medium for Left theorists and critics since it seemed to be the one most open to democratization. Unlike painting, theater, and literature, which had to contend with an ingrained cultural elitism, film was a relatively new medium that was often disparaged for its proximity and appeal to the working class. Film was struggling to establish itself as a valid, autonomous art form, a task made difficult because it seemed to contain so many contradictory tendencies and influences. It was a product of an industrial technology that seemed to threaten older art traditions, yet it strongly influenced the modernist experimentation occurring in the other arts. Was it the destroyer of fine art or its rehabilitator? Its mainstream production system seemed to be adaptable—it could work within a capitalist, a communist, or a fascist infrastructure. Film could be abstract, surreal, political, narrative, poetic, or, most often, a mixture of styles and genres. In the 1930s, film had yet to take on the mutually exclusive categorizations that would later arbitrarily isolate the documentary from the experimental, and either of those from the commercial. Hollywood could potentially belong to "the people" in the 1930s because film, at the time, belonged to no one.

Rather than regarding Hollywood simply as a proverbial "dream factory" that banished the Depression from its screens for Technicolor hal-lucinations of better times—the story relentlessly purveyed by traditional film histories—U.S. Left film theorists and critics increasingly viewed it as a site of socio-aesthetic conflict where progressive visions might actu-ally be enacted under the external and internal pressures of the Left. But this distinction often gets overlooked by traditional film history, since its scholars paint these critics, when they are noticed at all, as nothing more than a group of reactionary Marxists who blindly rejected Hollywood spectacle for Soviet-style filmmaking.[101] Such a view not only overlooks the theoretical transformations that U.S. Left film theory and criticism underwent throughout the 1930s, but also reduces the multivalent posi-tions and debates held by its theorists and critics into a one-dimensional caricature.

CONCEPTUAL REVISIONS

There are numerous reasons why U.S. Left film theory and criticism has been largely ignored by film studies. One stems from cultural historians' general dismissal of members of the 1930s cultural Left as nothing more than communist dupes. According to Michael Denning, the history of "fel-low travelers" who allied themselves with Marxism throughout the 1930s, and especially during the Popular Front years (1935–1939), is all too often "told as a morality tale of seduction and betrayal, utopian dreams and Cold War disenchantment," even by the most sympathetic of scholars.[102]

The Popular Front refers to a change in the Communist Party's po-litical stance, which was officially declared in 1935 at the Seventh Con-gress of the Communist International in Moscow. Instead of opposing other Left groups, like socialists, democrats, and anarchists, as it had previously done, the party initiated a coalition among them in order to collectively combat the rising threat of international fascism.[103] After all, political infighting between communists and socialists in Germany had al-lowed Hitler to ascend to power almost unopposed. Bourgeois democra-cies, once the declared enemies of communism, were now considered vital allies.

For many cultural historians, the U.S. Popular Front has all too typi-cally symbolized the Edenic fall of the American Left. Supposedly taking orders directly from Moscow, the Communist Party USA (CPUSA) infested domestic Left organizations and groups with its dogmatic platitudes and demands for lockstep political obedience. When all was said and done, a small core of communists secretly took hold of the political reigns of the U.S. cultural Left, opportunistically seizing the ideals of democracy to mislead fellow travelers while pursing their own self-interested goals. After 1939, when the Nazi-Soviet Pact threw the Communist Party on the defensive and initiated the dissolution of the U.S. Popular Front (named the Democratic Front domestically), fellow travelers were left reeling from the party's wake of shattered ideals and political bad faith, never to fully recover. Or so the story goes.

This outlook, however, has been increasingly discredited by scholars such as Alan Wald, Robin D. G. Kelley, Cary Nelson, Paula Rabinowitz, Barbara Foley, and Bill Mullen, who have challenged the center-periphery model that has typically framed debates concerning the U.S. cultural Left and the Popular Front in general.[104] Contrary to the belief that a small core of communists constituted the center of the U.S. Popular Front, Michael Denning argues that "the periphery was in many cases the center, the 'fellow travelers' *were* the Popular Front . . . The heart of the Popular Front as a social movement lay among those who were non-Communist socialists and independent leftists, working with Communists and liberals, but marking out a culture that was neither a Party nor a liberal New Deal culture."[105] According to Denning, one must stop treating the Popular Front and its multiple Left coalitions as an example of party politics as usual and instead consider them, in Gramscian terms, as a "historical bloc," which is a "complex, contradictory, and discordant *ensemble*" of social forces and groups vying for sociopolitical control.[106] The crash of 1929 should be viewed as a trigger for a crisis of hegemony in the United States, as "a moment when social classes became detached from their traditional parties . . . The years of the depression and war saw a prolonged 'war of position' between political forces trying to conserve the existing structures of society and the forces of opposition, including the Popular Front social movement, who were trying to create a new historical bloc, a new balance of forces."[107] Although the CPUSA must be given its due, since "it was without doubt the most influential left organization in the period and its members were central activists in a range of formations and institutions," it did not centrally control the U.S. Popular Front and the cultural Left.[108]

In a related vein, I argue that U.S. Left film theory and criticism must be regarded as a social formation that preceded the emergence of the Popular Front but eventually aligned itself with its antiracist and antifascist positions. I am specifically invoking Raymond Williams's definition of "social formation" to describe U.S. Left film theory and criticism: "those effective movements and tendencies, in intellectual and artistic life, which have significant and sometimes decisive influence on the active development of a culture, and which have a variable and often oblique relation to formal institutions."[109] Williams goes on to explain why the explication of social formations requires new analytical procedures: "Since such formations relate, inevitably, to real social structures, and yet have highly variable and often oblique relations with formally discernible social institutions, any social and cultural analysis of them requires procedures radically different from those developed for institutions."[110] Since traditional film studies mainly provided textual and institutional analyses, they were methodologically ill equipped to address the active role of social formations in defining film culture, at least until the widespread introduction of cultural studies into the theoretical framework of the field during the mid-1980s.

Pioneering studies of U.S. Left film theory and culture include William Alexander's *Film on the Left* (1981) and Russell Campbell's *Cinema Strikes Back* (1982), which focus on select organizations like the New York Film and Photo League, NYKino, and Frontier Films, and figures such as Joris Ivens, Pare Lorentz, and Willard Van Dyke.[111] However, both Alexander and Campbell underestimate the expansive origins and nature of Depression-era U.S. Left film theory and criticism, which exceeded narrow definitions of the Left, the confines of its cultural and political organizations, and even national boundaries.

Tom Brandon notes an example of this expansiveness: "Many of the critics who regularly wrote for the Left Press were also gainfully employed or contributed to such publications as *Esquire, The National Board of Review Magazine, Variety, The Nation, The New Republic,* and the like. Under their impetus, film criticism came of age in many of these publications as well as in the Left-publications proper."[112] *Collier's* liberal film critic Kyle Crichton also wrote radical film criticism for the *New Masses* under the pseudonym Robert Forsythe.[113] Harry Alan Potamkin wrote for the avant-garde cinema journals *Close Up* and *Hound and Horn,* the Marxist periodicals *New Masses* and *Experimental Cinema,* and mainstream publications such as the *New York Times* and *Vanity Fair.* This reveals some Left film theorists' and critics' understanding of the need to contribute both to independent, radical film journals that catered to a selective, politicized audience and to mainstream bourgeois publications with large readerships.

By middecade, the interests of liberal and radical film critics had converged. According to Myron Lounsbury, "Liberal critics began to encourage the scattered signs of social responsibility in the commercial movie and to point out precedents of political and economic issues found in the

American film tradition."[114] Similarly, radical critics tempered their tone with populist rhetoric and an intellectual willingness to explore the progressive potential of commercial film.

Because the origins and developments of U.S. Left film theory and criticism are found in both Left publications and bourgeois periodicals that were nonetheless sympathetic to some aspects of Left film analysis, I use the term "U.S. Left film theory and criticism" somewhat ambiguously in order to mirror the wide spectrum of socio-aesthetic positions held by various writers, who all nonetheless viewed film and film theory and criticism as central cultural implements for enacting progressive social change. It encompasses those theorists and critics who were self-identified with a specific brand of Left politics, those who advocated a progressive stance but refused to affiliate themselves with any specific Left ideology, and those who rejected the term "political" altogether but still felt that film's natural affinity with aesthetic experimentation could lead to radically egalitarian ways of envisioning the world. As Lewis Jacobs, a member of the NYF&PL and Left film historian, recounts: "We were all idealists. You know, which varied, some completely aesthetic, some partly aesthetic and partly political, some mostly political and a little aesthetic, it varied. And we were open more or less, to the combination of both the aesthetic and political, because the times were very political."[115] One must sacrifice the precision of the term "Left" for a broader definition and a fluid framework that can better map U.S. Left film theory and criticism as a multivalent social formation.

Anna Everett began to chart this new terrain in *Returning the Gaze: A Genealogy of Black Film Criticism, 1909–1949*. She explores the shared outlook between black and white Depression-era film critics about mobilizing "black filmgoers into a ready force of critical consumers forever on the alert for Hollywood films' 'ingenuity in anesthetizing oppression.'"[116] By excavating film columns found in the black and white presses, Everett identifies an interracial formation that was ignored by prior scholarship regarding 1930s U.S. Left film culture. As this study will show, this interracial solidarity became more pronounced during the Popular Front era, when antiracist and antifascist causes converged in the Left political imaginary, causing black and white film critics to collectively focus their attention on antilynching films.

Everett's work exemplifies Ella Shohat and Robert Stam's insistence that film and media scholars must think relationally about culture and its products: "Rather than taking cultural products and simply thumbing them up or down, cultural critique needs to see contemporary popular culture in a fissured, relational context, to ask who is producing and consuming what, for what purposes, in what situation, for whom, and by what means—always with an eye on the power of constellations and the emancipatory projects at stake."[117] By doing so, one is better able not only to identify how social formations always exceed the limits of organizational and institutional structures, but also to chart their multiple vectors that escape geographical and national boundaries.

A relational approach is particularly important for identifying how U.S. Left film theory and criticism had its theoretical origins in the avant-garde British film journal *Close Up*. During the late 1920s, Lewis Jacobs recalls, "There were no magazines that I knew of outside of one magazine that had come from England called *Close Up* that really dealt with film in a serious way."[118] Myron Lounsbury asserts that the journal "was the most significant attempt to establish lines of communication between artists and intellectuals of different nations," adding that it "presented a significant source of theoretical writing to American critics" throughout the 1920s and early 1930s.[119]

Close Up, founded in 1927, was the first English-language film journal. Yet its importance to the development of international film theory, and U.S. Left film theory in particular, has been consistently ignored by scholars, since the journal's eclectic style has made it difficult to categorize. As Anne Friedberg rightly observes: "Because the writing in *Close Up* crosses many borders—between literary prose and theoretical writing, between avant-garde manifesto and journalistic *feuilleton,* between film production and literary modernism—it effectively overruns the canonical boundaries of disciplinary republics."[120]

If anything, *Close Up* has been primarily classified by scholars as a modernist journal, with special emphasis given to the writings of H.D. and Dorothy Richardson. Because of *Close Up*'s links with high literary modernism, and because of disciplinary boundaries that foreclose relational approaches between literary and film studies, most film historians have missed the journal's importance as a forum for the development of Left film theory. Furthermore, problematic aesthetic assumptions concerning modernism in general have decontextualized *Close Up* from the Left political landscape, wrongly leading many scholars to believe that modernism represents an outright rejection of politics altogether.

This apolitical and extremely limited perspective of modernism has a particularly tenacious hold within literary studies. It is the product of Cold War-era critics like Clement Greenberg, Lionel Trilling, and Philip Rahv, who rewrote U.S. cultural history to dissociate their endorsement of modernism from their former Marxist politics, which were increasingly coming under attack. By decoupling modernism from Left politics, they effectively jettisoned history and modernism's divergent strains for a canon of select authors and a critical practice in which primary attention would be given to formal experimentation and biographical details. But as Haidee Wasson rightly critiques, this approach "explains little of the expansive series of ideas, practices, and political commitments designated by the umbrella term *modernism* and explains even less about the very conditions of possibility for modernist practice itself."[121]

Rejecting this approach, scholars like Fredric Jameson, Miriam Hansen, Haidee Wasson, and Ben Singer have recontextualized modernism into the sociocultural matrices of modernity and modernization to identify and historicize its multiple strains and practices.[122] Only by understanding the social, economic, and political upheavals of modernity can one fully grasp modernists' varied socio-aesthetic goals. Jameson writes, "Their own vocation for aesthetic change and new and more radical artistic practices finds itself powerfully reinforced and intensified at large in the social world outside."[123]

Additionally, by reconnecting modernism to its cultural moment, scholars have expanded our understanding of how its processes stretched beyond the remote confines of the literary and artistic avant-garde and into the sociopolitical and technological changes of everyday life. Miriam Hansen believes that modernism must be understood as a mass movement, since most people stood to benefit (as well as suffer) from its effects: "There were enough people who stood to gain from the universal implementation of at least formally guaranteed political rights; from a system of mass production that was coupled with mass consumption (that is, widespread affordability of consumer goods); from a general improvement of living conditions enabled by actual advances in science and technology; and from the erosion of long-standing social, sexual, and cultural hierarchies."[124]

Cinema stood on the cusp of modernization and modernism. A product of the scientific and technological advances that modernity ushered in during the late nineteenth-century, cinema represented a rupture with older forms of vision and living, as well as the promise of the new age that modernism, in its most utopian moments, embodied. For U.S. Left film theorists and critics, cinema logically drew together modernist experimentation and a collective social vision. According to Tom Brandon: "Film answered two contemporary needs—a more dynamic and imaginative form of expression to match the inventive new conceits of 'modern art' that were bursting old forms at the seams in all other spheres; and a social vision of our industrial world that could best be conveyed by the machine-oriented, collective medium which films are."[125] Aesthetics and politics converged within film, making it an increasingly relevant and influential mass medium for U.S. Left film theorists and critics as the Depression worsened.

As we will see, the intersection of modernist aesthetics and ideology was a central concern throughout 1930s U.S. Left film theory and criticism, anticipating the debates that preoccupied Marxist and feminist film theorists during the 1960s and 1970s. A transnational perspective dominated 1930s U.S. Left film theory and criticism: it continually looked abroad for socio-aesthetic models that might challenge American assumptions or be adapted to them. During the late 1920s and early 1930s, Soviet montage theory dominated the discussion. Theorists and critics used montage as a pliable concept for the ideological analysis of foreign, independent, and American films. They also championed it as a cinematic form that could challenge Hollywood's hegemonic style; this challenge was best exemplified by the works of Sergei Eisenstein and his Mexican film, *¡Que Viva México!* By middecade, after realizing that Soviet-style montage would never successfully unsettle Hollywood's domestic reign, Left theorists and critics turned to the work of Jean Renoir, specifically *La Marseillaise* (1938), as a new model of the progressive directions open to Hollywood filmmaking. In the interim, U.S. Left film theorists and critics turned their sights on the antilynching film and Fritz Lang's *Fury* to explore how some mainstream cinematic styles might be redeployed for progressive ends in both independent and commercial cinema.

By overlooking Depression-era U.S. Left film theory and criticisms' international origins and transnational influences, most film historians have underestimated its theoretical acumen and aesthetic scope. Paul Buhle and Dave Wagner have dismissed this entire body of criticism as "more political rage than intellectual advance."[126] Other scholars, like Russell Campbell, have interpreted 1930s Left film culture and criticism within the limited aesthetic criteria of socialist realism, a term that all too often assumes an opposition between Left film culture and modernist experimentation.[127] Only by studying this film theory and criticism relationally can we begin to adequately assess both its sophisticated international vision, which studied the developments of foreign cinema in order to inform its socio-aesthetic outlook, and its interracial stance, which harnessed the critical viewing strategies found in the black and white press to combat racism both on and off the screen.

MALE ANXIETIES: GENDER AND U.S. LEFT
FILM THEORY AND CRITICISM

Despite U.S. Left film theorists' and critics' fostering of critical spectators, interracial alliances, and general advances in the ideological analysis of film, they nonetheless maintained a rather reactionary stance toward gender issues. Unfortunately, all scholarship regarding 1930s U.S. Left film theory and criticism has failed to interrogate these gender assumptions. More generally, only within the last fifteen years has significant feminist scholarship been conducted regarding Depression-era Left culture.[128]

This book argues that a feminist framework is absolutely required when investigating the historical U.S. Left in order to undermine and politically rectify the chauvinism that all too often dictated its cultural and political programs and has plagued much academic scholarship on it. In regard to 1930s U.S. Left film theory and criticism, there are multiple reasons why gender must hold a prominent position within such an analysis.

Much recent feminist scholarship has revealed the centrality of women to the discussions and developments of consumerism and mass entertainment during the early twentieth century. Janet Staiger has shown that the domestic film industry actively courted female viewers as early as 1909.[129] Kathy Peiss, Nan Enstad, Lauren Rabinovitz, Miriam Hansen, and Anne Friedberg have documented the dialectical changes wrought by mass culture and consumerism upon older Victorian practices of womanhood.[130] Not only were women allowed access to new visual terrains and social spaces, but their very identities and actions were also being redefined by a heterosexual, commodity-driven gestalt. Rabinovitz describes the ambiguous ramifications resulting from women's new centrality as active consumers: "Movies and other [amusement] park attractions might have liberated young women, newly arrived in the city and cast adrift from their families, from familial supervision and Victorian sexual restraints. But they also exercised a new kind of cultural authorization of sexual objectification of women's roles as consumer and consumed."[131]

Accompanying women's newfound centrality within U.S. consumer culture was the socioeconomic disempowerment of white heterosexual men by the Depression. As Michael Kimmel writes: "With nearly one in four American men out of work, the workplace could no longer be considered a reliable arena for the demonstration and proof of one's manhood. And many men simply lost faith in a system that prevented them from proving their masculinity in the only ways they knew."[132] The Depression's destabilizing effects upon gender roles can most readily be seen within Hollywood cinema. As David M. Lugowski notes, "Hollywood is at its most queer from early 1932 to mid-1934, a period that corresponds to the worst years of the Depression."[133]

Not coincidentally, many of the Hollywood films that U.S. Left film theorists and critics analyzed, such as *Queen Christina* (Mamoulian, 1933), *The Scarlet Empress* (von Sternberg, 1934), *Fury* (Lang, 1936), and *Juarez* (Dieterle, 1939), problematize gender roles and place women in central narrative positions. Similarly, foreign Left films like *¡Que Viva México!* and *La Marseillaise* suggest that new gender roles are required if successful political change is to be enacted. Yet women's centrality within these films and the disruptive effects of the Depression on gender roles are notably absent from most of the 1930s U.S. Left film theorists' and critics' writings.

The effacement of gender issues from U.S. Left film columns speaks to both their writers' reliance upon a male gaze to structure much of their theory and criticism, and their gender anxieties. Gender was consistently supplanted by issues of class, race, and fascism. As we will see, those rare moments when issues of gender and sexuality slipped through their writing exposed the raw nerves of heterosexual masculinity in doubt. Despite women's centrality within Left and commercial film culture, and despite some 1930s Left writers' pleas to make gender more central to cultural criticism, Depression-era Left film theorists and critics remained silent, refusing to address the ways in which commercial culture itself had overturned many of their gender assumptions.

Their silence toward gender issues mirrored larger trends found within New Deal culture and the historical Left. Writing about New Deal public art and theater, Barbara Melosh argues that "New Deal gender representations suppressed contemporary sexual conflict through an image that insistently denied men's and women's separate interests." Instead, artists and playwrights "used gender metaphorically, that is, they incorporated images of manhood and womanhood as tropes in a political rhetoric directed to issues other than gender."[134]

This is precisely the same tactic that Paula Rabinowitz and Robin D. G. Kelley document within the 1930s U.S. Left. Kelley notes how masculine imagery and language dominated much Left literature and party propaganda.[135] Rabinowitz observes that "the prevailing verbal and visual imagery reveled in an excessively masculine and virile proletariat poised to struggle against the effeminate and decadent bourgeoisie."[136] The historical U.S. Left's metaphorical use of gender in its visual and written texts encapsulated the limits of its political programs, which often dismissed gender concerns as subsidiary to those of class and, to a lesser extent, race.

This metaphorical use of gender carries over into 1930s U.S. Left film theorists' and critics' discussions and evaluations of film culture, particularly in their celebration of male-centered genres like the biopic over more female-centered ones like the historical costume drama. In many ways, the male gaze of Left theorists and critics prevented them from evaluating female-centered commercial films as anything other than capitalist subterfuge. They believed that such films promoted a consumer-driven, highly individualistic conception of women's freedom and desires, and that such a conception drew attention away from the goals of organizing collectively and challenging the insidious practices of capitalism. According to many male Left theorists and critics, these films safely focused upon individual wants and needs because such a perspective left the social processes that informed such desires unchallenged.

Such an outlook so conflates female desire with consumerism that it overlooks the vital ways in which this desire exceeds commodification. As Lauren Rabinovitz warns, "These links between the department store, the screen space of the movie theater, and the objects of movie culture are speculative and tenuous, for there is no historical evidence that women's shopping gaze and identity at the department store was identical to women fans' consumption of movie culture."[137] Yet 1930s U.S. Left film theorists and critics continually saw them as indistinguishable—at times regarding women's very presence on the screen as nothing more than a symptom of the decadence of bourgeois culture as a whole.[138]

Left film theorists' and critics' gendering of progressive film culture as masculine and its reactionary tendencies as feminine strongly resonates with the sexist assumptions that still underlie many discussions in film and media studies. As Patrice Petro notes, "It is remarkable how theoretical discussions of art and mass culture are almost always accompanied by gendered metaphors which link 'masculine' values of production, activity, and attention with art, and 'feminine' values of consumption, passivity, and distraction with mass culture."[139] In comparison, 1930s U.S. Left film theory and criticism reveals at least a subtler sexist framework, wherein mass culture is not entirely dismissed as "feminine" but has its more "masculine" elements reclaimed by the Left.

These critics' ability to salvage the "masculine" moments of mass culture further reveals the sexist assumptions guiding their ability to discern the utopian impulses at work within commercial film. According to Fredric Jameson, works of mass culture cannot adequately function without harnessing "the deepest and most fundamental hopes and fantasies of the collectivity," even if they are presented in distorted and indirect ways.[140] Hollywood, notes Jane Gaines, often functions dialectically, "delivering the best hopes along with the worst tendencies, delivering them almost simultaneously."[141]

What a study of Depression-era Left film theory and criticism draws attention to is how the utopian project might be compromised by its advocates' sexist assumptions. It exposes how "the worst tendencies" of mass culture might nonetheless speak to desires that have remained unacknowledged by even the most progressive elements of society. By dismissing women's desires as nothing more than the embodiment of a capitalist ethos, 1930s U.S. Left film theorists and critics failed to acknowledge the liberatory yet deeply flawed impulses that consumer culture, and Hollywood cinema in particular, unleashed against reified gender practices. U.S. Left film theory and criticism should serve as an uneasy warning to contemporary cultural critics: take seriously all aspects of mass culture, particularly its seemingly most regressive forms, since deep within them might lurk those emergent hopes of the disempowered that have failed to gain a voice through legitimate political channels.

THREE MOVEMENTS

I have chosen to arrange this study chronologically rather than thematically because 1930s U.S. Left film theory and criticism naturally divides itself into three movements. Such a structure allows readers to follow its developments and multifaceted positions within each movement. The three periods are, first, 1927 to 1931, which saw the international emergence of montage theory and its deployment by U.S. Left film theorists and critics to initiate ideological analyses upon a wide range of commercial, foreign, and independent films; second, 1931 to 1935, when U.S. film theorists and critics focused upon the domestic mass distribution of ¡Que Viva México! in order to prove once and for all that a politically radical and aesthetically experimental film could be popular within the United States; and third, 1935 to 1939, when film criticism became more populist after the failure to mass-distribute ¡Que Viva México! During this final period, U.S. Left film theory and criticism switched its focus from radical montage theory to the investigation of styles that were more in accord with the demands of classical Hollywood cinema: emotional identification, character development, and linear narrative. The years 1934 to 1936 marked a pivotal moment in U.S. Left film theory and criticism as it moved from a vanguard radical position to a Popular Front orientation that explored Left film workers' ability to redeploy commercial cinematic conventions and themes in progressive directions in both independent and Hollywood cinema. These years establish the break between U.S. Left film theorists' and critics' earlier explicit theorization of a radical aesthetics via montage theory and their less formulated, more inductive approach of the Popular Front years, when detailed analyses of specific films were used to identify new progressive socio-aesthetic directions. The period saw a relatively coherent body of montage-derived Left film theory fracture into a criticism that sought new socio-aesthetic approaches through the close analysis of particular films and genres.

The failure to mass-distribute *¡Que Viva México!* cannot be overstated. Because of it, U.S. Left film theorists and critics were compelled to take Hollywood even more seriously than they had in the past. Whether this transition should be considered a failure of imagination on their part to domestically establish a widespread radical film movement, or a moment of insight in which they finally recognized Hollywood's centrality in regulating mass audiences' access to cinema is left for the reader to decide. But this divide in many ways speaks to recent discussions in film and media studies about the viability of and need for countercinematic media practices within a postmodern mass-commodified world. Should one still believe in the power of collective organization, oppositional politics, and radical aesthetics to delimit and repel capitalism's already intrusive forces, or must one work within its matrices to carve out ephemeral respites from its dehumanizing processes? Or is there some yet unimagined third way?

Chapter One identifies the journals and periodicals that were mainly responsible for establishing and promoting 1930s U.S. Left film theory and criticism. Furthermore, the chapter explores the multifaceted aspects of montage theory as U.S. Left film theorists and critics redeployed it to ideologically analyze films from a variety of backgrounds. As we will see, U.S. Left film theorists and critics did not use montage theory simply to defend Soviet cinema and rebut Hollywood, but also at times to critique the Soviets as well as recognize the progressive potential of commercial films. Finally, the chapter investigates the writings of Dorothy Richardson in order to identify a theoretical "road not taken" by U.S. Left film theory as a whole: a protofeminist montage theory.

Chapter Two investigates U.S. Left film theorists' and critics' advocacy of domestically mass-distributing a radical film, *¡Que Viva México!,* that would have challenged Hollywood hegemony. As doubts about the film's completion grew, however, U.S. Left film theorists and critics quickly confronted not only Hollywood's domestic monopoly over mass production, distribution, and exhibition, but also the inherent socio-aesthetic limits of montage, which prevented Eisenstein's film from being commercially viable and accessible to wider audiences. Finally, the chapter interrogates U.S. Left film theorists' and critics' general disregard of gender issues, which figured so prominently in the film's published scenario, its outtakes, and Eisenstein's correspondence. Eisenstein intended *¡Que Viva México!* to link political revolution with a radical denaturalization and transformation of gender roles. Despite having this information readily available, U.S. Left film theorists and critics chose to ignore it; by actively suppressing the radical gender insights that Left cinema offered, they retained their sexist authority, which implicitly gendered progressive culture as masculine.

Chapter Three examines U.S. Left film criticism's middecade transition to a Popular Front stance as it focused on the Hollywood antilynching film. In particular, Fritz Lang's film *Fury* served as a nodal point that drew together black and white film critics in their opposition to lynching and racial discrimination. By harnessing some of the critical viewing strategies employed by African Americans against the racism of mainstream cinema, U.S. Left film criticism promoted an interracial alliance that championed critical spectatorship, promoted collective organization in support of racial equality both on and off the screen, and explored Hollywood's ability to address systemic racism and other related social issues. However, U.S. Left film critics failed to identify the vital socioeconomic aspects addressed by *Fury*, which would have strengthened their ideological analysis of the film, because such an approach would have required a sustained focus on the film's gender issues (and its female protagonist); doing so would have undermined their male gaze and questioned their own positions of masculine authority.

Chapter Four charts U.S. Left film critics' endorsement of the films of Jean Renoir and William Dieterle. In the wake of the failure to mass-distribute *¡Que Viva México!* Renoir represented a director who could successfully transpose his Left vision into commercial forms. In particular, U.S. Left film critics used Renoir's film *La Marseillaise* (1938) as a model for politically sympathetic Hollywood directors to emulate in their own films. If some of Renoir's stylistic techniques could be translated into Hollywood films, then progressive content could reach mass audiences.

As the decade progressed, Left film critics increasingly considered the biopic an important genre in which to Americanize Renoir's progressive aesthetics, and William Dieterle represented a sympathetic Left Hollywood director who could actually implement such a strategy. As a result, U.S. Left film critics held out great hopes for Dieterle's *Juarez* (1939). If properly utilized, it could counter the reactionary, spectacle-laden tendencies of Hollywood cinema, best represented by the historical costume drama. Yet as we will see, critics' championing of the biopic over the costume drama was predicated upon their gender biases, which assumed masculine-centered genres were more politically progressive than feminine-centered ones. Their celebration of *Juarez* as a politically progressive film was dependent upon their repression of its female-centered, costume-drama elements for an exclusive focus on its male-centered, biopic ones.

Overall, Depression-era U.S. Left film theory and criticism represents a complex, and often conflicted, social formation. Schooled in the lessons of montage theory, which emphasized the need to analyze the ideological links between cinematic form and content, Left film theory and criticism reconfigured itself into a Popular Front stance by middecade with the realization that a reassessment of Hollywood filmmaking was necessary if progressive films were ever to reach mainstream audiences. This latter position was initiated by an expansion of racial scope that synthesized the critical viewing strategies of film critics from the black and white press into a body of criticism that promoted interracial alliances and audience organizations that fought against racial discrimination both on- and off-screen. Their focus on *Fury* and the antilynching film in general signals these critics' first sustained attempt to reevaluate the ideological potential of certain commercial cinematic forms for producing accessible, progressive mainstream films. As the decade progressed, their focus on Hollywood strengthened as the historical films of Jean Renoir and William Dieterle provided new models for Left commercial filmmaking. This aspect of U.S. Left film theory and criticism reveals an incredibly nuanced and fluid ability to deploy critical concepts in new configurations when required to do so by changing historical conditions.

However, at the same time, U.S. Left film theory and criticism trenchantly resisted a reevaluation of its problematic male gaze and other sexist assumptions that had haunted it since its origins, and that would continue into the 1940s, when its focus shifted to other male-centered genres and styles like the war film, the boxing film, and film noir. Seeing gender solely as a metaphor, if at all, and historical costume dramas as examples of reactionary spectacular excess, Left film theory and criticism failed to acknowledge the crucial ways in which gender identity was taking on new configurations. As a result, U.S. Left film theory and criticism held a contradictory ideological position: a utopian hope to create radical and progressive films that would allow audiences to envision themselves in more egalitarian and collectively empowering ways, and a reactionary desire to hold onto older structures of male privilege that the Depression, consumer culture, and Hollywood cinema were challenging. Ultimately, an analysis of U.S. Left film theory and criticism offers a way to begin identifying the multifaceted ways in which the historical Left viewed Hollywood, independent, and foreign films of the 1930s and subsequently attempted to influence future filmmaking and consumption in simultaneously progressive and reactionary directions.

Regardless of one's final assessment, the examination of U.S. Left film theory and criticism reminds us of the vital role that the study of any social formation serves in effectively challenging the conservative accounts of traditional, "top down" history. In the place of great leaders, the solidity of institutions, and the imprimatur of legislation stand the complex micromaneuverings of social formations arising from the collective actions, ephemeral publications, and utopian visions of the multitude, of those who were orphaned by official history but who nonetheless imprinted their invisible signature upon its every word.

In keeping with Walter Benjamin's admonitions, the study of social formations blasts apart the homogeneous course of history to expose its underlying contingencies, tensions, and unfulfilled possibilities. It reveals the secret histories of the dispossessed, which have been habitually repressed by history's official chroniclers. This study specifically blasts apart reified notions of Hollywood as a dream factory and dogmatic assumptions regarding the 1930s cultural Left to imagine a cultural moment when international and U.S. Left film theorists and critics believed that history belonged to them as much as it did to the elite, that cinema catered to their desires for a more just future as much as it pandered to Hollywood's desire for profits, and that film criticism could be used to foster critical spectatorship and collective action for not only better films, but also a more humane world.

When explaining the goals of his project, Tom Brandon fully realized the significance of such a "bottom up" approach to film history: "I hope that this effort to convey how it really was will be of help to those who want to do something in this art and medium of film about today and the future. For, in my opinion, much depends on the realization of those historical processes that are empowered from 'down below.' Much? It may be everything, perhaps the entire future of all people on this earth."[142] Although I reject Brandon's faith in the historian's ability to resurrect history,

I nonetheless share his belief that our future actions always hinge upon our knowledge of the past. This study assumes that our always partial and assembled knowledge of the marginalized social formations of the past assists us in recognizing the ideological fissures of the present, wherein we might pry open better futures. This study pays heed to Tom Brandon's unfinished promise to reclaim a forgotten time—orphaned by the chroniclers of homogeneous history and reluctantly abandoned by Brandon himself—not through any assertion of its final capture, but through the frank admittance of its provisional refraction through the warped lens of the present. This study is dedicated to better futures.

Chapter 1

Montage, Realism, and the Male Gaze

To fully grasp the nuances and developments within U.S. Left film theory and criticism, one must first recognize its intimate connection with international film theory and cinema. As we will see throughout this book, U.S. Left film theory and criticism always defined itself in relation to an international vision of cinema. For these theorists and critics, film served as an ideal medium for bridging national divides by familiarizing audiences worldwide with one another's cultural practices and attitudes in order to forge international solidarity against the exploitative tendencies of global capitalism.

This chapter situates U.S. Left film theory and criticism within the pages of international and domestic film journals and Left periodicals. A brief exploration of these primary sources reveals how writers from seemingly opposed film and political backgrounds—the avant-garde, Soviet socialist realism, and commercial cinema, to name only a few—influenced one another's writings. Furthermore, an international focus exposes a much more sophisticated theoretical background at work within U.S. Left film theory and criticism than has been typically assumed by film historians who have adhered to a more limited geographical and disciplinary scope.

Montage theory served as a key theoretical framework within which international and U.S. Left film theorists could develop their ideological analysis of cinema. Contrary to the belief that these theorists adhered to a narrow conception of montage that simply championed Soviet cinema over all other cinematic forms, a variety of montage theories proliferated throughout their writings. Montage functioned as an extremely pliable concept that Left film theorists and critics deployed to analyze a whole host of commercial and independent films, both international and domestic. It offered them a conceptual tool for examining how various filmic techniques could provide viewers with a radically new critical perspective for assessing their world.

New forms of representation, for many of these writers, were a necessary precursor to progressive political action. If one still thought and perceived within prescribed bourgeois conceptions of reality, then any political action could at best reform socioeconomic and political relations rather than radically challenge their underlying premises. Montage theory provided critics with a conceptual fulcrum that let them explore how certain cinematic stylistic choices could challenge the hegemonic hold of a limited and reactionary realism.

Additionally, this chapter argues that montage theory allowed many writers to conceptualize film's ability to counter the fragmenting and alienating processes of modernity by offering viewers a totalistic vision of the world. As Ben Singer has convincingly argued, "Social observers in the decades around the turn of the century were *fixated* on the idea that modernity had brought about a radical increase in nervous stimulation and bodily peril."[1] *The Education of Henry Adams* (1907) is a case in point. Within it, Adams attempts to map the vectors of industrialization, science, and monopoly capitalism that erupted from the late nineteenth century. But as the text progresses, Adams becomes increasingly aware that "a nineteenth-century education was a useless or misleading [training]" for interpreting the emerging socioeconomic forces of the twentieth century, leaving him on the edge of meaninglessness and chaos by the book's end.[2] Structured analysis succumbs to shattered descriptions of the vertiginous ruptures of modernity that both shock and fascinate Adams:

> The outline of the city became frantic in its effort to explain something that defied meaning. Power seemed to have outgrown its servitude and to have asserted its freedom. The cylinder had exploded, and thrown great masses of stone and steam against the sky. The city had the air and movement of hysteria, and the citizens were crying, in every accent of anger and alarm, that the new forces must at any cost be brought under control. Prosperity never before imagined, power never yet wielded by man, speed never reached by anything but a meteor, had made the world irritable, nervous, querulous, unreasonable and afraid.[3]

In the wake of such uncertainty and promise, Left film theorists viewed montage as one of the central methods for reassembling the fragments of modernity into a more totalistic and humane framework, thereby bringing "the new forces" under control.

Georg Lukács perhaps best describes how the concept of totality challenged the reified concepts and perceptions produced by modernity and bourgeois ideology:

The apparent independence and autonomy which they [bourgeois con-
ceptions] possess in the capitalist system of production is an illusion
only in so far as they are involved in a dynamic dialectical relationship
with one another and can be thought of as the dynamic dialectical aspects of an equally dynamic and dialectical process . . .

. . . For only this conception [of totality] dissolves the fetishistic
forms necessarily produced by the capitalist mode of production and
enables us to see them as mere illusions which are not less illusory for
being seen to be necessary.[4]

In a related fashion, Left film theorists and critics believed that montage,
if deployed skillfully within film, could supplant viewers' atomized vision
with a dialectical outlook and thereby reveal the mutually influential processes that exist between individuals and their social contexts.[5] Montage
could transform cinema, a product of the destabilizing forces of late capitalism and modernity, into a liberatory medium that would provide viewers with the necessary vision to realign the present moment into a more
utopian configuration.

Because of Left film theorists' and critics' concern with montage, this
chapter also argues that our understanding of the type of realism they were
advocating for must be more carefully theorized. Most 1930s Left film
critics were not demanding a classical Hollywood style of bourgeois realism that simply incorporated pressing political issues of the day. A new
style was also needed: one that allowed viewers not only to acknowledge
present political concerns, but also to envision them in new and more critical ways.

In its first period, 1927–1931, Left film theory argued for a montage-
based realism to counter classical Hollywood cinema's fragmented,
romantic realistic style. Montage provided for a thematically unified film
that explored the dialectical relations between individuals and their social contexts so that viewers could gain critical insights into the social
totality that the commodified processes of modernity obscured. As a result, montage-based realism exposed the connections between individuals
and their world rather than emphasizing individuals' alienation from it,
thereby reintroducing viewers to their world and the ways they could influence its composition.

In this chapter's final section, I will investigate U.S. Left film theorists' and critics' demand for a montage-based realism by exploring their
troubled relationship with director King Vidor, who was often considered
sympathetic to their causes. By examining Left criticism of Vidor's film

Street Scene, we gain a better sense of the type of realism these critics were advocating. Although the film possessed seemingly good political intentions, most U.S. Left film theorists and critics felt that Vidor's reliance upon a classical Hollywood style undercut the film's progressive content.

Furthermore, I will argue that if Left film theorists' and critics' reliance upon a montage-based realism is to be critiqued at all, it is not for their supposed dogmatic adherence to a Soviet model, but for their theories' reliance on a bourgeois male gaze that habitually marginalized gender issues and the role of women within their critical framework. I will examine how the very montage theories that provided them with a theoretically sophisticated critical apparatus with which to analyze a wide range of films nonetheless implicitly prioritized a male gaze, leading critics to overemphasize the male point of view, even when analyzing films that now are either regarded as female centered, like Josef von Sternberg's *Shanghai Express* (1932), or else, like *¡Que Viva México!* (1932), deploy gender as a central theme (for more on the latter film, see Chapter Two).

Yet there were a few exceptions to this male-centered montage theory. The chapter will conclude by focusing on Dorothy Richardson's unique brand of reformist montage theory, which incorporated gender into its analysis of commercial cinema. Richardson's criticism is enlightening for exposing how gender could be incorporated into a montage-inflected approach. Her criticism exposes a line of inquiry not taken by Left film theory and criticism as a whole. As we will later see, most U.S. Left film critics failed to acknowledge not only gender's importance in the films that they discussed, but also the ways in which sexist assumptions and anxieties caused their criticism to conflate women and their desires with the debased processes of consumer culture, and to subsequently dismiss any aspects of popular culture that smacked of being too feminine or female centered.

THE DAWN OF A POLITICIZED FILM THEORY

Because much contemporary film history has assumed that U.S. Left film theory and criticism rejected modernism and the avant-garde for a naïve social-realist aesthetic, it has dissociated it from important international, modernist debates concerning film theory. John Bodnar writes, "Social realism was certainly a key way in which critics judged films that concentrated on a solitary workingman."[6] He then cites the *Daily Worker* as a key Left publication, whose film criticism "decried portrayals of radicals as misguided or 'vile,' demanded that capitalist exploitation of labor be revealed in its full scope, and expressed much regret when it was not. Nothing was guaranteed to evoke complaints about films from this newspaper more than images of workingmen who were meek, compliant, or disinterested in collective action."[7] By limiting his focus to films solely concerned with the working class, as well as by relying primarily on the *Daily Worker*, Bodnar unintentionally simplifies the scope of U.S. Left film criticism by ignoring its complex theoretical origins, which challenge this vulgar realist account.

In *Cinema Strikes Back*, Russell Campbell even more explicitly contrasts social-realist film criticism with modernism. By problematically linking and limiting cinematic social realism with naturalistic and realist literary traditions, Campbell regards the advent of modernism as a threat to cinematic realism's very existence: "Social realism has also been rendered aesthetically old-fashioned by movements in modern art which attacked its legacy, beginning with the disjunction of coherent time and space and ending with a rejection of representation itself."[8] As a result, Campbell regards montage as the devil's bargain, "social realism's compromise with the twentieth century," rather than, as many Left film theorists at the time viewed it, as an advance in film form that united Left politics with modernist experimentation in a truly mass medium.[9]

Underlying Campbell's claims lurks a Lukácsian faith in realism that holds the particular and the universal, the individual and the social context, in dialectical tension and traces the outlines of a greater totalistic understanding by transcending the author's or director's personal political views. Modernism, in this account, represents nothing more than bourgeois decadence: a fractured, solipsistic, hyperindividualistic, subjective, and fully reified perspective that short-circuits any totalistic vision of the vectors of capitalism.[10] But as we will soon see, a thorough examination of Left film theory and criticism of the late 1920s and early 1930s reveals how aspects of modernism, Left politics, and the avant-garde were often intertwined within its corpus.

Recent Left scholars like Fredric Jameson, Paula Rabinowitz, Michael Denning, Saverio Giovacchini, Cary Nelson, and William J. Maxwell have challenged this monolithic notion of social realism, which supposedly dominated the cultural Left of the 1930s.[11] As Michael Denning notes, social realism has often been categorized and misinterpreted in three primary ways as an adherence to "the documentary aesthetic, a rearguard opposition to modernism, and a relatively straightforward representationalism in the arts."[12] Instead, Denning asserts that "the documentary aesthetic was actually a central modernist innovation; the cultural front was *not* characterized by an opposition to modernism; and the crucial aesthetic forms and ideologies of the cultural front were not simple representationalism."[13] Ultimately, he believes that the term social realism should be replaced with the concept of "social modernism," which more accurately defines the socio-aesthetic impulses of the 1930s U.S. cultural Left "to transcend and rebuild modernism" in politically radical directions.[14]

It is precisely a social-modernist perspective that we see at work during the emergence of international and U.S. Left film theory. But to observe it, we need to investigate film journals and Left periodicals that were dismissed by prior scholarship as not belonging properly to the radical Left. To reveal the mutually influential roles that modernist, avant-garde, and Left film theorists and critics had upon one another, we need to categorize their journals and periodicals other than by their ostensible political or aesthetic stances, since these categories all too often emphasize their divisions rather than their theoretical intersections.

Although each journal supported a diverse array of contributors who approached film in unique ways, I find it useful to categorize the journals in the following manner: those primarily concerned with film theory, those that mainly offered film reviews, and those that presented a mix of film theory and reviews. *Close Up, Experimental Cinema, Theatre Arts Monthly,* the *Left,* and *Modern Monthly* fit within the first category. The *New Masses,* the *Nation,* the *Daily Worker,* and the *New Republic* belong within the second category. Finally, *Filmfront* and *New Theatre* occupy the last category. By establishing categories that focus on how these journals approached film rather than on their ostensible political or aesthetic outlook, we are better able to see how film brought together seemingly opposing political or aesthetic stances. For example, *Close Up* is generally classified as an avant-garde film journal, whereas *Experimental Cinema* is often regarded as a political film journal. No film history examines these journals in relation to each other. But if one reexamines both journals' approaches to film theory, one begins to see how they were often addressing identical issues and placing themselves in a dialogue with each other. Archival sources reveal how often contributors from *Experimental Cinema* credited *Close Up* with strongly influencing their outlook. For example, the founder of *Experimental Cinema,* Lewis Jacobs, recounted in a 1974 interview that *Close Up* was the only journal before *Experimental Cinema* "that really dealt with film in a serious way."[15]

Furthermore, these categories emphasize how journals mainly dedicated to film theory were where cinéastes gathered to discuss in-depth, theoretical aspects of film among themselves, whereas periodicals addressing film criticism allowed writers to apply their theories to specific readings of films in order to expose general viewers to the ideological undercurrents of popular culture. The crossover journals were most useful in marking the transitional debates within U.S. Left film theory and criticism during 1934 and 1935 to a more Popular Front orientation.

The above categories do not imply that these journals and periodicals did not occasionally offer articles generally found in other categories of journals or that they were in any way consistently opposed to one another in their approaches to film. As mentioned earlier, not only did many of their writers personally know one another, but they also wrote for one another's publications. Kyle S. Crichton, who wrote reviews for *Collier's*, used the pseudonym Robert Forsythe to write film reviews for the *New Masses*. The radical Marxist film theorist Harry Alan Potamkin wrote for the avant-garde cinema journals *Hound and Horn* and *Close Up*, the Marxist journals *New Masses* and *Experimental Cinema*, and mainstream publications such as the *New York Times* and *Vanity Fair*.[16] These writers showed a remarkable ability to direct their attention to whatever issue they felt most urgently needed to be addressed at the time, and they published their views in whatever print venue they deemed appropriate. They held a rather sophisticated attitude toward the need to contribute both to independent, radical film journals, which catered to select readers, and to mainstream publications, which influenced large readerships.

In regard to the first category, the appearance of *Close Up* in the United States cannot be emphasized enough. Before this journal, U.S. readers possessed only limited critical resources on film. Both Vachel Lindsay's *The Art of Moving Picture* (1915) and Hugo Münsterberg's *The Photoplay: A Psychological Survey* (1916) were available, but both works still viewed film as an elaboration upon older art forms rather than as a distinct medium in its own right, and neither offered any type of ideological analysis.[17] At the same time, articles examining racial representations in both Hollywood and independent black films appeared sporadically in the African-American press.[18] Also, a five-part serialization of Willi Muenzenberg's pamphlet *Let Us Conquer the Film* ran in the *Daily Worker* in 1925, emphasizing the importance of film as a propaganda weapon by looking to Russian films as the vanguard and discussing ways to distribute and publicize such films.[19] But articles that addressed either the socio-aesthetic implications of film as a distinct medium were few and far between.

Close Up's appearance in 1927 was nothing less than sensational in this context. It was the first English-language journal dedicated entirely to the examination of film, and it introduced its readers to an interna-

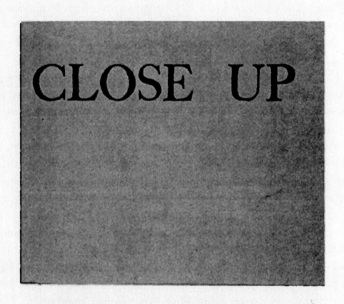

CLOSE UP

THE ONLY MAGAZINE DEVOTED TO FILMS
AS AN ART

Interesting and Exclusive Illustrations

THEORY AND ANALYSIS   NO GOSSIP

1 shilling or 5 francs (French) or 1 mark (German)
35 cents   1 franc (Swiss)   1½ shillings (Austrian)

Vol. III No. 4   OCTOBER 1928

Close-Up, *the first English-language film journal and a crucible for the development of U.S. Left film theory and criticism.*

tional group of well-known and not-so-well-known writers and directors, such as H.D., Dorothy Richardson, Marianne Moore, Hanns Sachs, Harry Alan Potamkin, Sergei Eisenstein, and G. W. Pabst, to only name a few. The journal's editor was Kenneth Macpherson and the assistant editor was Bryher (the pseudonym of Annie Winifred Ellerman), who used her family's money to support the journal, leaving it free from commercial constraints.[20]

The journal appealed to a wide range of readers who regarded cinema as a significant force for bringing about social change. Some contributors rallied against censorship in films, both in Europe and in the United States. Others advocated for independent film groups that would produce and distribute their own films as well as distribute other noncommercial films through local exhibitors. Dorothy Richardson examined how theaters provided working-class mothers refuge and envisioned the educational potential of film as a whole. Hanns Sachs offered one of the earliest translated essays on the dangers of film becoming kitsch. Eisenstein argued for the revolutionary structure of montage. By supporting heterogeneous positions on film as well as sustained analysis, the journal drew together varying socio-aesthetic explorations that would significantly shape U.S. Left film theory and criticism.

Experimental Cinema was a similarly theory-based journal, but one with a more consistently radical outlook than *Close Up*. The only U.S. journal devoted entirely to film, it ran from 1930 to 1934, publishing only one issue a year because of financial constraints. Each issue contained a large number of articles from Left artists, film theorists, directors, and writers like Harry Alan Potamkin, Vsevolod Pudovkin, Barnet G. Braver-Mann, Lewis Jacobs, Seymour Stern, Edward Weston, Sergei Eisenstein, and Theodor Dreiser.

Although some scholars have accused *Experimental Cinema* of dogmatism because it supposedly "did not recognize or even tolerate any possible alternative purpose or function of the cinema" than that promoted by the Soviet model, the journal had contributors who often disagreed with one another over film theory's and cinema's goals.[21] For example, the journal's move to Hollywood during its third issue upset some of its writers. Harry Alan Potamkin questioned not only the viability of its location within Hollywood, but also the lack of theoretical sophistication of its first two issues, to which he was a contributor:

> The novice-mind obstructs the road to valid criticism: social and esthetic, the esthetic in the social. If you want a compendium of the novice-mind refer to the first two issues of *Experimental Cinema* . . . The journal has trekked to Hollywood—the land of frustrated esthetes—with the intention of bringing a "fresh breath" into that morass. Young mystified mystics who have not been able to direct pertinent arrows toward even the periphery of Hollywood are going to influence the production there. Truncated boobs! Actually this is a rationalization of weakness and ego-centricity, of escape and a wish for success.[22]

Experimental Cinema, *a central forum for discussing the distribution and production problems surrounding Sergei Eisenstein's* ¡Que Viva Mexico! *(1932).*

But other writers, like Jacobs and Stern, although no cheerleaders for the studio system, believed that U.S. Left film theory and criticism was needed both within and outside Hollywood to effect progressive change.

More importantly, *Experimental Cinema* played a central role in publicizing the problems in mass-distributing Eisenstein's radical Mexican film *¡Que Viva México!* Leading the charge against Upton Sinclair's wish to reedit Eisenstein's film for mass distribution, *Experimental Cinema* dedicated its fifth issue to a three-article treatment of Eisenstein's original intentions for the film. Its editors had published manifestos in previous issues and in publications like *Close Up* in order to expose how the film's investors had prevented it from being released in its original form. Although these debates are discussed more thoroughly in Chapter Two, it is worth noting here that because of its sustained focus on *¡Que Viva México! Experimental Cinema* brought to the forefront of critical debate several crucial problems, including the dangers of independent Left films being co-opted, even those produced independently of Hollywood; the socio-aesthetic merits and problems associated with gaining a mass audience for radical montage; and the need for U.S. Left film critics and filmmakers to explore film styles other than montage if they ever hoped to have their films widely distributed and viewed.

In addition to *Close Up* and *Experimental Cinema,* there were a series of other journals—either short-lived or not entirely dedicated to film—that were nonetheless important to those interested in film theory. The *Left* appeared for only two issues in 1931, and was published in Davenport, Iowa, by George Redfield and Herbert Kline; contributors such as Seymour Stern, Sergei Eisenstein, Lewis Jacobs, and Barnet Braver-Mann expanded upon the stylistic differences and similarities between Hollywood and foreign films.[23] *Modern Monthly,* formerly the *Modern Quarterly* (1923–1940), offered in-depth analyses of *¡Que Viva México!* by Stern and others. *Theatre Arts Monthly* presented further information on the difficulties of mass-distributing *¡Que Viva México!* and published articles concerning montage, star studies, and Left directors like Jean Renoir. All in all, these smaller publications expanded upon the theoretical issues of montage and the development of progressive international cinema that had originated in more well-financed film journals.

The second category of magazines provided mainly in-depth analyses of individual films. This group included the *New Masses,* the *Daily Worker,* the *Nation,* and the *New Republic.* As mentioned earlier, many contemporary film historians have suggested that the writers for these magazines never worked out their own general film theories. But such an outlook ignores the ways that many contributors to these journals developed their theoretical positions in other venues: in their writings for other journals, in the film groups they attended, and, later, through audience organizations. Although articles concerning general film theory were few and far between within these magazines, their film criticism was informed by the theoretical debates occurring within the first category of cinema journals. Writers for these publications analyzed particular films ideologically but in ways that did not require an advanced understanding of film theory. Viewed dialectically, the *New Masses* and other such publications showed film theory "in action" for general audiences by assessing the aesthetic and ideological aspects of particular films, while journals like *Close Up* and *Experimental Cinema* developed film theory by and for people who were well versed in filmmaking and film analysis.

The most important of these "second category" magazines was the *New Masses*. Its ever-increasing popularity throughout the decade made it a significant cultural force. The magazine ran as a monthly from its inception in 1926 to September 1933, when it was revamped into a weekly. As David Peck notes, "From 1934 through the decade, during the period of the Popular Front, the weekly *New Masses* enjoyed its peak popularity," printing as many as 25,000 copies for a weekly issue.[24] It became one of the most important cultural organs of progressively minded groups throughout the 1930s, and its film column reached an audience untapped by any other independent papers or journals. Of all the publications, it offered the most in-depth focus on film for the longest duration.

Furthermore, the varying critical attitudes of the *New Masses*'s main film contributors toward Hollywood cinema often served as a barometer of the general changes taking place within U.S. Left film culture. The increasingly politically moderate stance of each new film critic suggested the overall movement of U.S. Left film criticism from a radical, montage-based aesthetics that often critiqued classical Hollywood cinema to a more Popular Front orientation that wanted to reach mass audiences by integrating montage within the traditional forms of linear narrative, mise-en-scène, character development, and audience identification.[25] Harry Alan Potamkin contributed from 1930 to 1933 and most often focused on the developments taking place in Soviet film. Nathan Adler and Irving Lerner contributed from 1934 to 1935. They tended to be critical of Hollywood productions while praising the Soviets' work. However, during the same years, Robert Forsythe also became a major contributor. He questioned his colleagues' assumptions that equated Hollywood with dreck and Soviet productions with the epitome of radical cinema. As he stated in one of his columns: "Every Hollywood product is not an abomination. It is neither sensible nor fair to consider everything on our side good because it comes from our side."[26] The simultaneous appearance of Adler, Lerner, and Forsythe within the pages of the *New Masses* was indicative of the factions developing within U.S. Left film criticism during the mid-1930s.

Lerner adopted the pseudonym Peter Ellis from 1935 to 1938 so that he could modify his earlier skeptical position toward Hollywood and champion some of its politically progressive films. In 1938, James Dugan supplanted Lerner as the main reviewer and wrote until 1941, mainly focusing on the progressive films coming out of the studios and on the stylistic and political developments within progressive foreign films that could be incorporated into the classical Hollywood style.

The *Daily Worker* began publication in 1924 and ended in the mid-1950s. Although it often lacked the subtlety of cultural analysis found in the *New Masses*, film criticism became an important focus in the late 1920s and early 1930s, when Sam Brody's film reviews and proposals for alternative film organizations began to appear.[27] Writers like David Platt and Tom Brandon regularly contributed throughout the decade. During the late 1930s, Mike Gold, a former editor of the *New Masses* who moved to California, contributed a regular column on Hollywood that could equally infuriate and amuse readers with its bombastic tone. As film grew in importance to the magazine, well-known Left directors like Sergei Eisenstein, William Dieterle, and Joris Ivens contributed an occasional piece.

The consistency and perception of its writers' film analyses drastically varied, but occasionally the *Daily Worker* offered an extremely influential article on film: Willi Muenzenberg's pamphlet *Let Us Conquer the Film,* Eisenstein's analysis of *Alexander Nevsky,* and Tom Brandon's account of the Legion of Decency and Hollywood censorship.[28] But of most importance was the sheer amount of information readers learned about Hollywood and independent film movements. The *Daily Worker* announced the creation of the New York Film and Photo League, offered analyses of the Screen Writers and Screen Directors Guilds' fight against studio-controlled unions, revealed the Soviet Union's desire to make a film about the treatment of African Americans in the South, agitated for boycotts of prowar and profascist films, and identified the sections censored from Soviet films in the United States.[29] The film column might have taken up only a quarter of a page, but it announced to its readers when something of importance relating to film was occurring and what audiences needed to do in response. The magazine possessed a much more activist stance toward film than did the *New Masses,* and suggested that audiences had significant power in shaping the types of films that would reach them.

Journals such as the *Nation,* the *New Republic,* the *Dial,* and the *Seven Arts* also published weekly film columns but from a less radical perspective. More moderate than the critics from the *New Masses* and the *Daily*

Worker, these journals' writers were mostly from an academic, middle-class background.[30] Although critical of Hollywood films, they shied away from class analysis and proselytizing about montage yet still argued that commercial film needed to develop more-sophisticated dialectical representations of individuals' relations to their historical contexts. Perhaps most useful for this study is the way in which many of these critics measured themselves against more radical stances, therefore providing an ongoing internal commentary on radical developments occurring within U.S. film theory and criticism. They provided an interesting moderating voice to complement the ideologically informed film analyses found in *Close Up* and *Experimental Cinema* and the more politically active film analyses found in the *New Masses* and the *Daily Worker.*

At the intersection of these two groups of journals and magazines were *Filmfront* (1934–1935) and *New Theatre* (1933–1937). *Filmfront* was the product of the Workers Film and Photo League (WFPL), which had emerged from the Workers Camera Club in New York City. The WFPL consisted of a group of men—David Platt, Tom Brandon, Sam Brody, Harry Alan Potamkin, Irving Lerner, Ralph Steiner, Leo Hurwitz, and Lewis Jacobs—who wanted to create a film group, controlled by amateurs, that would film political events like the 1932 Hunger March and the Scottsboro case, which had been ignored by commercial newsreels. *New Theatre,* the league's first journal, in which Hurwitz played a major editorial role, emphasized the need to create better-produced films and more-professional film units than the league was currently offering. *Filmfront,* created in 1934 under the editorship of David Platt as a breakaway from *New Theatre,* used Dziga Vertov's theories to emphasize the radical possibilities of film.[31] *Filmfront* argued for the production of American films without central protagonists or actors but relying instead on bold editing and documentary-like rawness to provide visual and dramatic appeal for audiences.

Filmfront was an amalgam of film reviews, research into Hollywood censorship, translations of Dziga Vertov's writings, and amateur, do-it-yourself filmmaking advice. Besides combining historical and theoretical analyses with a desire to offer alternatives to Hollywood filmmaking, the journal organized boycotts against certain Hollywood films deemed racist, prowar, or antilabor. Within in its mimeographed pages, *Filmfront* stirred together an eclectic mix of articles that had interesting but not necessarily all that productive results.

Eventually, the journal's rather doctrinaire adherence to a Vertovian aesthetic and its knee-jerk rejection of all things Hollywood began to annoy some of its readers. John Howard Lawson addressed this in a letter he wrote in its fourth issue:

> The Vertov article is fine, but the rest of the magazine is a little dry. The reviews of the current [Hollywood] pictures are not (in my opinion) either as clear or as vigorously approached as they might be . . . What is needed is a combination of an analytical Marxist approach with a lively popular style . . . To do this you need, more than anything else, meaty Hollywood stuff—and reviews which are surprising enough to create general interest, and yet not so sectarian as to repel the undeveloped sympathizer.[32]

Lawson is clearly arguing for a Popular Front style of writing that does not dogmatically reject Hollywood productions and keeps the general reader in mind. The mere inclusion of his letter suggests some sympathy from the journal's editors, but by this time there was a rift among the league's members over the relevance of "underproduced," raw films in relation to more professionally created films that could influence larger audiences.

This rift came to a head in *New Theatre* with the publication of two articles by former NYF&PL members Leo Hurwitz and Ralph Steiner, who criticized some U.S. Left film critics and filmmakers for their dogmatic adherence to a montage-based aesthetic and their intolerant dismissal of Hollywood cinematic styles (this is discussed more thoroughly in the next chapter). *New Theatre* not only provided a forum for socioaesthetic debates among U.S. Left film critics, but also exposed how some of those critics were turning to a more populist stance before the Communist Party's official declaration of a Popular Front in 1935. Contrary to the belief that U.S. Left cultural politics adopted a Popular Front position out of blind adherence to the dictates of Soviet cultural policy, U.S. Left film theory and criticism shows how domestic conditions and internal debates encouraged some writers to move in that direction months before the emergence of the Popular Front.[33] In many ways, the U.S. Popular Front grafted itself upon and unified already existing moderate, domestic socio-aesthetic tendencies in order to compose its cultural-historical bloc.

But what ultimately linked all the writers from these various journals and periodicals was cinema's ability to lend itself to both ideological and aesthetic analysis. Cinema, by its very nature, according to many Left theorists and critics, was the site where modernist aesthetics and progressive politics most logically converged. It is no wonder that journals like *Close Up* and *Experimental Cinema* promoted such diverse stances toward film, since the medium itself facilitated multivalent cross-communication.

Yet among these heterogeneous approaches, montage theory nonetheless emerged as the central conceptual framework for speaking about cinema.

FROM RUSSIA WITH LOVE: THE RISE OF INTERNATIONAL MONTAGE THEORIES

Seemingly from out of nowhere, the Soviets exploded onto the international film scene during the 1920s. Not only did they produce films that stunned critics and the public with their ingenuity, but they also extensively theorized about montage. Pudovkin's book *On Film Technique* (1929), Eisenstein's countless essays, and Vertov's manifestos regarding the "kino-eye" supplied multiple interpretations of montage.[34] While acknowledging the Soviets' different montage approaches, most Left film theorists realized that montage centered upon the fusion of modernist aesthetic experimentation with a socially committed cinema. As Lewis Jacobs states in *The Rise of the American Film:* "This stress on reality [by not using professional actors], together with deep purpose, serious subject matter, and grasp of cinematic form, gave the Soviet films a drive, conviction, and distinction that made non-Russian pictures seem petty."[35] Myron Lounsbury rightly observes that between 1929 and 1934, "the Soviet movie was the pivotal issue in the debate between 'radical' and 'liberal' [U.S.] critics," which mirrored the larger international debates occurring within *Close Up*.[36] Although film critics from various political backgrounds recognized the immense importance of Soviet film, only international film theory supplied the necessary theoretical space in which to investigate and debate the contours, promises, and problems associated with montage theory.

The four Soviet directors most often spoken about were Sergei Eisenstein, Vsevolod Pudovkin, Aleksandr Dovzhenko, and Dziga Vertov. Eisenstein and Pudovkin were especially central to international debates about montage because of their frequent theoretical contributions to various journals and magazines, which international theorists and critics utilized and debated in their own columns. Furthermore, by the early 1930s, both Pudovkin and Eisenstein had begun exploring their own films' relation to the sort of bourgeois modernist forms that most likely appealed to Western Left film theorists and critics, in an effort to supply those critics with a theoretical framework more suitable for the ideological analysis of commercial cinema. Vertov's hostility to Western art in general restricted his following to a small group of radical Left critics and filmmakers, mainly those belonging to the New York Film and Photo League. Dovzhenko, whose work was often regarded as the middle ground between Eisenstein's "intellectualism" and Pudovkin's "sentimentality," never wrote enough to make him too central a figure in international film theory.[37]

In the following section, I will examine three non-Soviet films to reveal how Soviet montage theory was used by Western Left film theorists and critics to analyze a wide variety of films as well as to explain how films that now seem to have little to do with montage were considered in the late 1920s and early 1930s to be intimately related to it. The three films are *Rain* (Ivens, 1929), *Borderline* (Macpherson, 1931), and *City Streets* (Mamoulian, 1931). The first is an abstract film without actors; the second is a character-centered avant-garde film; and the third is a classical Hollywood film. By juxtaposing the critical analyses of these three films, we begin to see the multifarious ways in which montage was applied to discuss similar socio-aesthetic issues from different film traditions. The ability of theorists and critics to use montage in such multivalent ways indicates that traditional demarcations between mass culture and high art, entertainment and politics, and formal experimentation and classical Hollywood cinema had not yet solidified into mutually exclusive realms for Left film theory and criticism. Also, we see how montage theory provided these critics with a conceptual tool for exploring how both independent and commercial cinema could be used to foster a domestic Left film culture.

MONTAGE IN THREE MOVEMENTS

One thing Western Left film theory highlights about Soviet montage is its ability to affect spectators in challenging ways. By employing such terms as "kino-eye" and "kino-fist" in their early writings, Soviet directors emphasized how montage could smash through spectators' reified perceptions and thoughts to enable a progressive, collective vision and way of life.[38] Rather than discussing cinema in such aggressive terms, international Western Left film theorists took a more moderate approach and an overtly Freudian perspective in discussing montage's ability to affect spectators. They drew more attention to montage's relation to character psychology than their Soviet counterparts did, since the Soviets at this time were more preoccupied with the "mass as hero" than with any focus on the individual.

Two seminal articles articulating this approach are Hanns Sachs's "Film Psychology" (1928) and "Kitsch" (1932), both of which appeared in *Close Up*.[39] For Sachs, popular culture was not the sole repository of kitsch as it would be for Clement Greenberg in his "Avant-Garde and Kitsch"

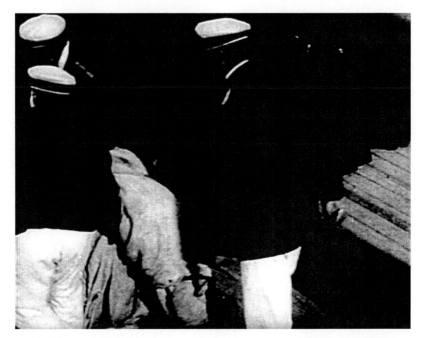

Sailcloth being used to cover mutineers facing execution in Battleship Potemkin *(1925).*

(1939).[40] According to Sachs, kitsch is "usually thought to be sugary sentimentality and omission of the painful and disgusting sides of reality, but this does not by any means exhaust the whole conception, for in addition to rose-colored Kitsch, there is a savage, brutal as well as an 'originality Kitsch' and also a 'refined Kitsch,' which seems to satisfy all the higher claims [of art]."[41] Any film could run the risk of containing bourgeois, kitsch-like aesthetics: "The difference [between art and kitsch] lies not in the subject but in the manner in which it is treated: the work of art creates new, hitherto unknown possibilities of inner experience, new approaches to the unconscious base; kitsch relies on safe and long familiar effects."[42]

For Sachs, kitsch prevents "the diverse possibilities of psychic decisions" because it guards spectators "against uncertainty and allusions to unpleasant recollections" by rendering their enjoyment as effortless as possible.[43] In other words, kitsch forecloses the spectator's ability to transcend limited understandings concerning the psyche and its relation to the world by confining aesthetic experiences to rote formulas that reinforce narrow, reactionary perspectives.

In "Film Psychology," Sachs illustrates how Eisenstein's film *Battleship Potemkin* (1925) uses montage to work against kitsch-like psychological representations. To emphasize how montage provides spectators with a deep psychological understanding of unconscious actions, the article examines the scene in which guards are about to execute the mutineers. According to Sachs, film's central focus on the movement of physical bodies offers spectators an acute psychological awareness of even the most seemingly insignificant human actions. Sachs cites Freud to explain that "so trivial and insignificant [human] movements . . . are in the highest degree indicative of the inner experiences of the subject, of his desires and emotions, and exactly of those desires and emotions of which he himself is unaware."[44] Film, in essence, can draw spectators' attention to the meaning behind a character's unconscious actions.

With regard to *Potemkin*, Sachs focuses on a close-up of a guard that precedes the moment when the ship's commander demands that the guards fire upon the mutineers:

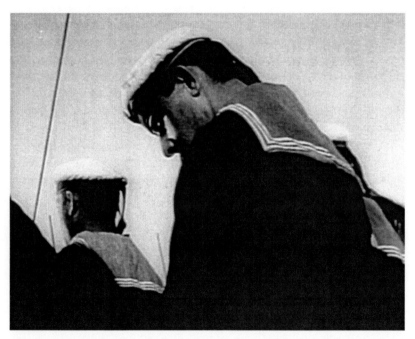

Solidarity expressed by a guard through a small gesture in Battleship Potemkin. *Western Left film theorists emphasized how montage could be employed to reveal the "unconscious optics" of cinema.*

Will the guard shoot or refrain? When at this moment one of the guard—whom so far we have considered as a creature bereft of individuality by drilling, a mere mechanically functioning unit—is dissociated from the group and, by means of a movement (independent and not dictated by discipline), by looking round at the sail-cloth as it is being carried past, betrays, however slightly, his character of a human-being involved in the proceedings, our question begins to be answered. We know that even the guard, in its totality an unfeeling machine, is made up of men capable of sympathy, and we begin to hope.[45]

The close-up exposes how the guard's gesture serves as a synecdoche for all the guards' sympathy with the mutineers even before they explicitly pledge their alliance with them. Sachs believes that this scene functions as "a kind of time-microscope, that is to say, it shows us clearly and unmistakably things that are to be found in life but that ordinarily escape our notice."[46] By visually juxtaposing the guard's relation to the group, *Potemkin* dialectically examines the dynamics between mechanistic training and human sympathy, which establishes much of the tension found in the scene.[47]

This psychological approach to montage was uniquely employed in analyses of abstract films. Although some contemporary film scholars regard the radical decontextualization produced by abstract film as anathema to the goals of Soviet montage, many international film theorists saw these films as pursuing similar ends to those of Soviet films, namely, directing the spectators' attention to overlooked phenomena that could influence their social outlook.[48] Zygmunt Tonecky's article "The Preliminary of Film Art" (1931) uses Eisenstein's concept of montage to investigate abstract film's radical reassemblage of spectator perceptions. Tonecky highlights Eisenstein's theory of intellectual film, which explains how cinema can direct the spectator's thought "by forcing him to reflect in a definite direction [and] ascribes to the montage association a great role for inciting comparison, for inducing to react, for formulating conclusions."[49] In montage, the spectator is shown "not only new distances but likewise new points of observation in dependence on the function of the objective."[50] But contrary to Eisenstein's belief in the scientific underpinnings of montage, Tonecky cites Béla Balázs's belief that the rhythm of montage's "relation to the plot may be very distant and irrational."[51] Tonecky's citation of Balázs is interesting in that it allows him to shift montage's focus from the intellect to more "irrational" film forms like abstract cinema (what Tonecky refers to as the "absolute film"), which does not play a role in Eisenstein's film theory.

Initially, it might seem as if Tonecky, by asserting that "singular objects in the so-called absolute film, thanks to the deforming actions of the camera, and the montage, differ much from what they are in everyday life and lose their usual daily character and aspect," is simply reinforcing contemporary observations about the formalist elements of abstract films.[52] But this defamiliarization of objects is not done mainly to draw the spectator's attention to the abstract forms of the objects themselves (by deconstructing their meanings), but to expose the psychic associations the film asserts between objects. According to Tonecky, "abstract psychic visions give purely visual associations . . . Single pictures are connected with each other not logically but psychologically—logic is here merely a means to facilitate understanding, its aim being psychological interpretation."[53] Abstract films maintain connections between their images through a psychological theme. For Tonecky, although single objects are physically decontextualized from their environment, they are still psychically linked to reality. Indeed, Tonecky implies that these objects must be decontextualized from their mundane surroundings in order to draw spectators' attention away from their literal meanings toward the psychological processes that organize the film's theme around them.

Clearly, for Tonecky and other early-1930s Left film theorists, abstract films were not simply formal exercises, but were linked to the project of creating critical spectators who could reenvision their world. Such an outlook can better assist us in understanding why Joseph Gollomb wrote in praise of Joris Ivens's abstract film *Rain* (1929) for the *Daily Worker*: "So he [Ivens] photographs rain with its infinite play of patterns in line and lights, on water, on the glistening street, on windows, umbrellas, automobile headlights and what not, until the homely phenomenon we ordinarily accept as a nuisance becomes a source of delight to see, if you have eyes to see; and Ivens's film, 'Rain,' helps open your eyes."[54] *Rain,* according to Gollomb, stands not in opposition to a Marxist cultural agenda in its use of abstraction but assists it by defamiliarizing reality for its viewers and, in essence, reconnecting them to their environment by making it "a source of delight."[55] Film, a product of the very industrialization that alienates humanity from nature, possesses the ability to defamiliarize reality and introduce it anew so that spectators become not only aware of intimate psychic connections, but also emotionally and sociopolitically reconnected to the world.[56]

But as well as fostering critical spectators, montage theory was also important in establishing a sophisticated representation of character psychology in film, which was to become an increasingly important concern for U.S. film critics and filmmakers as demand grew during the 1930s for the more widespread distribution and exhibition of progressive films. Montage offered filmmakers the ability to fuse experimental cinematic techniques with seemingly straightforward narratives. To use an analogy coined by Maya Deren, montage allowed film's "horizontal" movement of plot to temporarily stop and become "vertical" in the exploration of a specific cinematic moment, its meanings, nuances, and texture.[57] Within a montage-inflected film, one could have a character-centered plot that did not fetishize individuals as classical Hollywood cinema often did but that instead explored the nuances of personal psychology and the dialectical relationships between the characters and their social contexts.

This is perhaps best seen in Kenneth Macpherson's avant-garde film *Borderline* and in Macpherson's and H.D.'s analyses of the film. As Anne Friedberg writes, "*Borderline* contained everything that seemed important to the POOL group [which created it], combining, as it did, the psychological realism of Pabst, the psychoanalytic insights of Hanns Sachs, and the montage theories of Eisenstein."[58] In particular, the use of montage in the film was heavily influenced by Macpherson's reading of Sergei Eisenstein's article on overtonal montage, "The Filmic Fourth Dimension," which appeared in *Close Up*'s March 1930 issue.[59]

Overtonal montage, for Eisenstein, revealed how multiple elements within and between film frames resonated with one another. Unlike his earlier films *Strike* (1924) and *October* (1927), in which he used montage to emphasize dominant elements in the frames, Eisenstein felt that *The General Line* (1929) was his first film composed primarily of overtonal montage. Employing a musical metaphor, Eisenstein stated that along with the dominant tone of the film "comes a whole series of similar vibrations . . . Their impacts against each other, their impacts with the basic tone, and so on, envelop the basic tone in a whole host of secondary vibrations."[60] As a result, "this montage is built, not on *particular* dominants, but takes as its guide the total stimulation through all stimuli," which emphasizes the feeling of the shot as a whole.[61] Such use of overtonal montage allows the spectator to move beyond the simple responses of "I hear" and "I see" to a more nuanced dimension of feeling and thought.[62] In this essay, Eisenstein clearly shows how intellectual and emotional uses of montage needed to be intimately related to each other in order to create a deeply complex reaction in the spectator.

Although Eisenstein only later realized—while writing a treatment of Theodore Dreiser's *An American Tragedy* for Paramount—how overtonal montage might lead to a more sophisticated understanding of character

Astrid accusing Thorne of being a "nigger lover" in Borderline *(1930).*

psychology (see Chapter Two), Kenneth Macpherson was already using this concept to fashion a deep understanding of characters in his film. Unlike much avant-garde and Soviet work at the time that regarded character development as antiquated, *Borderline* blended montage theory with a concern for character psychology. Overtonal montage was important to Macpherson because it assisted his "subjective use of inference": "Instead of the method of externalized observation, I was going to take my film into the minds of the people in it, making it not so much a film of 'mental processes' as to insist on a mental condition. To take the action, the observation, the deduction, the reference, into the labyrinth of the human mind, with its queer impulses and tricks, its unreliability, its stresses and obsessions, its half-formed deductions, its glibness, it occasional amnesia, its fantasy, suppressions and desires."[63]

As H.D., who also stars in the film, notes in her pamphlet on *Borderline*, Macpherson's use of montage provides the film with a dreamlike and nightmarish quality. The film exposes how "that dream-nightmare permeates our consciousness although we may not know what it is or why."[64] She cites an example of this when Astrid (H.D.) accuses her lover of being a "nigger-lover," since he is sleeping with a mulatto woman:

"Subjective use of inference" in Borderline: *Astrid imagining Thorne lynched while the film simultaneously comments upon the hypocrisy of lynching.*

> Thorne, her faithless lover, by dream juxtaposition is seen posed as if a noose were dangling him from a floor . . . A small touch perhaps, to be noticed by a few only, but bound to have subconscious significance. Macpherson, it is obvious, in just that flash is demonstrating a tardy aphorism. If a black man is hanged for loving a white woman, why should not a white man be likewise lynched for loving a black one? Dream, I say. These conclusions happen only in the higher fantasy realm of dream value and of ultimate dream justice.[65]

H.D.'s analysis identifies the multiple uses of montage functioning throughout the film. She initially suggests that Macpherson uses montage for intellectual reasons to show the hypocrisy of a society that would hang a black man for his involvement with a white woman but not be similarly enraged about a white man's relationship with a black woman. This hypocrisy implicitly suggests the value placed on white womanhood while completely disavowing any "purity" for black women. Yet this intellectual point is made through "dream justice" that must break through the scene's objective "reality," suggesting how both the unconscious and the real converge.

Furthermore, implicit in H.D.'s analysis is Astrid's anger toward her lover, represented by her point-of-view shot that shows him hanging from a noose. The intellectual montage of "dream justice" also operates on the visceral level of Astrid's emotions, exposing the interpenetration of Astrid's feelings and Macpherson's belief about the hypocrisy of lynching. The scene, in essence, clearly yokes subjective character traits with a sociopolitical outlook that extends beyond the immediate narrative of the film, something that Eisenstein will pursue in his film adaptation of *An American Tragedy* and that will become a predominant concern for U.S. Left film critics and theorists during the tempestuous debates over *¡Que Viva México! Borderline* exemplifies how montage could be used for both political insight and the artistic need to create deeply realized characters.

It is worth highlighting H.D.'s primary concern with the scene's subconscious effects on the spectator, since it serves as a corrective to much contemporary theoretical work on montage that overemphasizes its intellectual and overtly critical aspects. H.D.'s insight reminds us that for some film theorists, montage's primary value lay in creating effects that spectators did not overtly notice. According to such theorists, the simple experiencing of montage in a film, regardless of a viewer's awareness of it, provides a significant moment in which reified sensibilities are disrupted by new relations and feelings that might provide the groundwork for a changed social vision. An emphasis on the spectator's unconscious reaction to montage led some Left film critics to identify the progressive potential in even the most commercial fare, since montage, no matter how bastardized, could still create perception-altering effects on some level and supply viewers with perspectives unavailable to them in any other medium.

As a result, montage theory, when used by these critics and theorists to understand commercial film rather than simply defame it, addressed the productive as well as problematic elements of Hollywood films. One of the most written-about and promising Hollywood directors during the early 1930s for U.S. Left film theorists and critics was Rouben Mamoulian. Mamoulian was a strange choice, since he was a director of mostly female-centered films in genres that most Left critics regarded at best as debased: maternal melodrama (*Applause*, 1929), horror (*Dr. Jekyll and Mr. Hyde*, 1931), romantic musical comedy (*Love Me Tonight*, 1932), romantic melodrama (*Song of Songs*, 1933), and costume drama (*Queen Christina*, 1933). However, despite Mamoulian's consistent choice of "trivial" subject matter, U.S. Left film theorists and critics could not help noticing his montage-inflected directing style.

For example, Mamoulian's counterpointing of visuals with sound in his films actualized some of the experimental tenets found in Eisenstein, Pudovkin, and Alexandrov's famous 1928 statement on sound.[66] The Russians wrote that sound, rather than being naturalized within talkies, had to be contrasted with the film's visuals in order to further develop the associational qualities of montage, and Mamoulian put this theory into practice in his Hollywood films. His second film, *City Streets,* a gangster picture, was often praised by U.S. Left critics for its intricate use of sound and visual montage. Seymour Stern wrote in a 1931 issue of the *Left:* "It is interesting to note that *City Streets* attains the highest standard of any talking-film in the matter of montage of its image-elements with sound. There is real organization, real purposive direction of photographic values, movement-forms and sound. The story is trite and insignificant, a gangster rehash, but the treatment of that story, such as it is, leaves nothing to be desired from a structural and technical standpoint."[67] Similarly, Harry Alan Potamkin, no fan of Hollywood, claimed that in *City Streets* "Mamoulian again separates himself from the trite story. He gives it a bold *Joan of Arc* treatment . . . a treatment far too heroic for the picture, but *per se* sensitive . . . [Even though the film "sags"], Mamoulian vindicates himself by doing a thriller which is as breathtaking as the railroad serial."[68]

As we can see, although critics of Mamoulian agreed that successful montage had to take into account both the film's formal structure and its content, they occasionally allowed for exceptions to this rule in their criticism when doing so was necessary to praise an innovative Hollywood director at the forefront of montage, even if he seemed to have intractably "bad taste" in film content. They were willing to modify their standards and classifications if doing so meant identifying and analyzing potential allies within the film industry. Mamoulian, according to these critics, was halfway to being a great Left director—and could make up the difference if he were to realize that a film's content was as important as its style. Potamkin chastised Mamoulian in a December 1929 issue of the *New Masses* for his maternal melodrama *Applause:* "Mamoulian has proved himself as a good a virtuoso as we have in America, but virtuosity we need no more. We need philosophers who seek great themes told with insight and ultimate import. We need artists who build structures."[69] But it was U.S. Left film critics themselves, rather than Mamoulian, who didn't adequately take into account his films' content. The "great themes" they constantly referred to often served as a euphemism for male-centered films that focused primarily upon traditional political content like class and racial issues, and they implicitly supported these types of films over those that addressed domestic, female-centered concerns.

Most critics regarded female-centered genres as either maudlin kitsch that "tear-jerked" spectators in the most conservative and predictable ways or as spectacular extravaganzas that celebrated materialism and hyperindividualism in order to deflect spectators' attention from streets filled with the Depression's unemployed and mounting political strife. As discussed in Chapter Four, these critics had a somewhat valid point in stressing the ways in which many female-centered Hollywood melo-dramas operated in an ideologically conservative fashion. But they missed how these films also addressed women and their desires. Female-centered genres like the historical costume drama and the maternal melodrama, in addition to being spectacular odes to materialism, exposed the intricate links that already existed between the domestic and the political, between gender differences and political equality. By trying to unify their readers under the banner of "the people" against the divisive individualistic and materialistic desires of capitalist ideology, U.S. Left film theorists and crit-ics ignored the importance gender differences played in establishing a so-cially progressive cinema. Just as they effaced the female-centered content at the heart of many of Mamoulian's films, time and again they ignored important gender issues within Left films by Sergei Eisenstein, Fritz Lang, Jean Renoir, and William Dieterle.

But despite U.S. Left film theorists' and critics' clear gender biases within their writing, their reliance on montage theory did not necessitate a wholesale rejection of non-Soviet films. As noted above, montage theory facilitated Left film theorists' and critics' discussions of the value of ab-stract, avant-garde, and even Hollywood films. Although their praise of montage could fall into dogmatic platitudes about the superiority of Soviet films, it could also supply intricate analyses of diverse genres and be used to explore the potentially politically emancipatory work occurring within each one. Hollywood was not immediately dismissed as a hopelessly cor-rupt bastion of capitalist cinema, since reactionary politics were not an in-herent element of the technology and cultural mode of production of the studio system.

Too many variables were at work during the 1930s for the studios' senior managers to fully consolidate their power and produce uniformly ideologically conservative films. As discussed in the introduction, those variables included the slump in box-office receipts caused by the Depres-sion, the formidable competition between studios for audiences, the Left political orientation of many film workers, the formation of progressive audience organizations, the competing independent and foreign films that influenced Hollywood films, and the film theory and criticism that transformed viewers into critical spectators. The real concern of many U.S. Left film theorists and critics was not the conservative ideology of Hollywood films but instead the question of who would control the studios' cultural mode of production and how the films could be situated to produce a critically informed reception. Such a project meant that U.S. Left film critics had to appraise all films, analyzing both their content and style, in order to prevent conservative kitsch from emerging from commercial and independent productions.

Montage, as a result, became the theoretical framework against which Left film theorists and critics could judge the rather ambiguous yet interrelated terrains of the popular and the avant-garde, the aesthetic and the political; it offered a way to dialectically juxtapose these realms with each other rather than to reject one for the other. U.S. Left film theorists and critics examined links across various film genres, styles, and cultural modes of production in order to conceptualize and enact a politically engaged and formally innovative cinema of the future.

REALISM AND THE MALE GAZE

For U.S. Left film theorists and critics, montage theory was important not only in restructuring spectators' perceptions and thoughts in progressive directions, but also in providing a coherent and meaningful explanation of a world that they felt was becoming increasingly fragmented and alienated because of the commodified processes of modernity. Rapid developments in science, technology, and advertising disoriented and dehumanized people through a barrage of competing discourses and social restructurings. In a 1930 issue of *Experimental Cinema,* David Platt noted the alienation modern science had produced: "For the first time in centuries man is without a *humanistic* system or theory of the universe potent enough to meet, cooperate with and give meaning and reality to the new naturalistic synthesis disclosed and still being disclosed by modern science."[70]

Interestingly enough, cinema, a product of modernity, could be used to combat this tendency. B. G. Braver-Mann explained in a 1934 issue of *Experimental Cinema* how montage, with its dialectical emphasis on social totality, provided spectators with a humanistic understanding of modernity: "A film director is an artist in a complete sense when he employs his tools to present a dialectic treatment of nature and man . . . ; he seeks to develop new aspects of cinematic design in time and linear patterns, and image relationships, with which to intensify artistically the deeply realistic content of his thematic material; he seeks new forms and methods not for their formal values alone but for their integration with an understanding of social phenomena."[71] According to this belief, film aesthetics are intimately tied to a unified humanistic social vision.

As mentioned earlier, regardless of the film form being analyzed—documentary, commercial, or avant-garde—the last thing Left film theorists, critics, and directors desired was a replication of bourgeois realism. The New York Film and Photo League, often regarded as the Left film group most adamant about social realism, understood reality in more complex terms than has often been assumed. Leo Hurwitz, one of the league's members, recounted how the league's notion of documentary was intimately tied to Vertov's idea of montage:

> I was fascinated by the mosaic character of film, by the capacity of documentary film to extract fragments out of the matrix of a visual-sound reality, then to weave these fragments into a form very different from the reality but capable of rendering the meaning and feeling of the real event. From this point of view, the documentary film was anything but a document. It did not "document" reality at all. Its tiny documents in the form of shots and sounds bore to the same relation to the film as the small pieces of colored stone and glass to the mosaic mural, the brushstrokes of painting, the individual words and phrases to the novel. The stuff was document, but the construction was invented, a time-collage. And it was clear that the question of truth or lie lay not in the stuff you were using but in the thoughts, responsibility, empathy of the filmmaker and his capacity to shape a form which could tell . . . how much of the truth.[72]

For Hurwitz and other U.S. Left film theorists and critics, cinema's main power was to restructure reality in socially meaningful and unified ways, not present it in a reified style that would naturalize spectators' perceptions by directing their thoughts and feelings only in accustomed channels.

In regard to Hollywood films, Left film theorists and critics often criticized them for being far too realistic—that is, for following the conventions of bourgeois filmic realism. U.S. Left film theorists' and critics' stance toward King Vidor is a case in point. His films were often concerned with the economic hardships of the lower or lower-middle class and tackled subject areas that Hollywood as a whole tended to avoid: southern blacks' experiences (*Hallelujah!* 1929), the working class (*The Crowd*, 1928, and

Street Scene, 1931), collective farming (*Our Daily Bread,* 1934), and corrupt medical practices (*The Citadel,* 1938). As William Troy wrote in the *Nation:* "He [Vidor] has always stood for a certain honesty, a certain originality, a certain ambitiousness in the handling of particularly and authentically American themes."[73] Yet many U.S. Left film theorists and critics questioned Vidor's realist style.

U.S. Left theorists and critics were particularly critical of Vidor's journalistic approach to filmmaking. B. G. Braver-Mann explains in *Experimental Cinema* in 1931: "From the point of view of King Vidor the functions of a film director are analogous to those of a journalist in that both report what they see, the difference between them being that the film director reports what he sees by means of the camera lenses and the film strip."[74] Braver-Mann believes that Vidor's documentary approach to film emphasizes the realism of each scene instead of establishing a unifying theme and montage structure that would develop the ideas at work in the film.

Braver-Mann's objection to Vidor's film style is not much different from Walter Benjamin's objection to the reified ways in which newspapers present their information: "If it were the intention of the press to have the reader assimilate the information it supplies as part of his own experience, it would not achieve its purpose. But its intention is just the opposite, and it is achieved: to isolate what happens from the realm in which it could affect the experience of the reader. The principles of journalistic information (freshness of the news, brevity, comprehensibility, and, above all, lack of connection between the individual news items) contribute as much to this as does the make-up of the pages and the paper's style."[75] The lack of connection between news items because of a paper's disjointed style could equally apply to Braver-Mann's critique of the inability of *Street Scene* to emotionally and intellectually connect with its viewers because of its fragmented structure. Braver-Mann feels that the spectator is unable to envision "the emotional content of the idea" in the film (namely, exploring the travails of working-class life), since the film is "incomplete or spurious in structure, scenes, implausible in meaning" through its lack of a coherent montage structure.[76] Vidor's realist style challenged montage theory because it emphasized the naturalized, documentary-like surface details of an individual scene instead of foregrounding ideas that should unify the film as a whole and thus present reality in coherent and meaningful ways to viewers.

In place of montage, Vidor relied on simplistic, sentimental stories. Harry Alan Potamkin notes this occurring at the end of *Street Scene.* After

the female protagonist's father kills her mother and is sent to jail, she decides to leave town so that her love interest will not sacrifice law school
in order to be with her. In the final shot, a high-angle camera focuses on
a group of children singing and dancing in a rotating circle. The camera
pulls back while mounting higher and higher as the children's song grows
faint, their circle gradually engulfed by the surrounding tenements. Potamkin regards the ending as clichéd and empty, reinforcing some empty plati-
tude like "life must go on."[77] He argues that the ending, unconnected to
the earlier parts of the film, merely reiterates the self-defeating generaliza-
tion that there is nothing to be done to improve tenement life.

In contrast, Left film critics felt that the film's focus on working-class
ethnic life required a montage structure that would emphasize the complex relations between individuals within the community, and how the
community was connected to a larger social context. Without this, there
could be no deeper understanding of the social causes of poverty. According to Seymour Stern, despite some "interesting shots of the posteriors of
washer-women," the film's lack of overall thematic unity prevents viewers
from comprehending the larger causes of the community's degraded living
conditions.[78] Alexander Bakshy adds that Vidor's disjointed photographic
style detaches individual characters from their backgrounds, and this de-
fect, along with "his insufficiently contrasted treatment of single episodes," splintered "the dramatic pattern of the play to a brightly colored
mosaic of a not particular clear design."[79]

Such criticisms resonate with contemporary film scholars' assessment
of the film. In *King Vidor, American,* Raymond Durgnat and Scott Simmon
claim that *Street Scene* emphasizes its two main protagonists, Rose and
Sam, at the cost of oversimplifying the rest of the ensemble cast into un-
sympathetic characters.[80] They write, "The film seems to condemn most of
its characters, to see them as sticks-in-the-mud deficient of life force, and
to give them some quick pity, maybe, but little interest in savoring their
quirks."[81] Even after the film ends, we don't feel as if we know these minor
characters any better than when we first met them.

One can observe the film's conflicted pull between the individual and
the group in a scene in which some of the tenants are discussing the affair
between Mrs. Maurrant (Estelle Taylor) and Steve Sankey (Russell Hop-
ton), and his run-in with her husband (David Landau). Two of the neighbors are speaking to a woman leaning out a window above them. The
film offers a high-angle, medium point-of-view shot of the woman looking down at one of the neighbors, Mrs. Jones (Greta Granstedt), who describes how Mr. Maurrant encountered Sankey walking down the street.

She explains that Sankey acted polite, but Mr. Maurrant shot him scornful glances, causing Sankey to leave, but then . . . The camera whip-pans to a medium shot of another neighbor, Filippo (George Humbert), who continues Jones's story: the Maurrants' boy, Willie (Lambert Rogers), comes home from school after being in a fight. As mother and father try to soothe the child, the father soon learns that the boy was defending his mother's character from another child's accusation of adultery. But before Filippo can continue, the camera whip-pans to a medium shot of Sam (William Collier, Jr.), the romantic interest of Rose Maurrant (Sylvia Sidney), as he protests against speaking behind the family's back. The scene emphasizes how this is a community brought together only by petty invective. The scene's sound track unites the various tenants by a continuous, unbroken narrative against the Maurrants, whereas the individual shots emphasize the characters' isolation from one another. Rose and Sam are championed as the only two people capable of a profound connection. The rest of the characters seem to deserve their miserable existence, since it externalizes their impoverished inner lives.

As this example shows, simply representing lower-class life on the screen was not enough. U.S. Left film critics believed that only a montage style could reveal the sociopolitical processes responsible for such poverty and suggest ways to alleviate them.[82] Although they valued Vidor's attempt to represent working-class ethnic life, they felt that his representation of it overlooked the needed unifying sociopolitical analysis. Instead, they were given a film that primarily focuses on a doomed love story between two members of a largely undeserving lower class.

Conversely, however, both international and U.S. Left film theorists and critics were blind to how complex representations of working-class ethnic communities could be found in the female-centered films that they marginalized. Durgnat and Simmon contrast the disjointed community in *Street Scene* with the more sophisticated conception of community that operates in Josef von Sternberg's *Shanghai Express* (1932). They assert that the film stresses "Marlene [Dietrich, the star] less than one might expect, and the Shanghai Express itself functions as a melting pot, in that initially self-obsessed individuals of diverse origin come to respect and help one another."[83] Although they overidealize the ensuing unity on the Shanghai Express, they correctly recognize how a dynamic and socially complex representation of community is at work.

Durgnat and Simmon emphasize how the film foregrounds the relationship between Shanghai Lily (Marlene Dietrich) and Hui Fei (Anna May Wong). They note how Hui even kills one of her own race for Lily's sake.[84]

This last comment is not entirely true and actually oversimplifies the two women's relationship by ignoring the overdetermined ways in which they are brought together. Hui's motivations for the murder of the revolutionary Henry Chang (Warner Oland) are complex. It could have been for the $20,000 reward or out of cultural pride, since she stated earlier how revolutionaries were a blight on the Chinese republic. But one definite reason seems to be as retaliation for Chang raping her, since her status as a prostitute justified it in his mind.

After Hui kills Chang, Lily says that she doesn't know whether she should be grateful for her actions. Hui responds that her gratitude does not matter. She continues, "Death cancelled his debt to me." A medium shot follows of Lily tapping her fingers on a suitcase. Her eyes glance around as she takes in Hui's response. Enigmatically, she begins to smile as her fingers slow and she looks over to Hui. Although Lily's thoughts remain unclear, she could be thinking that Hui's ultimate motivation was unimportant, since her actions nonetheless assisted Lily: both women occupy similar positions. Earlier in the film, Lily attempted to kill Chang, not for Hui's benefit but to save Captain Harvey (Clive Brook), her love interest. If Lily had succeeded, it would have also benefited Hui. Regardless of their intentions, Lily and Hui are a part of a community; the film takes pains to explore the social forces that place these women into nearly identical situations. The silence of Lily's thoughts in this scene signals that these two women do not need to talk to each other in order to come to an understanding. Their similar socioeconomic positions foster an inevitable understanding and community, and transcend their cultural differences. Unlike *Street Scene,* which never examines the conditions that create slum life, *Shanghai Express* relentlessly investigates these two women's common condition and the forces that threaten their autonomy. Their silences, pregnant with meaning and understanding, represent knowledge and a bond that the film viewer can only, at best, infer.

Yet early 1930s Left film theorists and critics were unable to see this complex representation of a working-class female community at work within von Sternberg's film, not solely because they considered his type of filmmaking anathema to a montage-based approach, but also because their reliance upon a bourgeois male gaze prevented them from doing so. In 1934, B.G. Braver-Mann noted the importance of montage techniques for *Shanghai Express*: "In *Shanghai Express* he [von Sternberg] flattered [Leonid] Trauberg and [Aleksandr] Dovzhenko, the former by imitating *China Express* both in genre and action while from Dovzhenko's *Arsenal* he adapted clichés from the freight sequence."[85] But Braver-Mann quickly dismisses von Sternberg's use of montage, since he ultimately believes that the director solely "concentrates on surface effects . . . and emphasizes the externals of film mechanics in a most inarticulate manner."[86] As a result, "Sternberg's distorted conception of the relation between man and his socio-economic background shows why this director is incapable of thinking the behaviour of his characters through to a logical conclusion."[87] Braver-Mann's last statement reveals the gender bias at work in his reading of the film. Although he analyzes von Sternberg's film in a seemingly nongendered way, his focus on problematic representations of "*man* and *his* socio-economic background" hints at the way many Left film theorists prioritized a male point of view, leaving their criticism unable to address complex cinematic representations of women and female communities.

In Braver-Mann's assessment of von Sternberg's oeuvre, he is incapable of seeing how all the director's films are concerned with representations of women and their surrounding communities. Instead, he assumes that von Sternberg's films merely objectify women as sexual lures for male spectators. In regard to *The Blue Angel* (1930), Braver-Mann claims that "Sternberg reveals such an abnormal interest in the singer's physical area below the hips that he succeeded in establishing Marlene Dietrich in the minds of filmgoers as the image of a slut."[88] Yet recent feminist film scholarship often cites this film for its remarkable portrayal, at least in the first half, of a female community that defies the structures of a male gaze. Judith Mayne argues that *The Blue Angel* has often been misinterpreted by contemporary film historians because of their unconscious theoretical reliance upon a male gaze when analyzing the film, and an identical assumption was at work within 1930s U.S. Left film theorists' use of montage theory to analyze von Sternberg's films.[89] As a result, a critic like Braver-Mann can make the astounding claim that von Sternberg's films reveal "his ignorance of the part played by economic determinism in the sex life of the capitalistic West," when, in reality, von Sternberg seems particularly adept at showing how women had to navigate the narrow channels of patriarchal capitalism in order to maintain a modicum of independence and actualize some of their desires.[90]

We can most clearly see how the male gaze structured Left film critics' analyses of von Sternberg's films by briefly returning to Hanns Sachs's article "Kitsch." Although Sachs claims that kitsch techniques operate in both commercial and independent cinema, he uses Soviet-montage films as examples of works that defy kitsch-like styles, whereas *Shanghai Express* becomes representative of bourgeois kitsch par excellence. Sachs believes that the film reinforces an audience's identification with the upper-class characters. Since Shanghai Lily wants to be rid of her notorious past in order to spiritually and sexually reunite with her former lover, Captain David Harvey, Sachs sees the film as setting up the couple as an ideal for audiences to emulate. As a result, "The lower, suppressed classes, in so far as they are not educated to independent class-consciousness, accept and firmly adhere to the ideals of the higher class which governs them."[91] Interestingly, Sachs's reading of the film overlooks the film's two primary protagonists, Shanghai Lily and Hui Fei, in order to prioritize Captain David Harvey as the film's narrative center.

Such a reading is surprising to a contemporary film viewer, since not only is Harvey denied the narrative agency to serve the heroic function of killing the film's villain, Chang, but the film also takes pains to expose Harvey's gross undervaluation of Shanghai Lily. At work within Sachs's reading of the film is his unconscious reliance upon the male gaze, which Laura Mulvey identified in her classic essay "Visual Pleasure and Narrative Cinema." According to Mulvey, classical Hollywood cinema presents women either as fetishized bodies or as individuals who must be punished or forgiven for committing threatening acts that symbolize castration for male characters and viewers.[92] But as Gaylyn Studlar points out in *In the Realm of Pleasure: Von Sternberg, Dietrich, and the Masochistic Aesthetic*, von Sternberg's films are notable for the ways in which they challenge the male gaze. Instead, male spectators and film protagonists are placed in masochistic positions: they do not fear castration but instead desire a powerful woman who symbolically represents a pre-Oedipal need for a strong maternal figure. Captain Donald Harvey is this type of male masochist. He carries a picture of Madeline (Shanghai Lily's old name) in his watch despite not having seen her for five years. He constantly grieves over his separation from her and her "betrayal" of his love, even though it was he who destroyed the relationship.[93]

Yet despite all of *Shanghai Express*'s structuring devices that challenge Mulvey's theory and the authority of Harvey's position, Sachs still overidentifies with Harvey by claiming that he has sole narrative control and serves as the film's central figure for viewer identification. Although Sachs correctly identifies how Shanghai Lily becomes the object of heterosexual male desire in the film, he is unable to theorize that she, rather than Harvey, wields narrative control and, therefore, "is not the passive object of the controlling look."[94]

Sachs's inability to see Shanghai Lily as an active participant in the narrative exposes how the male gaze structured many U.S. Left film theorists' and critics' theories of montage and film criticism: women were always regarded as objects, even in narratives in which they were clearly not so (see my discussions of *¡Que Viva México!* in Chapter Two, *Fury* in Chapter Three, and *La Marseillaise* in Chapter Four). Despite many Left film theorists' and critics' ability to provide complex ideological analyses of various types of cinema, they still aligned themselves with a heterosexual, white, bourgeois male gaze. This led to a pervasive shortsightedness regarding gender that plagued most of their theory and criticism: female characters were often either disregarded altogether or dismissed as representations of a corrupt bourgeois materialism; female-centered films and genres were labeled as conservative, bourgeois kitsch; and feminine aspects of celebrated Left films were purged from discussions in order to preserve the film's ideological strength and masculine autonomy.

One critic, however, did take notice of the importance of gender to film content, style, and spectatorship: Dorothy Richardson. Richardson is perhaps best known for her thirteen-volume novel *Pilgrimage*, but she was also an enthusiastic film critic for *Close Up*. She contributed more than twenty articles to the journal from 1927 to 1933.[95] Richardson created a hybrid brand of film theory that fused her reformist interest in cinema's power to culturally uplift the lower classes with her interest in montage's ability to alter viewers' perceptions so that they could gain a glimpse of the social totality that the fragmenting processes of modernity obscured. Furthermore, she often examined the importance of gender in her discussions of independent and commercial cinema. Even when gender was not at the forefront of her articles, her implicit gender awareness led her to see more democratic potential in commercial cinema than many of her male colleagues.

DOROTHY RICHARDSON: A THEORETICAL ROAD NOT TAKEN

Richardson's first film column, for the July 1927 issue of *Close Up*, indicates her initial reformist sensibility toward film. She views commercial cinema, with its ability to show better living conditions, as a potentially uplifting medium for the downtrodden. She particularly stresses the specificity of the audience — working-class mothers: "Their children, apart from the infants accompanying them, were at school and their husbands were at work. It was a new audience, born within the last few months . . . Many of the women sat alone, figures of weariness at rest. Watching these I took comfort. At last the world of entertainment had provided for a few pence, tea thrown in, a sanctuary for mothers, an escape from the everlasting qui vive into eternity on a Monday afternoon."[96] Richardson realized that the commercial theater provided a respite for mothers, who could temporarily break free of their daily routine of housework and motherhood (except for those with infants). She stresses that it was not necessarily all women but working-class mothers in particular who benefited from attending the cinema in midafternoon, since it broke up the drudgery of housework that consumed their daily lives.[97]

Richardson's initial focus on working-class mothers is important. As her film theory became gradually influenced by montage theory, her interest expanded from working-class mothers to working-class viewers in general. But she never forgot about audience specificity, even while speaking on a more abstract level about spectatorship, and frequently offered caveats that either acknowledged the limits of such abstract theorizations or reintroduced gender specificity in her articles.

In the aforementioned article, Richardson shows not only how the space of the theater serves as a momentary sanctuary for working-class mothers, but also how the films themselves provide these women with a sense of escape. Her initial conception of escape is somewhat opposed to the tenets of montage theory. Unlike proponents of montage theory, who viewed escapism as an all too common negative attribute of the uncritical spectatorship fostered by commercial cinema, Richardson argued that escape serves a positive function, namely, in diversifying the lower class's experiences. In "The Cinema in the Slums" (May 1928), Richardson states that film allows the lower classes to temporarily leave their cramped conditions and wretched lives through identification with the diverse experiences of the film characters. She states that regardless of the quality of the film, "civilization [is] working unawares" upon its lower-class viewers.[98] One can see her reformist sensibility at work in her feeling that the lower class needs "civilization" to guide its actions. Furthermore, one can speculate that Left montage theorists would have interpreted Richardson's program of cultural uplift as nothing less than a classist outlook that wanted to impose its bourgeois norms and restrictions on the "untrained" and "uncivilized" minds of the lower classes.

However, in "The Cinema in Arcady" (July 1928), Richardson revises her stance on escapism and retheorizes it through a montage perspective. Escape is now linked with cinema's potential to offer viewers the sort of new perceptions and experiences that allow them to see beyond their current socio-aesthetic limits. Escapism's main benefit is no longer that it establishes bourgeois ideals to emulate, but that it provides new perceptions, which override the limits of bourgeois individualism: "To cease for a moment to be just John or Mary carrying about with you where you go your whole known record, to be oblivious of the scene upon which your life is lived and your future unalterably cast, is to enter into your own eternity."[99] One notes how Richardson's conception of spectatorship has broadened to include all film viewers, not simply those belonging to a particular gender or class. Although she never mentions montage by name, her observation about film's power to unmoor viewers from their specific socioeconomic contexts is clearly influenced by montage theory's advocacy of a totalistic vision.

But unlike many montage theorists, Richardson believed that all films have the potential to provide such totalistic moments. Implicit in her writing is the belief that the primary audience for film is the lower class, which had rather limited experience with traditional art's ability to reveal the world in new and unaccustomed ways. What middle-class film critics might have found banal and bourgeois in commercial cinema had a strong perceptual and cognitive impact on members of the lower classes. Commercial cinema, even at its tritest, democratized art by catering specifically to lower-class audiences. As a result, film viewing could provide a broad, new aesthetic experience for people with little exposure to painting, literature, dance, or theater.

Richardson's position was in many ways not unlike that of Walter Benjamin in "The Work of Art in the Age of Mechanical Reproduction." One of Benjamin's central themes is how mechanical reproduction gives the general populace broad access to the arts: "With the emancipation of the various art practices from ritual go increasing opportunities for the exhibition of their products."[100] Accompanying this increased access is a qualitative change in both the artwork and its reception. Not only does mechanical reproduction strip art of its "aura," but it also turns viewers into cultural critics.[101] Film, according to Benjamin, represents the vanguard medium in this area. Although Benjamin stresses how the very concept of art changes because of mechanical reproduction, whereas Richardson leaves the status of art unquestioned, they are both interested in theorizing how cinema transformed working-class viewers' relation to the arts.

Richardson's theoretical development suggests the impact that Soviet montage had upon film theorists in the 1930s, including those who might not have explicitly identified themselves with a Marxist outlook, but were nonetheless influenced by its theories. Furthermore, her work shows that many 1930s film theorists considered cinema the central medium for helping mass audiences negotiate the traumatic effects of modernity. As Miriam

Hansen notes: "The juncture of classical cinema and modernity reminds us, finally, that the cinema was not only part and symptom of modernity's experience and perception of crisis and upheaval; it was also, most importantly, the single most inclusive, cultural horizon in which traumatic effects of modernity were reflected, rejected or disavowed, transmuted or negotiated."[102] We see this realization on Richardson's part as she fuses her growing knowledge about montage theory with her ideas about commercial cinema's impact on audiences.

By the time of "This Spoon-Fed Generation?" (December 1931), Richardson was asserting that commercial cinema has enough of a montage style at work within it to be able to offer spectators a unified and humane totalistic vision to set against modernity's fragmentation of human experience. Like U.S. Left film theorists David Platt and B.G. Braver-Mann, she understands that each generation "has had in turn to experience the break-up of a known world," but the modern generation has had to experience this at an increasing pace: "Uncertainty, noise, speed, movement, rapidity of external change that has taught them to realize that tomorrow will not be as to-day, all these factors have helped to make the younger generation shock-proof in a manner unthinkable to the majority of their forebears."[103]

People in the thick of this change and uncertainty are unable to obtain the required distance from their own lives to question their daily habits or contemplate the world as a totality. But montage places spectators at "the motionless, observing center," where such fragments could be "seen in full in their own moving reality."[104] Emerging "from our small individual existences and from narcissistic contemplation thereof," we "learn that we are infinitesimal parts of a vast whole."[105]

For Richardson, however, such a totalistic vision was not limited to Soviet films, but was also employed by commercial films, since they too were "arranged and focused at the distance exactly fitting the contemplative state."[106] She argues that this "remains *Borderline*'s utmost [goal] as well as that of [the commercial film] *The Policeman's Whistle*."[107] Richardson remained wary of film theories that condemned commercial cinema for not reaching high levels of artistic excellence or political insight, since such dogmatic positions ignored the stylistic similarities that nonetheless existed between commercial cinema and the most radical montage-based films.

Though montage theory influenced Richardson, she reminded its theorists that their standards (or anyone's, for that matter) were not absolutes but the product of a specific, limited perspective. In "The Thoroughly

Popular Film" (April 1928), she reminds the critical film community of this: "But when we condemn the inartistic let us beware of assuming aesthetic excellence as always and everywhere and for everyone the standard measure. If we feel we must condemn popular art let us know where we are, know that we are refusing an alternative measure and interpretation of the intercommunications we reject."[108] As we will see in later chapters, most U.S. Left film critics did not take heed of Richardson's warning. Although they offered many subtle interpretations of commercial and independent cinema, they still remained steadfast in their disavowal of female-centered films, which they regarded as hopelessly commodified and reactionary products, as well as of any feminine aspects of popular culture.

Richardson, on the other hand, was willing to give even the kitschiest and most clichéd filmic conventions the benefit of the doubt, since they often spoke to audiences' unconscious utopian desires. In particular, she focused on the most notorious aspect of commercial cinema—the happy ending:

> In some respects the worst criminal of all and certainly a thing-in-itself. It is demanded absolutely. They [mainstream audiences] won't, we are told, stand anything else. But there is good reason for their refusal, for their stern convention. Is it or is it not, the good ending, the truth, perhaps crudely and wrongly expressed, of life, and their refusal to have it outraged based deeply in the consciousness of mankind? They welcome even the most preposterously happy ending not because it is in contrast to the truth as known in their own lives, but because it is true to life. The wedding bells, the reconciled family, the reclaiming of the waster, all these things are their artistic convention and the tribute of love paid to them by the many is a tribute to their unconscious certainty that life is ultimately good.[109]

For Richardson, to condemn such conventions because they did not meet the criteria of montage theory for a unified and coherent filmic whole was to miss the more important point that such kitsch conventions speak to mass audiences' unconscious utopian desires for a better life, for a new future.

Richardson's brilliant observation resonates with recent film scholarship that suggests Left film theory needs to move beyond a negative critique of mass culture (embodied by Frankfurt School theorists Theodor Adorno and Max Horkheimer and by Althusserean apparatus theory) in order to better theorize about the utopian elements lurking within commercial cinema (found in the work of Walter Benjamin and Ernst Bloch). This was succinctly elaborated by Fredric Jameson in his brilliant essay "Reification and Utopia in Mass Culture": "The works of mass culture, even if their function lies in the legitimation of the existing order—or some worse one—cannot do their job without deflecting in the latter's service the deepest and most fundamental hopes and fantasies of the collectivity, to which they can therefore, no matter in how distorted a fashion, be found to have given voice."[110] Or as Jane Gaines even more succinctly puts it: "If it did not offer us something, mass culture *would not be able* to deceive."[111]

Along similar lines, many Left film theorists and critics were unable to see how seemingly female-centered films and the feminine aspects of mass culture might have been speaking to desires and issues more complex than the simple bulwarking of a reactionary bourgeois outlook. Richardson, on the other hand, because she always remained aware of specific audiences even while engaging in abstract theories of spectatorship, was better able to explore the limits of montage theory, which all too often ignored the very viewers (and their sociocultural backgrounds) that it was attempting to politically liberate.

Finally, and most ambitiously, Richardson began to theorize how silent and sound cinema might be gendered. In "The Film Gone Male" (March 1932), Richardson identifies the newly emergent talking cinema as male, whereas the silent cinema was representative of a female sensibility. Speech, according to Richardson, is men's domain, since they are the ones who have dictated its rules, its theorems, and its logic. Language itself is incapable of fully grasping female reality or "being," as Richardson calls it.[112] In a related fashion, talking cinema is problematic not only because of its dependence on the spoken word, but also because its linear narrative formally eschews women's experience. On the other hand, Richardson praises silent cinema for its non-linear quality: "Being nowhere and everywhere, nowhere in the sense of having more intention than direction and more purpose than plan, everywhere by reason of its power to evoke, suggest, reflect, express from within its moving parts and in their totality of movement, something of the changeless being at heart of all becoming, [silent cinema] was essentially feminine."[113] Despite Richardson's essentializing of "feminine" Being and "masculine" Becoming, she nonetheless perceptively stresses how cinematic styles themselves might be gendered.

As a matter of fact, Richardson felt that since sound cinema was increasingly "becoming a medium of propaganda, it [was] doubtless fulfilling its destiny"—"but," she hastens to add, "it is a masculine destiny."[114]

Although I take issue with Richardson's assertion that propaganda cinema is inherently "masculine," one can see how international and U.S. Left film theorists were positioning montage film and theory as a masculine-oriented form of cinema and analysis. As we will see in the following chapter, even in a montage-based film like *¡Que Viva México!* in which gender revolution is a central theme, U.S. Left film theorists and critics systematically ignored this aspect because of their theoretically limited male gaze and male-oriented criticism. As a result, one can understand why Richardson would perceive montage-based propaganda films as innately masculine, since the film theory and criticism surrounding them incessantly positioned them so.

CONCLUSION

It has been the goal of this chapter to situate the emergence of U.S. Left film theory and criticism within the pages of international and domestic film journals and Left periodicals. This has revealed a much more sophisticated theoretical background at work than has often been assumed. In particular, "montage" served as a pliable term to assist Left film theorists and critics in analyzing both commercial and independent cinema. It offered critics a conceptual tool with which to compare films from divergent backgrounds and examine how they employed related stylistic techniques to help viewers break free from rote bourgeois perspectives to radically new interpretations of the world.

Montage theory also articulated the necessity for cinema to offer a totalistic, humane vision that would counteract the alienating and fragmenting processes of modernity. International and U.S Left film theorists' and critics' demand for realism must be understood within this theoretical outlook. They desired a montage-based realism that would use a dialectical style to counteract Hollywood realism and reveal the mutually influential relations between individuals and their sociopolitical context. Their call for realism was far from being a naïve endorsement of a strict documentary-like representationalism.

However, despite the insights offered by montage theory for the ideological analysis of a wide variety of films, an implicit male gaze directed its practitioners to celebrate male-centered genres and the masculine aspects of mass culture at the expense of female-centered ones and the "feminine" elements of film culture as a whole. Because of their sexist gaze, most international and U.S. Left film theorists and critics ignored the importance of gender representations in independent and commercial cinema and dismissed any aspects of mass culture that struck them as too femi-nine. Regardless of their desire to forge socio-aesthetic links between commercial and independent cinema, and between domestic and inter-national cinema, in the name of creating a politically progressive cinema of the future, these theorists and critics were unable to address the impor-tance of gender issues in their plans.

This first period of U.S. Left film theory and criticism was unique in its reliance on montage theory to provide a central framework for interna-tional and domestic discussions of cinema. As we will see in the following chapter, its development would be drastically altered by events in indepen-dent political filmmaking. In the years between 1931 and 1935, U.S. Left film theory and criticism gradually split itself into two opposing camps as a result of the controversy surrounding Sergei Eisenstein's film *¡Que Viva México!* One group consisted of those critics who advocated the use of radical montage by independent Left cinema against the conciliatory and hopelessly compromised outlook of Hollywood. The other group com-prised those who felt that Hollywood styles had to be incorporated into Left filmmaking (and vice versa) so that its products could reach a wider audience. The only major theoretical consistency between these factions remained a general refusal to analyze the importance of gender within *¡Que Viva México!*—a film that offered one of the most striking examples of how the formation of a classless society was inextricably linked to a gender revolution.

Chapter 2

Eisenstein in America

THE *¡Que Viva México!* DEBATES AND EMERGENT POPULAR FRONT U.S. FILM THEORY AND CRITICISM

In the early 1930s, a group of U.S. Left film theorists and critics banked their hopes on the mass distribution of Sergei Eisenstein's *¡Que Viva México!* within the United States in order to prove once and for all that modernism was not the sole province of cultural elites but could serve both political and aesthetic revolutionary ends for mainstream audiences. The film's use of radical montage to expose the relations between the political and the personal, between the individual and his or her socioeconomic context, served as a corrective to the conservative ideology and reified representations of many Hollywood films. Yet as these theorists and critics promoted Eisenstein's film, they became increasingly aware of Hollywood's stranglehold on all channels of mass distribution, especially when producers demanded that Eisenstein's film be reedited in a style that was in more accord with the forms of classical Hollywood cinema. Widespread debates arose in the critical community about the problem of mass distribution in the United States, about the ability of montage to address both social issues and character psychology, and about whether film should shock audiences into intellectual engagement or use emotional identification with characters to prevent viewers from becoming completely alienated from the subject matter. By examining the influence of Eisenstein's theoretical articles on U.S. Left film theorists and critics, and these theorists' and critics' failed attempts to mass-distribute *¡Que Viva México!* we can observe a shift in U.S. Left film theory and criticism from a radical position that was often skeptical of Hollywood's formal conventions to an emergent Popular Front stance that acknowledged the need of Left films to adopt some commercial conventions in order to gain access to the mass audiences that Hollywood had carefully guarded.

Additionally, this chapter argues that Eisenstein's Mexican footage reveals how montage could be used to show that political equality depended directly on a radical transformation of gender roles. Although one does not want to underestimate the difficulty of theorizing about such a tentative, incomplete film project, a careful analysis of Eisenstein's script, working notes, and outlines, along with the reconstructions of the film by his student Jay Leyda in the 1950s and his assistant Grigory Alexandrov in the 1970s, suggests that *¡Que Viva México!* might have become one of Eisenstein's most sophisticated works to investigate gender's relation to radical political transformation. Eisenstein's notion of overtonal montage serves as a useful conceptual tool for analyzing the Mexican footage, since it draws attention to the importance of evaluating the dominant and residual montage elements operating within each shot as well as those operating between them.[1] As Vladimir Nizhny, Jacques Aumont, and David Bordwell suggest, mise-en-scène and mise-en-shot (montage-within-the-shot) became central in Eisenstein's teaching after his experience filming *¡Que Viva México!* suggesting that these elements were important when he was working on the film.[2] The incomplete Mexican footage provides ample evidence of mise-en-shot and thus, when analyzed in conjunction with Eisenstein's and his contemporaries' writings on the film, allows one to make some inferences about the overall montage structure that his film might have taken if he had completed filming and edited the film.

Furthermore, 1930s U.S. Left film theorists' and critics' writings on Eisenstein's Mexican footage (and its Hollywood-release version, *Thunder over Mexico,* assembled from outtakes taken by Edward Tisse and Eisenstein, and edited by Hollywood producer Sol Lesser) help elucidate how they continued to marginalize gender issues. In accord with the work of such feminist scholars as Deborah Rosenfelt, Paula Rabinowitz, and Nan Enstad, who examine the problematic attitudes of the historical U.S. male Left toward gender politics and women's liberation, this chapter exposes how most 1930s U.S. Left film theorists and critics used gender, at best, as a metaphor within their columns to help critique censorship of Eisenstein's film.[3] Rarely did they note the central importance of gender in structuring *¡Que Viva México!* despite all of them having had access to Eisenstein's film scenario and some of them having interviewed Eisenstein both on and off location and gotten the chance to view his outtakes. Although one could rightly claim that limited viewing access and the incomplete nature of the film hindered the ability of some U.S. Left film theorists and critics to identify gender as a central theme, the marginalization of gender in their columns stemmed in fact from three pervasive sources: as mentioned in Chapter One, a male gaze that minimized women's narrative importance and ignored gender within cinema; a political strategy that primarily viewed the championing of female desire and agency as nothing more than a consumption-based framework that jeopardized class solidarity and collective action; and a male fear of how the Depression's economic instability and the consumerist discourses of the 1930s challenged their own masculine identities and privilege.

EISENSTEIN AND U.S. FILM THEORY

Before engaging in a close analysis of *¡Que Viva México!* and the theorists' and critics' responses to it, I first want to briefly address the context that made Eisenstein a significant figure for 1930s U.S. Left film theory. Not only was Eisenstein a prolific writer, but U.S. film theorists and critics of the period also felt that much of his theory and filmmaking represented the most advanced stage of Left cultural work on and in film. *Close Up* published nine translations of Eisenstein essays from 1929 to 1933; *Experimental Cinema* published fifteen articles by or about Eisenstein from 1930 to 1934.

By the early 1930s, Eisenstein had significantly revised his filmic strategy of the early 1920s, which focused on portraying the mass as hero and forsaking any concern with character psychology. By 1929, he gradually became more interested in the individual's relation to the masses, as seen in *The General Line*'s focus on a peasant woman's struggle to form a cooperative in her village. Furthermore, his experience reading James Joyce's *Ulysses* in early 1928 encouraged Eisenstein to contemplate using Joyce's notion of internal monologue within a Marxist cinema. By the time of his six-month stay at Paramount studios in the summer of 1930, Eisenstein finally had the opportunity to create a project that used internal monologue to develop characters' psychology while still situating them within broader socioeconomic contexts. His scenario for Theodore Dreiser's *An American Tragedy* provided a model for U.S. Left film theorists and critics on how to combine a political and experimental style within a conservative Hollywood film structure that emphasized linear narrative and individualized characterization. Eisenstein addressed how ideology affects the structure of personality by using internal monologue to represent how the psychological state of his protagonist, Clyde Griffiths, was shaped by the surrounding culture.

According to Eisenstein, film was the ideal medium to present internal monologue because of its visual and aural nature, "for only the sound film is capable of reconstructing all the phases and the specific essence of the process of thought."[4] In *An American Tragedy*, Eisenstein used highly experimental forms to represent Griffiths's psychological state within a typical classical Hollywood narrative. By linking Joyce's internal monologue with a sociological theme, Eisenstein felt that the scenario achieved "greater psychological and tragic depth," since it exposed the link between personal psychology and the social forces that, in this case, push a character to a predestined failure.[5] Unlike most Hollywood films, which emphasized the individual's separation from and triumph over his or her social surroundings, *An American Tragedy* was to show how the individual emerged from the social, and the social from the individual.

Eisenstein's desire to fuse character psychology with social analysis served as a corrective to his earlier beliefs related to montage, which often resulted in his objectifying individuals for the sake of representing collective action. As we will see later, Eisenstein's use of internal monologue anticipated some of the objections made by U.S. Left film theorists like Leo Hurwitz and Ralph Steiner concerning how some montage films objectified people in ways analogous to the forces of capitalism, which reified both laborer and consumer. The problem of how best to represent people in film became increasingly important as the decade progressed, since it signified U.S. Left theorists' and critics' theoretical shift from a radical stance on montage that saw characters only as products of socioeconomic forces toward a greater concern with character psychology and classical Hollywood forms.

Even before Eisenstein published an account of his experiences with *An American Tragedy,* a few U.S. Left film theorists noted in their columns the importance of Eisenstein's work in Hollywood, since it not only suggested how a Hollywood film could address the relationship between the psychological and social, but it also indicated Eisenstein's increasing ability to address in his own works the individual's relation to social forces. Harry Alan Potamkin had often criticized Eisenstein for ignoring character psychology in his films. In an article for *Experimental Cinema* in 1930, Potamkin presciently claims, "He [Eisenstein] does not penetrate the individual and there is a question in my mind whether he has penetrated the social inference contained in the mass-expression," which must take into account its effects on individuals' psyches.[6] But in "Novel into Film: A Case Study of Current Practice," an article published in *Close Up* in December 1931, Potamkin states that Eisenstein's script work on *An American Tragedy* represented the first time Eisenstein revealed an ability to make both personal and political elements contribute to "the total structure of the film."[7] For Potamkin, internal monologue allowed Clyde, the film's protagonist, to function dialectically between the sociological and psychological. Since this technique broke down the barriers between Clyde's surrounding social context and his subjective thoughts and feelings, viewers would experience the inextricable links between the political and personal. As a result, the Eisenstein script for *An American Tragedy* proved a pivotal text for U.S. Left film theorists like Hurwitz and Steiner, who believed that montage had to take into account character psychology if it were to remain a viable film style within mainstream cinema. The script for *An American Tragedy* represented the most explicit attempt by a radical Left director to reconcile the political and experimental with the demands of a conservative Hollywood system that foregrounded conventional narrative and individual character psychology. Although the film was never shot using that script, it provided a useful model for critics, since its script suggested what could be attempted in Hollywood, encouraging them to demand that similar projects actually get made.

But it was Eisenstein's next venture, *¡Que Viva México!* that truly excited U.S. Left film theorists and critics. Unlike *An American Tragedy*, which was rejected by Paramount in part because of its radical indictment of the American political and judicial system, this independent U.S.-funded project seemed guaranteed to be completed because of its freedom from studio control. Most theorists and critics felt that Eisenstein would use techniques he developed for *An American Tragedy* on this project. According to Seymour Stern: "The picture that Eisenstein brings with him from Mexico will no doubt make history enough for our Hollywood-ridden Western hemisphere," since the completed film would expose the genius Hollywood denied.[8] Stern was seconded by Adolfo Best-Maugard: "Modern cinema is *Viva México!*, a new achievement of a new technique, a more amazing technique than that of *Potemkin*, perhaps most adequately described, I should say, as 'symphonic cinema.'"[9] In part, such optimism by U.S. Left film theorists and critics made them react so vehemently when everything about Eisenstein's Mexican film went wrong.

Unfortunately, multiple factors prevented Eisenstein from completing *¡Que Viva México!:* his political and aesthetic disagreements over the film's composition with Upton Sinclair (a key financial backer of the film); the difficulty of arranging mass distribution of the film; and Stalin's demand that Eisenstein stop filming and immediately return home or else be deemed a deserter to the Soviet Union.[10] At the time of Stalin's ultimatum, Eisenstein had shot only five of the six episodes of *¡Que Viva México!* all of which he eventually shipped to Upton Sinclair. Despite Eisenstein's subsequent pleas to gain access to the footage in order to edit it, Sinclair refused, believing that Eisenstein might try to smuggle this footage abroad, never to be seen again. Instead, Sinclair hired Hollywood producer Sol Lesser to condense Eisenstein's raw footage into a film with a ninety-minute running time, resulting in the film known as *Thunder over Mexico*.

Before the release of *Thunder over Mexico* in September 1933, Left film theorists and critics mounted one of the most organized campaigns against it and for *¡Que Viva México!* There were two major points of contention: *¡Que Viva México!* represented the possibility of mass-distributing a radical film in America for the first time ever and thus of challenging the hegemonic hold Hollywood had on theaters and audiences; and *¡Que Viva México!* demonstrated montage's superiority to the Hollywood cutting found in *Thunder over Mexico*. Together, these two points helped illuminate a fundamental paradox within 1930s U.S. Left film theory and criticism: while arguing for montage's superiority over Hollywood cutting as a means to reenvision the multiple relations between social and political processes, these theorists and critics grew increasingly aware that if they wanted progressive films ever to be widely distributed in America, they would have to work with a studio system that denied the merits of radical montage. Furthermore, as we will see, *¡Que Viva México!* critiqued bourgeois institutions while recognizing the need to work within them in order to realign their structures for the benefit of progressive political goals. Like Eisenstein's later films and theories, *¡Que Viva México!* emphasized the need for an aesthetics that incorporated classical cinematic styles like character development into Left film techniques like montage-within-the-shot—an aesthetics more inclusive than most U.S. Left film theorists and critics would have recognized while they were defending the radical structure of *¡Que Viva México!*

As mentioned in Chapter One, montage served as a central concept in structuring the debates of emerging Left film theory during the late 1920s for two main reasons: it was a pliable enough term that Left film theorists could use to pursue the ideological analysis of a wide variety of films; and its emphasis on the inextricable links between film form and content provided a sophisticated method not only for analyzing the overall structure of specific films, but also for exploring cinema's ability to offer spectators a more coherent vision of modernity's fragmenting socioeconomic processes and to explore how spectators could alter such processes in humane and egalitarian directions. In regard to the debates over *¡Que Viva México!* U.S. Left film theorists and critics feared that the Hollywood-style continuity editing of *Thunder over Mexico* would emphasize one-dimensional characters, melodramatic events, and visual eye candy over *¡Que Viva México!*'s social content and themes.

In 1933, Seymour Stern, who had once been a production assistant for Universal, mapped out how the Hollywood and montage styles of editing differed and what was at stake in those differences. Hollywood relied not only on the formulaic application of such technical tricks as wiping and the dissolve, which often took little or no account of the film's content, but also on spectacular mise-en-scène within a realist narrative in order to give audiences a familiar filmic structure that simplified content by making it both pleasing and natural to the eye. Backgrounds had to be scenic. Close-ups were meant to highlight the actors' features. Above all else, strict continuity dictated that the narrative follow a progression that seemed to represent everyday temporal and spatial relations. So although the content of the film was often spectacularized through the mise-en-scène, the narrative flow of events was based on a rigid notion of temporal and spatial realism that failed to acknowledge Stern's main contention: film "has its own reality. And the film has this autonomous filmic reality to the extent it departs from the norm of actual reality."[11]

On the other hand, montage, for Stern, acknowledged film's own intrinsic reality in order to disregard causal temporal links and spatial continuities for the sake of creating associational links between units of content. Despite Soviet directors' various theories of montage, Stern indicates that they all believed montage provided the central organizing principle for film as a whole. They asserted the relation of content to film style by exploring how each shot was connected to another in order to reinforce the film's central theme or themes: "[The Soviets] regarded the cutting-process rather as an *assembling-process,* and the division of the master scenes into long shots, close ups, etc. not really as a division, but as a *geometric building-up* and unification of vital elements inherent in the scene."[12]

Montage, as a result, challenged audience members' perceptions and thoughts by presenting radical content in a way that suggested the limits and constructed nature of realism. Stern cites the opening sequence of *Katorga* (1928) by Yuli Raizman as an example of montage's radical re-envisioning of reality: "This *summation* montage . . . consists of elements (prisons, churches, facades, religious symbols, etc.) which have no geographical connection with each other or with the action projected, but which are coordinated as essential elements in the *explicit* symbol-relationship formulating the association of church and prison."[13]

Stern illustrates the two approaches to film construction by showing how Hollywood defined "excess footage" as any shot not related directly to character or the film's narrative action.[14] But footage that was excess to Hollywood was necessary for Soviet montage, since it was needed to create subtle associational links (as exemplified in the opening of *Katorga*) that built up the film's complex dynamic, which challenged spectators' naturalistic way of viewing the world. Stern's comments about "excess footage" are particularly germane for grasping U.S. Left film theorists' and critics' problems with *Thunder over Mexico*.

As mentioned earlier, Eisenstein originally intended *¡Que Viva México!* to comprise six episodes, each chronicling a different epoch of Mexican history. He described the structure of the film as like that of a Mexican serape:

> So striped and violently contrasting are the cultures in Mexico running next to each other and at the same time being centuries away. No plot, no whole story could run through this Serape without being false or artificial. And we took the contrasting independent adjacence of its violent colors as the motif for constructing our film: 6 episodes following each other—different in character, different in people, different in animals, trees and flowers. And still held together by the unity of the weave —a rhythmic and musical construction and an unrolling of the Mexican spirit and character.[15]

But the film's very lack of a singular plot or story, which Eisenstein saw as a cinematic breakthrough, prevented Hollywood executives from wanting to mass-distribute the film. Upton Sinclair explained Hollywood's point of view to Eisenstein in a letter: "He [a man at MGM] then wanted to know the 'story' and pinned me down about it. He explained that a 'story' means one set of characters running all the way through the picture. If you haven't that, then you have a travelogue, and there is nothing in between, from the trade point of view. I tried to explain your idea of a group of stories, and when I got through explaining, the man was absolutely cold . . . You are making the kind of picture that Hollywood does not want."[16]

THUNDERING TROUBLES

Without a unified story running throughout the film, Hollywood viewed the entire project as nothing more than "excess footage," a "travelogue," to use their euphemism, all of which Stern warned about in his column. As a result, when Sol Lesser became charged with transforming Eisenstein's Mexican footage into a Hollywood film, he centered the story on *¡Que Viva México!*'s most dramatic episode, "Maguey": the execution of Sebastian, a peon, and his friends, who revolt against a hacendado (landowner) after Sebastian's wife, Maria, is raped by one of the hacendado's men. As Marie Seton explains: "Edited according to established Hollywood methods, the Maguey story, originally intended by Eisenstein to occupy but *two* reels in the total film, was spun out to six reels—seven including the Prologue and Epilogue."[17]

U.S. Left film theorists and critics were well aware that "Maguey" was only one of six episodes of the film, since *Experimental Cinema* and other Left film journals and columns had been chronicling the developments of Eisenstein's Mexican film since its inception in 1931 and had published Eisenstein's written scenario (among other pieces on the film) in February 1934.[18] As a result, Sol Lesser's *Thunder over Mexico* seemed nothing more than a desecration of Eisenstein's original Mexican footage. In a manifesto in defense of *¡Que Viva México!* the editors of *Experimental Cinema* clearly laid out their problems with *Thunder over Mexico:* "Thus, Eisenstein's great vision of the Mexican ethos, which he had intended to present in the form of a 'film symphony,' has been destroyed. Of the original conception, as revealed in the scenario and in Eisenstein's correspondence with the editors of *Experimental Cinema,* nothing remains in the commercialized version except the photography, which no amount of mediocre cutting could destroy."[19] By eliminating three of the six episodes and not allowing Eisenstein to edit the film, those responsible for *Thunder over Mexico,* according to these critics, ensured that the film lost all thematic unity and development.

U.S. Left film theorists and critics who were familiar with Eisenstein's scenario understood that the "Maguey" episode was supposed to symbolize a failed peon revolt against the economic and social injustices fostered under Porfirio Díaz's regime—the rape of Maria representing just one form of oppression among many, such as the exploitation of peons' labor in extracting pulque and their limited access to the hacienda. But by having *Thunder over Mexico* center on this episode, thereby undercutting its relation to the rest of the film, "Maguey" lost all of its political symbolism and became nothing more than a clichéd action sequence. As film critic William Troy notes: "What little of the celebrated Eisenstein camera symbolism is retained appears totally disjointed and meaningless."[20]

As a result, Left film critics felt that *Thunder over Mexico* used banal action sequences and empty stylistic effects to cover for a lack of imagination and ideas. Samuel Brody and Tom Brandon emphasize the meaninglessness and stupidity of *Thunder*'s focus on action in a rather lengthy plot summary of the film:

> The rape (?) of a peon's girl by a guest of the *hacendado.* Attempt to save the imprisoned girl by a guest of the *hacendado* [actually, it is one of the peons who attempts this]. Failure. Chase. More chase. Still more chase.

And chase again. The *hacendado*'s daughter is shot. The hero is captured. "And for you, the punishment of the horses!" Burial of Sebastian and two other peons up to their necks. Soldiers on horseback trample on their heads. Grafted sound effects that might have been taken from a "Silly Symphony." Dark, dark skies. Composite shots of peons listlessly climbing, climbing, climbing. More composite shots. More superimpositions. More "wipe-offs."[21]

Brody and Brandon's choppy writing style accents the film's fragmented and action-oriented style. They continue: "[W]e are 'wiped-off,' 'overlap-dissolved,' and 'super-imposed' into Mr. Sol Lesser's idea of a 'Revolt!' A puff of smoke, some fireworks sparkling meaninglessly in the night, and a small pile of burning straw! There is your revolution!"[22] William Troy similarly claims, "Its [*Thunder*'s] appeal, based on the elements of rape, violence, and physical torture, is to the sensations rather than to the mind," making the film into nothing more than a "sadistic melodrama."[23]

Therefore, *Thunder* was shaped in complete opposition to Eisenstein's intentions, which did not necessarily entail a rejection of sensationalism but saw it as subsidiary to the film's thematic impulses. Troy notes as much: "But these things [the film's sensationalism], we may feel confident, were not intended by Eisenstein to be offered for their own sake. Necessary to the dramatic elaboration of his theme, they would undoubtedly have been made to seem less sensational by being placed in proper relation to other elements of his subject. In Sol Lesser's production both theme and subject are dislocated to produce a volume of selections which resembles nothing so much as a collection of 'gems' from some masterpiece of literature or music."[24]

As a result, for U.S. Left film theorists and critics, *Thunder*'s sensationalistic simplicity not only jettisoned Eisenstein's intended symbolism, but also offered both a gross simplification of Mexican history and a disempowering representation of Mexico's lower class. For example, the editors of *Experimental Cinema* note: "Eisenstein's original prologue, which was intended to trace the sources and primitive manifestations of Mexican culture, thus projecting the most vital cultural forms among the Aztecs, Toltecs, and the Mayans, has been converted into a pseudo-travelogue."[25] Furthermore, by integrating material of the conquistadors within the prologue, Lesser made it historically inaccurate. A second manifesto on the film explains: "Apart from every other blunder committed, the false placement of these shots robs Eisenstein's material of its cultural and ethnic authenticity."[26]

Because the Mexican people serve as little more than a backdrop in Lesser's film—an interesting compositional element rather than a thematic subject whose history, tradition, and struggles would be emphasized and investigated in their own right—U.S. Left film theorists and critics viewed *Thunder* as an insult to the Mexican people as a whole. In discussing "Maguey," Brody and Brandon write: "The peons are at all times shown as characterless 'passive resisters' (a direct slander against the heroic traditions of the Mexican masses!)."[27] As a result, *Thunder*'s epilogue, which emphasizes Mexico's revolutionary transformation into a land of equality and justice, seemed completely hollow to Left film critics, who felt that the emphasis on the masses' powerlessness throughout the film in no way prepared the viewer for such an idealistic ending. William Troy writes, "Without any sort of transition, these events [within "Maguey"] are succeeded by a tritely symbolic evocation of the new Mexico—great public buildings, men working, military parades. One has assisted at an orgy of sadistic melodrama only to be thrown a sop of old-fashioned mystical 'progress' at the end."[28] *Thunder*'s epilogue implies that a benign government suddenly emerged after the harsh Porfiriato. The editors of *Experimental Cinema* write that Eisenstein intended the original epilogue "to anticipate the revolutionary urge dormant in the descendants of those ancient races . . . [but Lesser has converted it] into a cheerful ballyhoo about 'a new Mexico,' with definite fascist implication."[29]

The fascism that U.S. Left film critics were referring to in *Thunder* was mainly due to its out-and-out glorification of the Mexican military and army. Such depictions fulfilled Upton Sinclair's well-known promise to the Mexican minister of foreign affairs that "the film would not show the people of present-day Mexico as mistreated or unhappy."[30] Herman G. Weinberg quotes a letter from Seymour Stern in order to show how such an ending undercut Eisenstein's original intentions: "Anyone who has seen the rushes, except the blind fools who backed the picture, could have seen at once, *even without the 'rushes' being cut*, that Eisenstein had taken the shots of the Mexican army, the Mexican police, etc., in a bitter satire, rivaling the most satirical moments of *Ten Days that Shook the World!* All these shots, however, have been distorted under Lesser's idiotic supervision into a super-glorification of everything that makes present-day Mexico despicable."[31]

Furthermore, such an ending overlooked the very real problems that still plagued working-class Mexicans. Brody and Brandon elaborate, albeit in hyperbolic terms, on some of them: "This about the Mexico where not a foot of soil remains unstained with the blood of oppressed peons! This about the 'new Mexico' that suppresses the Communist Party and murders its heroic leaders! This about the Mexico where the feudal-reactionary Catholic Church is daily regaining its foothold thanks to the Wall Street inspired policies of the Rodriguez military dictatorship!"[32] Therefore, according to them, *Thunder* uncritically celebrates the new Mexican state without acknowledging its still-reactionary tendencies and by ignoring the importance of people's revolutionary collective action for bringing about progressive reform.

Although sympathetic with radical film theorists' and critics' interpretations of *Thunder*, some liberal U.S. film critics like William Troy and Pare Lorentz did not find Brandon and Brody's argument entirely convincing, since it overlooked Eisenstein's own habit of creating disjointed symbolism in earlier films like *October* (1927), over which he supposedly had full editing control.[33] As a result, Troy and Lorentz partially blamed Eisenstein himself for Sol Lesser's fragmented symbolism in *Thunder over Mexico*. They believed that such abstraction was an inherent tendency in all of Eisenstein's films. Most interestingly, these critics supported their charges against Eisenstein by citing other radical film theorists' earlier critiques against Eisenstein's reliance on abstraction. In "Selections from Eisenstein," William Troy reworks Harry Alan Potamkin's charge that Eisenstein's films were often abstract, formalistic filmic exercises. Troy deploys Potamkin's argument from "Eisenstein and the Theory of Cinema," published in *Hound and Horn* in 1933. In this article, Potamkin claims that because Eisenstein had overdogmatized his belief in montage-as-conflict in his earlier writings, he overlooked aspects of film besides editing, like "the human actor as the material of experience."[34] For Potamkin, the dialectical processes of film concern issues of both content and form, "and to eliminate the former is to go abstract, as Eisenstein most often does."[35] However, instead of reinforcing Potamkin's belief that Eisenstein's past themes and films were hampered by an overly reductive conception of montage, Troy poses the problem in more auteurist terms: Eisenstein's vision versus that of a universal social theme. Although Troy believes that Eisenstein's social commitment was genuine, he notes that "Eisenstein's technical virtuosity is so great that he does not always resist the impulse to play with pictorial effects that have nothing very definite to do with his theme or with anything else."[36] As a result, Eisenstein's films often turned completely abstract because of his unbridled enthusiasm for technical virtuosity. Troy concludes his article with a troubling question: "Is it possible that even Marxism will not save us for long from the perilous attractions of absolute art?"[37]

Troy's disconcerting conclusion completely detaches Eisenstein's abstract tendencies from their historical and political context. Potamkin, in his article, takes pains to locate Eisenstein's concept of montage-as-conflict within the debates he had with other Soviet filmmakers like Vsevolod Pudovkin and Dziga Vertov in the 1920s. To distance himself from their theories, Eisenstein took an extreme approach that saw montage as conflict. But as these debates grew less strident, Eisenstein was better able to assess his own theories of montage in relation to, rather than against, those of other Soviet directors. As a result, Potamkin believes that Eisenstein came to a better understanding of the relations between the human subject and montage in his later theoretical writings.[38] But Troy's article instead highlights Eisenstein's individualistic artistic qualities, implying that they were an essential aspect of Eisenstein's creative personality rather than results of specific aesthetic and historical contexts. Troy assumes that Eisenstein's individual artistic vision was hopelessly at odds with his ideological beliefs—and that this could be seen in *Thunder over Mexico* even though Eisenstein did not edit the film. Unlike Potamkin, who sees Eisenstein as learning from his ongoing experiences with Soviet and capitalist cinema, Troy naturalizes Eisenstein's artistic vision as always in conflict with Marxist politics, since Troy can envision the individual only as opposed to his social context rather than as a product of it.

Troy's appropriation of Potamkin's earlier radical critique of Eisenstein opened up the possibility that the socio-aesthetic problems of *Thunder over Mexico* might have been at least in part due to Eisenstein's own longstanding formalistic tendencies. Defenders of Eisenstein's original intentions for *¡Que Viva México!* therefore emphasized its thematic coherence. They argued that the film's thematic unity would have organized such seemingly abstract elements into a cohesive structure.

A central theme that U.S. Left film theorists and critics addressed in *¡Que Viva México!* was religion. By juxtaposing their analyses with my own close readings of the film's religious themes, we will begin to see how *¡Que Viva México!* offered a much more complex account of religion than most critics were able to identify at the time. In particular, *¡Que Viva México!* despite its critique of religion, held a much more accommodating view toward religion than most early 1930s U.S. Left film theorists and critics noticed or held. In many ways, *¡Que Viva México!*'s stance toward religion anticipated a political paradigm shift that occurred in the mid-1930s, when many U.S. Left film critics adopted an accommodating, Popular Front attitude toward bourgeois institutions like Hollywood and religion.

I recognize the controversy in offering any analysis of Eisenstein's Mexican footage, since he did not finish shooting the film's final episode, "Soldadera," and was unable to edit the material he had shot. Yet as Ian Christie points out, it is impossible for film scholars to identify any Eisenstein film as an urtext, since Soviet silent films were liberally reedited for both internal political reasons and the commercial mandates of appealing to foreign markets.[39] A few examples of how Eisenstein's films were tampered with: the loss of the original titling of *Strike;* the disappearance of the original negative of *Battleship Potemkin;* the Stalinized reediting of *October, Ivan the Terrible, Part I* and *Part II;* the destruction of *Ivan the Terrible, Part III* and *Bezhin Meadow;* the missing reel from *Alexander Nevsky;* and the three-year gap between the initial shooting of *The General Line* in 1926 and its final shooting and rushed editing in 1929, when it was renamed *The Old and New* and significant differences between prints resulted. It is impossible to identify any film in Eisenstein's entire oeuvre that is untainted by similar alterations.[40]

October, usually considered Eisenstein's most experimental work, is, according to Christie, "essentially uncompleted" because of Stalin's visit to the cutting room just before the premiere, when he ordered the removal of several important scenes, totaling about 3,000 feet of film.[41] Even though we can never ultimately determine the overall montage structure the film would have taken without Stalin's intervention, *October* remains an important testament to how Eisenstein attempted to implement his developing theories on montage.

My point here is that *¡Que Viva México!* differs in degree rather than in kind from Eisenstein's other films. It hovers between his unshot projects like *An American Tragedy, Sutter's Gold, The Glass House, Kapital,* and his Haitian film, among others, and his more nearly completed works like *Strike* and *Nevsky.* But to disregard the material Eisenstein shot for *¡Que Viva México!* as being too incomplete to support any inferences at all about the possible final form of the film strikes me as being based on incorrect assumptions regarding how we must approach Eisenstein's oeuvre in particular and silent cinema as a whole. Christie rightly notes, "Because individual copies of films could be and were easily altered for many different reasons in the course of their circulation, it makes little sense to search for a unique original or authentic version of each production."[42] As a result, one must, if possible, contextualize the appearances of the various prints of a film and the reasons for their differences. In regard to *¡Que Viva México!* I take a stand similar to Harry M. Benshoff's in claiming that I am not so much offering a reading of the film, which lacks a singular textual authority, as discussing "some of the visual connotations that arise from individual shots, and how these images relate to individual episodes and across the film as a whole."[43] Furthermore, I second Benshoff's belief that the suppression of *¡Que Viva México!* by the film's backers and American distributors lends credence to the idea that Eisenstein intended the final film to be radical in structure and content.[44]

My analysis of *¡Que Viva México!* relies on Alexandrov's 1979 reconstruction of the film and Jay Leyda's assemblage of Mexican outtakes in *Eisenstein's Mexican Film: Episodes for Study* (1955). Of all the versions of the film, Alexandrov's comes closest to Eisenstein's written scenario. Additionally, Alexandrov worked intimately with Eisenstein during the original shooting, and since his own development in film production was significantly shaped by the events of the Russian Revolution, the two men shared a similar cultural background. The latter point becomes particularly important in regard to the development of gender issues in his reconstruction, since one can't help seeing the film's gender representations as being influenced by the Bolsheviks' stance toward "the woman question" immediately following the revolution.[45] Leyda's reconstruction remains important because of its singular focus on showing Eisenstein's and Tisse's outtakes in their entirety, which allows for the most thorough examination of montage-within-the-shot of Eisenstein's Mexican footage. Also, Leyda's reconstruction helps us better identify some of the outtakes that guided 1930s U.S. Left film theorists' and critics' discussions of *¡Que Viva México!*[46] For the most part, I refer to Alexandrov's version in my analysis, so I will indicate whenever certain insights gleaned from Leyda's footage have been woven in.

THE DIALECTICS OF RELIGION

In an October 1933 article in the *Modern Monthly*, Seymour Stern emphasizes how religion was linked to death throughout the outtakes of *¡Que Viva México!* His article chronicles the countless ways that the film represented religion as a life-denying force used by priests to subjugate the lower class.[47]

Stern's lack of concern with the positive aspects of religion in the film can partially be explained by his assumption that Soviet citizen Eisenstein was an antireligious director, as exhibited in Eisenstein's earlier films: *Battleship Potemkin*'s critique of the conservatism shown by the priest who attempts to prevent the mutiny, and *October*'s gods sequence, which exposes the primitive and mystical origins of antirevolutionary religion. But more importantly, Stern was one of many Left film critics who were concerned with critiquing those bourgeois institutions that mainstream film critics often celebrated no matter what the film or who the director. As Tom Brandon recounted in a 1974 interview, the function of 1930s Left film theory and criticism must always be read "against a backdrop that showed so much emphasis on the other side of all great qualities, all acceptance [of bourgeois institutions]; . . . A good deal of Left criticism was an attempt to bring into the forefront those aspects that were not being dealt with by other [that is, bourgeois] criticism."[48] Stern's emphasis on the negative elements of religion was a part of this political agenda of Left film analysis. Whether Stern couldn't see the film's positive representations of religion or whether he simply chose to ignore them remains unclear.

To take one example: on first viewing, the "Fiesta" episode of *¡Que Viva México!* certainly seems to link religion with the oppression and death caused by the Spanish conquest. The episode concerns the festival of the Virgin of Guadalupe, during which the Catholic Church subjugates Aztec and Maya cultures. The episode's critique of Catholicism is heightened by the way in which ritual functions throughout it as well as throughout the film. Although Eisenstein never mentions the importance of ritual in any of his articles, *¡Que Viva México!* clearly shows that he valued it, since ritual provided a way for him to move easily from the literal to the abstract, a technique he endorsed in his theories of montage. One can observe Eisenstein's concern with the abstract and literal elements of cinema in his 1929 article "The Cinematographic Principle and the Ideogram," in which he theorizes about the similarities between the operations of the Japanese language and filmic montage. Just as two hieroglyphs with literal, distinct meanings can combine to produce a concept that transcends the literal meaning of either one, montage provides a dialectical conflict between a film's separate shots in order to create abstract associational concepts that transcend the literal aspects of each shot. As Eisenstein notes: "Each [hieroglyph or shot], separately, corresponds to an *object*, to a fact, but their combination corresponds to a *concept*."[49] He elaborates even more explicitly on the ramifications of montage's dialectic abilities in his article "Perspectives":

> To restore to the intellectual process its fire and passion.
>
> To plunge the abstract reflective process into the fervor of practical action.
>
> To give back to emasculated theoretical *formulas* the rich exuberance of life-felt *forms*.[50]

Eisenstein's use of montage-within-the-shot in ¡Que Viva Mexico! *(1932) to reveal how the Catholic Church oppresses the Mexican people.*

Similarly, ritual, for Eisenstein, simultaneously operates on both imma-nent and abstract planes and allows him to highlight either or both of its tendencies as necessary.

For example, throughout "Fiesta," we see three men who represent Christ and the two thieves carrying their crosses to the crucifixion. They are naked from the waist up and have saguaro trunks lashed to their backs and outstretched arms. One shot is particularly revealing. It shows how the symbolic image of the Trinity accentuates the literal oppression of peons by Catholicism. In a medium shot, one of the men walks away from the foreground. In the background stands a large white church. The shot is backlit by the sun, so the man's body is shadowed. Yet as the man walks away from the foreground, the distant church's central doorway becomes visible—dead center with the man's body. As his size diminishes, his shad-owed body merges with the dark doorway. Only his arms extend against the church's white walls, making him into a walking crucifix, engulfed by the church's edifice. The image reminds the viewer how the abstract sym-bolism of the crucifix is connected with the actual suffering of Mexico's underprivileged population. It is not all that different from scenes in

Eisenstein's earlier films in which he employed Christian imagery of the martyr to depict the suffering of the lower class at the hands of the bourgeoisie, such as the Bolshevik who is stabbed to death by the parasols of the aristocratic women in *October*. The scene in *¡Que Viva México!* emphasizes how such asceticism did not improve the cross bearer's own plight but bulwarked the strength of a church that remained indifferent to such suffering.

Furthermore, in this shot we see Eisenstein employing the overtonal montage that he discovered while filming *The General Line* (1929) and theorized about in his article "The Fourth Dimension in Cinema" (1929). No longer was montage to be conceptualized only as dominant conflicts between shots, but also as those occurring between secondary stimuli like lighting, texture, spatial arrangements, and movement within a shot.[51] Both spatial arrangements (the church dwarfing the human form) and lighting (the man merging into the darkness of the door, his shadowed arms forming a walking crucifix against the church's white edifice) allow Eisenstein's mise-en-scène to hold in tension the scene's literal meaning (a man serving penance) with its more abstract concept (the church's oppression of the peasants). Ritual, in other words, provides Eisenstein with one of the most effective methods of using overtonal montage in *¡Que Viva México!*

But to claim that the religious symbolism in the film is only negative, as Stern suggests, is to oversimplify matters. More liberal film critics who did not come to the film with the idea that Eisenstein was antireligious were better able to assess the film's positive religious overtones. In an article for *Theatre Arts Monthly* in 1932, Adolfo Best-Maugard, an official chaperon of Eisenstein in Mexico, observed Eisenstein's thrill at filming the fiesta of the Virgin of Guadalupe, which Best-Maugard felt was reflected in his footage of it.[52] Pare Lorentz notes in a 1933 article for *Vanity Fair* that regardless of who cut *Thunder over Mexico*, the film exudes a religious quality, especially in its characters, "because he [Eisenstein] surrounds them with beauty and dignity; he chooses them for their native grace."[53] As contemporary Eisenstein scholars like Rosamond Bartlett and Mikael Enckell observe, religious imagery permeates all of Eisenstein's work; for example, in *Potemkin,* Vakulinchuk's corpse symbolizes a resurrected image of working-class oppression as it is raised from the waters.[54] Marie Seton similarly notes in her 1960 biography of Eisenstein, "Filled with hatred towards what he felt to be the false practices of the Church, he was yet irresistibly fascinated by the inner philosophic aspects of religion and the primary figures and symbols which men worshipped."[55] But unlike

Revealing the native population's appropriation of Catholic imagery in ¡Que Viva Mexico!

Eisenstein's earlier films, in which religious imagery was either cloaked or subsumed by revolutionary imagery and ideology, *¡Que Viva México!* explicitly addresses how religion, when in the hands of the people, could be harnessed for revolutionary purposes. In part because of his freedom from Soviet control, which demanded that religion be portrayed in a negative light, and in part because of his experiences in Mexico, where religion was central to peasant life, *¡Que Viva México!* boldly examines the nuances of religion's relation to revolution, which his earlier films only implied.[56]

Pare Lorentz's observation that Eisenstein links a religious overtone with human dignity is perceptive, since it hints at how Eisenstein consciously or unconsciously believed that religious ritual could be used by Mexico's downtrodden to assert and express themselves as much as it could be used against them by the hierarchy of the church. This is seen in Eisenstein's representation of the festival of the Virgin of Guadalupe in "Fiesta." As Eisenstein himself realized, because the churches were built on old Aztec temples, the Maya, Aztec, and Catholic religions had merged in Mexico, making it unclear whether the festival participants were celebrating a Catholic ritual or a pagan rite. We see this fluidity among religions during a close-up of an Indian dancing in an Aztec costume. At the center of his headpiece is a tiny statue of the Virgin of Guadalupe. By suggesting that the natives have appropriated Catholic imagery for their own religious ceremonies, the image reverses the earlier representation of Catholicism as having been imposed on the indigenous people. It exposes how the natives' own religious culture allows them to maintain their traditions in spite of the cruelty and oppression of the conquest. But this subversion of the Virgin's use is masked by shots of the natives seeming to honor the Catholic holiday. The scene exemplifies the uses of religion that Eisenstein both loathes and celebrates: the religion of the elite Catholic minority, which was imposed on the lower class, and the religion of the people, who appropriated Catholic iconography for their own purposes.

Because of the multifarious ways that religious ritual and symbolism are employed, *¡Que Viva México!* does not simply oppose Catholicism to native religions, but shows how Catholicism was used by Mexico's underclass to enunciate its own oppression. This is particularly the case in the film's use of the Trinity. Although "Fiesta" represents the Trinity as oppressive with its images of the saguaro men, a later episode, "Maguey," complicates such a monolithic representation. After Sebastian and two

The Virgin Mary as totem in ¡Que Viva Mexico!

The figure of the trinity, connecting the revolutionary potential of Christianity with class struggle in ¡Que Viva Mexico!

other peons are rounded up, they stand in an attitude like that of Christ and the two thieves. While holes are dug for their execution, Sebastian stands in the center. Countless associations occur from this moment. The oppression that the peons suffer is linked to the religious oppression seen in "Fiesta." Yet the literal oppression visited upon Sebastian and the peons is also connected with the symbolic oppression visited up Christ, showing how the Catholic imagery imposed by the conquest could be used to speak to contemporary Mexico's socioeconomic conditions. *¡Que Viva México!* draws parallels between the ways in which the Mexican people and the film itself incorporate Catholic iconography for revolutionary purposes. Just as the Aztec appropriates the Virgin of Guadalupe in his headpiece, *¡Que Viva México!* incorporates Catholic iconography into the execution scene to suggest how the symbolic suffering of Christ is made real in Sebastian's suffering, while Sebastian's suffering transcends its setting and is aggrandized by its connection to Christ's life. The literal and the abstract, as a result, are held in a tension that speaks to oppression that is both particular and transhistorical. Ritual, in effect, allows both historicity and symbolic transcendence to occupy the same plane and suggests a potential link between religion and revolution. Christ, after all, was a rebel in his own time. Just as Christ's death allows Catholics to enter the kingdom of heaven, the remembrance of the symbolic crucifixions visited upon Sebastian, Maria, and other peons allows for a revolutionary vision that will transcend their present historical oppression.

Eisenstein's exploration of the many uses of Catholicism in *¡Que Viva México!* anticipates a general trend among U.S. Left film theorists and critics from 1934 to 1936 to reexamine what were generally considered conservative, bourgeois institutions in order to see how they could be used to benefit a politically progressive agenda. In "Cinematography with Tears" (1933), Eisenstein examines Alexander Dumas's bourgeois novel *The Count of Monte Cristo* not only to show how the interpreting of ideologically conservative works could benefit radical art, but also to demand that the cultural Left's theoretical response to bourgeois works of the past be more sophisticated than a simple rejection.[57] Similarly, a year later, Robert Forsythe, a film critic for the *New Masses* wrote that dogmatic Marxist film criticism was not useful, since it ignored a film's actual qualities by quickly associating the film with either the regressive products of Hollywood or the progressive films of the Soviet Union.[58] In 1935, John Howard Lawson encouraged *Filmfront*'s Marxist critics to employ a lively, popular style that would appeal to a larger audience by not seeming so ideologically rote.[59] Increasingly, other U.S. film theorists, critics, and historians, such as Lewis Jacobs, James Dugan, Peter Ellis, Kenneth Fearing, and Margaret Thorp, analyzed how Hollywood itself might be encouraged to produce politically progressive and formally experimental films.

Yet during the debates of 1932 and 1933 on *¡Que Viva México!* and *Thunder over Mexico,* U.S. Left film theorists like Seymour Stern were too involved in defending Eisenstein's film according to certain preset ideas about the director and his work to notice how Eisenstein and film theory were changing. In some ways, it is unfortunate that most U.S. Left film theorists and critics did not see *¡Que Viva México!*'s reevaluation of traditional institutions like the church, since it provides an interesting analogy to the ways in which many of them were going to reinvestigate the potential of Hollywood after 1935. Just as Eisenstein saw that Catholicism was harmful when controlled by the hands of the few but potentially liberatory when used by the masses, U.S. Left film theorists and critics began reassessing Hollywood: left in the hands of Wall Street executives and studio heads, Hollywood would continue producing mediocre films that supported the status quo, but under the pressure of audience groups, Left film reviews, and progressive film workers and organizations within the studios, Hollywood films could begin to experiment and to introduce styles and content that would challenge viewers' reified perceptions.

Despite their limited reading of religion within *¡Que Viva México!* U.S. Left film theorists and critics, armed with the uncut rushes of Eisenstein's Mexican footage, his written scenario, and their correspondence with the director, still felt fairly adept at identifying some of the film's central themes, including revolution and religion. Yet it strikes one as odd when examining these very same sources from a contemporary perspective that barely any U.S. Left film theorists and critics noted the thematic importance women and gender held in *¡Que Viva México!* Although one can argue that the footage these theorists and critics might have seen did not emphasize gender issues or women, Eisenstein's written scenario clearly suggests their centrality: two of the six episodes focus on women—"Sanduga" and "Soldadera"—and "Maguey" sets itself off by self-consciously drawing attention to its virile and masculine environment. Only one critic, Morris Helprin, dedicated an entire article to the importance of gender in Eisenstein's Mexican film. Seymour Stern, on the other hand, who organized the campaign against *Thunder over Mexico,* knew Eisenstein's work better than any other U.S. Left film theorist, and had seen the most rushes of the film, mentioned the role of women only in passing. The other U.S. Left film theorists and critics remained silent about the issue altogether.

Before investigating how Helprin addresses gender issues and women's centrality within Eisenstein's Mexican film, and exploring the reasons for U.S. Left film theorists' and critics' general silence on such matters, I first want to explore some of the ways gender might have structured a completed *¡Que Viva México!*

GENDERING REVOLUTION WITHIN *¡Que Viva México!*

As mentioned earlier, Eisenstein's film was supposed to use an elaborate six-part structure to offer a sophisticated representation of the historical factors that eventually led to a revolutionary outbreak in Mexico in 1910. By exploring the protosocialist tendencies in preconquest indigenous society, which would eventually be harnessed for revolutionary action, as well as the various types of exploitation of the lower class by conquistadors, the church, landowners, and the Porfirio Díaz regime, all of which exacerbated class tensions between the peons and the bourgeoisie, *¡Que Viva México!* links revolutionary action with the collective will of the people while acknowledging the complex and diverse historical processes that led up to it and would carry on its tradition in the future. Unlike *Thun-*

der over Mexico, which offers an individualistic interpretation of a conflict that emerged between some peons and a hacendado, *¡Que Viva México!* provides a dialectical and historical understanding of the revolution as being dependent upon both individual and collective action throughout multiple historical epochs.

Equally important, Eisenstein's Mexican footage represents the revolution's success as being dependent upon radical transformations of gender hierarchies into more-egalitarian structures, which clearly suggests resonances with the Bolsheviks' own stance toward "the woman question" immediately following their revolutionary takeover of Russia in 1917. As a result, by studying Eisenstein's Mexican footage, we can not only gain an understanding of how montage potentially allowed for more-sophisticated representations of revolutionary action and representations of women than classical cinematic forms provide, but also see how residual elements of the Bolsheviks' radical stance toward women's liberation, at least during their early days of coming to power, influenced Eisenstein's representation of the Mexican Revolution.[60]

¡Que Viva México!'s fourth and fifth episodes, "Maguey" and "Soldadera," most centrally deal with the growth of revolutionary consciousness and its outbreak, and explore its intimate relationship with gender issues. "Maguey" concerns the exploitation of the peons by the hacendados during the time of the Porfirio Díaz regime (1877–1911). "Soldadera," which takes place during the revolution of 1910–1911, is filmed from the point of view of a woman, Pancha, who fought alongside the revolutionaries of Pancho Villa and Emiliano Zapata. I will first focus upon "Maguey" and its relation to the film's first episode, "Sanduga," since these two episodes establish the primary causes of revolution—including the role played by women's exploitation—and then examine how "Soldadera" and the "Epilogue" show radical transformations in gender roles to be necessary for successful revolutionary action.

Overall, *¡Que Viva México!* situates a patriarchal male gaze as the product of a capitalist economy and class system, therefore suggesting the contingent nature of such patriarchal and class-based relations and the potential to replace them with a more equitable and socially just ideological structure. In his script for "Maguey," Eisenstein emphasizes "aggressiveness, virility, arrogance and austerity"—and this masculine focus sets "Maguey" apart from the other episodes, which either address women's importance in Mexican civilization or take a more gender-neutral approach.[61] The episode establishes the dominance of the male gaze with a medium shot of a painting of the uniformed Porfirio Díaz looking sternly

A portrait of Porfirio Díaz, tyrant of Mexico, in ¡Que Viva Mexico!

The upside-down U *in* ¡Que Viva Mexico! *that links the oppression of the Porfiriato with that of the conquest.*

A native bowing in submission to conquistadors.

out from the hacienda's wall. There is a cut to a close-up of his face. The top part of the painting's oval frame is cut off to form an upside-down U shape, subtly suggesting a critique of the masculine gaze in a period of Mexican history linked with exploitation during the Spanish conquest. An earlier episode, "Fiesta," presents an Aztec warrior bowing in submission before a group of conquistadors with a ceremonial band forming an upside-down *U* in his hands. As a result, "Maguey's" opening upside-down *U* suggests similarities among the recurrent types of violence, supplication, and oppression in the narrative.[62]

"Maguey" reinforces the ubiquity of the male gaze not only through repetitive close ups of Díaz's portrait, but also when the hacendado displays the peon's bride, Maria. A long shot shows the hacendado sitting in a throne-like chair near the top of an open courtyard as Maria walks past him and stands to his right. A medium shot follows of Maria removing her kerchief so the hacendado can see her face. In close-up, the hacendado examines her body, looking her up and down. A medium shot switches to the man who will eventually rape her, as he examines her and drinks his pulque. She looks back skeptically at the man in a medium shot. A longer medium shot frames the rapist, sitting back in his chair, left leg

Maria on display before the hacendado and his men.

The hacendado sitting on his throne before Maria.

Maria's rapist staring at her from a distance.

arched as his foot rests on another chair. His crotch is in the center of the frame, suggesting not only the assault that will soon follow, but also how the male gaze of this episode is inextricably linked to the phallus. But this shot also deconstructs the abstract male gaze with a literal cock shot of the rapist. Here male heterosexual desire is self-consciously and critically marked as the determining factor in women's oppressed position in the narrative. Although the hacendado never touches Maria, the linking of his gaze with that of the rapist suggests that their views of Maria are part of the same visual economy of gender (and perhaps class). Furthermore, by initiating the episode with Díaz's stare, Eisenstein symbolically links the political economy that Díaz represents with the sexual economy that leads to Maria's rape. The connection between Díaz's look and Maria's rape is further emphasized when she walks offscreen in this scene and stands against the hacienda's inner wall. As the sunlight enters a buttressed doorway, its light frames an upside-down *U* around her, showing how she is a part of the political and sexual economy that frames Díaz's portrait in the episode's opening.

By focusing on how Maria's family gave her to Sebastian, Leyda's footage emphasizes how bourgeois familial structures as well as heterosexual

Linking political and sexual exploitation through the upside-down U motif.

Maria enduring the collective suffering resulting from Sebastian's death.

desire lead to the exploitation of women. Maria's father rides on a mule, Maria follows him on foot, and her mother walks even farther behind, picking up loose sticks for kindling. Here we see the father's privileged position and how the mother must still engage in domestic labor (gathering kindling) even when she is out of the domestic realm. Similarly, Maria seems to occupy a liminal gender realm: not yet a full-fledged wife but no longer an androgynous child. In a long shot, we see the family meet Sebastian in the desert. Sebastian follows patriarchal protocol by first kissing the father's hand, then the mother's, and then bowing to Maria. After Maria kisses her mother, she briefly kisses her father's hand, which then immediately waves her off to Sebastian. After a quick sign of the cross, the father turns and leaves, and the mother follows. The cross serves as an interesting gesture, since it suggests a link between the patriarchal structure of the family and the church, which places a woman's symbolic importance as wife, mother, virgin, or saint over her individual presence and desires.[63]

In the family, women are made to occupy the symbolic position of wife, which we see occur immediately after Maria's family leaves. Alone with Sebastian, Maria never directly looks at him, suggesting a submission that emulates her mother's submission to her father. She is already taking on the role of a "good," submissive wife. Sebastian then places her on the burro he has brought. This gesture can be seen as either a challenge to traditional gender roles, if one assumes that he is offering her the position that her father denied her mother, or as a reinforcement of them, if one assumes that he is, in a sense, placing her on a pedestal, elevating her above the earth as a living symbol of his own good fortune. The latter view closely resembles that of the Catholic Church, except that it excludes women's presence from its highest institutional workings and uses them only as a symbol, ironically, of its orthodox power. Yet, clearly, aspects of the relationship between Sebastian and Maria are emulated in the hacienda scene between the hacendado and Maria. In both cases, Maria does not have the right to look back at the man who observes her. In both cases, a woman is exchanged like an object: between father and husband, and between husband and hacendado. The patriarchal position of the father is figuratively reinscribed in the hacendado. Therefore, the heterosexual-male economy that determines both familial and work structures is exposed as a central agent in causing woman's oppression.

By situating the male gaze within the "historically shifting economic conditions" of the Porfiriato, Eisenstein is further able to expose an alternative looking relation at the end of the episode.[64] Sebastian, Maria's husband, and his friends have been executed by being trampled to death. Maria is crouched down by his side. A medium shot frames her looking at her husband's crushed body. She does not have an expression of grief or shock. She is merely taking in what has happened. From a distance, in the maguey fields, we see a medium close-up of a peon who has survived. The peon lowers his head, his sombrero covering his eyes, as Maria lowers her face to the desert, lying beside Sebastian. After a cut back from Maria, there follows a series of extreme close-ups of other peons who are observing the scene clandestinely—where from, we are not entirely certain. The eyes multiply, taking in this moment of defeat under Díaz's rule. It seems as if all of Mexico's downtrodden observe this event, since none of their gazes are linked to an identifiable place. But now, both the peons' and Maria's visions are united by their identical stoic expressions, suggesting a shared emotional state. She no longer represents a sexualized object but a person who suffers from the common oppression that plagues them all, emphasized by the scene's mise-en-scène: her face in the lower-left corner of the frame next to Sebastian's trampled torso, which juts out center frame against the clear sky. Maria shares the space with Sebastian, but she is not fetishized as she was with the hacendado, since Sebastian's corpse dominates the frame and our vision.

Additionally, Harry M. Benshoff explains how the episode, by presenting men "as helpless victims," inverts the representations of them found in classical Hollywood cinema.[65] For Benshoff, the scene's religious evocation of the crucifixion, with Sebastian standing in for Christ and his two friends as the thieves, "invokes a heady mixture of sadomasochism and homoeroticism that marks so many depictions of Catholic icons/martyrs."[66] But unlike traditional Catholic imagery, whose religious connotations can serve to mask such sadomasochistic impulses, "Eisenstein foregrounds these sadomasochistic signifiers, and in so doing, de-represses the impulses that lurk beneath the signifieds of Christianity."[67] As a result, one can observe how "Maguey" represents Sebastian's fall from a privileged male subject position to that of a literal object, a corpse, whereas Maria moves from an objectified status to that of a subject by the end of the film. Yet the presence of the peons within the scene prevents it from being interpreted merely as a reversal of gender roles but a unification of men's and women's looks into a collective and egalitarian observation of the tragedy that has befallen Sebastian, his friends, and themselves as a people. Furthermore, as Benshoff rightly notes, Sebastian's object status nonetheless transforms him into a powerful symbol for all of those who observed the tragedy: "Sebastian has become part of the land, the land that the Spaniards have stolen, raped (both literally and metaphorically), emasculated, and trampled down."[68] It is this transformation and unity of vision that serves as a necessary precursor to the revolution that will take place in the next episode.

But *¡Que Viva México!* goes even further than suggesting that revolution is dependent upon more-equitable looking relations in the future. It shows that more-equitable looking relations existed in the past with its focus on female labor in the matrilineal society of "Sanduga." The episode's primitive community serves as an alternative to the patriarchal relations in "Maguey" by showing how unalienated labor and independence must be intertwined for women to gain autonomy. The episode functions in the film much as primitive communism functions in Friedrich Engels's work *The Origin of the Family, Private Property, and the State*. Engels relies on the findings of ethnologist Lewis Henry Morgan to argue that matrilineal kinship relations predominated before the emergence of private property and exchange relations, which reconfigured such societies into patrilineal forms. Engels does not argue for a return to such earlier societies, but uses them to expose the transitory and limited existence of patriarchal, capitalist relations. Eisenstein similarly situates "Sanduga" near the beginning of the film to show how such a society predated the Porfiriato's patriarchal, capitalist regime, which forms the context of "Fiesta" and "Maguey." These two episodes are then followed by "Soldadera," which addresses the Mexican Revolution and shows many of the ways in which it used some aspects of matrilineal culture to effect change after the Díaz regime.[69]

"Sanduga" also dramatizes Engels's belief that many of the tendencies of communism existed in incipient form in primitive communities. Production in these communities was tied to both the individual and the community. Items were produced for direct consumption and use. "Sanduga" shows a civilization in which production is still in the hands of the producers. Concepción and the other women of Tehuantepec sell their locally grown fruits and vegetables in the market in order to obtain gold pieces for their dowry necklaces. But the gold necklace does not simply represent some abstract unit of exchange that other commodities are measured against: it is subsidiary to the ultimate goals of unifying the community. The gold coins are connected to the community through lap dissolves that link them to the U shape of flower necklaces and the hammock in which Concepción's future husband lies. Furthermore, the emphasis on women's labor in this episode suggests women's importance in this type of society. As Engels notes, "People whose women have to work much harder than

Using the U to idealize matriarchal society in "Sanduga."

Concepción, the protagonist of "Sanduga."

we would consider proper often have far more real respect for women than our Europeans have for theirs."[70] Women's equality depends upon their having access to the means of production, which affords either equal or superior status in the community. "Sanduga"'s focus on female labor emphasizes that the means of production are intimately connected with the equitable looking relations occurring throughout the episode.

Yet "Sanduga" can also be seen as Eisenstein's overidealization of the two central but interrelated tenets that the Bolsheviks proposed for the emancipation of women: the abolition of private property and full integration of women into the workforce.[71] Indeed, "Sanduga" exposes both the value of communal life and the importance of women's work, but it tends to show the men doing nothing at all except lounging in hammocks. Harry Benshoff reads such gender representations in progressive ways, since they allow for a homoerotic gaze of "the naked male torso" and show respect for matriarchal society and women's active roles, all of which undercuts the traditional homophobia and sexism that underlies much of classical Hollywood cinema.[72] All of this is true. Yet the episode is troubling to me in the way that it mostly reverses gender positions by making women more active and men more passive rather than showing them sharing labor equitably. By having the women conduct all the labor and men none, "Sanduga" resonates with the very same problems that the Bolsheviks had in creating women's emancipation: women were introduced into the workforce, but the necessary infrastructure for socializing domestic work away from the private sphere never materialized, therefore creating a "double burden" of work for women.[73] Yet "Sanduga" represents this "double burden" in the most idealized way: smiling women who connect with one another across generations and families and gaze at beautiful male bodies while the men lay back and rest. It fails to represent a mandatory ingredient for equality: men contributing their own labor to a truly communal endeavor.[74]

To be fair to Eisenstein, it must be recalled that the episode was supposed to represent only primitive communism at work, not communism proper, so one can read the episode's shortcomings in regard to the equitable division of labor as one of the points it is in fact trying to make. And as we will see in my analysis of "Soldadera," the revolutionary gender roles and labor issues represented there are quite different from those in "Sanduga," yet are still not entirely unproblematical. Yet the very filming of "Sanduga," with its soft-focus, halo-like lighting and curving, sensuous male and female bodies and faces, tends to undercut seeing the episode as anything other than a depiction of a fallen paradise.

The idealized shooting of "Sanduga," however, serves a more thematically significant purpose: it jarringly contrasts with the hard-focus, angular, phallic forms that dominate "Maguey." If "Sanduga" represents primitive communism, "Maguey" represents its destruction by capitalism. It exposes how, with the growth of capitalism, producers gradually lost control of their products as an exchange system began to determine all social relations. Producers no longer knew what became of their products, "and the possibility arose that the product might some day be turned against the producers"—a possibility that "Maguey" exposes with the peons' harvesting of pulque.[75] Initially, most noticeable is how the female labor of "Sanduga" has been replaced by the all-male labor of pulque production, which indicates that the Díaz regime removed women from the means of production and further suggests that women lost their liberty precisely when primitive communal life was transformed into relations of private property. Patriarchal society transforms women from ends in themselves to sexual commodities for men's desires, as my earlier analysis of "Maguey" supports.

For the male workers, close-ups and medium shots accentuate the peons' intensive labor of extracting the juice from the maguey plants, which is fermented into pulque. But rather than fermenting the juice themselves, they take it to the hacienda, where the hacendado oversees the production of pulque. After fermentation, the pulque is sold back to the peons, for whom, according to Eisenstein's scenario, it "drowns sorrows, inflames passions and makes pistols fly out of their holsters."[76] But these sorrows and passions are often caused by the alienating production system for harvesting pulque, which keeps the peons dispossessed of their land and in a constant state of abject poverty.

The phrase "pistols fly out of their holsters" is a double entendre that further emphasizes how the pulque consumed by one of the hacendado's men encouraged his rape of Maria and led to Sebastian's armed rebellion. "Maguey" reveals how economic and sexual exploitation are a part of the same economy. The peons' inability to own the means of production not only keeps them in a perpetually destitute state, but also allows the hacendado's men to believe that they own both the pulque and the laboring bodies that produce it. The commodity and the producer are conflated, making the peons a disposable product for the upper class's amusement. This general conflation of the human being with the commodity further explains the display of Maria before the hacendado's men. Eisenstein's intercutting of the hacendado's men drinking pulque while gazing at Maria suggests the similar place that both pulque and Maria occupy: things to be consumed either orally, visually, or sexually.

The film's next episode, "Soldadera," which strikes me as the film's most interesting section because of its focus on the women who fought beside the revolutionaries between 1910 and 1911, is also the most problematic to analyze. Since Eisenstein was unable to shoot this episode, we have only his written scenario and random accompanying notes on it as sources for what might have appeared on film. Yet as Harry Benshoff observes: "It is interesting to speculate whether this sequence would have proven to have been one of the earliest statements of feminist action to be seen in Soviet film."[77] Based on Eisenstein's written scenario, "Soldadera" would have emphasized the importance of women's action and labor to enact revolutionary change. Yet rather than deeming such an outlook feminist, I consider "Soldadera" to be representative of an antifeminist Bolshevik position that nonetheless acknowledges the importance of women's liberation through class struggle. The episode represents one particular Bolshevik stance toward the woman question that dismissed feminism as bourgeois feminism, regarding it as a liability that would remove focus from the class struggle and undermine collective political action. Therefore, instead of "viewing the liberation of women as a desirable object in itself," this stance treated "the mobilization of women in more instrumental terms as a potential contribution to the larger revolutionary struggle," which is exactly what "Soldadera" seemed to set out to do.[78] Yet the scenario of "Soldadera" is interesting because it focuses on the women while visually minimizing the men's importance. So even though the episode adopts an antifeminist Bolshevik position toward the woman question, its structure highlights the importance of women's actions and community in ways that the usual adherents of such a position did not.

In contrast to Maria in "Maguey," the women of "Soldadera," on the whole, take a more active stance, aiding the Mexican Revolution with an interesting mixture of masculine and feminine traits. They take empty gun cartridges and allow their children to suck on them for a lack of candy; they apply tortillas to the men's wounds and fasten them with willow fibers.[79] In essence, the women take military objects and domesticate them while seizing on the domestic for military uses. Much like the unity of visions at the end of "Maguey," which establishes a revolutionary perception, the mixture of the domestic and the public suggests that the masculine and feminine spheres in revolutionary action are no longer mutually exclusive but must be fused for social progress to take place. This conflation of the masculine and feminine is particularly noteworthy when one keeps in mind that Eisenstein typically "uses the crossing and blurring of traditional gender lines to caricature figures he does not like [in his films]."[80] Al LaValley cites the "masculinized" women's death battalion in *October* as well as Efrosinia's "mannish" features and Vladimir's "feminine" look in *Ivan the Terrible* as examples.[81] Although some exceptions to this rule can be found, such as Marfa's final "masculine" image in *The Old and New* and Fyodor's gender-bending dress and actions in *Ivan, Part II,* "Soldadera" offers Eisenstein's most sustained and nuanced focus on the need to problematize traditional masculine and feminine roles in order to foster revolutionary activity.[82] And because "Soldadera" refuses to separate gender spheres, it shows women who were no longer forced to choose between having either a family or a career, as patriarchal, capitalist ideology asserts, but were allowed to do both once again, as in "Sanduga."

Yet, like "Sanduga," "Soldadera" exposes a double burden of work for the soldaderas, who must tend to domestic labor and fight in the revolution. Rather than lounging around, as in "Sanduga," men here are busy fighting. Yet "Soldadera" seems more aware of the double burden imposed on women than "Sanduga." We see this in Eisenstein's description of Pancha, the main soldadera in the episode: "a machine-gun ribbon hangs across her shoulder, a big sack containing household utensils weighs heavily on her back."[83] Pancha's image represents how this double burden literally weighs on her. "Soldadera" tends to emphasize the hardship, privation, and suffering inflicted on women by the revolution. This is not the fallen paradise of "Sanduga" but a transitory hell on the way toward liberation. Yet through such suffering and pain, "Soldadera" seems to suggest how revolutionary activity nonetheless transforms traditional gender and familial roles in ways that are necessary for a more egalitarian and just future.

¡Que Viva México! ultimately aims at transcending the limited categories of "masculine" and "feminine" by exposing how the experience of ecstasy allows all people to move beyond their gendered, racial, and socioeconomic limits. During ecstasy, the self is no longer divided from its surroundings. It is not, however, simply the incorporation of the external into one's "I," but an "excorporative" dissolution of the self into its surroundings, as Kaja Silverman deems it.[84] As many Eisenstein scholars have noted, Eisenstein primarily viewed ecstasy in religious terms, "like the saint's loss of self in the Other."[85] Personal control no longer exists as the experience becomes totalistic, fusing consciousness with processes that exceed and determine the ego's gendered, racial, and other socioeco-

nomic boundaries. The fiesta, for ¡Que Viva México! becomes an important site for temporarily gaining access to ecstasy, which is why the film ends with the Day of the Dead.

The holiday highlights the Mexican *vacilada,* in which the ridiculous and the sublime, the masculine and the feminine, the spiritual and the animal, intermix.[86] By challenging the categories and logic of patriarchal, capitalist Mexican society, the Day of the Dead provides the potential to access a collective ecstasy in which people can reenvision society as a totalistic whole in which more-equitable and more-pleasurable structures can be established out of the exploitation of the present. In *The Labyrinth of Solitude,* Octavio Paz clearly noted the revolutionary potential of Day of the Dead: "It is . . . a sudden immersion in the formless, in pure being. By means of the fiesta society frees itself from the norms it has established. It ridicules its gods, its principles, and its laws: it denies its own self."[87] In ¡Que Viva México! the Day of the Dead reveals how revolutionary potential lurks in the present moment—within every sugar skull, at the bottom of every cup of pulque, in between every musical chord.[88] Although the conflation of the masculine and the feminine seen in "Soldadera" is still far from the transcendence of such categories, the episode indicates a desire to move toward a better, more equitable future. What exactly this future will look like is not entirely certain, but the film suggests that it most definitely will not resemble those class and gender positions that constitute the bulk of "Maguey."

As we can see from my close analysis of ¡Que Viva México! U.S. Left film theorists and critics were correct in asserting the importance of montage in their columns, since it indeed offered a more complex and radical structure for Eisenstein's film than Hollywood continuity editing could provide. As stated before, when Upton Sinclair and Sol Lesser released *Thunder over Mexico,* Left film theorists and critics denounced it as having reduced the complexity of the original film into "a single unconnected romantic story" by making "Maguey" the central focus rather than only one of six episodes, as Eisenstein had intended.[89] Although "Maguey" is a pivotal episode in ¡Que Viva México! since it suggests the emergence of revolutionary perception and consciousness, it is still only a brief episode in the overall film. *Thunder,* therefore, overindividuates the episode into a melodramatic conflict between good peons and a bad hacendado without accounting for the wider sociohistorical processes that led to the forms of exploitation shown. And in regard to gender issues, the male gaze that ¡Que Viva México! questions is no longer presented within *Thunder* as historically class contingent but is established as a transhistorical gendered norm. Because alternative socioeconomic structures and looking relations are not addressed, the male gaze is unproblematically naturalized.

GENDER ASSUMPTIONS WITHIN U.S. LEFT FILM THEORY AND CRITICISM

Despite many 1930s U.S. Left film theorists' and critics' perceptive analyses of how Hollywood's reliance upon continuity editing, spectacular mise-en-scène, and limited characterization would efface the radical politics of *¡Que Viva México!* they largely ignored the significant role that gender played in the film's overall structure. One might argue that they simply did not possess a theoretical outlook that would enable them to clearly articulate how patriarchal capitalism constructed female identities, but as one searches through the archives of the *New Masses,* the *Daily Worker,* and other periodicals and literature of the time, one notices female writers such as Meridel Le Sueur, Josephine Herbst, Martha Millet, Mary Heaton Vorse, Rebecca Pitts, and Grace Hutchins, who theorized the complex connections between gender and Marxist politics.[90] Ella Winter traveled to the Soviet Union and reported on the abolition of sex discrimination in her book *Red Virtue: Human Relationships in the New Russia* (1933).[91] Grace Hutchins offered a survey of women's labor in the United States in her book *Women Who Work* (1934), in which she distinctly places her work in the Marxist tradition: "They [Marx and Engels] included in their analysis the first basic treatment of women's status under capitalism and their statements are as true today as when they were made some eighty years ago. It remained for Lenin and the Soviet Union to point the way with inescapable clearness toward the true freedom of women in socialist society."[92] Meridel Le Sueur reported on the travails of unemployed women for the *New Masses* and the *American Mercury* in the early 1930s, suggesting that the Depression has affected them as significantly as men.[93] Such writings are important: as Paula Rabinowitz points out, although no historical Left institution of the 1930s, including the Communist Party USA, the American Federation of Labor, or the Congress of Industrial Organizations, ever emphasized a feminist program within its structure, "the early years of the decade had seen a surge of demands resonant with feminist goals."[94] Yet such feminist goals were entirely absent from most U.S. Left film theorists' and critics' columns at the time, suggesting either a disconnection between these critics and the writers, mainly women, who investigated gender issues, or a failure on these critics' part to see how a focus on gender might benefit their ideological analysis of film.

Rebecca Pitts's article "Women and Communism" (1935) offers a particularly remarkable Marxist analysis of female exploitation, which parallels the same observations made by *¡Que Viva México!* Pitts also uses Engels's *The Origin of the Family, Private Property, and the State* to explore the importance of female labor in establishing women's equality within the community. One of Pitts's observations could stand as a summary of "Sanduga": "In primitive times, and, indeed, until shortly before the dissolution of tribal communities, women were free, productive members of the group" because exchange relations had not yet usurped use value, which placed people, not profit, at the center of the community.[95] And as "Maguey" follows "Sanduga," Pitts likewise follows her observation about women's freedom with one about its loss: "It is very interesting and important to notice that women lost their liberty precisely when primitive communal life broke down and *private property* developed."[96] Removed from the workforce and regarded as items of exchange between men, women were seen as men's "own property, made for his personal use and pleasure."[97] And as Pitts also noted, "From an end in herself she became a sexual commodity, a means to an end," an observation echoed in "Maguey's" focus on the rape of Maria.[98] Communism is the only way to help women regain their status as ends in themselves, since it is the only political system that acknowledges the need for new economic and psychological foundations if women were to truly realize their full potential.[99] Pitts looks to the Soviet Union not as an embodiment of communist principles but as a nation offering "embryonic hints of the future," just as *¡Que Viva México!* looks to Day of the Dead as a harbinger of a new future in which the economic and social orders must change for class and gender equality to take place. In essence, Pitts's article tracks the exact trajectory that *¡Que Viva México!* takes, even though it is unclear whether Pitts was familiar with the film.[100]

Pitts's article is important for highlighting how some members of the early 1930s U.S. Left were familiar with Engels's text and its sophisticated Marxist analysis of gender, which could have served as a productive theoretical tool for analyzing the gender implications of *¡Que Viva México!* Yet such an analysis was largely absent from U.S. Left film theory and criticism on the film. Since Pitts's article was published a year after the *¡Que Viva México!* debates subsided, U.S. Left film theorists and critics could not have used it in their analyses of the film. But one can safely infer that at least some women on the U.S. Left were discussing gender equality before the appearance of Pitts's article; some of their works that analyzed gender from a Marxist point of view include Agnes Smedley's *Daughter of Earth*

(1929), Grace Lumpkin's *To Make My Bread* (1932), and Tillie Olsen's *Yon-nondio: From the Thirties*.[101] Yet U.S. Left film theorists and critics show no evidence of having engaged in a dialogue or even of having been familiar with such socialist-feminist discourses.

The closest U.S. Left film theory came to noticing the importance of gender in *¡Que Viva México!* was Morris Helprin's 1934 article for *Experimental Cinema*. Helprin spent several months in Mexico observing Eisenstein, which provided him with a more in-depth knowledge of the film than most other Left film theorists and critics possessed. In his article, Helprin claims that Eisenstein discovered "the importance of woman's position in that country," a realization that moved the film "from [originally being] a dimensionalized fresco to the presentation of a socio-logical problem" about the role and influence of women in various Mexican epochs.[102] Helprin cites "Sanduga" as representing female labor in a matrilineal society. Woman "tills the fields, barters in the market place and rules the home. Her husband is a procreative force and no more."[103] Furthermore, he notes the drastic change in gender focus in "Maguey": "Here a phallic symbolism is engaged to emphasize the complete *masculinity* of the terrain" and episode.[104] His use of the term "phallic" to describe the episode is surprising, since it indicates a vague awareness that gender is not limited to human bodies but includes milieu—that gender is a part of the environment and its ideologies as well as of the characters. Ultimately, Helprin notes that Eisenstein "has recognized the part that woman plays in the social and economic life of the country and around this has constructed his film."[105] Although her physical presence might not dominate all of the film's episodes, "her influence is as subtle as the Indian's overconquest and swallowing-up of his Spanish conqueror."[106] Helprin's last statement is revealing, since it connects women's presence in the film to the anticolonial struggle, suggesting that at least one U.S. Left film theorist saw how the two themes were intertwined.

But this general silence on U.S. Left film theorists' and critics' part is not entirely surprising if we keep in mind how the male gaze structured most of their writings. Since their theoretical lens inherently marginalized women and gender issues, a film like *¡Que Viva México!* was quite simply unassimilable by their conceptual frameworks; therefore, all aspects of the film relating to women and gender were either ignored or subsumed under more-"revolutionary" issues pertaining to class and nation.

Because of this underlying sexist gaze, male Left film critics could only see, at best, the film's metaphorical use of women to represent revolution, thus supporting Paula Rabinowitz's observation that the 1930s male Left often considered gender issues to be subsidiary to class issues.[107] When gender was brought to the forefront by the male Left, it was usually used metaphorically to represent class conflict by juxtaposing a masculine proletariat to an effeminized bourgeoisie.[108]

U.S. Left film theory and criticism supports Rabinowitz's general observation about the historical Left's metaphorical use of gender, with one important difference. On the rare occasion when these theorists and critics did mention woman's importance within Eisenstein's film, they highlighted her as a metaphor for revolution, thus inverting the traditional way in which the historical Left often associated the "masculine" with the proletariat and the "feminine" with the bourgeoisie. In other words, although Eisenstein's film provoked Left film critics to reverse women's metaphorical role in revolution, it failed to make them take notice of the complex ways in which women operated nonmetaphorically in the film's episodes.

For example, in regard to "Soldadera," Seymour Stern highlights women's metaphorical role by seeing its central character, Pancha, as representing the growing revolutionary consciousness of Mexico in traditional feminine ways. Pancha initially marries a man in Pancho Villa's regime. Eisenstein viewed Villa as a problematic revolutionary figure because he revolted more for his own self-interests than for Mexico as a whole. Unable to suppress his egocentrism for the sake of the revolution, Villa warred unnecessarily against Zapata's troops for the spoils of victory. After Pancha's husband dies about three-quarters way through the episode, she immediately marries a Zapatista soldier and gives birth to a child. Pancha's new marriage represents, for Eisenstein, "the conception that strength does not reside in dispute, but uniquely in the union of all the people against the forces of reaction."[109] Stern emphasizes Pancha's role as child bearer by indicating that the climax of "Soldadera" "is the birth of a child by one of the soldadera[s] hiding in a freight car, intercut in parallel montage with the triumph of the 1910 Revolution in the desert through which the train is speeding."[110] Stern's article, which does not even mention Pancha by name, highlights her "motherly" role as a child bearer at the expense of effacing her complex actions that challenge the mutual exclusivity of masculine and feminine realms.

Because Pancha hovers between gender binaries, she occupies a liminal position that most working-class women held and that the male historical Left had difficulty identifying: "not fully feminine because she works, neither is she a worker, because she does women's work. Her body is a site of the dual labor of productivity and reproduction and so appears outside the divisions constituting knowledge."[111] This effacement by U.S. Left film theorists and critics of women's complex roles in *¡Que Viva México!* was representative of their common belief that gender had to function traditionally or in a limited metaphorical way in order to serve class solidarity. If gender became a point of investigation in itself, critics risked disrupting its metaphorical use in defining social classes. Pancha had to remain unnamed in Stern's article because an assertion of her individuality would have deemphasized her metaphorical role in the revolution.

Rather than investigating the metaphorical role of gender in the film, Left film theorists and critics metaphorically gendered their descriptions of the film. Sol Lesser's editing of *Thunder over Mexico* was considered "THE RAPE OF ¡QUE VIVA MEXICO!" which turned *Thunder over Mexico* into "an emasculated fragment of Eisenstein's original scenario."[112] Thus violated, *¡Que Viva México!* was reduced from its original "manly" state to become the effeminized *Thunder over Mexico*. Yet other critics considered *¡Que Viva México!* an object of feminine beauty that had been despoiled by Lesser's editing. Herman G. Weinberg believes that *¡Que Viva México!* possessed "ravishing physical beauty" that "'died of an abortion' performed by murderous hacks."[113] Yet Weinberg describes those "murderous hacks" as people "who had no more feeling for its [*¡Que Viva México!*'s] greatness of conception than so many mercenary 'mid-wives.'"[114] The various uses of feminine language in Weinberg's article indicate that the feminine could be metaphorically applied both positively and negatively by U.S. Left film theorists and critics. The feminine is both violated and violator. It is the pristine object to be gazed at, but it is vulnerable to violation because of its objectified status. But if the feminine becomes active, it is then deemed a "mercenary mid-wife." Within these descriptions of the film, we notice the gender assumptions made by many Left film theorists and critics: the feminine is associated with the objectified, but is also seen as a threat when it takes on an active status—hence the threat of the bourgeoisie, which is deemed feminine by the Left yet nonetheless actively controls U.S. politics and economics.

Male Left film theorists' and critics' desire to position the feminine in such limited ways suggests a tendency to reductively "pin down" women and the feminine in response to the newly proliferating discourses of Hollywood, fashion, and the cosmetics industry, which destabilized gender identities. By asserting women's ability to purchase a certain gendered look, these materialistic discourses undercut the older belief that gender was "naturally" connected to one's sex. As various feminist scholars like Kathy Peiss, Janet Staiger, Nan Enstad, and Shelley Stamp have shown, women became a central focus for the new consumer culture that flourished from 1880 to 1920.[115] Sarah Berry notes how Hollywood marketing became intertwined with the fashion industry in the 1930s, which "contradicted older notions that a woman's social status was defined by her father's or husband's social position."[116]

A few U.S. Left film theorists and historians were well aware of how Hollywood's growing links to new fashions destabilized traditional representations of women on the screen. For example, Lewis Jacobs observes in *The Rise of the American Film* (1939) that "short skirts, boyish figures, silk stockings, step-ins, cigarettes, and drinking not only emancipated the modern girl from 'woman's passive role' but freed her for masculine pursuits as well."[117] Although Jacobs's observation suggests a role reversal more than a destabilization of the categories themselves, he indicates that masculine gender positions were open to women because of the consumer discourses found on the Hollywood screen.

Despite consumerism's ability to emancipate women from passive roles, 1930s U.S. Left film theorists and critics realized that such independence came with a price: a self-commodification that precluded either collective action or a systematic understanding of capitalism's processes as a whole. By prioritizing individual desires over collective action, the "women's independence" promulgated by consumer discourses was seen by many Left theorists and critics as belonging to a conservative ideology: women could safely focus on their individual wants and needs because such an attitude left the social processes and structures that created such desires, along with the concept of the individual, unexplored. Yet the critics and theorists largely failed to see the dialectical nature at work in women's attraction to consumer discourses: "Women's embrace of style, fashion, romance, and mixed-sex fun could be a source of autonomy [from patriarchal familial structures] and pleasure as well as a cause of their continuing oppression." And for working-class women, aspects of commercial culture could function as both a form of escape and a means to productively inform their political practices and foster a politicized community.[118]

Despite the legitimacy of some of their ideological objections to a consumer-based practice of liberation, U.S. Left film theorists and critics were also personally unsettled by the numerous representations of powerful female figures in women-centered films, which challenged their patriarchal authority and heterosexual assumptions. As a result, "the new leisure culture changed the definitions of female identity in relation to the family, superimposing the values of motherhood and domesticity with the appeals of pleasure, glamour, and eroticism."[119] Mike Gold, who reported on Hollywood during the late 1930s, vented his frustration in a May 1937 column for the *Daily Worker* in which he critiqued the stage mothers who dragged their little girls to Hollywood to become the next Shirley Temple. Instead of learning proper "feminine" roles, these girls have "been taught all the worst mannerisms of a ham actress—to be consciously coquettish, vain, cute, and cunning."[120] Hollywood infused these girls with a sense of "artificiality," as Gold deems it, the kind of knowledge about the performativity of femininity that, Gold assumes, did not exist outside the culture industry's influence. But Gold's real concern is not for the girls' well-being but for the men who will have to deal with them later in life. He asks: "Will any hard-working man want to marry a wife who has graduated from such training?"[121]

Similarly, Robert Forsythe, normally one of the more sophisticated U.S. Left film critics, throws a veritable tantrum about Mae West in his revealingly titled article "Mae West: A Treaty on Decay." According to Forsythe, West's overt sexuality represents nothing less than "the breakdown of capitalist civilization . . . [and] symbolizes the end of an epoch."[122] He represents female sexuality and desire as not having any value in themselves, but only as symptoms of a decaying bourgeois age in which "real" men have lost control. His column continues in an increasingly homophobic bent, seeing West's sexuality as opening the door to homosexual license: "If I make a point at all in this respect it would be to indicate that introversion [homosexuality] is essentially a class ailment and the direct result of a sybaritic life which finally results in profound boredom for lack of any further possible stimulation or titillation."[123] Therefore, anything other than heterosexual male desire is deemed aberrant, a metaphor for all that is wrong with capitalism. One can perhaps better understand, but not defend, Forsythe's volatility by keeping in mind that "Hollywood is at its most queer [in terms of filmic representations] from early 1932 to mid-1934, a period that corresponds to the worst years of the Depression."[124] So Forsythe was writing at a time when heterosexual males felt vulnerable and disempowered, both economically and socially.[125]

I highlight Gold's and Forsythe's articles because they represent extreme examples of a general male anxiety that permeates the writings of U.S. Left film theory and criticism. As I have shown, there were other critics, like Lewis Jacobs and Morris Helprin, who held more accommodating attitudes toward the analysis of gender in their writings. Yet by juxtaposing U.S. Left film theory and criticism with insights made by Rebecca Pitts and with the representations in Eisenstein's Mexican footage, we can see that it never accessed any of the more sophisticated discourses of the time that interwove gender and class analysis. Although U.S. Left film theorists and critics for the most part correctly identified the reified ways in which leisure discourses asserted women's independence, their reluctance to adopt a materialist understanding of gender was also related to their own masculine anxieties. At a time when mass unemployment displaced many men from their traditional breadwinning positions, at a time when new consumer discourses emphasized women's independence from the home and men, at a time when Hollywood offered numerous queer representations of gender in film, the absence of gender from male U.S. Left film columns might have been an intentional silence, a way to ignore how these conditions challenged their very sense of masculinity. To distance Eisenstein's anti-Hollywood film from such practices, these theorists and critics might have, consciously or unconsciously, minimized the importance of gender (and homoeroticism) in the film's scenario and footage.

"THE 'LESSER' OF TWO EVILS": DEBATES CONCERNING DISTRIBUTION

Before the release of *Thunder over Mexico* and the subsequent critical lamentations regarding the emasculation of *¡Que Viva México!* U.S. Left film theorists and critics concentrated on the problems of distributing Eisenstein's Mexican film. Ultimately, they asked whether the film should be commercially or selectively distributed. Although the former option could deliver potentially larger audiences, the film's structure would inevitably have to be altered to a more traditional, commercial form that would appeal to both exhibitors and general audiences. In a letter written to *Modern Monthly* in July 1933, Herman Weinberg notes how *¡Que Viva México!* was "suffering from a species of 'maladjustment' typical of all great films which find themselves at the mercy of the commercial channels of distribution—a necessary evil, we suppose, but one which should be definitely waived [*sic*] aside in this case because it means the artistic annihilation of the world's greatest film and the most resplendent artistic creation of the twentieth century."[126] Although Weinberg was dismayed by the mandates imposed on films by commercial distribution, he was not challenging commercial distribution altogether but merely suggesting that it recognize exceptional, unconventional art films and ease its fiscal mandates in those cases. For Weinberg, the problem with commercial distribution was that it prioritized sales over the inherent aesthetic quality of a film. With films that challenged conventional genre categories, mass distribution was able to register them only as a loss of sales.

Other theorists and critics noted how the compromises of mass distribution could have been ameliorated if the backers had simply accepted limited distribution of *iQue Viva México!* Because the backers did not choose this option, certain theorists and critics questioned these backers' underlying motives, especially after the Soviet Union offered $60,000 for the rights to the film. In an October 1933 article for *Modern Monthly,* Seymour Stern mentions how "[Upton] Sinclair and Co. spurned this offer and held out for a flat cash sum of $100,000. They were not concerned over the artistic fate of *iQue Viva México!* and they apparently did not trust the Soviets on a percentage-arrangement."[127] Stern had a valid point: since Sinclair publicly wrote that he cared about the artistic integrity of the film, it was unclear why he did not accept the Soviet's initial offer, which would have allowed him to break even with the film. But the longer Sinclair and the backers waited to strike a better deal with the Soviets, the colder the Soviets became about buying the film. Eisenstein was becoming persona non grata in the Soviet Union over the supposed "decadent" formalism of his films.[128] When Eisenstein's political enemy Victor E. Smirnov took control of Amkino, the Soviet film outlet in New York City that negotiated rights for the film, the Soviet government withdrew its offer to buy the film.[129] In a 1933 article for *Modern Monthly,* Herman Weinberg quotes an unnamed speaker who indicated that the Soviet government was no longer interested in Eisenstein's film. Just as a great many Hollywood executives were indifferent to Eisenstein's originality, a significant number of Soviet bureaucrats also "dislike[d] Eisenstein personally or ha[d] no understanding of the significance of his work."[130]

This change of attitude by the Soviets toward Eisenstein's film was disturbing to U.S. Left film theorists and critics, since the Soviet Union was the one country that seemed to be free from commercial mandates in filmmaking. But now even the stronghold of experimental film—one that these theorists and critics often championed when challenging Hollywood to make experimental and original films—showed its indifference to radical art. Not only were independent producers exposed as being no different from commercial ones, but the Soviet film industry's bureaucracy also seemed to resemble that of Hollywood more and more, with its concerns about auteurist aesthetic flourishes and content censorship.[131] Suddenly there seemed no place to turn to guarantee any type of distribution for a radical film.

Because of the many problems associated with mass-distributing *¡Que Viva México!* and maintaining its radical form, U.S. Left film criticism of *¡Que Viva México!* and *Thunder over Mexico* brought to the forefront issues that came to have increasing importance for a Popular Front stance regarding film. Fed by the Eisenstein montage debates of the early 1930s, later U.S. Left film theory and criticism emphasized progressive film's relation to Hollywood while suggesting that Left theorists, critics, and filmmakers move away from their earlier radical assumptions if they wanted their films and ideas to reach a wide audience. After the discussion of *¡Que Viva México!* one of the first and most significant groups to reevaluate its previous stance toward film was the New York Film and Photo League. This reexamination of its practices was somewhat surprising, since the league often prided itself as being the most radical American film group. Yet by 1934, the league was beginning to publicly question the use of experimental techniques in its films and to reconsider audiences' reception of their work. Leo Hurwitz, a league member, hinted at these concerns in a 1934 article for *New Theatre*, suggesting that the league problematically "presupposed on the part of the audience a knowledge and sympathy with our point of view."[132] By not taking into account the possibility of reaching a more diverse audience, the league failed to see how its approach to filmmaking could alienate potential audience members from its politically charged subjects. The implicit question was whether the league wanted to keep preaching to the already politically converted or to reach a larger audience, which might be encouraged to take a more progressive social view by the league's films. Undoubtedly, the problems with distributing *¡Que Viva México!* / *Thunder over Mexico* forced the league to recognize that if it truly desired a wider audience, it would have to alter quite drastically how its films were made, since their amateur style and lack of narrative were two major impediments to mass distribution.

By 1935, league members such as Leo Hurwitz and Ralph Steiner became more vocal about how their films' reliance upon montage often led to a cinema that was "depersonalized, inhuman."[133] Using arguments found in Harry Alan Potamkin's and William Troy's articles, Hurwitz and Steiner claimed that this depersonalization was often due to an overreliance on montage by some filmmakers as an aesthetic end in itself rather than a means to further the film's content.[134] As a result, since the films' characters were regarded only "externally," as formal properties of light, shape, and movement, they became "objects rather than . . . human beings," a status that duplicated the very reification of humanity found in the Hollywood films they criticized.[135]

Audience identification became the necessary corrective to such abstraction. Hurwitz and Steiner acknowledged the importance of someone like Eisenstein because he investigated the links between film's dramatic elements and montage, but since there was no equivalent film director in America, they turned for inspiration to theater workers like Lee Strasberg, who had also thought deeply about film.[136] Perhaps the most important concept they learned from Strasberg was to focus on a film's dramatic construction in order to ensure the audience's emotional involvement with the material, since without it, no matter how profound and socially important the film's themes, they "will be [regarded as] lifeless and socially ineffectual."[137] Thus, some members of the league no longer considered plot, character, dramatic re-creations, and professional acting to be simply unnecessary conventions of bourgeois art, but treated them instead as elements to be considered in relation to the lessons of montage theory.

THE FOURTH PERIOD OF SOVIET FILM AND
RAPPROCHEMENT WITH HOLLYWOOD

Furthermore, Left film theorists and critics for the *New Masses,* the *Daily Worker, New Theatre,* and other periodicals were noticing the movement in Russian films toward a greater use of dramatic conventions. Georgy Vasiliev's *Chapayev* (1934) was praised by critics for its ability to address biographical material as well as historical issues. Similarly, Leonid Trauberg's *The Youth of Maxim* (1935) was noted for its development of psychologically subtle characterization.[138] Yet unlike the executive in charge of the Soviet film industry, Boris Shumyatsky, who viewed Eisenstein's radical aesthetics as "formalist" and at odds with the precepts dictating the construction of socialist-realist films, most U.S. Left film theorists and critics felt that Eisenstein was still on the cutting edge of fusing of Left politics with a radical aesthetics. Although some U.S. theorists and critics critiqued Eisenstein for his formalist tendencies, many recognized how Eisenstein's ongoing development of his theories and film styles often showed a revision of his earlier positions. The *¡Que Viva México!* debates suggest that the Americans still valued the importance of certain major Soviet avant-garde directors, even though the Soviet film industry as a whole followed an alternative impulse to purge avant-garde aesthetics from its screens.

By 1935, Left publications were offering translations of Eisenstein's own accounts of the changes occurring in the Soviet film industry. In his article "The New Soviet Cinema" for *New Theatre,* Eisenstein explains that Soviet "socialist realist" cinema was not simply emulating the styles of Western commercial cinema, but also fusing commercial styles with the radical discoveries of montage. He divided the Soviet cinema into four periods: the first provided for the necessary economic stabilization of the cinema after the Russian Revolution; the second manifested the silent avant-garde's challenge to all commercial styles and narrative; the third produced films that demanded "penetration into the inner problems of the individual, psychoanalytic treatment of the human material, and an integral plot, strictly confined to its story"; and the newly emergent fourth period fused the avant-garde discoveries of the second period with the classical structures of the third.[139] He believed that *Chapayev* was indicative of the ideal fourth-period picture, since it "succeeded in achieving unforgettable portrayals of living human beings [the third period] and in presenting an unforgettable picture of the epoch [the second period]."[140] But Eisenstein wanted to be clear that *Chapayev* was not a return to "classical" bourgeois models but instead "a movement 'forward to a new form of plot.'"[141] Mere emulation of Western, commercial plots would not adequately allow Soviet films to dialectically address the individual's relation to his or her social context. Although one might rightly debate whether Soviet films ever successfully carried out this political and aesthetic mission during its fourth period, U.S. Left film theorists and critics could not help noticing the changes taking place in both Eisenstein's attitude and Soviet film as a whole during the mid-1930s.

By 1936 many U.S. Left filmmakers, theorists, and critics pursued two related ideas: creating progressive narrative films that focused mainly on individual characters, and examining how Hollywood films could strike a balance between character identification and social context. Leo Hurwitz and Ralph Steiner left the New York Film and Photo League to create NYKino and then Frontier Films, where they developed scenarios, hired professional actors, and used some Hollywood techniques along with experimental montage in various film shorts and their full-length film *Native Land* (1942).[142] At the same time, progressive dramatists and theater workers seeking larger audiences than the ones available on Broadway were moving in droves to Hollywood in the hope of infusing its films with their political vision and avant-garde techniques. With people like Clifford Odets, Paul Muni, John Howard Lawson, Rouben Mamoulian, Paul Green, Ring Lardner, Jr., Lester Cole, Dorothy Parker, John Bright, Paul Jarrico, and Dalton Trumbo moving to (or already in) Hollywood in the mid-1930s, U.S. Left film theorists and critics could not help believing that Hollywood might become a more viable political and cultural force in Left film culture than they thought possible during the late 1920s and early 1930s.

In any case, Hollywood, by necessity, had to become a focus for U.S. Left film theorists and critics by the mid-1930s. As tensions mounted in Europe and the Soviet Union, the distribution of foreign films lessened. Also, most of the important international film journals like *Close Up* and *Experimental Cinema* went under, making it difficult for Americans to find international artists' and theorists' discussions of film. But the knowledge they had gained from reading and writing for such journals as *Close Up* and *Experimental Cinema* readied U.S. Left film critics to offer more-complex understandings of both independent and Hollywood films than they had previously been capable of.

CONCLUSION

It has been the goal of this chapter to reveal that the debates surrounding *¡Que Viva México!* were central for U.S. Left film theory and criticism's transition to a Popular Front stance by forcing its writers to confront some of the troubling links between independent production and Hollywood. These debates exposed the problems of distributing a radical film on a mass scale in the United States, and encouraged a subtle analysis of montage that emphasized both the merits and disadvantages to Left filmmaking. Among the merits: classical Hollywood continuity editing paled in comparison with the sophistication of radical montage. Ironically, Hollywood, by paying Eisenstein to write a scenario for *An American Tragedy,* assisted him in developing a sophisticated montage theory that addressed character psychology. Additionally, *¡Que Viva México!* allowed Eisenstein to explore the progressive potential within even the seemingly most repressive ideologies, like Catholicism, a move that anticipated the attitude that U.S. Left film theorists and critics adopted toward Hollywood soon after the failure of his film. Yet most U.S. Left film theorists and critics missed this subtlety because of the film's partial nature and their central concern with advocating for its completion.

A more serious theoretical limit, however, was U.S. Left film theory and criticism's reductive metaphorical reading of gender within *¡Que Viva México!* Although one might claim that these theorists' and critics' limited access to Eisenstein's outtakes impeded their ability to properly see how gender functioned within the film, Eisenstein's written scenario and the articles and books produced by Marxist female writers of the period provided U.S. Left film theorists and critics with the necessary theoretical framework and evidence to make such conclusions, as Morris Helprin's article verifies. Their metaphorical use of gender stemmed from deeper, systemic problems with how international Left film theory implicitly rested on a male gaze that reduced gender issues to matters of class and dismissed women's desires as nothing more than a fully reified outlook. Even in a film like *¡Que Viva México!* in which gender revolution was central to an articulation of class equality, it could only, at best, invert U.S. Left film theorists' and critics' metaphorical use of gender, rather than shatter such presuppositions for a more materialist approach. Although willing to question the centrality of montage, U.S. Left film theory and criticism still held adamantly to an exclusive male gaze.

By questioning the tenets of montage theory, U.S. Left film theorists and critics were left in search of a theory by middecade. By losing montage as a central framework as well as theoretical journals, like *Close Up* and *Experimental Cinema,* in which new film theories might by posed, U.S. Left film criticism analyzed specific films even more closely than before in a search for trends that might suggest a new theoretical approach. Film criticism begins to supplant film theory, which is not to say that U.S. Left film critics were not influenced by international film theory, but instead they tried to assemble a new theoretical approach from the mass of films that they reviewed. With its central conceptual orientation lost, U.S. Left film criticism not only became better at close analysis, but also significantly extended its racial focus as the Popular Front began.

Chapter 3

Screening Race

THE ANTILYNCHING FILM, THE
BLACK PRESS, AND U.S. POPULAR
FRONT FILM CRITICISM

With the collapse of *¡Que Viva México!* and the hopes of domestically mass-distributing radical films, U.S. Left film criticism lost its galvanizing framework of montage theory. The only remaining certainty was that a popular film criticism needed to be established in its wake. In the February 1935 issue of *Filmfront*, John Howard Lawson explained that film criticism needed to be "a combination of an analytical Marxist approach with a lively popular style" to produce "a revolutionary film magazine with a really wide circulation."[1] He continued: "To do this you need, more than anything else, meaty Hollywood stuff—and reviews which are surprising enough to create general interest, and yet not so sectarian as to repel the undeveloped sympathizer."[2] What exactly constituted this "meaty Hollywood stuff" remained unclear. But within a year the antilynching film would emerge as the answer.

The reason for the antilynching film's centrality in U.S. Left film criticism was largely the result of the U.S. Popular Front's ability to draw together divergent political interests into unified coalitions. As mentioned in the introduction, the Popular Front was an international movement initiated by the Communist Party to combat the rise of fascism, which had been seen in Italy, Japan, and, more recently, Germany. Disavowing its former sectarian approach, the Seventh Congress of the Communist International in 1935 permitted its members to form alliances with former political enemies: socialists, liberals, anarchists, etc. No longer were bourgeois democracies conflated with bourgeois fascism, but were instead regarded as important allies in combating it. Because of such policies, the Popular Front gained significant strength in England, France, Spain, and the United States.[3]

In the United States, the Popular Front consisted of "a vast array of disjointed, fractious, highly differentiated sub-groups [that] could be united in a series of overlapping organizations."[4] In general, it took three political forms: "a social democratic electoral politics; a politics of anti-fascist and anti-imperialist solidarity; and a civil liberties campaign against lynching and labor repression."[5]

It was precisely these three political stances that converged around the antilynching film and drew together Left critics from both liberal and radical backgrounds. As Myron Lounsbury observed, "Between 1935 and 1939, liberal and radical film criticism joined together to evaluate the American motion picture of the past and the present . . . Liberal critics began to encourage the scattered signs of social responsibility in the commercial movie and to point out precedents of political and economic issues found in the American film tradition."[6] Similarly, radical critics modulated their tone into a more populist stance. Furthermore, the antilynching film fostered a coalition between African American and white film critics, with many of their reviews crossing between the black and white independent presses. Overall, the Popular Front catalyzed the development of a new interracial formation within U.S. Left film criticism that focused on the antilynching film.

In the first half of this chapter, I map the separate but related critical trajectories of U.S. Popular Front film criticism by examining the black press's concern with lynching and its representations in film, as well as the historical Left's attitudes toward race and its relation to film. In its second half, I offer a case study of Fritz Lang's *Fury* (1936) in order to show how antilynching rhetoric provided Left film critics with a theoretical framework for reading repressed racial histories back into white mainstream productions. Furthermore, these critics trained audiences to be critical viewers so that they could collectively mobilize demands for more-progressive Hollywood films and push for federal antilynching legislation. *Fury* is a particularly interesting text because it exposes how U.S. Popular Front criticism co-opted a reactionary, antidemocratic film for a progressive, antilynching agenda, thus revealing not only the selective reading practices of 1930s Left film critics, but also the force of their interpretation, which still unconsciously influences many contemporary scholars' understanding of Lang's film. Additionally, *Fury* reveals how Left film critics' masculine anxieties prevented them from engaging in a substantive economic analysis of the film, since doing so would have required acknowledging the narrative importance of both Katherine (Sylvia Sidney), the film's female protagonist, and men's emasculation by the Depression.

THE AFRICAN AMERICAN PRESS

As Christopher Waldrep has shown in *The Many Faces of Judge Lynch,*
during the 1880s and 1890s, "black journalists persuaded Americans to
think of lynching as racial" and as primarily associated with the South.[7]
Until then, lynching had broadly stood for western frontier justice meted
out against Anglos, Hispanics, and Asians, and multiracial attacks erupt-
ing in the South.[8] Waldrep cites the journalism of T. Thomas Fortune and
Ida B. Wells as being most influential in initiating this crusade.[9] Thanks to
their work and that of other African American leaders and writers, lynching forever afterward would most often be associated with the abuses and
terror visited upon black male bodies.

The black press was instrumental in drawing lynching to the forefront
of liberal and socialist debates. In November 1919, the first issue of the
Crisis provided an editorial written by W. E. B. Du Bois against the lynching of two Italians in Florida, thus revealing lynching's multiracial vengeance.[10] According to George Hutchinson, "lynching became a kind of
national icon [within the *Crisis*], and one mission of the magazine was to
expose the moral bankruptcy and hypocrisy of 'nigger-hating America.'"[11]
The *Call* associated the 1919 race riots with pogroms, thus initiating the
links between antiblack racism and anti-Semitism that would become
a staple of Left discourse during the 1930s. Lynching was also a persistent theme in the *Liberator*.[12] And the *Messenger,* A. Philip Randolph and
Chandler Owen's socialist black newspaper, "insistently analyzed lynching in the context of class division and exploitation, arguing that lynching
'is used to foster and to engender race prejudice to prevent the lynchers and
the lynched, the white and black workers from organizing on the industrial and voting on the political fields, to protect their labor-power.'"[13]

Furthermore, the black press's ability to link lynching with the antiblack racism of *The Birth of a Nation* (1915) provided a template for many
of the strategies employed by Left film critics during the 1930s. As Anna
Everett has shown in *Returning the Gaze,* "it was common for black newspapers to carry reports on lynching and news of the suppression campaign
against *Birth* in the same editions . . . to remind the nation's cinephiles
that this film more than any other demonstrated beyond a doubt that the
cinema was not simply a matter of box office receipts predicated on, or
delimited by, high ideals of aesthetic and artistic-evolution."[14] Similarly,
some critics also critiqued the film by juxtaposing the history of Reconstruction against the distortions of the film.[15] These mutual strategies of
article placement and a historical analysis used to expose how African

American histories had been repressed or distorted in commercial films would become key techniques employed by 1930s Left film critics when discussing the antilynching film.

Simultaneously, in response to the insidious racial representations of *The Birth of the Nation* and U.S. commercial cinema as a whole, independent black filmmaker Oscar Micheaux began cinematically interrogating various lynching practices in such films as *Within Our Gates* (1920) and *Gunsaulus Mystery* (1921).[16] If, as Cedric J. Robinson contends, "motion pictures appear at that juncture when a new racial regime was being stitched together from remnants of its predecessors and new cloth accommodating the disposal of immigrants, colonial subjects, and insurgencies among the native poor," Micheaux's films unwove this racial regime from a uniquely critical black perspective.[17]

For example, the lynching sequence that ends *Within Our Gates* has rightly been regarded by numerous film scholars as a tour de force in deconstructing the white barbarity underlying such practices. Jasper Landry (William Stark), a black tenant farmer, is wrongly accused of killing his boss, who was actually shot by a disaffected poor white tenant farmer. A white mob forms and apprehends Landry and his family. Within the mob, white women and children wield sticks, beating the Landrys as the preparations for the lynching are being completed. As Jane Gaines notes, Micheaux's inclusion of white women and children in the scene provides a bold stroke to expose the white savagery that underlay lynching, and undermines its moral justification as a retaliatory measure to protect the defenseless. "The accusation of 'primitivism' is turned back onto White Southern culture," which inevitably led to the film being banned by most white censors as revealing "too much truth."[18] As will be shown later in this chapter, Depression-era black and white film critics similarly stressed how such critical representations of lynching seeped into Hollywood antilynching films like *Fury* and *They Won't Forget*. Although these critics might or might not have been aware of Micheaux's films, they nonetheless shared his antilynching stance, which unveiled the white barbarity and lust that fueled lynching.

The black press was crucial in encouraging such critical perspectives from independent black film-production companies. As Charlene Regester observes, "Between 1918 and 1929, African-American newspapers exerted a positive influence by applauding the efforts of companies that produced films appealing to black audiences."[19] Yet, unfortunately, the majority of "race film" companies produced a mostly bourgeois cinema. As Cedric Robinson notes, Micheaux was the exception rather than the rule: "When Black nationalism, Black radicalism, Black resistance, or Black insurgencies did erupt, they were either absent or caricatured in race movies. Black melodramas might employ referents to the social ideology of Booker T. Washington, but with respect to the Niagara movement, the NAACP, Black Socialism, the Universal Negro Improvement Association, or Black resistance to lynching, there was almost total silence. The one anomaly was Oscar Micheaux."[20]

Nonetheless, the black press emphasized "the idea of a coalition politics between the races" in order to combat racism both on and off the screen.[21] One way it did so was by reprinting critiques of *The Birth of the Nation* made by sympathetic whites. This revealed a shared political stance between races that directly opposed the film's reactionary, divisive politics.[22] This strategy was utilized by both black and Left presses during the 1930s, providing some writers and critics with a highly fluid role among diverse audiences. This fluidity was in many ways facilitated by a Popular Front discourse in which fascism served as a binding metaphor linking racist U.S. practices and attitudes with those of anti-Semitism abroad. As a result, antifascist rhetoric was used to create national and international coalitions between races and ethnicities. U.S. Left film critics adopted such strategies in their film columns to speak to readers of different ethnicities and races.

Although it is unclear how much Left film critics of the 1930s were directly influenced by the black press—though it was certainly to some degree—many of the techniques established by the black press for analyzing film became key strategies with which Depression-era Left film critics uncovered the repressed racial histories lurking within the antilynching film and used film criticism, in general, as an antiracist organizing tool.

THE WHITE LEFT AND FILM JOURNALS

Scholars such as Robin D. G. Kelley, Mark Solomon, Barbara Foley, and William J. Maxwell, among others, have well documented the growing importance of racial politics within the Communist Party throughout the 1920s and 1930s. As Kelly notes, "The Fourth Congress of the Comintern in 1922 adopted a set of theses describing blacks as a nationality oppressed by world-wide imperialist exploitation."[23] In 1925, the party founded the American Negro Labor Congress in order to combat the racist practices of the white labor movement as well as to harness the collective power of black workers.[24] In 1928, the Sixth World Congress of the Comintern asserted that African Americans in the black belt "constituted an oppressed nation and therefore possessed an inherent right to self-determination."[25] In 1930, the League of Struggle for Negro Rights, a Communist Party auxiliary, was founded. It supported black self-determination, militant resistance, and campaigns against lynching and white terror.[26] The increasing centrality of race within the Communist Party produced a ripple effect in other white Left organizations. Suzanne Sowinska observes: "Once the Communist Party began to take up strategic discussions of the Negro Question and launched an enthusiastic campaign to include race as part of its radical agenda, other branches of the Left also began to move beyond their color blindness to define racial persecution as a matter of tremendous importance."[27] She continues: "A utopian vision of racial equality combined with that of the eradication of class oppression fed the imaginations of many white radicals, who for the first time consciously attempted to undermine both their own assumptions about racial difference and the all-pervasive racism prevalent in white society."[28]

However, no event proved more decisive in garnering black support for the Communist Party than its defense of the Scottsboro Boys in 1931. William J. Maxwell writes: "Scottsboro made Communism a household word in African-American clubs, beauty shops, and churches and added color to the party's rank and file throughout the United States."[29]

On March 25, 1931, nine black boys got into a fight with some whites while hopping a train to Memphis. One of the whites, who had been beaten and thrown from the train, reported the incident to the local police, who then caused the train to be halted in Paint Rock, Alabama. As the boys were apprehended, two white women dressed in men's clothes emerged from a boxcar several cars away. Suddenly, rape charges were pressed against the boys, despite evidence suggesting otherwise. Without adequate counsel and under constant threat, the boys were rushed through trial in April 1931. After three days, all were sentenced to death except Roy Wright, who at thirteen years old was given life imprisonment.

In the meantime, the Communist Party USA was on the scene, reporting events in the *Daily Worker* and coming to the defense of the boys through its legal arm, the International Labor Defense (ILD). The ILD represented the case not as a mere incident of backward southern racism, but instead as a metonym for the racist machinations of the entire capitalist system and its judicial apparatus. Dan Carter writes:

> The fight for the Scottsboro boys' freedom would be inextricably joined with the class struggle. The constant linking of Scottsboro with the Sacco-Vanzetti case by Party publicists often gave the impression

that the nine defendants had been not only class conscious members of the proletariat, but also revolutionary activists. In general, however, Party leaders made more modest claims. "The issue of the oppression of Negroes is obviously an economic question," said one official of the International Labor Defense. The bourgeoisie, terrified at the growing solidarity of the Negro masses with their white co-workers, had decided to execute the nine defendants in order to crush this new black and white militancy.[30]

From such a perspective, the case had to be fought on two fronts: within the courtroom and through mass action. The latter was necessary, according to the ILD, "since the capitalist ruling class controlled the state and federal judiciary."[31] Freedom for the boys could be achieved only if the case were "linked up with the struggle against the whole system which breeds similar Scottsboros."[32] Only by highlighting and challenging the systemic processes of U.S. racism could the racism of this specific trial be successfully overruled.[33]

On the one hand, the Scottsboro case represented a sea change for the way blacks perceived whites. The ILD consistently outmaneuvered the NAACP for control of the case, not simply because it acted more promptly on the boys' defense, but also because of its more humane treatment of them. Unlike the NAACP, which made a series of condescending comments about the boys' low intelligence, the ILD asked for both the boys' and their mothers' input. As Dan Carter writes, "For the first time in their lives, white men were not telling them what to do, but asking their support, on the basis of complete equality."[34] It was through such words and deeds that the ILD gained the general support of blacks. Robin D. G. Kelley notes: "The ILD was not just one additional voice speaking out on behalf of poor blacks; it was a movement composed of poor blacks. It not only provided free legal defense and sought to expose the 'class bias' of racism in the South, it gave black working people what traditional middle-class organizations would not—a political voice."[35] Furthermore, and this cannot be stressed enough, the Communist Party USA, which the ILD was clearly supported by, offered many black people for the first times in their lives "a framework for understanding the roots of poverty and racism, linked local struggles to world politics, and created an atmosphere in which ordinary people could analyze, discuss, and criticize the society in which they lived."[36]

On the other hand, some blacks and less radical whites worried that the ILD might simply be using the boys for its own propagandistic purposes.

Many worried that the communists, by overemphasizing the class character of the trial, might unnecessarily antagonize the southern jury and judge against the boys. William Pickens, the NAACP's field secretary in Kansas City, announced to a group of black citizens: "It has since developed that their [the ILD's] chief aim is communistic propaganda, and that the plight of these youths is only a vehicle for that propaganda . . . I even suspect that it is their feeling that if justice should miscarry or if the boys should be lynched, it would further play into their hands and give them material for still more sensational propaganda among the more ignorant of the colored population."[37]

I want to argue that these two poles of African American response to the Scottsboro case encapsulate the overall contours of black opinion toward the white Left at the time: a constant ebb and flow between embracing the promises of an interracial utopian vision and uncovering the dangerous residual crags of structural racism that haunted such traditionally white organizations. Yet as the historical Left, and the Communist Party USA in particular, became more active in assisting blacks in their fight for equality—doing things such as establishing a sharecroppers' union in Alabama; defending Angelo Herndon, who was sentenced to twenty years in prison for handing out leaflets during an unemployment rally in Atlanta; analyzing the socioeconomic reasons behind the 1935 Harlem riots; fighting white chauvinism in the party itself; and nominating James Ford, an African American, as the Communist Party's vice presidential candidate in 1932—many African Americans could not help being persuaded that an interracial coalition with the white Left might be to everyone's benefit.

As "the Negro Question" gained prominence among the historical Left, race also became more central to film theory. The August 1929 issue of *Close Up* dedicated itself to the issue of blacks in film, drawing together white and black writers and intellectuals like Geraldyn Dismond, Harry Alan Potamkin, Walter White, and Paul Green. As mentioned in Chapter One, *Close Up*, a British publication, provided a forum for U.S. Left film theorists and critics and often defined their theoretical stances.

Harry Alan Potamkin's "The Africamerican Cinema" is an important article not only because its depoliticized, modernist analysis of African American cinematic representations provoked a direct response from Left film critics, but also because it identified the origins of Potamkin's racial analysis, which he would eventually incorporate into his later Marxist film criticism.[38]

Potamkin clearly despises the limits placed on black representation within commercial cinema, yet he voices his objections in an extremely vulgar and essentialized way:

> As for me, I shall be assured of the white man's sincerity when he gives me a blue nigger. I want one as rich as the negroes in Poirer's [*sic;* the reference is to French filmmaker Léon Poirier] documents of Africa. I am not interested primarily in verbal humor, in clowning nor in sociology. I want cinema and I want cinema at its source. To be at its source, cinema must get at the source of its content. The negro is plastically interesting then when he is most negroid. In the films he will be plastically interesting only when the makers of the films know thoroughly the treatment of the negro structure in the African plastic, when they know of the treatment of his movements in the ritual dances, like the dance of the circumcision, the Ganza.[39]

Despite Potamkin wanting blacks in film who are like "the negroes in Poirer's documents of Africa," he does not advocate the documentary film, since the form was often misused by white directors to portray blacks in a paternalistic anthropological light. Even the social-problem film is inept because white directors often lacked familiarity with African American contexts, leading to the development of yet more dull, misleading films.[40] Although Potamkin's primitivist stance deserves rebuke, he uses it to suggest how repressed African American histories and traditions need to be employed to combat the racist stereotypes that were projected by a white-controlled industry onto mainstream screens. He evokes his own positively valued stereotypes to attack the Eurocentric viewpoint that dominated Hollywood's view of blacks.[41]

Furthermore, Potamkin believes that black characters must be intimately intertwined with the film's form and content rather than merely serving as spectacle for white audiences' racist pleasures. According to Potamkin, the artist must "evaluate the relevant data [that is, the plasticity of blacks] [so] that he may be better able to know its potentialities."[42] Once again, although it is disturbing to hear Potamkin refer to African Americans as "relevant data," it is noteworthy that aesthetic considerations could lead artists to expose the "potentialities" of African Americans that make them a part of the "human-esthetic problem" rather than a projection of white fears.[43]

Potamkin was by no means alone in regarding an aesthetic approach to race as fundamental for undermining white racist perspectives. A year later, Kenneth Macpherson, the editor of *Close Up,* released his film *Borderline* (1930), starring Paul Robeson, which primarily dealt with infidelity and miscegenation. In a pamphlet for the film, H.D. addresses its racial dynamics in terms very similar to those found in Potamkin's article:

> He [Macpherson] is, in no way whatever, concerned personally with the black-white political problem. As an artist, he sees beauty, "take it or leave it," he seems to say again and again, and, "I'm not busy with party politics." Nevertheless, in his judicious, remote manner, he has achieved more for that much mooted and hooted Problem (with a capital) than if he went to gain specific sympathy. He says, "here is man, he is black," he says "here is a woman also of partial African abstraction." He says, not "here is a black man, here is a mulatto woman," but "here is a *man*, here is a *woman*." He says, "look, sympathize with them and love them" not because they are black but because they are man, because they are woman.[44]

Instead of appealing to racial origins like Potamkin, H.D. suggests that the abstract concern with beauty alone produces a sophisticated understanding of the complexities of racial relations. Beauty recognizes the desires and fears common to all races and nationalities. This stance implies an implicit resignation by whites of ever understanding blacks, which Macpherson gives voice to within his own article for the 1929 race issue of *Close Up:* "Our idea of the negro is as negroid as Al Jolson and no more . . . Let the negro, then, film himself, be free to give something equal to his music, his dance, his sculpture."[45] Beauty, as a result, provides the only way to transcend the racial divide between whites and blacks.

Potamkin, on the other hand, employs a more dialectical analysis in his film theory than H.D. Although Potamkin's appeal to a "human-esthetic" problem, like H.D.'s appeal to beauty, effaces race for an abstract concept, he also recognizes that African American traditions serve an equally important part in facilitating the accurate representation of blacks on screen. Potamkin realizes, unlike H.D., that equitable representations depend on both an appeal to a transcendental notion of humanity and on the specific coordinates of African American traditions. By keeping these conditions in tension with each other allows for the simultaneous recognition of racial differences and commonalities.

Yet it is precisely Potamkin's essentialism and appeal to aesthetics that later U.S. Left film theorists attacked. In a February 1931 article for *Experimental Cinema*, Samuel Brody quotes at length Potamkin's reference to Poirier's documents and his theory of sources. Brody asks, "Am I to accept this as a new brand of discrimination?"[46] He then reveals how the racist assumptions that underlie Potamkin's film theory are similar to the ones found in Eugene O'Neill's *The Emperor Jones:* "Only a thin veneer separates the American Negro from his African origin (read 'source'), and under primitive conditions will revert to the fears, hysteria and superstitions of his tribal forefathers."[47] Overlooked by both Potamkin and O'Neill is material reality, which discredits such an atavistic perspective: "Capitalist America has created a new Negro who in virtue of his position in the American social structure is as far removed from his African origins as his so-called 'white-nordic superiors' are from theirs."[48] To further stress Potamkin's complete ignorance of contemporary African American life, Brody ponders "how strange these fairy-tales must seem to the Negroes in the steel-mills of Pittsburgh, the packing-houses of Chicago, and the coalpits of Pennsylvania!"[49]

Brody finds Potamkin's rejection of a sociological approach equally reactionary: "I want Potamkin to inform me how we would go about the matter of making a film on the American Negro without consideration for the socio-political motive that underlies every phase of Negro life in the United States."[50] Brody observes that in regarding blacks as only "relevant data," Potamkin dives "headlong into the polluted waters of art-for-art's-sake."[51] For Brody, "the construction of any concrete theme in art in which human material is involved strictly implies the drawing up of definite social relationships as a prerequisite."[52] The problem with Potamkin's theory is that "an esthetically abstracted Negro essence in the film has become the thing for him."[53] Devoid of a historical-materialist framework, Potamkin's theory dangerously slides into a reactionary outlook that engages an abstract "theory of sources" in order to avoid any formative analysis of the racist realities of the present.

Despite the accuracy of Brody's critique, it was a relatively cheap shot, since Potamkin had already begun to significantly revise his theory into a more Marxist framework. For example, in "Lost Paradise: *Tabu*" (1931), he notes how the representations of the natives in *Tabu* as either grotesque or overidealized were "a concession to the apperception and preference of the western white audience" for a clichéd plot of "love forbidden."[54] Potamkin continues: "Had the approach been through the avenue of [the natives'] experience, rather than of sentimental showmanship, the selection would have been from the quotidianal and most constant of the experiences of the society of the Society Islands."[55] The film would have answered such questions as how do these people commonly live? What are their means of livelihood? What are their social categories? Potamkin reveals how this problem exposes Hollywood's inability to "respect the experiences of a people as something to draw upon seriously for theme and plot."[56]

One observes how Potamkin has shifted away from his abstract theory of sources toward more-material concerns about the lives of the natives, which he does not pretend to know. Rather than appealing to some essentialized cultural heritage, Potamkin now urges readers to understand that the natives' experiences have been structurally effaced through Western cinematic conventions. All Potamkin can do is ask the questions about the natives that he would have liked the film to answer, but he makes no pretences about what the answers should have been.

Potamkin concludes his article by noting how such visual clichés present the natives as defeated and quasi-pathetic, as if representing nothing more than the vestiges of a dying community. Instead, he argues, they should be presented heroically, since they managed to persevere despite the exploitation of Western imperialism. The film continues this imperialist tradition by harnessing the natives' lives as fodder for Eurocentric expectations rather than investigating the natives on their own terms and showing how imperialism has affected them.[57] In essence, the film's formulaic structure prevents it from achieving two vital goals: providing a non-Eurocentric perspective on other cultures and offering a self-critique of Western imperialism's oppressive forces. At best, "suggestions of exploitation, of imperialism—*the* universal experience of an oppressed people—loiter weakly and incidentally within the film."[58]

Another article from *Close Up*'s 1929 race issue that provoked a response among the Left was Geraldyn Dismond's "The Negro Actor and the American Movies." In it, Dismond recounts the multiple ways in which blacks were either barred from or stereotyped by Hollywood. Therefore, she argues, the rise of African American independent films, along with black actors' gradual entry into Hollywood, will challenge white racist perceptions: "Because of the Negro movie, many a prejudiced white who would not accept a Negro unless as a servant, will be compelled to admit that at least he can be something else; many an indifferent white will be beguiled into a positive attitude of friendliness; many a Negro will have his race-consciousness and self-respect stimulated. In short, the Negro movie actor is a means of getting acquainted with the Negro and under proper direction and sympathetic treatment can easily become a potent factor in our great struggle for better race relations."[59]

It was this observation that Robert Stebbins (Sidney Meyers) took to task in "Hollywood's Imitation of Life" (1935). He begins his article with the above quotation from Dismond. He then comments: "Off-hand it would be difficult to hit upon another example of wishful prophecy so precisely unfulfilled."[60] The rest of the article recounts the numerous racist representations of blacks in films such as *Hallelujah!* (1929), *The Emperor Jones* (1933), and *Imitation of Life* (1934).

Yet Stebbins's critique is not entirely fair, since Dismond's own quotation slips from speaking about black independent films to black actors, so it is unclear whether she is ultimately speaking about black actors within black independents, or about black independents *and* black actors in white films. Furthermore, Harry Alan Potamkin had already astutely revealed how some African American Hollywood films had challenged white viewers in spite of the films' racist outlooks. For example, in the pamphlet "The Eyes of the Movie" (1933), Potamkin notes how *Hallelujah!* despite its stereotypically agrarian, lower-class black perspective, caused southern white upper-crust audiences to object to the film, since they did not appreciate being placed in the submissive viewing position of "customers" of a "black star" on the screen.[61] Potamkin further notes: "The Negro was not ridiculous enough (no 'Amos 'n Andy'), a little too romantic for the southern boss, worried by signs of working-class solidarity."[62] Although one might rightly question some of Potamkin's assumptions, he nonetheless reveals how audiences could react in quite unexpected ways. Formal analysis of a film was not enough; one needed to take into account its sites of consumption, a fact that Stebbins seems not to have learned.

Not only was race gaining greater prominence within U.S. Left film columns, but also within white independent Left filmmaking. Interracial unity was emphasized in films such as *National Hunger March* (1931), *Bonus March* (1932), *Strike, Detroit UAW* (unknown date), and *Communist Rally in Michigan* (unknown date) by various Film and Photo Leagues in New York, Chicago, Detroit, and Los Angeles. Furthermore, members of the New York league went to Scottsboro to document the trial; they also filmed national rallies in support of the boys, producing such film as *Scottsboro Trial* (1932), *Scottsboro Demonstration* (1932), and *Washington Scottsboro Demonstration* (1932).

But no film drew more notice from African Americans than *Black and White*, a Soviet-German coproduction concerning the oppression of African American workers in the United States and their subsequent proletarian revolt. The Soviet Union hired twenty-two African Americans to travel to the Mezhrabpom Film Company to participate in production. Langston Hughes, Loren Miller, and Ted Poston, among others, set sail on June 14, 1932.[63] The *New York Amsterdam News* announced that the film would be "devoid of sentimentality as well as buffoonery" and would trace "the development of the Negro people in this country, their work, their play, their progress, their difficulties."[64]

However, a series of miscalculations caused filming to be halted. The lack of professional actors in the group made for embarrassing performances. Inadequate technical facilities delayed filming. But mainly, the script was wildly constructed, causing Langston Hughes "to weed out the burlesques, including a white mill owner who dances with his black serving maid, a lynching that is advertised over the radio, a Negro who calls for Yankee help over the radio, and a crusade of Northern workers who rush southward to join their black proletarian brothers."[65] All in all, a total lack of adequate preparation undermined the making of *Black and White*.

Yet very different reasons for the film's delay initially circulated in the African American press. The *Atlanta Daily World* announced that "the Soviet authorities suppressed the film for fear that its appearance would prejudice American opinion against the Soviet Union," since the Russians were trying to receive diplomatic recognition from the United States in order to ward off the Japanese threat from the east.[66] Accusations surfaced similar to the ones hurled against the ILD for its supposed manipulation of the Scottsboro Boys for solely communistic purposes: "The great lesson to be learned from this is that, all professions here to the contrary, Communism is interested in the Negro only as a propaganda medium for its own advancement in the world. We have said this all along. When the results of this propaganda have been beneficial to us we have not failed to say so, as in the Scottsboro and Euel Lee cases; but there is very little difference between the economic exploitation of oppressed groups and the exploitation of the same groups for propaganda purposes alone."[67] *Black and White*, for some in the African American press, served as yet another example of white mendacity and the exploitation of blacks for whites' purposes.

However, other accounts refuted the initial rumors. The *Atlanta Daily World* reported on October 5, 1932, that there were four reasons for the film's delay: an unsatisfactory scenario; "the types of players were unsuitable for production; the "South Russian tribe of Negroes" was not then available for filming; and "Meschrapbpom [*sic*] lacked the technical facilities."[68] In the February 1933 issue of the *Crisis*, Louise Thompson, who had arranged travel plans for the African American crew of *Black and White*, offered the most thorough defense of the film. She writes that problems arose because the Russians sent "for our group before the necessary preparations for the production of the picture had been completed."[69]

She mentions that Langston Hughes tried to rewrite the scenario, but "the conference ended with no agreement being reached," thus causing filming to be postponed for a year because of "winter weather conditions."[70] She optimistically added that the film "is on the calendar of productions for Meschrabpom-Film for 1933," with all the original members of the film crew to be rehired if they are available.[71] But this was never to be.

Despite the ultimate failure of *Black and White,* its very appearance showed, once again, that communists were in the vanguard of race relations on the white Left. Regardless of African Americans' doubts about their ulterior motives, communists provided them with opportunities that were largely unavailable through all other political venues. As Anna Everett correctly points out, African Americans' involvement with *Black and White* "illustrate[s] unequivocally black radical intellectuals' resolve to go literally to the ends of the earth on the slightest chance that they might intervene in Hollywood's intractable racist discourse."[72] This also held true when white Left film critics finally addressed the antilynching film. Blacks were not only well positioned to assist in the fight, but also eager to take advantage of a moment in Hollywood's history when its films could actually aid their fight for equality.

CONVERGENCE

In the May 1931 issue of the *New Masses,* Jacob Burck provided an illustration of a sheriff holding guns at the backs of two prisoners he was releasing to a lynch mob dressed in Ku Klux Klan regalia. Barely discernible, standing secretly amid the mob, are three fat cigar-wielding caricatures of bosses, portrayals typical of Left iconography of the time. One prisoner is in profile. He seems to possess African American features and a dark hue. The other prisoner has his back to us. The only clues to his racial identity are his lighter complexion and the chains wrapped around his powerful forearms, a symbol of labor ruthlessly shackled by capital. The sheriff tells both men as he escorts them out, "We treats Reds and Niggers alike!" A deputy dressed in a Klan robe and holding a shotgun observes from the door.

This picture condenses many attributes typical of white U.S. Marxist thought at the time. The inability to clearly identify either prisoner suggests the related oppression that blacks and white radicals experienced at the hands of the law, capital, and domestic fascists. The bosses' secretive presence within the Klan reveals how capitalism fostered racism to divide workers. Furthermore, the law is revealed as nothing more than

SHERIFF: "We treats Reds and Niggers alike!"

Jacob Burck

A Marxist emphasis on racism's systemic link with a capitalist mode of production.
"Sheriff" by Jacob Burck © Estate of Jacob Burck.

capitalism's agent, infected with the same racism as the townspeople—
with its deputy donning a Klan robe. Essentially, the illustration seems
to say, black and white workers are already united, except in their own
consciousnesses.

Burck's clever use of scale within the drawing reveals how only a Marxist perspective can provide a remedy for the injustices depicted. In graphi-
cally minimizing the presence of the capitalists, the drawing forces the
Marxist viewer to give them undue attention. Marxism offers the needed
conceptual lens for identifying and stressing the machinations at work
within both the drawing and everyday reality. To the undiscerning reader,
the picture might just seem like a random lynching of a black man and a
white laborer. To a Marxist, it reveals capitalism's reliance on racism and
violence to prevent working-class unity.

Because of its radical vision of racial equality, Marxism maintained a
strong presence among Left-leaning African Americans during the early
1930s. In 1932, W.E.B. Du Bois dedicated two issues of the *Crisis* to black
editors' views on communism. The general attitude was mixed. Often, editors were sympathetic to a Marxist viewpoint, but in general they viewed
it as a useful threat that made their liberal racial demands seem all the

more reasonable. C. A. Franklin writes: "I look for a more tolerant age to let the door of opportunity respond to our thrust. If not, then some change, possibly Communism."[73] W. P. Dabney notes: "There will be no Black Communists in America when fair play rules, merit is recognized, race prejudice ostracized. Will Pharoah [*sic*] Heed?"[74]

Most editors' problem with Marxism was that despite its vision of racial equality, it seriously challenged their other deeply cherished bourgeois beliefs. Roscoe Dunjee writes: "Jim Crow, segregation, anti-marriage laws, yes, everything which has hitherto separated the white and the black here in America, is denounced by this poor white," but, he continues, "with one mighty arm he draws me into his embrace, while with the other he casts bombs at our existing governmental system. His economic nostrums are anti-individualistic."[75] This mixed attitude toward communism led Du Bois to identify two main fears held by most of the editors: "In the case of American Negroes, 'Communism is planned and worked from without.' It does not make an experimental survey based on the problems of the American Negro as a minority group"; and "What will happen when they grow in numbers as they hope to grow and when they attempt to permeate the mass of American labor? What will they do when they are faced with the temptation of gaining a million white laborers by ousting and ignoring a hundred thousand colored ones?"[76] Although scholars like Mark Naison, Robin D. G. Kelley, William J. Maxwell, and Mark Solomon have shown the multivalent ways in which African Americans influenced U.S. Communist Party politics and policy, these editors' fears that Moscow somehow dogmatically controlled its American adherents reveal a pervasive concern among the black bourgeoisie, which was voiced during the ILD's defense of the Scottsboro boys and the abandonment of *Black and White*.

Du Bois chimed in with his own dialectical view of Marxism in the May 1933 issue of the *Crisis*. His brilliant article "Marxism and The Negro Problem" represents the most sophisticated use of Marxism to analyze African Americans' lives up to that time. As Cedric Robinson has observed: "It was in those then irreconcilable roles—as a Black radical thinker and as a sympathetic critic of Marx—that Du Bois was to make some of his most important contributions concerning Black social movements."[77] The article addresses some of the essential contradictions that a Marxist framework confronted radical African American thinkers with.

Du Bois initially illustrates the importance of the concept of surplus value for understanding the source of economic exploitation: "Surplus value arises from labor and is the difference between what is actually paid laborers for their wages and the market value of commodities which the laborers produce. It represents, therefore, exploitation of the laborer, and this exploitation, inherent in the capitalistic system of production is the cause of poverty, of industrial crises, and eventually of social revolution."[78] "Labor," he continues, "is the sure foundation of value and whatever we call it—exploitation, theft or business acumen—there is something radically wrong with an industrial system that turns out simultaneously paupers and millionaires and sends a world starving because it has too much food."[79] As a result, Du Bois reveals how Marxism provides a vital framework for theoretically grasping the fundamental economic inequalities that came to a head worldwide during the Depression.

However, once race enters the picture, Marxism becomes a much more problematic model: "While Negro labor in America suffers because of the fundamental inequities of the whole capitalistic system, the lowest and most fatal degree of its suffering comes not from the capitalists but from fellow white workers."[80] The reason for this is that ethnic workers adopt white, racist identities in order to psychically distance themselves from their shared economic exploitation with blacks. Du Bois observes: "The Irish climbed on the Negroes. The Germans scrambled over the Negroes and emulated the Irish. The Scandinavians fought forward next to the Germans and the Italians and 'Bohunks' [a derogatory term for Central Europeans] are crowding up, leaving Negroes still at the bottom chained to helplessness, first by slavery, then by disenfranchisement and always by the Color Bar."[81] Sixty years before David Roediger coined the phrase "the wages of whiteness," Du Bois identified it in his article by rejecting the communist notion that racism was merely propagated from the top down by white capitalists in order to divide workers and undermine unionization efforts.[82] Du Bois notes how the wages of whiteness were systematically instilled by the labor movement itself: "It is no sufficient answer to say that capital encourages this oppression and uses it for its own ends . . . William Green and Mathew Woll of the A.F. of L. have no excuse of illiteracy or religion to veil their deliberate intention to keep Negroes and Mexicans and other elements of common labor in a lower proletariat subservient to their interests as theirs are to the interests of capital."[83]

Additionally, race also undermined capitalist hegemony, according to Du Bois. The black bourgeoisie "bear the brunt of color prejudice because they express in word and work the aspirations of all black folk for emancipation."[84] The color bar, therefore, prevented this class from joining "either white capital, white engineers, or white workers to strengthen the color bar."[85] Furthermore, "the revolt of any black proletariat could not

. . . be logically directed against this class" because of their shared aspirations and abject racial status.[86] Although one might take issue with Du Bois's belief that the black bourgeoisie represent "the aspirations of all black folk," a position that rationalized his own privileged background and elitist belief in the talented tenth, he was ultimately correct in asserting how the wages of whiteness and race in general undermined any vulgar binary Marxist notion of capital versus labor. The psychic economy of race had to counterbalance any theory of economic exploitation. As Du Bois concludes: "Exploitation comes not from a black capitalist class but from the white capitalists and equally from the white proletariat."[87]

The rise of the Popular Front and its populist antifascist discourse, which pushed class issues into the background, helped mitigate the tensions between racial and class analysis found in the white Left. Although many on the Left emphasized fascism's economic roots, the term itself served as a broad metaphor for linking the horrors of fascism abroad in Germany, Italy, Japan, and Spain with those perpetrated domestically by groups like the Ku Klux Klan, the Liberty League, and the Black Legion. In regard to race, the term "fascism" supplied an international perspective for interrogating the connections between racism in the United States and anti-Semitic practices in Germany. Harold Preece made this connection in the December 1934 issue of the *Crisis:* "If fascism triumphs in this country, the Negro will become the national scapegoat. Germany had no colored race upon which it could unload the sins of the ages, hence the children of Israel were singled out for persecution. The Negro, because of his different color and his different folkways, developed through segregation, will be a more fitting object of fury for the American fascists than the white Jew."[88] Jacob J. Weinstein wrote in the July 1934 issue of the *Crisis* about the shared psychological dysfunctions of Jews and African Americans that arose from their oppressed status: "There are in both groups, all the variations of the oppression psychosis from the sense of noble martyrdom to that paranoic [*sic*] delusion of persecution."[89]

This specific emphasis upon shared Jewish and black oppression attempted to mitigate some of the tensions and resentment that more-reactionary members of the African American community felt toward Jewish business owners in predominantly black neighborhoods like Harlem, as well as toward the Jews who controlled Hollywood, which produced a steady output of films that slandered blacks. For example, J. A. Rogers, a widely read black journalist, wrote an article in 1933 entitled "Negroes Suffer More in U.S. than Jews in Germany." He claims that "Hitler, at his worst, is but a poor imitator of cracker methods."[90] He concedes that "Nazi treatment of the Jew is brutal and unjustified," but nonetheless "most of what is told about Jewish treatment in Germany is propaganda, since the Jews control to a great extent the international press."[91] In order to counter such interracial hostility, Popular Front writers used an antifascist discourse designed to smooth over racial and economic divisions by enlisting all readers into a common cause.

Domestic antiblack fascism was particularly stressed in order to validate African Americans' sense of racial outrage. David H. Pierce identifies the racist practices of the New Deal in order to reveal how the U.S. federal government sanctioned them, thus giving it a worrisome resemblance to the governments of Germany and Italy: "His [African Americans'] closed banks have not reopened. New jobs have not been created for him. Mr. Roosevelt has not employed his personal charms of his political influence to promote the Costigan-Wagner anti-lynch bill. Proposed federal housing schemes are everywhere segregation projects. Federal emergency relief measures permit a lower dole for Negro unemployed."[92]

At the same time, the *New Masses* provided countless articles on domestic fascism that chronicled the incipient fascism in early New Deal policies, the Liberty League's desire to overthrow Roosevelt, and William Randolph Hearst's megalomaniacal publishing empire.[93] On December 17, 1935, the *New Masses* produced a forty-eight-page "Anti-Fascist Number" that chronicled anti-Semitic events in Germany, Mussolini's invasion of Ethiopia, and the Angelo Herndon case, implying that the three had underlying fascist similarities.

As the decade progressed, fascism and racism became gradually more intertwined in Left discourses. In *The Perils of Fascism: The Crisis of American Democracy*, A. B. Magil and Henry Stevens state that "the situation of the Negro in the United States is in many respects startlingly analogous to that of the Jew in Nazi Germany. There are, in fact, sections of the South where without doubt the Negroes are even worse off than are the Jews under Hitler's dictatorship."[94] They then go on to indict the sharecropping system, which produced "vagrancy laws, chain gangs, lynchings, [and the] Scottsboro and Herndon cases."[95] And they stress that lynchings, "the sharpest and most barbarous expression of anti-Negro terror, jumped from 7 in 1929 to 20 in 1939."[96] In 1939, William Pickens wrote in the *New Masses* that the reason behind blacks speaking either in favor of Hitler or against Jews was due to either ignorance or spite: "from ignorance of the true nature of Hitlerism, which is at least as much anti-Negro as it is anti-Jewish, or from spite at the hypocrisy of Americans, who get so 'het up' about the horrors over the Rhine while remaining so indifferent to similar or worse horrors down the Mississippi."[97] Like Magil and Stevens, he ends his article with lynching statistics: "We have over five thousand recorded lynchings in America, more than four thousand of the victims being Negro and the other thousand being poor whites or whites whom our fascist lords did not like."[98]

What both articles reveal is how antilynching rhetoric had been successfully incorporated into antifascist discourse by the late 1930s. This is because the antilynching campaign, forged during the early to mid 1930s, drew together Left-wing blacks and whites in an interracial campaign. Armed with information from books such as *Rope and Faggot: A Biography of Judge Lynch* (1929), *Lynchings and What They Mean* (1931), *The Tragedy of Lynching* (1933), and the works of Ida B. Wells, whites and blacks initiated a fervent antilynching campaign that would eventually find its way into their film columns.

Yet this shared terrain also led to schisms between political groups, as can best be seen in two antilynching shows of 1935. The NAACP hosted "An Art Commentary on Lynching" at the Arthur U. Newton Galleries in Manhattan in February 1935.[99] According to Amy Helene Kirschke, the exhibit was intended "to bring attention to the issue of lynching and garner support for the Costigan-Wagner Bill, new anti-lynching legislation which had been introduced to Congress in 1934."[100] A day after the NAACP exhibition closed, the Artists' Union and other Left organizations opened their own antilynching exhibition, "Struggle for Negro Rights," at the American Contemporary Gallery in Greenwich Village.[101] It attempted to garner support for the "Bill of Civil Rights for the Negro People," a radical antilynching bill brought to Congress that advocated the death penalty for lynchers.[102] Despite their related aims, which could have allowed them to pool their resources into one show, each group deemed the other too different in ideological outlook to make any concessions.

The two exhibitions stand as a metonymy for how black and white Left film critics addressed the antilynching film. Although they shared many of the same socio-aesthetic commitments and outlooks, their reviews at times diverged into parallel but related tracks produced by the fissures of political or racial differences. Nonetheless, the antilynching film provided black and white film critics with the needed cultural ballast to transform their emergent arguments about radicalized spectatorship into material reality.

THE RADICAL SPECTATOR

Tom Brandon observes that what differentiated 1930s Left film critics from the bourgeois film press was that the former "never lost sight of the place of film in society, its role as a force for reform and revolution—film was to be a weapon in changing the world."[103] They saw film criticism as a deeply politicizing tool that could encourage critical spectatorship in their readers and foster collective organization that would push for the distribution of independent and foreign films, the production of progressive films by Hollywood, and support of domestic and international Left causes like antifascism, antilynching, and unionization.

As Anna Everett points out, David Platt was one of the first critics in the black press to encourage critical spectatorship. He wrote a regular column for the *Harlem Liberator*. On September 9, 1933, he invited his readers "to send notes, comments and criticism of films they have seen, liked and disliked. Keep a sharp lookout for bits in movies that misrepresent the lives of Negro and white workers and send them to me."[104] By encouraging readers to become cowriters of his column, Platt not only reveals his willingness to listen to their ideas, but also suggests the collective efforts needed to produce insightful ideological film criticism.

Everett has also shown how Platt offered readers "a primer on how to decode films laden with submerged anti-worker, pro-government content" by providing them with lists of films and their reactionary politics.[105] In turn, he highlighted films that provided humane racial and working-class representations. In an article published on April 29, 1933, he praised the Russian film *The Return of Nathan Beck* for doing just this: "In this Soviet movie we have for the first time in the history of film a portrait of an American Negro worker, a bricklayer, in the Soviet Union—an honest, living, breathing conscious human being, depicted as a true equal with his white brethren, who are building a new world, where segregation, jim-crow, and racial superiority does not and cannot exist."[106]

Platt highlights not only the film's portrayal of the black worker, but also the context that allows such equality to bloom. Furthermore, he encourages readers to "enroll in film courses sponsored by the Workers Films and Photo League" in order to learn the skills that will allow them to produce their own radical films.[107] Overall, Platt showed how both film criticism and film production belonged to everyone. Only through collective mobilization could the consumption and production of films move in progressive channels.

Along similar lines, a reviewer known only as L.E.H. explained how the practices of international distribution revealed the need for blacks to unite with whites in order to combat racism on the screen. In an article that appeared both in the *Harlem Liberator* and the *Daily Worker,* L.E.H. explains how Hollywood's monopolistic distribution practices ironically undercut its ability to stereotype some cultures: "There was a time when Mexicans, Japanese, Chinese and others were the victims of this form of 'easy' writing. Mexicans were villains, Japanese were spies and Chinese with long pig-tails were kicked around by cowboys. But during the final epoch of imperialist expansion, Hollywood gained a stranglehold on the world's film trade, and respective governments threatened American films with boycotts if these libels of their people continued. This method succeeded, for today the Negro alone, denied the right of government protection, remains the 'goat.'"[108] Denied protection by their own government, blacks had to team up with "the Worker's Film and Photo League, and other worker's film groups to combat this form of attack against Negroes, by presenting their own films which will show the Negro in his proper status, and up, from the frowsy and vicious caricatures sponsored by the mongrel productions of Hollywood."[109]

Yet the most sophisticated analysis of critical spectatorship to emerge from the black (and white) press at this time was Loren Miller's "Uncle Tom in Hollywood," which appeared in the November 1934 issue of the *Crisis.* Miller was a young attorney and newspaperman from Los Angeles. According to Bruce M. Tyler, Miller "emerged as one of the city's first radicals on the cultural front against Hollywood film stereotypes of blacks."[110] His article not only offers one of the lengthiest film discussions designed for a general readership, but also analyzes both consumption and production practices in order to expose their intimate links.[111]

Miller begins with his experience of watching the white expeditionary film *Trader Horn* (1931) in a Negro theater.[112] After being captured by a "savage" African tribe, the blonde heroine is rescued by the white protagonist. Miller is amazed by the crowd's reaction: "At this particular showing the audience burst into wild applause when the rescue scene flashed across the screen. I looked around. Those who were applauding were ordinary Negro working people and middle class folk. Hollywood's movie makers had made the theme so commonplace and glorious that it seemed quite natural white virtue should triumph over black."[113] Even worse than the film's content, according to Miller, was the indoctrinated racist position that black viewers unconsciously held: "Obviously those spectators were quite unconscious of the fact that they were giving their stamp of approval to a definitive pattern of racial relationships in which they are always depicted as the lesser breed."[114] The audience, absorbed by the film's immediate "entertainment," was unable to see its systemic links with the racist ideology central to its narrative, representations, and mise-en-scène as well as to the Jim Crow practices that created the need for segregated theaters in the first place.[115]

According to Miller, protest was the only weapon that could challenge such racist films and their insidious indoctrination techniques. Audiences "must be taught to recognize and resent anti-Negro sentiment in such a manner that their feelings can reach the box office. They must let Hollywood know that they object vigorously to being shown as buffoons, clowns or butts or jests. They must stop applauding for such imperialistic jingoism as *Trader Horn*."[116] Although protest organizations such as the Legion of Decency had already banded together to purify Hollywood's screens, Miller realized that "hardly an organization enlisted in the present purity drive is opposed to Jim Crow and all that it means."[117]

Instead, a radical film criticism had to be harnessed to help black audiences "adopt a critical attitude."[118] First of all, this meant sustained criticism, not one that only sporadically flared up when "some monstrosity such as *The Birth of a Nation* is announced."[119] Second, it meant abandoning a bourgeois film criticism that either mimicked studio publicity or "pump[ed] up some Negro bit actor up to the dimensions of a star": "Such criticism is worse than useless; it is the abjectness of a beggar fawning over a penny tossed him by his lord," reinforcing the very warped consciousness exemplified by the black audience viewing *Trader Horn*.[120] Instead, viewers needed to be "armed with an intelligently critical spirit" that could become the base for a "'little movie' movement" that would produce pictures reflecting "their own lives and aspirations."[121] Miller concludes: "It's time we took up arms on the Hollywood front. We might get in some telling blows just now when the movie makers are already under fire."[122]

It was precisely the antilynching film that resonated with Left film critics' desire to reinvent spectatorship. Countless critics highlighted how *Fury* problematizes the sort of traditional modes of identification that suture film viewers into a racist gaze. Furthermore, the film served as a catalyst for emergent audience organizations like the Associated Film Audiences, which materialized Miller and Platt's call to arms on the Hollywood front. The antilynching film finally provided the nodal point where Popular Front film criticism actualized its demands.

Yet *Fury* represented an odd choice for Left film critics to champion, since its very structure opposes many of the tenets that the Left hold dear, such as democracy, the belief in collective organization, and a virile white masculine pose. The ability of Left film critics to position *Fury* as an antilynching film exemplifies the power of antilynching, Popular Front discourse at the time, which could successfully gloss over the film's reactionary elements in order to highlight its momentary progressive tendencies. This final section first explores some of the contemporary misinterpretations of the film. I then show how these misinterpretations actually stemmed from 1930s Left film critics' positioning of the film. After exploring how the Left embedded the film within an antilynching agenda, I conclude by showing how Left film critics effaced the film's economic insights, since to have done otherwise would have forced them to confront the gender anxieties that underlay all of their film criticism.

FURY: AN INTERPRETATION IN THREE ACTS

Fury is one of Fritz Lang's most written-about yet least understood films. For decades, it has been interpreted as an antilynching film by scholars like Lotte Eisner, Paul M. Jensen, Robert A. Armour, and Nick Smedley.[123] Often, it is positioned as a part of Lang's "social trilogy," which also includes *You Only Live Once* (1937) and *You and Me* (1938).[124] Much of the confusion that has fueled these interpretations can be traced to Lang's wild fabrications concerning the film's production and his supposed intentions.

At the time of the film's release, Lang explained the film in rather apolitical terms. In an article in the *New York Times* in 1936, Lang stated: "*Fury* is the story of mob action. Lynching happened to be the result. People the world over respond in the same way. I've been through four revolutions and have made an intimate study of how people react. They often start out in the best of spirits. Suddenly you realize that humor has given way to hate and violence. I attempted to picture that imperceptible line where the change comes. Mob psychology fascinates me."[125] In Lang's mind, the film has little to do with lynching or the United States. His description of the film is so nondescript that it could equally apply to the mobs found in *Die Nibelungen* (1924) or *Metropolis* (1927). Furthermore, Lang understands mob psychology in the most abstract terms—regardless of context, race, class, or gender, hate and violence can break out from people who are "in the best of spirits."

Although one might argue that Lang had to speak of the film in apolitical terms because the *New York Times* would be hostile to a Left interpretation (a problematic assumption, since the *Times* actually did offer Left interpretations of the film), it is still the most accurate self-assessment that

Lang offered of the film. The interviewer reinforces the idea of Lang as an apolitical filmmaker while dismissing the film's subsequent political interpretations as mere projections of willful audiences: "Lang has no interest in propaganda; if it is contained in *Fury* it is because the audience has willed it. He merely told a story and the public can make of it whatever it wants."[126] Yet it wasn't "the public" that was willing a propagandistic reading of the film, but Left film critics from both black and white presses, as we will soon see.

The antilynching angle on the film received such good press that Lang himself soon adopted its terms in discussing the film, even though it often contradicted his original, and never completely abandoned, explanations. This made Lang's antilynching explanation implausible, even incoherent. He explained to Peter Bogdanovich in 1967 that "if a picture is to be made about lynching, one should have a white woman raped by a colored man, and with this as a basis, still prove that lynching is wrong."[127] But Louis B. Mayer supposedly rejected Lang's idea of a film starring a black man because the racist Mayer assumed that "colored people can only be used as shoeshine people or as porters in a railroad car."[128] This is the explanation often used to prove that *Fury* was supposed to be a thorough antilynching story, but because of studio and Production Code Administration interference, Lang could only allude to the racial, antilynching angle of the film.

Yet as Barbara Mennel has shown, even Lang's story taken at face value contradicts the notion of an antilynching picture: "Lang claims that a 'white woman raped by a colored man' would constitute a story line that is politically more progressive than *Fury*, yet this narrative is, on the contrary, instead the racist justification of lynching, as, for example, presented paradigmatically in *Birth of a Nation*."[129] The problem is that later film scholars have willfully misinterpreted Lang's line as meaning "a black man *accused of* raping a white woman," instead of what it actually says, which seems to support the lynchers' rationale. Regardless of whether Mennel is making a bit too much of Lang's imperfect English and awkward syntax, she still offers an excellent observation, and until her article appeared, no one had questioned Lang's account.

Patrick McGilligan, through extensive archival research, has revealed the absolute falsity buried beneath Lang's claim. Spencer Tracy was always scheduled to play the film's lead, not a black actor. The various drafts of the script offer no indication that it featured a black protagonist. Furthermore, Lang's repeated racist jokes to the press regarding blacks when he first arrived in the United States suggest his lack of racial sympathy.[130] And the fact that African Americans never played any significant role in any of the other forty-three films Lang directed shows his lack of commitment to even the vaguest notion of civil rights.

I. Contemporary Misreadings

But Lang never needed to be entirely convincing on this point, since it was never his point in the first place. Left film critics had already done all the interpretative work for him. The strength of antilynching discourses of the 1930s provided these critics with the rhetorical power to seize upon a film essentially concerning fascism and selectively reinterpret it to fit their campaign against racism. As mentioned, Left writers had begun conflating racism and fascism in their columns by the early 1930s. The Popular Front strengthened such links, so by the time of *Fury*'s release in 1936, Left film critics could easily seize upon the film's critique of fascism and remold it into an attack on lynching.

But Left film critics' role in establishing *Fury*'s antilynching message has been undervalued, since many contemporary film scholars have all too readily accepted Lang's own absurd anticommunist accounts, which push the historical Left into the background and thus make Lang seem the sole originator of the film's liberal message. Lang offered two variations of this account. In the first, during a drunken interview with Gretchen Berg in 1965, Lang recalled how the communists had fooled him: "It was 1934, I had just arrived [in America] and didn't speak, nor write, nor read a single word of English. I received a letter, a pamphlet from some American Democratic Society which asked me to sign I don't know what. I saw there were other signatories, I saw Thomas Mann and some others. I said, 'Perfect, Thomas Mann and Democracy, I feel strong about democracy, that's perfect.' I signed. I discovered later that it was a cover for a Communist organization."[131] The problem with the story, however, is its logistical impossibility. There were no Left Hollywood organizations during 1934 that could have fulfilled this function. The Hollywood Anti-Nazi League wasn't founded until 1936. If Lang meant the Motion Picture Democratic Committee for his fictitiously named "American Democratic Society," it didn't exist until 1938. And neither of these organizations was communist.

Most likely realizing his first story's complete implausibility, Lang constructed a revised version during a 1969 interview with Charles Higham and Joel Greenberg. Lang recalled events that occurred during the shooting of *Scarlet Street* (1945): "I got a letter from a very famous actress asking for contributions to such-and-such an organization. I instructed my secretary to send them a hundred dollars and thought no more about it, until I

suddenly found myself described as a sponsor on the letterhead of an organization latter characterized as pro-Communist."[132] In this version, Lang
at least had a plausible date for implicating some vague Left organization
in the plot against him. Also, the organization was no longer described as
communist but instead as "pro-Communist," thus leaving the organization's actual political affiliation unknown.

Regardless of which variant one heeds, Lang's basic tale of political
deceit was ridiculous, nothing more than a paranoiac delusion straight
out of one of his films in which an innocent man suddenly finds himself
enmeshed in a web of conspiracy and shadows. In fact, Lang belonged to
a series of Left organizations, such as the Hollywood Anti-Nazi League
and Films for Democracy, throughout the 1930s. His hallucinatory recollections are most likely nothing more than alibis from the days when Lang
was accused by the House Un-American Activities Committee of being
sympathetic to communism. To take Lang's word for granted is not only
to overlook Lang's connections with the Left, but also, and more importantly, to ignore the Left's importance in promoting and defining *Fury*.

Yet, as mentioned earlier, *Fury* seems a rather unlikely choice for the
Left to champion. As Anton Kaes notes: "The experience of the exile is
the historical unconscious" of *Fury*.[133] This places the film rather at odds
with a U.S. Popular Front perspective, particularly in regard to its concept of the "people." As Michael Denning has shown, both the "people"
and "Americanism" were broad terms used to unify diverse interests into
a strategic collective configuration to fight for democracy across racial,
ethnic, and class divides.[134] These terms "were attempts to imagine a new
culture, a new way of life, a revolution."[135] However, for German émigrés
in general and Lang in particular, the "people" held more-ominous connotations. As Saverio Giovacchini writes, "Many Hollywood Europeans
remained convinced that the 'people,' at least in Germany, was [*sic*] a con-
sensual partner of Nazism rather than its victim."[136] And it is this essential
distrust of the "people" and democracy that is seen throughout *Fury*.

This is not to suggest that Hollywood ever provided an unadulterated
celebration of collective organization. As Martin Rubin has shown in his
excellent essay "The Crowd, the Collective, and the Chorus: Busby Berkeley and the New Deal," Depression-era films reverberate with the tensions
found in New Deal society, which attempted to uneasily balance a defense
of individuality against the dehumanizing effects of the newly emergent
consumer society while promoting new forms of collective organization
that would curb the ills produced by laissez-faire capitalism and rugged
individualism run amok. Ultimately, the individual-collectivist split repre-

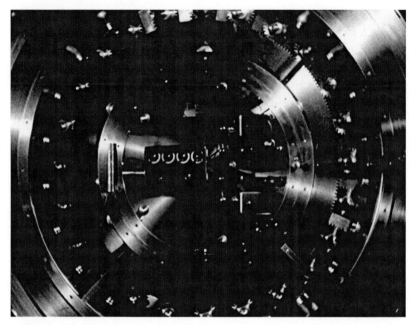

The bank vault serving as an analogy for the well-oiled administration of the bank in
American Madness *(1932).*

sented "two value systems . . . placed side by side, yoked together in a very
steady balance without really coming together."[137]

The director who best portrayed such New Deal tensions between the
individual and the crowd was Frank Capra. In Capra's world, a collective
without a strong leader will eventually metastasize into a mob. In *American Madness* (1932), for example, Capra emphasizes the hierarchal structure needed to keep the Union National Bank functioning properly. Bank
owner Thomas Dickson (Walter Huston) is the benevolent patriarch who
not only oversees all his employees' actions, from making sure that they
are not smoking on the job to prodding their romantic relationships, but
also provides members of the surrounding community who lack any financial assets with needed loans to outlast the Depression. Underneath
Dickson is Matt Brown (Pat O'Brien), the assistant cashier, who oversees
all the tellers' actions and generates camaraderie among his men through
his good humor. Capra repeatedly uses the bank's safe as a metaphor for
the well-oiled operation resulting from the bank's hierarchal structure.
As Matt opens the safe, we see an inner shot of its door with all the gears
and pins visible. The pins move in unison, unlocking the door smoothly,

effortlessly, silently. The shot then cuts to the front of the safe, where the cashiers are standing outside and observing Matt. The cut equates the mechanism of the safe with the working of the cashiers. Just as the pins in the door ensure the trouble-free operation of the safe, each man functions in synch with the bank's inner logic and the oversight of its leaders.

Yet outside the purview of Dickson's centralized control, rumors circulate that he stole several million dollars from the bank. Gossip about the bank spreads across town: its frenzy is visualized as an ever-increasing montage of faces in close-up that grows more grotesque as low-key lighting and canted angles come to dominate; sentences degenerate into clipped phrases like "that dirty dog," "bank's broke," "hurry up." We are watching individuals deteriorate into a mob as a bank run begins.

Yet even during the worst parts of the run, Capra focuses on small, persistent examples of humanity, refusing to completely dehumanize the mob. For example, an old woman pleads with a Union National guard, "But you said it was safe. It's his life insurance money. Oh, please, I'll go to the old ladies' home if you don't do something." She faces us, an act that humanizes her as we witness her panicked reaction. The guard places his arm

Matt Brown (Pat O'Brien) providing lower-management leadership in American Madness.

Capra humanizing the mob with close-ups of individuals in American Madness.

around her, saying, "Take it easy. Everything will be all right," as he makes room through the crowd to help her reach a teller. It is in moments such as these, when compassion surmounts the inexhaustible frenzy of the mob, that Capra seems to be signaling to us that all is not lost, that underneath the temporary insanity our humanity endures.

Fury, however, offers a very different perspective. Lang's mob is nothing more than a group of unrelenting sadists. Unlike Capra's mob, which might have lost its reason but never entirely loses its humanity, Lang's never had any humanity in the first place. At best, its individual members fearfully yet resentfully subscribe to the laws that guide everyday life. But given the right opportunity, a bestial glee erupts from them, tearing aside the veneer of civilization as it succumbs to violence and depravity. The mob is so comfortable with its own inner perversities that we see mothers bringing their children to watch a man be burned alive, sanctioning this collective monstrosity as a rite of passage. A man casually eats a hot dog as the smell of Joe Wilson's (Spencer Tracy) flesh fills the air, suggesting the mob's cannibalistic lust for suffering. As Tom Gunning points out, this perverse lust is made visible after the mob has supposedly killed Wilson:

it possesses "a still, almost spent, quality" that Gunning has rightly identified as "post-orgasmic."[138] A sheriff tries to stop the mob from breaking inside the jail where Wilson is held. In Capra's world, such an authoritative figure would most likely succeed in calming the mob. In Lang's, he is held down and bashed unconscious with a two-by-four. Lang's mob is without redemption. At best, its members can only later scuttle behind their facades of humanity and hypocritically deny that such actions ever took place.

Although many film scholars have used the concept of destiny to explain Lang's pessimistic vision, I think it is more useful to see Lang as a practitioner of naturalism.[139] I am particularly thinking of its American literary variant, which was influenced by Charles Darwin and his sociological interpreter Herbert Spencer.[140] As Louis J. Budd has observed, one of American literary naturalism's distinctive traits is its concern with exploring "humankind's animal sides," as when instinct overpowers conscious will.[141] He continues, "Most distinctively, they [the naturalistic writers] pushed further toward determinism—economic or biological or cosmic— than American novelists had cared or dared to go before."[142] It is this focus on biological instinct that centrally concerns *Fury* and leads to the film's deterministic fatalism.

Lang emphasizes the biological impulse for violence during the film's barbershop sequence. Hovering over a customer with a straight razor, the barber explains, "People get funny impulses. If you resist them, you're sane. If you don't, you're on your way to the nuthouse or the pen." The camera suddenly glides in to a medium-close two-shot of the barber and his customer. The barber stares at his customer's neck, his hand on the man's breastbone, explaining in a lusty, low voice his own violent impulses: "Now, Mr. Jorgensen, you've got one of the levelest heads in the county. Would you believe in the twenty years that I've been stroking this razor across throats here that many a'time I've had an impulse to cut their Adam's apples wide open?" The barber then makes a slicing motion just in front of the customer's neck, saying, "Shhhht. Just like that. Yes, sir." When the town's deputy, Bugs Meyers (Walter Brennan), asks the barber whether he has that impulse now, the barber approaches him, razor lifted as if about to strike. The barber suddenly stands in front of Bugs, his back to us, hand on Bugs's left shoulder, razor on his right, precariously close to Bugs's neck. He explains as Bugs looks on with alarm, "An impulse is an impulse. It's like an itch. You've got to scratch it." As the barber explains, we see his reflection in the mirror behind Bugs. From the mirror's per-

Fury (1936) and the dark mirror: exposing the naturalistic impulses to kill.

spective, the two men seem to be having just a normal conversation based upon their body language and position. Yet from our side, we seem to be witnessing the prelude to a murder.

The mirror's presence in the scene is important because it emphasizes the film's primary concern with appearance versus reality or, more precisely, with the superficial veneer of civilization and the naturalistic violent impulses that lurk within everyone. The balance between the two states is always precarious. At any moment we expect the barbershop to quickly tip from being a meeting place to the site of a bloodbath. The film itself adopts a mirror structure. Its first half represents Joe Wilson as average, upstanding American, naïvely believing in democracy, justice, and the law. In its second half, after Joe resurrects himself from his near murder, he transforms into the living-dead embodiment of naturalism. His bloodlust and sadistic impulses symbolize those repressed desires that pervade all aspects of American life—from the barbershop to the mob to the reporting of events to the courtroom. All are tainted. Lang's film is less a warning about lynching than an exposure of how Americans were no different from the fascists and Nazis whom Lang had recently fled from. Although the purported ideals of the two societies might differ, the perverse impulses of their citizens remained the same.[143]

II. Converting Fury to an Antilynching Film: Popular Front Film Critics

One way in which both black and white presses positioned *Fury* as a progressive film was by juxtaposing reviews of the film with other antilynching and antifascist articles, photographs, and drawings. The visual proximity suggested their intimate links. A review of the film in the *New York Amsterdam News* was placed adjacent to an article chronicling Samuel Leibowitz's ability to remain the main defense counsel in the Scottsboro case.[144] By linking the film with Scottsboro, the *News* revealed not only how Hollywood effaced African Americans from its films, but also how the film's events could be read against the actual racist practices at work in the Scottsboro case. The layout implicitly suggests the complex mediations and repressions that Hollywood employed to translate contemporary racist events into commercial fare.

Similarly, the issue of the *New Masses* that came out the same day placed a drawing of a lynching in the center of a review for the film.[145] The silhouettes of two black bodies hang from two trees. At the foot of one are two mourning women. In the background stand three members of the Ku Klux Klan, observing. Once again, the drawing emphasized both the film's links to and effacement of African American disenfranchisement. Furthermore, the same issue contained an article by John L. Spivak on the Black Legion, the infamous midwestern "pro-white" organization that repeatedly murdered blacks and labor organizers.[146] Spivak describes the group's role in Michigan politics through its leader, Harry Bennett, the "head of Henry Ford's secret service."[147] By juxtaposing the Black Legion, antiblack lynching by the KKK, and *Fury* in a single issue, the *New Masses* used its layout to establish what Walter Benjamin refers to as a "monad" in which the flow of thoughts is suddenly arrested to establish "a configuration pregnant with tensions."[148] Through such a juxtaposition, new meanings arise, producing "a revolutionary chance in the fight for the oppressed past" to emerge from the homogeneous, official history that serves the status quo and the privileged.[149] In this issue of the *New Masses,* the monad serves two primary functions: it uses articles and illustrations to draw attention to Hollywood's repression of African American histories; and it exemplifies how the juxtaposition of diverse sources like film, art,

The Screen

"Fury"—Anti-Lynch Film

ALL of you movie hopheads taking the cure under Prof. Fearing, how many of you can remember as far back as *Fugitive From a Chain Gang?* It's not likely that many can. The cinema addict who can come out of his coma in front of the theater and remember how he got there, let alone recall the title and plot of the film that has been enthralling him for the last 60 minutes, really belongs in some other, less-serious ward, possibly the revolutionary dance. But if you do have a dim and confused recollection of *Fugitive From a Chain Gang,* M-G-M's current *Fury* is just like it, only better and it's a pretty good picture.

To be accurate, it's one top-notch picture with two or three mediocre ones tossed in on top of it just to make sure the basic story doesn't make too much sense. Nobody knows what we movie-goers would do if confronted with a film that took a substantial theme and followed it through to its logical end. Maybe we wouldn't know the difference. Or we might explode. There might even, as some say, be a revolution.

Lynching is the subject of *Fury* and the first half of it is so realistic that when flames leap up the old courthouse and encircle the caged victim, you actually smell the burning flesh. It's really as savage and convincing and as good as that. If you think of the story as ending there, where it always does end in fact and if you also imagine the victim to be Negro, as he usually is and not white, then this is a film that will haunt your dreams for many a night and make the ordinary Hollywood thing seem tamer than a vacation postcard.

But there are a lot of "ifs" barring *Fury* from being the great picture that it might have been, and not even Spencer Tracy's fine, electrically-charged acting convinced me that a man so starkly burned to death could manage, by a simple miracle in the scenario, to come back to life. Saint Metro-Goldwyn-Mayer, be with me in my hour of need! You can avert famine, war and pestilence by a close-up of Garbo singing a presidential proclamation; you might even, I imagine, pass a liberal law that wouldn't be declared unconstitutional.

Considered strictly as melodrama, however, *Fury* is still an exceptional film. Some day in the future some great master of the cinema art, possibly myself, will write a serious treatise called "Evasion and Exposition: The Essential Methods of Each, with an Analysis of Their Relative Values, Purposes, Habits and Habitat." It will run to at least six volumes and undoubtedly be the opus your son works his way through college on. The principles advanced in the first three of them will be that evasion is the essential element of any art in a society based upon exploitation, that evasion's inner secret is the business of building improbability upon improbability whereas the process of exposition is the opposite, building probability upon probability and lastly, that although evasion predicates a stagnant art, it also forces increasingly brilliant technical innovations.

Fury has this technical ingenuity, this time simply in the field of plotting. After the realism of the lynch scene has built up the picture's tension, the remaining half of it is kept going by a series of surprises—the victim's survival, his self-concealment that leads on to a trial of the lynchers, the seeming collapse of the case against the lynchers until the dramatic introduction of motion-picture evidence and so on—each improbable, but not impossible, event skilfully connected to the next. Nothing but good acting could put the latter half of the film across and the cast was extremely good. It's amazing, seeing how much technical perfection alone can do for a picture.

But the real story lies wrapped up in the first part of it and it's fine anti-lynch stuff, though not as pointed as it could have been —remember, we have to sell these pictures in the South. See the film, and imagine what might have been done with it.

KENNETH FEARING.

From *Hol' Up Yo' Head* by Herb Kruckman

Using layout as a Benjaminian monad to expose the racial political unconscious of commercial cinema. Herbert Kruckman, Hol' Up Yo' Head *(1936) Courtesy © The Kruckman Estate.*

and history is necessary in order to grasp the hidden forces of capitalism that foster racism, violence, and antiunionism and delimit what ultimately can be represented within mainstream cinema.

Black and white Left film critics also contextualized *Fury* within their columns to draw out its relevancy to African American and Left histories. An advertisement in the July 1936 issue of *New Theatre* explicitly ties the film to an antilynching stance. The background of the ad shows a series of photographs of antiblack lynchings along with articles describing similar events. In the middle of the ad, the magazine's editors list a series of lynching statistics: "A lynching occurs in the United States on an average of every three days. Over 5,000 men and women, most of them Negroes, have been lynched in this country since 1882."[150] They note that very few convictions have taken place, because of collusion among citizens to protect the guilty, "as is shown in *Fury*." They further link lynching with the Ku Klux Klan and the Black Legion, emphasizing that labor disputes, not "sex crimes," as was commonly assumed, were more often behind it. By stressing lynching's economic roots, the editors delegitimize the myth of the black male rapist while reiterating that most lynching victims were African American. By juxtaposing their ad with a review for the film, the editors provided a valuable history of lynching that supplied context for the film and its accompanying review.

In the June 9, 1936, *Daily Worker*, Ben Davis, Jr., offered an even more, though slightly reductive, Marxist analysis of the film. In general, Davis highlights the moments in the film that reveal the systemic causes for lynching: "A scene in the office of the Governor showed the intimate connection between politics and lynching. Acting on the advice of his chief political friend, the Governor refused to send the national guard to 'protect' the prisoner."[151] He also observes the forces of capitalism at work within the film's riot sequence. Davis observes that a strikebreaker incites the riot. Furthermore, "the film shows the lynch mob to be organized and led by the 'leading business men of the town.'"[152] Despite the film's limited racial perspective, achieved by effacing "a background of 'race-superiority' poison, lynch terror and rape frame-ups against the Negro people," which inhibits an analysis of "the whole economic and social structure . . . [that] gives rise to lynchings," Davis believes that the film will nonetheless "open the eyes of people who are accustomed to regard lynchings as a barbarous practice entirely unconnected with the political and economic structure of the capitalist system."[153]

R.O. of the *New York Amsterdam News* similarly explains lynching in *Fury* as a systemic problem: "Its details are patterned after countless hundreds of typical outlines, and therefore the main current of the picture is an accurate analysis of a phase of our social scene."[154] R.O. continues by recounting the lynching statistics given in the film: "America witnesses one lynching every three days."[155] And the reviewer highlights the collusion between the law and the lynchers, which keeps the perpetrators safe from justice: "The sheriff, of course, when brought as a witness against the lynchers swears he can't recognize anyone who participated in the mob."[156] But all is not lost: "A newsreel account of the lynching is their downfall." The power of mass media to assist in rectifying racial injustices was shown in the ILD's use of newspapers and radio to expose the racism inherent in the Scottsboro trial, just as it was in *Fury*'s depiction of lynching on commercial screens and in R.O.'s analysis of the film in the black press.[157] New forms of mass media were equally important factors in combating lynching because of their ability to disseminate information quickly to large audiences. The function of newsreels in the film became an apt metaphor for Left film critics' desire to publicize the history of lynching to their readers.

Most interestingly, R.O. highlights the film's mundane representation of the lynching: "In swift moving shots all the characters are recognized. Some of the women carry babies and hold them up to see the spectacle of a man — burning alive. (This scene is a duplicate of a drawing by Reginald Marsh and another by Spinkle Alston). Men with moronic faces eat apples as they witness the revolting scene. Others smile with satisfaction. Women and children join in jeering the man, who grapples with his bars as he is being burned."[158] Rather than seeing the lynching as an anomaly provoked by outside agitators or the riffraff of the town, the film emphasizes its communal structure. This reveals how the racism inherent in antiblack lynching not only pervaded white culture, but was also consciously passed on from generation to generation.

Reginald Marsh's drawing cited by R.O. illustrates this dynamic at work. A crowd looks on gleefully at something out of frame. A mother holds her little girl in the air to offer a better view. The crowd's enthusiastic reaction suggests a scene found at any typical community event, such as a parade, play, or concert. The drawing's imagery resonates with the American ideals of community and intergenerational bonds, of the sort typically found in the saccharine work of Norman Rockwell. Yet the drawing's title reveals the crowd's lurid focus: *This Is Her First Lynching* (1934). Its title draws distinct attention to the little girl as spectator, a corporeal site where perversion corrupts innocence. The jarring contrast between visual expectation and textual reality, American ideals and racist reality, throws

"This is her first lynching."

Contrasting American ideals with racist reality. This Is Her First Lynching, *Reginald Marsh © 2009 Estate of Reginald Marsh / Art Students League, New York / Artists Rights Society (ARS), New York.*

the observer off balance as lynching is uncloaked as a publicly sanctioned American institution.

Marsh's drawing was displayed in the January 1935 issue of the *Crisis*.[159] R.O.'s highlighting of it within the film review indicates not only how anti-lynching imagery had an impact on *Fury*'s visuals, but also, and more generally, how the visual rhetoric found in the black press was manifesting itself within mainstream, white-controlled culture. For an industry that was well known for its seemingly indomitable racist practices and representations, any small allusion to antiracist rhetoric and African American influence signified a monumental step forward.

One of the more unexpected ways that white Left film critics contextualized *Fury* was in relation to the Sacco-Vanzetti trials of 1927. Nicola Sacco and Bartolomeo Vanzetti were apprehended on May 5, 1920, in a police trap set against foreign-born radicals. They were accused of a robbery and murder that had occurred three weeks earlier. Enraged not only by the unconstitutionality of the raid in which Sacco and Vanzetti were apprehended, but also by the unfair conduct of their trial—prosecution witnesses perjured themselves, the judge was openly biased against the defendants—the U.S. Left quickly came to the pair's defense. Sacco and Vanzetti's trial and eventual execution symbolized the failure of American justice, making U.S. democracy seem "as flawed and unjust as many of the older societies of the world, no longer embodying any bright ideal, but once again serving the interests of the rich and the powerful."[160]

Ben Davis, Jr., criticized *Fury* for its idealistic representation of courtroom justice: "Was it not Judge Thayer in the Sacco and Vanzetti case, Judge Wyatt in the Herndon case, and Judge Callahan in the Scottsboro case who incited a lynch-hysteria against the accused?"[161] The belief in an objective judiciary could be sustained only if one overlooked how the courts had historically been used against radicals, immigrants, and African Americans. Robert Stebbins (Sidney Meyers) creatively employed Vanzetti's voice to question some of *Fury*'s faults: "Vanzetti would have pointed out that the institution of lynching has an economic and racial background that is necessary for a complete understanding of the problem and that the film was faulty for the want of it. He'd have proceeded to point out that almost eighty percent of the lynched are Negroes. And lastly, he'd scorn the likelihood of the innocent, dead or alive, receiving legal justice."[162] Both critics used the Sacco and Vanzetti case to not only highlight how courts had persecuted radicals and blacks, but also to expose Hollywood's celebration of justice, which bore little relation to the legal travesties repeatedly visited upon working-class immigrants and racial minorities in America's courtrooms.

Identification served as a central concept with which black and white Left film critics framed the film. Many white Left film critics criticized *Fury* for featuring a white protagonist and predominantly white cast, thus effacing the racial aspect of most lynchings. As mentioned above, Robert Stebbins conjured the ghost of Vanzetti to reprimand Lang for not adequately addressing the economic and racial background of lynching.[163] Similarly, Ben Davis, Jr., chastised the film for making "the whole lynch atmosphere appear to be engendered by the tongues of gossipy women" rather than economic and racial motives.[164] Otis Ferguson of the *New Republic* commented that "there is no race angle . . . there is no mutilation and the man escapes."[165] Kenneth Fearing recommended that if his viewers "imagine the victim to be a Negro, as he usually is and not white, then this film will haunt your dreams for many a night and make the ordinary Hollywood thing seem tamer than a vacation postcard."[166]

The most insightful analyses of filmic identification emerged from the black press. Unlike white Left film critics who condemned the film's focus on a white protagonist, R.O. of the *New York Amsterdam News* emphasized the benefits of such a setup: "We feel that, in choosing a white man, many factors were eliminated which complicate the fight against lynching in its interracial aspects."[167] For example, the film's erasure of African Americans from its narrative had the benefit of implicitly dismissing the myth of the black male rapist as a primary cause for lynching. *Fury*, R.O. observes, instead highlights the flimsy circumstantial evidence used against lynching's victims as well as the collusion of the law and townspeople to protect the lynchers' identities. By focusing on a white male, the film could better address lynching's systemic causes and results without having to counteract racist assumptions regarding African American males supposedly innate criminal tendencies.

Furthermore, according to R.O., the film's focus on a white protagonist ensured "a wider and more sympathetic audience."[168] Since lynching was largely associated with African American victims, the film's focus on a white protagonist serves both as an important reminder that "fully 20 per cent of all lynch victims have been white" and as a strategic narrative device to force white audiences to indirectly identify with the oppressed.[169] Blacks, on the other hand, "will have no difficulty in identifying with Joe Wilson and appreciate his bitter experience," since Joe provides them with what Ella Shohat and Robert Stam refer to as an analogical structure of feeling, which is "a structuring of filmic identification across social, political, and cultural situations, through strongly perceived or dimly felt affinities of social perception or historical experience."[170] Because of Hollywood's refusal to present African American experiences and peoples on its screens, black viewers were forced to create sophisticated forms of spectatorship that allowed them to cross-identify between races, classes, genders, and so forth.[171] Identifying with white characters, as Loren Miller showed in his disturbing audience analysis of *Trader Horn*, became a mandatory coping strategy for many black viewers. With a film like *Fury*, whose white protagonist holds an oppressed position typically associated with blacks, African American audiences should have had no problem in identifying with him.

Whites, on the other hand, were ideologically trained to identify with actors on-screen according to a Jim Crow logic in which the racial characteristics of characters and viewers had to closely correspond. To explicitly breach this implicit cultural mandate was to undermine Hollywood's Eurocentric mode of identification. As mentioned earlier, Harry Alan Potamkin noticed this occurring when "the southern upper crust objected to [the] all-black musical *Hallelujah!* [since] they did not like this relation of the Negro as 'star,' and themselves as 'customers.'"[172]

The limits of white identification often extended into the Left press itself. An unnamed writer for the *Chicago Defender* observes how *Fury* was listed on the *Nation*'s 1937 honor role for its indictment of lynching, yet no African American contribution was mentioned at all. Although the writer praises the *Nation* for honoring men "who pushed along a movement in our favor," he hopes "that as time goes on [the] *Nation* will take notice of some of the fine achievements of the members of the Race, feeling certain its editors will find some one among our people who 'deserve the applause of his countrymen,' for courageous service."[173] The fact that the *Nation* editors praised a film that challenged lynching yet failed to see how their own racist selection process reinforced the very practices that the film critiqued reveals the limits of identification of even liberal whites.

When even whites who were sympathetic to black causes overlooked African American contributions to them, it is understandable why R.O. felt that only a white protagonist in *Fury* could create the necessary identification among white audiences. Although an African American protagonist would have added complexity to the depiction of lynching in the film, R.O. rightly notes its historical impossibility, since it would have challenged the Jim Crow spectatorship that governed Hollywood cinema and most white audiences at the time.

Joe (Spencer Tracy) accusing the audience watching Fury *of enjoying sadistic pleasures.*

Unlike the aforementioned Left critics, who focused on the film's white protagonist, Frank S. Nugent emphasized how audiences were pushed into multiple, often contradictory, points of view toward lynching: "We see it as the victim sees it, as the mob sees it, as the community sees it, as the law sees it, as the public sees it."[174] Although *Fury* features white protagonists, it does not represent them in a particularly favorable light. As Tom Gunning has written: "Lang's Hollywood films frequently rub against this assumption of identification and sympathy with a protagonist, creating strategies of distance that undermine the dominant Hollywood narrative approach."[175] There are two primary ways in which *Fury* problematizes identification: equating viewers with the mob and transforming its central protagonist into a monster.

The film continually equates its viewers with the mob, both through direct address and point of view. At one moment, while speaking about the members of the lynch mob in medium close-up, Joe looks directly to us, hurling his accusation: "I'm legally dead, and they're legally murderers. That I'm alive is not their fault. But I know 'em. I know a lot of 'em. And they'll hang for it, according to the law, which says if you kill somebody, you've got to be killed yourself. But I'll give them the chance they didn't give me. They'll have a *legal* judge and a *legal* defense. They'll get a *legal* sentence and a *legal* death." As Joe says, "But I know 'em," he points his finger accusingly at the audience, jabbing us with his indictment. At the end of his speech, the camera backs slightly out as Joe turns toward his brothers. The fact that his brothers are positioned to Joe's side, away from his gaze, reveals that no one else but the audience could be Joe's addressee. The conflation of our own and the mob's sadistic desires is further stressed when Joe speaks about sitting in a movie theater where he watched a newsreel of himself getting burned alive "over and over again": "The place was packed. They like it. They get a big kick out of seeing a man burned to death. A big kick." Although not direct participants of the lynching, the sadistic spectator is equally implicated for his or her scopophilic desire for violence and misery. This is underlined as the film's courtroom is transformed into a theater when newsreels are used as evidence to indict the participants of the riot.

Lang's film shows that identification might be more indebted to sadistic desires on the viewer's part than to any sense of sympathy or shared humanity with the characters on the screen. It shows how such base desires extend from the screen and into the courtroom and community itself. The role of mass media in *Fury*, as a result, has less to do with the diffusion of information and understanding than with the extension of a sadistic gaze across wider audiences.

The film also locks the viewer into the mob's point of view. For example, as the mob approaches the jail where Joe Wilson is held, we are sutured into their look, staring toward the sheriff and his deputies as they stand guard in front of the jail's entrance, and then stopping directly before them. Tom Gunning stresses that the shot holds "no one person's point of view; rather, the smooth forward thrust of the camera out in front and somewhat above the mob expresses its force."[176] I would further add that it suggests a fury beyond anyone's control, as if the mob's collective anger and sadistic impulses have transcended any individual point of view and gained a momentum all of their own, relentless, inhuman.

Along similar lines, the film initially establishes Joe as the average American, whom audiences are supposed to identify with. But by its second half, Joe has become a mirror of his lynchers, sharing their own sadistic impulses as he watches them suffer in the courtroom and then be sentenced to death. Joe's brother Tom (George Walcott) comments, "You're as bad as they." His other brother, Charlie (Frank Albertson), pleads, "Be human, Joe." Paul M. Jensen argues that Joe ultimately becomes worse than the lynchers. Unlike the lynchers, "who in one moment of weakness had combined into something temporarily devoid of logic . . . , Joe develops a permanent one-track mind and pursues his end with cold calculation. His method seems to be more cruel, because he acts consciously and tortures his victims over a longer period of time."[177] Joe, in essence, becomes naturalism incarnate, giving full expression to the repressed sadistic desires articulated by the barber in an earlier scene. Joe is the unreleased fury of the id, the dark mirror reflecting back the audience's own perverse desires in full view.

Despite the film's seemingly normative point of view (white, male, heterosexual), it actually bores from within, undermining this hegemonic perspective by exposing the utter depravity and sadistic desires lurking beneath its rational exterior. As Patrick McGilligan shows, Lang was well aware of how Joe's characterization undercut traditional identificatory practices. During a story conference on September 7, 1935, Lang became concerned that Joe might not be sympathetic enough. To compensate, Lang argued that *Fury* needed "to be equally a woman's picture—told from Katherine's perspective as much as Joe's."[178] As we will see, however, Left film critics failed to note the importance of Katherine's position, since doing so would have necessitated an analysis of the Depression's effeminizing effects upon white men, a fact that hit too close to their male anxieties regarding their own uncertain positions of authority.

Rather than addressing how Katherine becomes increasingly central to the narrative during the film's second half, Left film critics instead dismissed that part of the film altogether. Although the second half of the film provides some valuable insights into the antilynching cause—revealing, among other things, the townspeople's collusion against naming the lynchers in court, the government's political justification for refusing to prevent a riot, and statistics on lynching—Left film critics considered it mainly a concession to the Hays Code and the box office. Kenneth Fearing of the *New Masses* claims that "the first half of it [the film] is so realistic . . . If you think of the story as ending there [with the lynching], where it always does end in fact . . . then this is a film that will haunt your dreams for many a night and make the ordinary Hollywood thing seem tamer than a vacation postcard."[179] The reason the second half of the film neuters much of the critique of the first half, according to Fearing, was the racist demands of the southern box office: "Remember, we have to sell these pictures in the South."[180]

Robert Stebbins of *New Theatre* rightly notes how the film's shift in identification in its second half undermines its antilynching stance: "The second half of the film almost renders invalid its object [of lynching] by shifting the emphasis of guilt from the lynchers to vengeful Joe Wilson." But he assumes that these compromises within the film were most likely "demanded by the box-office experts and not of Lang's making."[181] Robert Geroux of the *Nation* sarcastically summarizes the film's happy ending, pointing out that it trivializes lynching as nothing more than a simple case of misinterpretation: "Nobody's hurt; Joe and his girl are ready to marry and start life over, and the lynchers had a big scare. The whole business is, I suppose, just one of those messes which human beings are always getting in and out of."[182] Otis Ferguson writes that by the film's second half, "they are trying to change a lynching picture into a love and personal vengeance story," making "lynching and the Hays office come out even."[183] In other words, the film's second half, according to most Left film critics, reverted back to formulaic, melodramatic cliché in order to appease censorship mandates and conservative, even outright racist, audience demands.

Yet at the same time, Left film critics could not simply dismiss the film's melodramatic aspects, since they were some of its most effective parts. Kenneth Fearing notes: "Considered strictly as melodrama, however, *Fury* is still an exceptional film."[184] As time passed, *Fury*'s melodrama made it increasingly attractive to Left film critics, especially in comparison to later antilynching films. Peter Ellis compares *They Won't Forget* (1937), a much more realistic film regarding lynching, with the melodramatic pyrotechnics of *Fury:* "But in spite of the fact that the line of the story is straighter in the current film, in spite of the fact that the victim is lynched and the district-attorney questions the man's guilt only after lynching, *They Won't Forget* doesn't have the impact or the emotional drive that gave *Fury* all its force."[185] Similarly, David Platt praises *Fury* for its "profound psychological insight into the minds of the members of a lynch mob."[186] *They Won't Forget,* on the other hand, offers "attention to the inner workings of the minds of the District Attorney and the politicians without achieving the profundities of the Lang film."[187] In other words, despite the later film's more realistic portrayal and systemic analysis of lynching, two aesthetic attributes normally assumed to be endorsed by the historical Left, Left film critics actually were more concerned with conventions that would emotionally engage audiences and draw them into the film.

Furthermore, Left critics understood that melodrama rather than realism might be needed to emotionally convince audiences of the urgency of an issue. In the same article, David Platt criticizes *They Won't Forget* for possessing "too much understatement for a subject that can hardly be overstated. Fritz Lang may have sensationalized certain things in the

courtroom scene in *Fury,* but he never understated the case. Leroy's courtroom scene was probably much more authentic, much more reportorial,
but it was also much less imaginative and dynamic."[188] These debates
about *Fury* and *They Won't Forget* are important for revealing how U.S.
Left film critics juxtaposed analyses of related films as they developed
their own aesthetic criteria in the wake of montage theory. The debates
not only suggest a much more self-conscious analysis of film aesthetics
than is typically assumed, but also identify the willingness of U.S. Left film
criticism to reinvestigate earlier films at a later date to further hone socio-
aesthetic judgments.[189]

Despite some of *Fury*'s ideological limits, most Left film critics praised
it. Robert Stebbins called it "the most forceful indictment of lynch justice ever projected on a screen."[190] Otis Ferguson perhaps most succinctly
identified *Fury*'s target audience:

> For those who already have all the dope on lynchings, *Fury* will have
> nothing to say, and will not say all of that . . . But, if you will be patient
> with me in a crusading moment, who in God's name is to be educated
> around here anyway? That handful of liberals and last-gaspers who have
> known all the answers these many years? The people to get to are those
> who don't even know the questions yet, and on these little will be lost by
> a movie company's trying to eat its cake and sell it to the chains, too, so
> long as on the one subject they treat, however obliquely, terror is made
> true and the truth terrible.[191]

By pointing out both Hollywood's relatively horrible track record on addressing lynching and white audience's general ignorance of lynching altogether, these reviews highlight how *Fury* served as a vital conduit to
introduce antilynching discourse to the general public.

The Left used *Fury* to garner collective support for a federal antilynching bill as well as the formation of audience organizations. An ad for *Fury*
in *New Theatre* explained how the Costigan-Wagner antilynching bill had
been delayed in Congress by filibustering, but urged "readers to demand
of their Congressional representatives that they support the bill" when it
was introduced in the next session.[192] An unnamed reviewer in the *Atlanta
Daily World* explained how support for a federal antilynching bill was dependent upon the emergence of more progressive films from Hollywood:
"Since the NAACP and certain congressmen are pushing the fight for a
federal statute against the mob evil, these [anti-lynching] pictures are ap-
pearing at a psychological time. Colored Americans owe it to themselves
to give such films their entire support, and it wouldn't hurt if several thou-

sand wrote to the picture companies expressing their thanks at this significant change in policy."[193] According to the reviewer, "producers with starch in their backbones can do much to abolish the crime of lynching and at the same time correct many white misconceptions of the Negro and improve race relations" by making antilynching films.[194] A review in the *Chicago Defender* urged "anti-lynch workers everywhere to see the film, to ask their favorite theater to book it, and to write Metro-Goldwyn-Mayer, commending the company for its courage in dealing with lynching on the screen."[195]

Ben Davis, Jr., tied *Fury*'s very existence to the dual collective efforts against lynching and reactionary films: "*Fury* itself is a result of the growing sentiment against lynching, a sentiment which is organically connected with the thousands of picket lines which have marched in front of movie theaters which were showing anti-labor, anti-Negro and war-whooping films."[196] The success of this tactic served as "a mandate for workers and progressives to strengthen their boycotts, picket lines, strike actions, and all other types of struggles designed to counteract the steady stream of vicious poison which flows from Hollywood."[197]

And strengthen their forces they did. In 1936, the audience organization Associated Film Audiences (AFA) was founded. In addition to screening "revolutionary, propaganda, anti-war and anti-fascist pictures" to its members and discussing them, the AFA also issued "a bulletin reviewing films and discussing film and ideological problems."[198] For example, during a screening of *The Emperor Jones* (1933) at the New School for Social Research on March 22, 1937, AFA asked its members: "Does the film portray the Negro honestly? Does any commercial film do so?"[199] The AFA moderated discussions, sent out questionnaires, and distributed bulletins in hopes of encouraging audiences to become critical viewers and to use their collective influence to push Hollywood in progressive directions. *Fury* was regularly cited by the AFA as a model Hollywood film. In the *Daily Worker*, an anonymous writer in 1937 argued that it was AFA's job "to popularize fine films like *Winterset, Fury, Black Legion,* and *Mr. Deeds Goes to Town*."[200] David Platt stated that "constant agitation by audience organizations for better films has been responsible for films like *Life of Zola, Make Way for Tomorrow, Fury, Informer, These Three, Dead End,* [and] *Black Legion*."[201]

In 1938, Fay M. Jackson, a studio correspondent and theatrical editor of the *California Eagle,* founded the Cinema League of Colored Peoples (CLCP) in Los Angeles. The league sought to create an interracial global membership. According to Jackson, "One of the main objectives of this league will be to serve as a clearing house for the helpful exchange of ideas and facts pertaining to Negro people offered in solution of the motion pictures in which they are cast."[202] Modeling itself partially on the Production Code Administration, the league served as a clearinghouse and censorship organization addressing the misrepresentations of black history and culture in Hollywood cinema.

The reason audience organizations like the AFA and CLCP felt that they could influence Hollywood was because the industry itself was becoming increasingly sympathetic to Left causes. The Hollywood Anti-Nazi League was formed in 1936, with Fritz Lang as one of its founding members.[203] The Motion Picture Artists Committee for Loyalist Spain was founded in 1937, and the Motion Picture Democratic Committee, which endorsed liberal political candidates, in 1938.[204] Furthermore, after four years of dormancy, the radical Screen Writers Guild fought for union recognition in 1937. It was this double front of audience and internal studio pressure that led some Left film critics to conclude "that Hollywood has produced more progressive films in the past twenty-five months than in the entire past twenty-five years of the movie industry."[205] David Platt argued that "no one will deny that one of the chief reasons for this change for the better has been the tremendous growth of unionism and anti-fascism in the country, particularly in the movie industry itself."[206] These efforts converged in 1938 in the formation of Films for Democracy, which acted as a pressure group on Hollywood and a producer of Left films, enlisting the assistance of Hollywood progressives like Walter Wanger, Dudley Nichols, Fredric March, and Fritz Lang.[207]

Black film critics were also well aware of the importance of audience groups. Edgar Dale writes, "We must make motion pictures unprofitable which show these stereotypes, and make those movies which are honest and accurate in their portrayal of race and nationality relationships successful at the box office. This means, frankly, the organization of the movie consumer."[208] But because of segregation, black audiences had been prevented from wielding much collective power on their own. Dale observes, "Negro groups have not yet been able to establish consumer pressure due primarily to the fact that they have been quite effectively barred from attendance at many motion-picture houses throughout the United States."[209] In fact, the houses that they were able to attend represented only 1.5 percent of the total. As a result, blacks were encouraged to join groups like the AFA, which already had large memberships and were sympathetic to African American causes. Dale cites an AFA-produced bulletin, dated April 2, 1937, in which David Selznick was questioned about the production of *Gone with the Wind*. Selznick attested that "the treatment of the Negro characters will be with the utmost respect for this race with the greatest concern for its sensibilities."[210] Although Selznick's assurances rang hollow after the film appeared, the AFA nonetheless took a leading role among audience groups by questioning the racist ideologies at work within past and present films and taking proactive measures to derail their appearance in future productions.

As can be seen, then, a focus on the antilynching film, and on *Fury* in particular, represented an important intervention on the part of black and white U.S. Popular Front film critics. Reviews of antilynching films served as a nodal point in popular culture where critics could contextualize the practices of lynching by exposing the repressed racial histories that lurked underneath Hollywood's all-white contexts. In addition, the reviews allowed critics to retheorize the uses of identification and melodrama in progressive cinema. Finally, Left critics who analyzed these films encouraged their readers to support federal antilynching legislation and join audience organizations like the AFA and CLCP to combat the politically reactionary tendencies in Hollywood cinema.

Yet, surprisingly, all these critics overlooked one of the main points in *Fury* that coincided with a Left outlook: how the economic effects of the Depression led to the lynching of Joe Wilson. How, one might ask, could U.S. Left film critics, with their focus on class and economics, miss the film's explicit references to the Depression? The final section of this chapter explores how a possessive investment in masculinity foreclosed U.S. Left male film critics' ability to grapple with the film's economic issues.

III. Fallen Men and the Empathetic Gaze

Class and economics were always central concerns for U.S. Left film critics. In regard to *Fury*, Ben Davis, Jr., Robert Stebbins, and others emphasized some of the economic and class elements of lynching that the film either alluded to or repressed. This type of analysis has a long history, starting with U.S. Left film criticism's initial focus on lynching in film, as can be seen in Harry Alan Potamkin's review of *Cabin in the Cotton* (1932) for *Close Up*:

> For the first time, in my immediate recollection, the movie has dared to approach lynching as a contemporary American custom. Here the victim is a white peasant who has been sorely driven to the murder of a planter. More should have been made of the scene since it submits

the climax to the hyphenate's evolving attitude. We must recognize also that this is not a typical instance. The typical instance is lynching not on a "real" but a framed charge; the most frequent instances are the organized mob murders of Negroes, but this is an indisputable fact to which our conscience is too sensitive—we can argue the lynching in *The Cabin in the Cotton* as rare and therefore chance. Still, the incomplete presentation of the pursuit and lynching of a white man by wealthy men of his own race is an incipient suggestion of the fact that lynchings are economic. Therefore, for all its distortion of the social theme it particularizes, *The Cabin in the Cotton* is an advance in the movie's content.[211]

What was truly amazing Left critics' analyses of *Fury* was their ability to map the subtle aspects of class evoked in the film while missing its most obvious point: Joe Wilson's inability to provide economic security for Katherine (Sylvia Sidney) jeopardizes his marriage and ultimately leads him to his own untimely death. *Fury,* in other words, is a film not simply about lynching, as U.S. Popular Front film critics would have it, but more centrally about the disenfranchisement of white males by the economic and gender upheavals of the Depression and consumerism.

During interviews, Lang often underplayed the film's economic focus, yet he could not entirely rid it from his descriptions. For example, during an interview with Peter Bogdanovich, Lang indirectly let slip that repressed economic motives often led to riots. He described a man in Paris who was walking in front of a fence with a stick, knocking it against each post. A crowd followed behind him. Lang continued, "Then the fence ended, and he came to a display window. He started to knock on it, and after he had knocked it two or three times with his cane, he broke the window. And this started a riot. The crowd became a mob."[212] Although Lang attempted to frame the formation of the mob as a spontaneous eruption, the presence of the display window is highly symbolic, as was shown by its centrality in *Fury.*

As Judith Mayne has observed, display windows often serve a prominent function in films as metaphors for the screen itself, a contradictory site marking both a threshold and obstacle for its observer.[213] The display window invites the observer to fantasize about possessing the pristinely displayed object while also physically distancing it with a protective wall of glass. In many ways, the display window draws to the forefront the politics of envy, which Carolyn Kay Steedman defines as "the proper struggles of people in a state of dispossession to gain their inheritance."[214] Envy should not be seen "as sordid and mindless greed for the things of the mar-

A seemingly traditional portrayal of a wedding in Fury.

Introducing viewers to the style of the new woman.

The androgynous couple in Fury.

ket place, but attempts to alter a world that has produced in them (dispossessed people) states of unfulfilled desire."[215]

Lang effaces the economic motives of envy by repressing the class status of the mob and the man who attack the display window, and substituting instead a naturalized description of violence and human nature. Not surprisingly, this is a common technique found in naturalistic literature in regard to what June Howard identifies as one of its central themes: "proletarianization"—the anxieties that ubiquitously haunt the middle class about a sudden and unforeseeable loss of its class privileges. Rather than explicitly address these anxieties, naturalism translates them into universal signifiers concerning "the destruction of the intellect, humanity, even civilization itself."[216] I want to argue that it is precisely this fear of proletarianization that haunts Joe Wilson from the very beginning of *Fury,* and that it is this fear that the film then unsuccessfully attempts to derail with its growing focus on sadism and mob fury. Typical of naturalism as a genre, *Fury* generalizes the white male anxieties of Joe Wilson into an allegorical tale concerning the utter depravity of human nature.

Fury begins with a display window. Within it we see a wedding book with "The Fall Bride" written across its open pages. Flowers stand next to the book. This traditional image of heterosexual union, however, is undercut by a sound track that plays a jazzy version of Mendelssohn's "Wedding March." The grandiosity of the original arrangement is replaced with a swing rhythm accented by a trumpet. Veneration has given way to Tin Pan Alley casualness, even outright flippancy, toward the key institution of heterosexuality. This is verified as the camera pulls back to reveal a female mannequin in a modern wedding dress with a garish tapered waist, a baroque torso, and extravagant silver streamers hanging from the bouquet. Tellingly, no husband is present. Marriage no longer represents heterosexual union, but a pageant of styles.

This opening scene indicates how consumerism has altered traditional heterosexual relationships. The absence of a husband in the display window suggests the newfound independence consumerism has provided women. The bridal mannequin embodies the tensions found within the New Woman, whose sexual independence is paid for at the cost of self-commodification.[217] Overall, new fashions and the emergence of jazz have redefined heterosexuality in gender-ambiguous ways. We witness this as the camera pans left to show Joe and Katherine standing in front of another display window, this one of a wedding bedroom that says "For Newlyweds." They both stand with their backs to us, identical in pose and look: a hat, trench coat, short hair. It is impossible to decipher their genders except from Katherine's telling gesture of hooking her arm through Joe's.

The display window represents a threshold to their happiness, with marriage serving as their goal. Yet we quickly learn that Joe's economically disempowered status and Katherine's New Woman independence have temporarily blocked their entrance. Because of Joe's inability to provide for both of them, Katherine decides to move away for a better job. When Joe whines, "Why can't you stay with your job here?" she calmly explains, "We've been all through that, darling. I'll be saving for us, too." This places Joe in an infantilized role, which is emphasized when Katherine corrects his use of the word "momentum" for "memento" and sews his coat's pocket in the train station, chiding him that he won't repair it on his own. Katherine has essentially taken the typical masculine position in the relationship, revealed when she offers Joe her mother's wedding ring. Inscribed within its band is "Henry to Katherine / Katherine to Joe." Bequeathed from her father to her mother, Katherine now places Joe in the feminine position as its new recipient. However, Joe's inability to fit the ring on his finger symbolizes his failure to consummate their union. Once aboard the train, Katherine looks out through its window.

Her image is trapped behind the glass, which becomes a moving display window as Joe looks on and she vanishes into the night.

Laid out before us is how the forces of the Depression, consumerism, and the New Woman have all converged to place Joe in an effeminized position. His fear of proletarianization initially manifests itself in his loss of masculinity and will culminate in the second half of the film, when his very humanity unravels. Unmoored from privileged gender and class positions, Joe regresses into the ultimate figure of abject femininity: the hysteric. In a sense, the film's introductory sequence serves as an allegory for the fears of many white heterosexual males impoverished by the Depression. Yet the material causes for Joe's anxiety are eventually displaced and condensed into naturalized scenes of violence and mob fury. The Depression recedes into the background as the film attempts to naturalize Joe's hysteria, assuring its viewers that such reactions are transhistorical. By assuming that everyone innately holds the potential for uncontrollable sadism, *Fury* tries to efface the material processes of the Depression that sent U.S. white heterosexual men reeling into a hysterical state.

Needless to say, U.S. Left film critics refused to discuss Joe's hysteria. Instead, they deflected attention away from Joe by focusing on Katherine's witnessing of Joe's death. Frank S. Nugent writes that "Wilson's sweetheart arrives in time to see him being burned alive."[218] Otis Ferguson similarly notes that "his girl finally arrives to witness what they are doing to him with fire and smoke and mob frenzy."[219] These readings reinforce traditional gender categories by displacing Joe's hysteria onto Katherine. Tellingly, U.S. Left film critics focused on Katherine's most vulnerable moment in the film in order to efface her powerful narrative function throughout it, particularly in its later half. If, as mentioned earlier, *Fury* serves an allegorical function for white heterosexual male fears, it simultaneously allegorizes these men's dependence on the New Woman to come to their rescue.

Katherine's complex position in the film is indicated by an ad for the film that ran in the *New York Times* on June 4, 1936. Katherine looks out from the ad, imploring the reader, "You've *got* to listen to me!" She is flanked on both sides by scenes from the first half of the film, which she narrates:

> [Box 1] Joe and I loved each other. We intended to marry.
> [Box 2] We set the date. It was to be tomorrow night—but now—
> [Box 3] Of course, I had heard about this horrible crime. But how was I to know—

An advertisement in the New York Times, *June 4, 1936, positioning Katherine (Sylvia Sidney) as a central protagonist.*

[Box 4] Then poor, innocent Joe was taken to jail. At first, I thought they were trying to fool me—

[Box 5] But it was all true! I rushed to the jail—it was blocked by a gang of howling men!

[Box 6] Flames shot up through the building! The mob had struck![220]

Much as U.S. Left film critics did in their reviews, the ad emphasizes Katherine's function as a witness of Joe's murder. The increasingly lengthy descriptions accompanying each scene suggest her growing hysteria as Joe's demise approaches. However, unlike Left film critics, the ad also reveals the narrative centrality of Katherine. Contrary to reading her increasingly melodramatic descriptions as the onset of hysteria, one can instead see them as her growing ability to seize control of the story. As Patrick McGilligan observes, after Joe's death, "the weight of the drama would also shift—to Katherine."[221]

However, many later analyses of the film have consistently missed the significance of this shift. Barbara Mennel writes that "it is her character that allowed the writers to conceive of the film partly as melodrama, since they considered that 'there is a great possibility of making this not Spencer Tracy's story but a woman's story.'"[222] Mennel concludes: "Thus, morality and the law are associated with the white male and the melodrama associated with the female character and the mob."[223] Although Mennel is correct that Katherine's character allowed Lang and the writers to conceive of the film in melodramatic terms, she oversimplifies Katherine's melodramatic function by relying upon a binary logic that assumes the film associates white males with morality and the law, and Katherine with melodrama.

To give Mennel credit, Katherine does function in some typically melodramatic, feminine ways, like the one repeatedly emphasized by U.S. Popular Front film critics: her witnessing of Joe's death. Eyes open, mouth agape, Katherine is overloaded with the sensory input of the lynching. Joe's death is indelibly imprinted on her memory. Afterward, she lapses into a catatonic state, imprisoned within the traumatic images that run incessantly before her eyes. Yet the film's emphasis on Katherine's trauma is needed to obscure an even more melodramatic and sustained aftereffect of the lynching: Joe's hysteria. In many ways, Katherine functions as a temporary diversion from Joe's complete descent into irrational fury and lunacy.

Using women as decoys to draw attention away from the traumas visited upon men is not an uncommon technique in Depression-era Hollywood films. Martin Rubin identifies the fallen-woman genre as serving this exact purpose. Underneath the stories of heroines who have been degraded and humbled, "one finds frantic distress signals of masculine self-confidence and an implicit indictment of patriarchal society, which, after all, had just laid a large egg called the Depression."[224] This description is equally applicable to *Fury*, since it initially establishes how white men's economic dispossession and the rise of the New Woman and consumer culture all converge to jeopardize the institutions of heterosexuality and white masculinity. To make Joe not seem completely effeminized and impotent, the film contrasts Katherine's catatonia with his hysteria in order to underplay Joe's absolute vulnerability.[225]

Yet unlike Joe, Katherine suffers only a rather brief moment of vulnerability. Furthermore, her witnessing function provides more than a diversion from Joe's hysteria: it reveals how she is the only character in the film to witness the lynching from outside a sadistic perspective. Unlike its participants and commentators, Katherine was present and absorbed by the moment itself. Much like the newsreel cameras that witness the event through their indifferent lenses and will project the cruelty and inhumanity of Strand's townspeople back to themselves in the courtroom, Katherine similarly absorbs the lynching to become "the film's moral point of view."[226]

Yet her gaze is superior to that of the news cameras, which only selectively focus on the lynchers. Katherine's ability to observe and empathize with all those concerned provides her with the morally superior position in the film. She explains to Joe: "I understand how you feel, and I understand why you feel that way. When I thought you were dead, when I thought of what killed you, I wanted revenge, too. But now I don't. Now I want to be happy again. I want what we always promised each other." When Joe responds, "You ought to have a couple of violins when you talk like that," she implores him to see his connection with the mob: "Don't you realize that what you felt for a few hours, they had to face for days and nights and weeks. Wishing with all their souls that they could have that one day to live over again."

Although Joe does not initially heed Katherine's advice, her voice inscribes itself into his consciousness. It first manifests itself as Joe stands once again before the "For Newlyweds" display window, where his fear of proletarianization initially appeared. He hears her ask him, "Are you planning to do a lot of running around in this room?" a question she asked earlier in the film. The empty hopes for matrimonial bliss still haunt him. Later on, Joe stands before another display window, this one full of

Joe embalmed by his guilt.

flowers. However, rather than looking in with Joe, the camera looks out to him, framing him in a medium shot behind its glass. With the display's flowers surrounding Joe as he crosses his hands and stands still, he seems embalmed behind its glass, a living corpse. Suddenly superimpositions of the lynchers appear before Joe as Katherine says, "Do a good job of it [sending the lynchers to their deaths]. What does it matter? Twenty-two, twenty-three, twenty-five?" The consumer has now become consumed by his own hysteria, making him into nothing more than an object.

To accent Joe's helplessness is Katherine's voice-over, an extremely rare instance within classical Hollywood cinema. As Kaja Silverman notes, normally the voice-over is reserved for male characters, aligning them "with transcendence, authoritative knowledge, potency, and the law—in short, with the symbolic father."[227] To provide a woman with this function is extremely dangerous, "since it would disrupt the specular regime upon which mainstream cinema relies; it would put her beyond the control of the male gaze, and release her voice from the signifying obligations which that gaze sustains."[228] But in a world where the Depression and consumerism have disrupted white male hegemony, it is not surprising that a New Woman would occupy the authoritative position previously reserved exclusively for men. As Joe becomes increasingly objectified and imprisoned behind his hysterical fury, Katherine ascends to the narrative's forefront, becoming its godlike moral force.

Katherine's narrative authority is intimately linked with her empathetic gaze, that is, with her ability to comprehend and empathize with diverse groups and individuals. Out of all the characters in the film, Katherine is most allied with the interests of U.S. Left film critics. After all, these critics were employing the empathetic gaze themselves as they used antilynching discourse to analyze the film and establish interracial coalitions that could fight for federal antilynching legislation as well as demand more-progressive representations on mainstream screens. As we saw earlier, U.S. Popular Front film critics distinctly used *Fury* to investigate questions of identification and spectatorship. Yet with all their focus on Joe Wilson, they refused to see Katherine as the true embodiment of an empathetic Left gaze. Doing so would have required them to both critique the white male gaze and ally themselves with a female viewing position. Despite their desire to draw race to the forefront of their criticism of the antilynching film, U.S. Popular Front film critics would not jeopardize their masculine authority to form an interracial socio-aesthetic vision.

CONCLUSION

As we have seen, many vectors of African American and white political traditions converged in U.S. Popular Front film critics' focus on the antilynching film. African Americans' assertion of the racial dimensions of lynching during the 1880s and 1890s, along with the black press's popularization of antilynching discourses and its ability to fuse them with critiques of racist Hollywood films, provided the template for U.S. Popular Front film critics' discussion of the antilynching film. At the same time, the historical Left's growing concern with racial justice throughout the 1920s and 1930s, white film critics' increasing attention to cinematic depictions of race, and the Soviet Union's desire to make a film regarding the conditions of African Americans catalyzed interracial formations between blacks and whites. By the early 1930s, Marxism was being openly discussed in journals like the *Crisis,* and by middecade, the antifascist rhetoric of the Popular Front synthesized itself with an antiracist stance.

On the film front, both black and white Left film critics had been theorizing the need to create resistant spectators and audience organizations since the early 1930s. The arrival of *Fury* in middecade provided these critics with the chance to enact their theories. By contextualizing the film within African American and Left histories, exploring its uses of identification and melodrama, and critiquing Hollywood's racist practices, film critics used it to collectively mobilize audiences to support federal antilynching legislation and to pressure Hollywood to produce progressive films concerning racial issues.

The fact that *Fury* is still predominantly read as an antilynching film attests less to the power of the film itself than to the discursive power of Popular Front film critics. Their use of antilynching and Marxist discourses to position the film caused Fritz Lang to partially adopt their interpretation as his own, thus coloring future readings of the film by later scholars. If anything, critics' ability to incorporate the film's naturalistic readings of fascism into a Left framework addressing racism exemplifies the successful synthesis of antifascist and antiracist stances by the Popular Front. Although a rather reactionary film on its own terms, *Fury* has been consistently misread as an antilynching film because of the enduring strength of Poplar Front film critics' interpretation of the film.

However, as they did when analyzing *¡Que Viva México!* U.S. Left film critics consistently ignored *Fury*'s gender issues, even when such an analysis would have benefited their understanding of the film's class issues and clarified their concern with progressive uses of identification. The obviousness of Joe Wilson as a fallen man of the Depression and industrial consumerism resonated too strongly with their own masculine anxieties. Better to sacrifice their economic analyses of the film than to question their own male gaze and masculine authority. As we will see, these sexist assumptions reached a crescendo when U.S. Popular Front film critics focused on Jean Renoir, the biopic, and the historical costume drama to better theorize and envision what a progressive Hollywood cinema might actually look like.

Taking Hollywood Back

Chapter 4

GENDERED HISTORIES OF THE
HOLLYWOOD COSTUME DRAMA,
THE BIOPIC, AND JEAN RENOIR'S
La Marseillaise

As we have seen, U.S. Left film criticism had coalesced around an anti-fascist and antilynching Popular Front stance by 1936. A few remaining radical Left film theorists sourly noted the changes taking place in film criticism—changes that seemed to lead to a lack of ideological rigor. In a 1936 article entitled "The Bankruptcy of Cinema as Art," Seymour Stern, a key critic in defending *¡Que Viva México!* remarks on how many of his colleagues had compromised their critical faculties by celebrating certain Hollywood films as an advance in film form: "It is the fashion nowadays, especially among the young intellectuals who write for the liberal magazines, to temporize agreeably with current film production, and they have even managed to discover a number of self-styled 'classics' in the course of their new rapport with the industry . . . But the acclaim . . . pictures receive from the intellectuals is painful evidence of the laxness and vaguemindedness of U.S. film criticism."[1]

Criticisms such as these, however, were becoming increasingly rare among U.S. Left film theorists and critics by 1936. Rather than seeing Left film criticism as having sold out to the commercial mandates of Hollywood, newer critics felt that Hollywood itself was growing more receptive to Left cultural practices because of the increasing number of liberal film workers, the growing power of audience organizations that demanded socially conscious films, and the willingness of producers like Walter Wanger and Darryl Zanuck and studios like Warner Bros. to produce progressive films (see the introduction for a full discussion of these developments). Radical theorists like Stern saw the Popular Front shift in Left film criticism as part of the Left's ongoing failure to create a viable alternative radical film culture in the United States, a failure emblematized by the wreckage of *¡Que Viva México!* Although middecade Left film critics were well aware of the *¡Que Viva México!* fiasco, they underplayed its significance by instead examining how the denial of a radical film movement had trained their sights upon Hollywood and its films. As Margaret Thorp wrote in 1939: "The [Hollywood] industry delights to win the approval of the 'class' audience, the 'intellectuals,' as it politely calls them, who want 'art' in their movies and 'content' as well as escape and excitement and glamour."[2] Many U.S. Left film critics were taking up the challenge of ensuring that the industry moved in such a progressive direction.

The focus of mid-1930s U.S. Left film critics on Hollywood, however, should not be interpreted as a sign of provincialism or a move away from international to domestic, commercial cinema. Although the demise of film journals like *Close Up* and *Experimental Cinema* made it difficult for critics to gain access to international directors' and critics' thoughts on film, and although the escalating conflicts in Europe and the Soviet Union limited distribution of foreign films in America, U.S. Left film critics nonetheless discerned an international film trend that—like the best Hollywood films—fused Left politics with a more commercially viable and accessible film style. The Soviets were praised for films such as *Chapayev* (1934) and *The Youth of Maxim* (1935), which created complex characterizations within relatively straightforward narratives. French directors like Julien Duvivier, Jacques Feyder, and Jean Benoit-Lévy were championed for creating films that were both popular and intellectual. Indeed, the most popular foreign director to emerge during the late 1930s for U.S. Left film critics was Frenchman Jean Renoir.

This chapter investigates U.S. Left film criticism's interrelated critique of Hollywood's historical costume dramas and praise for its historical biopics. The focus is on two central points: how critics' close readings of Jean Renoir's films led to new theoretical discoveries that advanced their discussion of producing politically progressive commercial films; and how the male gaze guided their attention toward antifascist themes within male-centered genres, a stance that would carry over into their work during and after World War II.[3]

The first part of this chapter establishes U.S. Left film critics' ideological critique of the costume drama and their positioning of Jean Renoir's *La Marseillaise* (1938) as a film that counteracted the genre's reactionary tendencies. For many U.S. Left film critics, Renoir's film signaled the first instance of a Western director employing mainstream cinematic conventions to produce a film that addressed complex historical and contemporary issues from a predominantly working-class perspective.[4] According to these critics, *La Marseillaise* revealed how studios could create politically progressive historical films, provided that there were people willing to take on such a task. William Dieterle was one such person. A committed Left director who occasionally contributed pieces to periodicals like the *Daily Worker*, Dieterle became a hot commodity in 1937 after his biopic *The Life of Emile Zola* won three Academy Awards.[5] For Left film critics, Dieterle possessed not only the political commitment but also the needed studio prestige to make progressive historical films in Hollywood, as Renoir had done in France. Therefore, the second part of this chapter explores the growing importance of the biopic within Left film criticism with a particular emphasis upon Dieterle and his 1939 film *Juarez*.

In addition, this chapter continues to investigate the male gaze and persistent gender anxieties as forces that pushed U.S. Left film criticism to consistently favor a male-centered, "masculine" genre over a female-centered, "feminine" one. As a result, U.S. Left film criticism embodied a conflicted socio-aesthetic position. While this criticism provided viewers with a sophisticated ideological understanding of mainstream cinematic conventions and attempted to mobilize viewers into audience groups that could pressure Hollywood to turn out progressive films, Left critics nonetheless reinforced traditional gender hierarchies that the costume drama in particular and consumer culture in general were challenging.

THE COSTUME DRAMA, WOMEN, AND SPECTACLE

Left film critics' desire to establish a clear demarcation between the historical costume drama and "legitimate" historical films began as early as 1928 with the release of Carl Dreyer's *The Passion of Joan of Arc*. Writing for the *National Board of Review Magazine* in January 1929, Harry Alan Potamkin observes, "*The Passion of Jeanne d'Arc* is an historical film, but not a costume film."[6] He reasons that the film possesses "no specious prettiness, but [a] hardness" that organizes all the film's images around a central idea: dedication to God over the state.[7] Joan, therefore, according to Potamkin, embodies the thematic conception of the film, operating as a metaphor for its central idea rather than merely representing the literal plight of an individuated woman battling the church.

In this early review, Potamkin established a central dichotomy that would structure all later U.S. Left film criticism's demarcations between the costume drama and legitimate historical films: spectacle versus theme. According to Potamkin, Dreyer rejects "specious" spectacle by using each detail within the film to develop its theme. Form and content remain intimately intertwined. Spectacle, on the other hand, as found within the costume drama, distracts spectators from a film's themes by engrossing them in the empty effects of the mise-en-scène's surface details. Form, thus, supersedes content through an orgy of images that possess no thematic coherence.

Yet around the same time, another critic drew attention to the troubling gender implications found in Dreyer's film and, by implication, embedded in U.S. Left film criticism's prioritizing of theme over spectacle. In the July 1928 issue of *Close Up,* H.D. critiques Dreyer's film precisely for its complete lack of spectacle. Although recognizing the film's artistic importance, H.D. argues that its rejection of spectacle ultimately dehumanizes Joan: "This [portrayal of Joan] is an Athene stripped of intellect, a Telisila robbed of poetry, it is a Jeanne d'Arc that not only pretends to be real, but that is real, a Jeanne that is going to rob us of our own Jeanne."[8] The film is "real beyond realism" because it offers the calculating and overly rationalistic insight of a microscope, dissecting Joan like a specimen on a slide but failing to take into account the human aspects—like her visions and beliefs—that make her into a particularly powerful woman.[9] As a result, the film's lack of spectacle, for H.D., does not emphasize its central theme but instead sadistically guides its very form to highlight Joan's suffering: "Do I *have* to be cut into slices by this inevitable pan-movement of the camera, these suave lines to the left, up, to the right, back, all rhythmical with the remorseless rhythm of a scimitar?"[10]

Unlike Potamkin, who could view Joan only as a metaphor for the film's theme, H.D. identified with Joan as a woman, refusing to see gender as a secondary issue. Therefore, H.D.'s criticism of Dreyer's film exposed a recurrent theoretical failure underpinning most U.S. Left film criticism: by viewing gender only as a metaphor for the class and theoretical issues it deemed more important, U.S. Left film criticism not only failed to identify gender as a central term in the construction of radical and progressive films, but also remained unaware of how traditional gender hierarchies structured both its celebration of films and genres that often punished strong women in the name of historical causes, and its condemnation of films that failed to do so.

Despite its problematic gender assumptions, U.S. Left film criticism nonetheless sharpened its critique of the spectacle found in historical costume dramas as the genre gained prestige within Hollywood. Two main objections guided their criticism: historical spectacle's reactionary idealization of the past diverted attention from the disturbing socioeconomic effects of the Depression and spectacle's stupefying obsession with the details of mise-en-scène forestalled its films' ability to develop nuanced themes and sociohistorical contexts.

Irving Lerner's 1934 review of *Queen Christina* (1933) in the *New Masses* well illustrates the first objection. Before addressing the film, Lerner quotes at length from Philip Lindsay, the historical adviser on the British costume drama *The Private Life of Henry VIII* (1933), since his statement represented "an expression of the ideology that governs the bourgeois film generally and its costume films specifically":

> We have been pushed too close to the shoddy, vulgar, and brutal things of today; we are tormented by memories of the last war, frightened at the menace of another war; we have gone to the film for relaxation, for inspiration, for pleasure, and we have returned shocked and a little ashamed of our civilization. In the future, however, we will be shown the great achievements of man in the past; we will see the heroic deeds and splendid women, and thus we will be taught that our civilization is not a crude, sudden growth—not a 'system' as the Communists, in defiance of history, will call it . . . This is what costume films can make us realize . . . Costume films . . . will bring back a sense of honor and honesty . . . We need romance terribly today. Half of our present sense of futility is based on the lack of these old values that man has most carefully formed and treasured for centuries.[11]

Straight from the enemy's mouth: Lindsay starkly articulated the reactionary ideology that U.S. Left film critics suspected the historical costume drama embodied. With its idealization of the past, the genre conjured up a tradition of honor and love to placate contemporary viewers' anxieties.

Yet for Lerner, actual history suggested otherwise. In regard to *Queen Christina*, he observes how Hollywood transformed "the ugly, sickly, and sexually abnormal Queen of Sweden" into the glamorous image of Greta Garbo and made Christina's abdication seem to result from her love for her Spanish lover (John Gilbert) instead of from "the threatened revolt of the peasants against the extravagance and oppression of nobility."[12] A true historical film, for Lerner, must abandon genre conventions of love and glamour and instead represent the collective power and historical oppression of the people. In place of a love story, *Queen Christina* should have instead exposed how the "people who dared protest against the exploitation of the peasants were tortured, quartered, and beheaded," which indeed "would have pushed us closer 'to the shoddy, vulgar, and brutal things of today.'"[13] Overall, for Lerner and Left film critics in general, historical costume dramas transformed actual histories of mass resistance, which would resonate with contemporary events and working-class audiences, into spectacles of doomed love and idealized pasts from reactionary, aristocratic perspectives that ideologically served the powers that be.

Yet even in regard to the historical costume dramas that weren't intentionally duplicitous, Left film critics felt that their spectacular attention to mise-en-scène foreclosed their ability to adequately represent sociohistorical contexts. In a fairly sympathetic review of *Romeo and Juliet* (1936), Peter Ellis notes that the film's obsessive attention to historical detail actually precludes its ability to capture Renaissance Verona: "All [this] research and care has given us a Renaissance Verona accurate in many details, but as dead as a museum piece. The actors recite their lines with respect and sometimes feeling, but they are members of this huge pageant instead of living human beings."[14] Subsumed by the film's mise-en-scène, its actors become mere accoutrements rather than representatives of a specific age.

Joseph von Sternberg represented the worst habitual offender of such spectacular excess. William Troy deemed *The Scarlet Empress* (1934) "an elephantiasis of the imagination," since "hardly a square inch of background in certain scenes is free from these swollen phantoms of Von Sternberg's."[15] Von Sternberg's art-for-art's-sake attention to detail contradicted all the lessons that montage theory had instilled in Left film critics. According to B. G. Braver-Mann, a film director "seeks new forms and methods not for their formal values alone but for their integration with an understanding of social phenomena," yet von Sternberg's "concern with the pictorial for its own sake is one of the reasons why no Sternberg film ever presents an image with a relationship to another image for the purpose of developing an independent image idea in the mind of the spectator."[16] For Left critics, directors like von Sternberg, as well as the historical costume drama in general, failed to see that history was not simply the sum of its physical parts but also comprised abstract ideas and belief systems. The "image idea," which could relate such abstractions within film, was absolutely necessary to make history a viable force for the present instead of an empty "pageant" that actors paraded through. From a misguided belief that an accumulation of historical details alone could suffice, spectacle short-circuited the development of complex forms of sociohistorical representation. Hollywood consistently missed this point. Jean Renoir, however, did not.

THE FRENCH RESISTANCE: JEAN RENOIR

While Sergei Eisenstein was a central figure for Left film theorists and critics during the late 1920s and early 1930s, Jean Renoir had become their new figurehead by the late 1930s. Unlike Eisenstein's radical montage, Renoir's style was more suitable for creating commercial productions that promoted a Left agenda. The fiasco of *¡Que Viva México!* clearly exposed how Eisensteinian montage was too radical ever to become a politically and aesthetically viable style in popular filmmaking. But after they abandoned montage, U.S. Left film critics needed a new theory with which to establish an alternative yet accessible filmic style. They found one with the release of Jean Renoir's *Grand Illusion* (1937).

Renoir was an important figure for Left filmmaking in France long before U.S. Left film critics took notice of him in 1938. Although contemporary Renoir scholars still debate Renoir's politics of the 1930s—asking when exactly did he affiliate himself with the French Left, what was the degree of his political commitment to the Left, and when did he gradually move away from Left politics—most agree that somewhere between *La Chienne* (1931) and *The Crime of M. Lange* (1935), Renoir's films began exhibiting a clear sympathy with Left political issues.[17]

Before the release of *Grand Illusion*, U.S. Left film critics were largely unaware of Renoir's background. *Grand Illusion*'s international release in 1938 caught them off guard, since Renoir's style was distinct from the montage-derived practices that these critics had been expounding for the past ten years. Although Left film critics had been arguing for the importance of character development in progressive films since 1934, they had never seen a director employ it in a popular form as skillfully as Renoir did in *Grand Illusion*. As James Dugan wrote in the *New Masses:* "Renoir has scorned stereotyped characters. His German jailors are kindly men, victims of the same illusion as their prisoners."[18] For Dugan, Renoir's populist belief in a common humanity was profound. Although class and politics might divide individuals, they are ultimately united by their shared humanity: "[Renoir] believes in the nobility of man and he hates the traps laid for men by their stupid conditions of life—classes and castes, boundaries and nationalisms, are in the way of human brotherhood."[19]

Although Renoir himself, along with later film critics like André Bazin, pointed out that psychology is often the least important aspect in his films, Renoir's refusal to typecast actors and his emphasis on a character's connection to his or her social and physical environment pushed the acting beyond stereotype and one-dimensionality. As Bazin observes in his posthumous book on Renoir, by casting actors in roles they were unaccustomed to playing, Renoir forced them to go beyond rote acting: "At moments like these the actor is pushed beyond himself, caught totally open and naked in a situation which no longer has anything to do with [traditional] dramatic expression."[20]

In his autobiography *My Life and My Films,* Renoir recounts how he intentionally trained actors to move beyond cliché through his Italian method of reading lines before shooting:

> It consists of seating the actors round a table and getting them to read their lines without any expression whatever . . . What happens is that the actor learns his part in this way, denying himself all reaction until he has explored all the possibilities of every phrase, every word and every gesture . . . So we get together, actors and director, and we go through the text two or three or even twenty times. And suddenly, in this lifeless reading of lines, the director discovers a tiny spark. That's it! Starting from there the actor has a chance to achieve an original interpretation of the role.[21]

As the actors and director become familiar with the multiple meanings of the lines, they decide on the most effective ways to approach the material. Despite U.S. Left film critics' unawareness of such acting techniques in 1938, James Dugan implies in a 1939 article for the *New Masses* that non-clichéd acting is a key component of *Grand Illusion:* "Renoir seems to be allowing his material to shape itself—the great actors, Gabin, von Stroheim, Fresnay, Dalio, Dita Parlo, and the beautiful child."[22]

But in addition to great acting, Renoir's ability to embed his characters in physical, intellectual, and socioeconomic contexts enabled his films to express depths of feeling and avoid clichés. In a 1939 article for *Theatre Arts Monthly,* Richard Rene Plant quotes Renoir on the connection between people and their physical environment: "It has become clear to me that man is rooted in the soil that nourishes him. He is bound to the conditions that form his body and soul and chained to the landscape that dazzles his eyes."[23] Although Renoir's assertion of a connection between people and the land clearly had a populist impetus behind it, it did not imply for U.S. Left film critics an anti-intellectual agrarian stance. *Grand Illusion* revealed a dialectical connection between people and their environment that was, in part, achieved through background research. As James Dugan notes, the plot was constructed from "interviews with veterans of German prison camps."[24] Richard Plant further claims that part of the film's appeal lies in its general stance toward war as a whole: "Here is a film that does not eschew intellectual discussion. Renoir dares to make his characters speak of the problems which confront men, and whose contemporary significance [for the impending world war] is obvious."[25] Although contemporary film histories portray Renoir as a humanist who strongly distrusted intellectuals and politics—in opposition to someone like Eisenstein, who engaged frequently in theoretical debates—the Renoir of the 1930s, for U.S. Left film critics, appeared to be as intellectually and politically engaged as a figure like Eisenstein. Left film critics' championing of Renoir as their new favorite auteur, in place of Eisenstein, did not signify an apolitical move on their part, but rather their desire to have an intellectually and politically committed Left filmmaker whose style was more adaptable to commercial conventions than Eisenstein's.

But more important than Renoir's ability to place his characters in an intellectually relevant and well-researched context was his technical virtuosity in visually and aurally linking his characters dialectically with their socioeconomic contexts. U.S. Left film critics, in a limited sense, understood Renoir's radically new technical approach, but they lacked the critical vocabulary to clearly describe it. After discussing montage for ten years, they realized that whatever Renoir was doing formally, it was nothing that they were accustomed to. James Dugan comments: "His film [*Grand Illusion*] knocked a lot of my theories for a loop. Where is what I once called film language? Renoir moves along a straight narrative line, without the brilliant tricks of Hitchcock or René Clair."[26]

Furthermore, Dugan realizes that Renoir's use of mise-en-scène, despite its simplicity, provides the spectator with a radically new way of envisioning the mundane: "The camera work by Claude Renoir, which is really superb, seems no more unusual than a writer constructing the word 'love' out of a vertical bar, a circle, an open wedge, and a combination of a circle and a crossbar."[27] Dugan's analogy reveals his awareness of how Renoir used the everyday, the literal, to construct deep and abstract meanings. André Bazin makes a similar point when defining Renoir's "realism": "But simply being realistic is not enough to make a good film. There is no point in rendering something realistically unless it is to make it more meaningful in an abstract sense . . . Renoir the moralist is also the most 'realistic' of film makers, sacrificing reality as little as possible to the thrust of his message."[28]

Despite Bazin's moralistic description of Renoir, he, like the U.S. Left film critics before him, notes how Renoir's style of fusing the literal (or realistic) with the abstract differed radically from the technique of earlier filmmakers, who would have created such links through montage rather than mise-en-scène. Early in his career, Eisenstein, for example, would have created such abstract links between literal, plastic elements with montage—and thereby disturbing the narrative flow of events. Renoir, on the other hand, considered mise-en-scène, with its combination of aural and visual elements, an aspect of narrative fluidity. He attempted to avoid montage as much as possible in order to keep his films moving in a rather smooth temporal fashion while suggesting the broad social implications that are a part of his narratives. Eisenstein used montage to fracture narrative in order to suggest the social whole that standard narrative forms elided. Both directors were concerned with dialectically linking the abstract with the literal, the individual with his or her socioeconomic context. Whereas Eisenstein felt (at least throughout the 1920s and early 1930s) that classical narrative had to be disrupted in order to address systemic socioeconomic concerns that the form was incapable of revealing, Renoir believed that classical narrative could be used to facilitate deeper socioeconomic understandings.

Bazin's article "The Evolution of the Language of the Cinema" helps explain the radical transformation of cinematic style that Renoir's films marked during the late 1930s and early 1940s. For Bazin, before 1938 or 1939, Hollywood cinema was largely dominated by a montage style. Clearly, as Chapter Two shows, Hollywood was not receptive to radical uses of montage; nonetheless, Bazin sees "invisible" editing as a form of montage at work within most Hollywood films: "scenes were broken down just for one purpose, namely, to analyze an episode according to the material or dramatic logic of the spectator."[29] Bazin views this type of montage as highly manipulative, since it forces the spectator to accept the director's point of view. Although some Hollywood directors like Eric von Stroheim, F. W. Murnau, and Robert Flaherty worked against a montage style in their films, they were marginal to classical Hollywood cinema. But by the late 1930s, because of technical developments like the widespread use of panchromatic film, which was more light sensitive than earlier black-and-white film stock, and the innovations of directors like Renoir, Orson Welles, and William Wyler, a new aesthetic style developed, one based on mise-en-scène and culminating in films like Renoir's *Rules of the Game* (1939) and Welles's *Citizen Kane* (1941). Bazin's article reminds contemporary film historians that directors like Renoir and Welles, who now seem to represent the apex of classical narrative cinema, were originally considered innovative, modernist directors whose styles were only beginning to constitute a new classical style.

U.S. Left film critics identified by example some of the new techniques that Renoir used, but it would take someone like Bazin, fifteen years later, to formally label such techniques: depth of field, the long panning shots, and elaborate tracking. The importance of such techniques from a Marxist point of view has been pointed out by Renoir scholar Christopher Faulkner, who notes how Renoir's style worked both within and against classical Hollywood cinema. Temporally, Renoir's style created individuated linear narratives, yet spatially through his use of depth of field, panning, and tracking, it collectivized the film's protagonists within their physical and sociohistoric contexts. In these ways, Renoir's 1930s films "socialize space."[30] As a result, although they temporally rely on classical Hollywood narrative conventions, they articulate a dialectical understanding of the individual's relation to his or her socioeconomic context.

It was precisely Renoir's ability to work both within and against classical Hollywood cinema that made him particularly appealing to U.S. Left film critics. Although they could not clearly articulate the dialectical forces at work in Renoir's films, they realized that his works could serve as models for progressive Hollywood cinema. As Barbara Stavis observes: "[Renoir] reiterated his belief that fundamental social relations could be set into commercial films, by getting the spectator to reflect on the direction of his own life and of others like him, confronting him with a broader conception of the oneness of society, shaking loose some of the provincial ideas, digging into the crust of prejudice accumulated through years of commercial films."[31] Stavis implies that spectators' emotional identification with characters operates on two planes at once: with the characters in the film and with the social contexts that surround the film characters and the spectators. Rather than locking the spectator solely into identification with a romanticized and dehistoricized character, as in a typical Hollywood film, Renoir's films create forms of emotional identification that recognize the dialectical interaction between individual and social context, and between spectator and characters. Moreover, they do so without sacrificing a traditional character-centered narrative approach—a sacrifice that Eisenstein's films often entailed.

Yet many U.S. Left film critics' advocacy for a mise-en-scène-based style did not yield so much an overthrow of older montage-based styles as a fusing together of newer techniques with older ones. In "Post-classical Hollywood," Peter Kramer offers a good summation of Bazin's description of what was actually occurring in "post-classical" U.S. cinema of the late 1930s and early 1940s: "[It is a cinema] which is described as an impure, less rigorous, highly flexible cinema, characterized by the coexistence of contradictory aesthetic strategies (classical editing, expressionism, realism) rather than a strict and exclusive adherence to the continuity system; by the extension, embellishment, playfulness, and mixing of its genres rather than by generic purity; and by an engagement with topical issues and controversial subject-matter even in its most conventional generic offerings."[32]

We see such hybridity at work in William Dieterle's historical film *Juarez* (1939). It uses both montage and mise-en-scène, mixes the genre conventions of historical biopics and costume dramas, and engages in such topical issues as the sovereignty of the Mexican nation and imperialism. In many ways, *Juarez* represents the ideal hybrid product of "post-classical" Hollywood cinema. But the film's very hybridity disturbed many U.S. Left film critics, who demanded a purified, "masculine," male-centered, and political biopic that lacked any traces of the "feminine," female-centered, and commodified costume drama. In their advocacy of *Juarez*, Left film critics effaced the film's female-centered, costume-drama elements, since focusing on them would have exposed the film's hybridity and contradicted their contention that its success was solely due to the conventions of the "masculine," male-centered biopic.

U.S. Left film critics believed that it was possible for Hollywood to obtain biopic purity partly because Renoir's next film, *La Marseillaise* (1937), represented their ideal historical film. The film's production and distribution alone offered an alternative to commercial cinema's control.[33] Barbara Stavis observes how *La Marseillaise* was "financed by hundreds of thousands of tiny contributions from rank-and-filers in the Front Populaire."[34] She also mentions how the independently controlled Les Films Populaires acted as the film's distributing organization: "[The film] has had to find its exhibitors outside ordinary commercial channels; clients include trade unions, the Communist and Socialist Parties, cultural clubs, and independent exhibitors mainly in Paris and environs. An important function of Les Films Populaires is the bringing of social pictures to the village and countryside by traveling caravans, equipped for screening sound films in rural halls."[35]

U.S. Left film theorists and critics failed to domestically mass-distribute and exhibit Eisenstein's radical *¡Que Viva México!* but France seemed more open to alternative forms of film production, mass distribution, and exhibition. Equally important, *La Marseillaise* was a sophisticated Left historical film that could be used by critics to counter and critique the growing popularity of the Hollywood costume drama. If aspects of *La Marseillaise* could be incorporated into Hollywood historical films, as many Left film critics believed, perhaps the costume drama could be exposed as the consumer-driven kitsch that they felt it was. Yet *La Marseillaise* also had its share of so-called costume-drama elements, which most U.S. Left film critics ignored in their columns. The "purity" of *La Marseillaise* was more the invention of its critics than the truth of its content.

VIVE LA FRANCE: *La Marseillaise*
AS THE IDEAL HISTORICAL FILM

First and foremost, U.S. Left film critics felt that *La Marseillaise* counter-acted the historical costume drama's reliance on spectacle. According to them, all the film's details serve a specific purpose. They avoid becoming fetishized props that are unrelated to one another. James Dugan cites the scene when the Royalists begin running through a rainsquall. One of them leans over and throws his coattails over his head. Dugan observes: "This happens in the background and has no significance except to illustrate that the director understands that historical costumes actually had a certain use, and are not merely masquerade ball props."[36] Renoir's emphasis on his props' use value rather than their look is important. As Guy Debord notes: "The spectacle is the money which one only looks at, because in the spectacle the totality of use is already exchanged for the totality of abstract representation."[37] Renoir's use of costumes in his films, for Dugan, repre-sents the director's desire to pull them from the "abstract representation" of spectacle into the social realm, where they serve a practical purpose.

Additionally, U.S. Left film critics felt that *La Marseillaise* challenged the historical costume drama's dependence upon a star system that over-individuated historical events, usually from an upper-class point of view. As Irving Lerner showed in his 1934 analysis of *Queen Christina*, the cos-tume drama presented history as top-down, organized by heroic leaders who directed the people's actions, rather than as bottom-up, created by the people themselves, some of whom eventually became prominent leaders. James Dugan saw a similar dynamic operating in MGM's 1938 cos-tume drama *Marie Antoinette*, which seemed to side with the aristocracy: "MGM's posthumous obsequies to the frivolous lady from Austria are in the best manner of noblesse oblige."[38] Marie is represented in the film as a victim of the Duke of Orleans's deception, not as a callous ruler indiffer-ent to the suffering of the peasants. She refuses to buy a necklace for a mil-lion and a half francs because she thinks indulging in such extravagance would be wrong while a majority of her people suffer economic hardship. Nonetheless, the duke arranges for some of the queen's crooked council-men to purchase the necklace, which he then uses to convince the people that the queen is indifferent to their plight. Although the queen attempts to prove her innocence in a court of law, the verdict goes against her and further reinforces the duke's charges.

Moreover, because the film upholds the queen's point of view, it de-monizes the leader and the masses who took part in the revolution. Dugan

The socialization of space in La Marseillaise *(1938).*

notes: "The revolutionary crowds are seen through the eyes of the Queen herself: Robespierre and Danton are shown as tools of the Duke d'Orleans."[39] The revolutionary crowd in the film is represented as an undifferentiated mob full of rage and hatred, blindly following the duke's commands. In one scene, we hear a voice-over of the duke, his tone growing more frantic and hysterical as he incites the people to rebel: "You furrow the soil in the heat of the day, but the soil is not yours. It has never been yours. Why, you work like rats in the bowels of the earth. For whom? A queen . . . who came from afar hating the people of France, throwing its gold away, the minted drops of your blood. Will you not listen? Will you not rise? Will you not demand the abolition of the aristocracy and its privileges?" As he speaks, we see documentary-like medium shots of peasants tilling fields and miners at work. But as his speech increasingly incites the people, the laborers are gradually framed in medium close-ups and then close-ups, looking eagerly into the distance as if stopping their work to heed the duke's call for revolution. This is top-down history, in which only select leaders organized the mob's actions—a mob that had no thoughts of its own. Marie absolves the mob members of their judgment against her when she states that they act on "things they don't understand," and one thing they don't comprehend, as MGM wants the viewer to believe, is Marie's innocence.

For Left film critics, *La Marseillaise*, in part because of its casting of unknowns, represented the people as the sole originators of the revolution. The film centers on two lower-class men, Jean-Joseph Bomier (Edmond Ardisson), a mason, and Honoré Arnaud (Andrex), a tall clerk and writer. Arnaud rises through the ranks to become a leader, while Bomier remains a foot soldier, exposing how the people themselves constituted the various ranks of the revolution. The film frequently shows Bomier and Arnaud discussing the purpose of the revolution among themselves and with other revolutionaries. Cultural historians Dudley Andrews and Steven Ungar observe how the film was influenced by "the new spirit of historiography that was just then coming into existence under the name of 'Annales,'" which chronicled the common people and the quotidian details of their lives rather than the majestic ascent and narratives of great leaders.[40] James Dugan notes how the film worked against Hollywood's portrayal of revolutionaries and the people "as swine and leering hogs, and the queen with pity."[41] He emphasizes Renoir's mise-en-scène, claiming that "the picture needs the closest attention because of these Renoir touches, which constantly remind you that the revolution is made up of people, not MGM extras."[42] Rather than reifying the people into an undifferentiated mob of mass hatred as MGM did, Renoir used his mise-en-scène dialectically to show how the people acted simultaneously both as a collective and as individuals.

This use of mise-en-scène is perhaps best illustrated when the revolutionaries seize a fort in Marseille. A long shot shows, on the right side of the frame, the Republican guards, led by Arnaud, and their prisoners in the fort's courtyard. A well-placed center frame balances the mise-en-scène. On the left side stands one Republican guard, who has just recognized a prisoner as a former childhood friend. They hug and ask about each other. The guard then explains to Arnaud, "We both come from the same place." The well's circular shape accentuates how Arnaud's and the guard's differing points of view (Arnaud sees the prisoners as enemies, whereas the guard realizes his connection to them) are a part of the same continuum. Although the Republican guards must oppose the king's troops, their actions are ultimately guided to unify the people. *La Marseillaise*'s temporal narrative exposes the divisions between the revolutionaries and the king's army, and between the guard's agrarian and populist stance and Arnaud's erudition and links to leadership. But the scene's mise-en-scène socializes space by showing how all these seemingly opposing stances are ultimately visually unified.

Additionally, U.S. Left film critics emphasized *La Marseillaise*'s ability to counter the historical costume drama's romance plot, which deflected attention from the historical issues surrounding popular resistance and its connections with contemporary political concerns. For example, *Marie Antoinette*'s first half centers on the Duke of Orleans's seduction of Marie, who is pursuing an affair with Count Axel de Fersen (Tyrone Power). According to James Dugan: "The picture implies [the Duke of Orleans] cooked up the Revolution because the Queen wouldn't go beddy bies with him."[43] Similarly, Lauren Adams saw the love story between Mary (Katherine Hepburn) and Bothwell (Fredric March) in John Ford's *Mary of Scotland* (1936) as smoothing "over Mary's [counterrevolutionary] political ambitions and offer[ing] her as a woman who is every inch a mother, a sweetheart and a queen."[44] In these ways, revolution served only as a backdrop for the romantic melodrama of thwarted love between Marie and Axel, or Mary and Bothwell.

By contrast, U.S. Left film critics considered *La Marseillaise* a picture absorbed not by romance but by political ideas. James Dugan listed some of the film's concerns: "the immediate problems of revolution, looting, mercy to the ignorant enemy, the status of women, and the patriotic aspect of revolutionary fighting."[45] For Dugan and other Left film critics, the concerns of the film were important not only because they conveyed a more sophisticated historical understanding of the revolution to audiences, but also because they alluded to related contemporary issues of the Popular Front. However, if one were to read Left critics' accounts of *La Marseillaise,* one might think that the film is devoid of a romance plot altogether. This is far from being the case. Unlike the historical costume drama, though, which centers on a love story and sees politics as a threat to romance, *La Marseillaise* connects its two love stories (which involve Louis XVI [Pierre Renoir] and Marie Antoinette [Lise Delamare], on the one hand, and Bomier and Louison [Nadia Dibirskaïa], on the other) to political events. The king's dysfunctional relationship with Marie represents the monarchy's increasingly problematic relationship with the people, whereas Bomier's blossoming romance with Louison marks the increasing power of the people to form coalitions and take control of the state.

One might think that U.S. Left film critics would have accentuated the film's ability to draw connections between the personal and political, since such an association directly relates to their politics of linking the indi-

vidual to the social whole. *La Marseillaise* is particularly apt in presenting well-rounded characters without forsaking the sociopolitical contexts
that produced them. Bomier dies at the end of the film, but this is not considered a failure of the revolution, since his spirit and thoughts live on in
others who are still fighting for democracy. Arnaud verbalizes the importance of Bomier's and other dead Jacobins' sacrifices for the revolution in
the film's closing romantic metaphor: before the revolution, people stared
at liberty like a lover afraid to approach his beloved. But now the lover embraces his beloved: "Of course, she's not yet his mistress, and he'll have a
difficult time winning her over. But even if they're parted, they know each
other now, and one day or another they'll be reunited." The film's final
emphasis on such a romantic metaphor makes it remarkable that no U.S.
Left film critic noticed the film's ability to not only connect the personal
and political, romance and politics, but also use a romantic device to do
so. Such an observation would have helped these critics recognize how
Hollywood films could function both as a love stories and as progressive
historical narratives.

But the silence of U.S. Left film critics on this point becomes understandable when we recall their desire to use *La Marseillaise* as a corrective
to the Hollywood-style costume drama's emphasis on personal, supposedly depoliticized, issues. By ignoring *La Marseillaise*'s romantic plotlines,
these critics found it easier to distinguish Renoir's approach from Hollywood. Yet at the same time, through their advocacy of Renoir's films as
models for progressive commercial cinema, they fostered certain links between Renoir's and Hollywood's films. This proximity led a few Left film
critics to conclude that "the historic costumes and trappings cramped his
[Renoir's] realistic style and the film [*La Marseillaise*] did not live up to expectations."[46] The attempt to influence Hollywood while also criticizing it
was a pervasive concern of many U.S. Left film critics as they attempted to
distinguish the "genuine" historical film from the gaudy Hollywood historical costume drama.

GENDER REDUX

One reason U.S. Left film critics remained silent on *La Marseillaise*'s
ability to fuse the personal and the political was because of their belief
that the political should always take precedence over the personal. Romance veered too near the emotions. Better to ignore its presence in a film
than to have it potentially derail or deflect the political focus of one's film
criticism. Either these critics lacked the critical vocabulary with which to

discuss such interconnections adequately, or they simply resisted such an analysis, since it would have problematized their prioritization of political issues over personal ones. The Hollywood-style costume drama, as a result, was a political no-man's-land for these critics. It was better to castigate the films for their conservative politics than to run the risk of being drawn into their spectacular allure and confusing hybridity.

The domestic realm was a particularly prevalent and troublesome aspect of the historical costume drama. U.S. Left film critics had difficulty doing anything other than dismissing it as a hopelessly compromised site of bourgeois ideology. *La Marseillaise* itself is a deeply divided film as far as the relationship between the political and the domestic. As much as it attempts to link the political with the personal, it also banishes the personal from the political when it comes to its portrayal of female-centered domestic life. By focusing on such a sequence, we can better understand the way in which many male U.S. Left film critics held a similar view. Both the film's and Left film critics' desire to marginalize such issues reveals a pervasive anxiety not only about addressing personal desires that might undercut one's politics, but also about acknowledging woman-centered spaces as a viable arena for political change.

In *La Marseillaise*, Jean-Joseph Bomier sits in an auditorium listening to a revolutionary speak about forming battalions to storm Paris. The speaker tells the men that he is now accepting enlistees. Bomier becomes excited about joining until the speaker mentions that all enlistees must be debt free. His friends question him about why he is not enlisting. Bomier cryptically states that he simply cannot join. Arnaud derisively comments, "You talk about the king's dependence upon the queen. You sacrifice honor and dignity for a woman, too." The unspecified woman mentioned refers to either Bomier's mother or his girlfriend, Marie. A woman divides Bomier from the collective political space of the revolution, as the scene suggests through its camera work. The scene begins with a medium shot of the speaker asking for enlistees. The camera tracks back, locating the speaker among a crowd of revolutionaries, then pans left and up to a group of women who begin singing, encouraging the entire room to follow their lead. The camera then pans down and to the left, observing the first man signing up. It then pans left and up to Bomier sitting dejectedly. The lack of cutting suggests the solidarity between the revolutionaries and emphasizes that Bomier's narrative is only one of many in the film. After Bomier tells his friends that he cannot join, the scene dissolves into an interior shot of Bomier's mother's house.

Renoir dramatically contrasts the domestic space with the earlier scene

Jean-Joseph Bomier (Edmond Ardisson) breaking free of domestic inertia.

The domestic as self-excluded from the political realm.

to emphasize the domestic as a threat to progressive politics. The first shot shows Bomier's mother closing a door, punctuating the confinement that Bomier feels within the domestic sphere. He sits at the table, unable to eat. The camera remains static, cutting between various two-shots of mother and son, suggesting a claustrophobic link between the two. The scene represents his mother as the conservative of the family. She refuses to sit at the table and eat with him because her deceased husband deemed it inappropriate for women and men to eat together. She is relieved when Bomier tells her that he cannot join a battalion. She says, "Believe me, there will always be rich and poor. Your friends can't change that." In a medium shot, Bomier moves to the window and opens it while speaking about his friends who are joining. In deep focus, we see two workers singing, building a roof. The shot subtly suggests the community that Bomier wants to join but cannot because of his debt. We soon learn that his debt arose because he lent Marie money to open a shop. She is noticeably absent throughout the film. Unlike his mother, who is representative of the conservatism of the domestic space, Marie represents a threat to male autonomy by breaking free of the private sphere while simultaneously preventing Bomier from joining his comrades in the political public sphere. Her link to the bourgeois shop contrasts with Bomier's desire for working-class solidarity. As part of the exploiting class now, she has relinquished her connection with working-class people like Bomier.

However, despite the threat of the domestic sphere to Bomier's political mission, his mother's conservatism ultimately works against her. Since she recognizes Bomier as the head of the household, she tells him that they own a vineyard, which they can sell to free him of debt. Bomier thanks his mother and begins singing as he leaves. A passing maid closes the door he opens. In one of the few fluid camera movements in the scene, we see Bomier's mother in medium close-up sitting sadly at the table. The maid embraces her until the mother directs her to shut the window. As the maid leaves the frame, the camera tracks left, slowly moving over domestic items like a vase, a pot, a rack of chestnuts, and, most symbolically, a caged bird. The camera pans right to the window, where the maid stands. It tracks forward so that the window's frame is no longer visible. We hear Bomier singing as the camera hangs on a long shot of the roofers and then tilts down into the street, where we see Bomier skipping and passing through busy crowds. He is part of the community once again. As he disappears from sight around a corner, the maid's hand slowly pulls the window shut. The singing is silenced by the sound of the window's lock being latched.

The scene emphasizes that the domestic must be quarantined. Women confine men's actions, so they (women) must in turn be confined. Bomier the revolutionary cannot coexist with Bomier the son. Trying to convert the domestic space into a politically progressive realm is hopeless. The mother is too set in her ways, as is shown by her constant desire to have doors and windows shut, as if she fears the intrusion of politics into her private sphere, not realizing how they already define her very notion of privacy. The domestic, in other words, is considered too suffused with bourgeois ideology to be worth troubling over. Not surprisingly, histori-cal costume dramas that center on women and thus feature the inevitable convergence of the domestic and the political especially challenged most U.S. Left film critics' dismissal of the domestic. Rather than seeing such films as a potential means to hone their political and cultural analyses, these critics often dismissed them as meaningless spectacles—as kitsch, even though it was the critics themselves, rather than the films, who often limited the domestic space's meanings.

As mentioned in Chapter One, when U.S. Left film critics noticed women outside the domestic realm, it was often in the denigrating sense of exposing how women's newfound independence was inextricably linked with the rise of materialism and commodity culture. We also see this at work in *La Marseillaise*. In an early scene, Bomier, Arnaud, and an old man named Anatole Roux camp on a hill. As Leger Grindon observes in *Shadows of the Past*, *La Marseillaise*'s open landscapes and nature are often associated with the revolution and its liberating tendencies.[47] This early scene with the three men represents an idyllic bond between them, a true fraternity. But one of the men wishes that the group could have ac-cess to alcohol, tobacco, and women. Arnaud, however, warns that if they allow any of these commodities to intrude upon them in the country, then the place will become just as compromised and commodified as the city. Women, although acknowledged as part of city life, are, at this moment in the film, considered inimical to the revolutionary project of democracy, since they are seen as being no different from any other commodity used to dull the revolutionaries' senses. The film's politics becomes particularly regressive here: women are seen only in relation to men's desires and fears. Women's possible desire to be a part of the revolution or the newly democ-ratized country is ignored altogether.

This attraction, yet fear of spectacle, interestingly enough, also occa-sionally surfaced in U.S. Left film critics' columns in the rare moments when they spoke personally. Robert Forsythe explicitly states his fear of contamination in the *New Masses*. Writing in response to a reader who suggested that Hollywood films might have dulled his critical capacities, Forsythe willingly concedes that the reader has a valid point. Although he once was extremely critical of most Hollywood films, after five years of film criticism, Forsythe finds himself more accepting of them: "Instead of saying, 'This is terrible; let me out of here,' I was saying, 'Well, it isn't so bad; it's better than Jean Harlow last week.'"[48] He gives backhanded praise to a Joan Crawford and Clark Gable vehicle, *Chained* (1934), for its lush costumes and designs: "It was said to be a Clarence Brown production but in reality it belonged to Adrian, the dress designer," suggesting how spectacle often trumps the narrative development and cohesion that the director is supposed to impose.[49] He goes on to account for the various dresses Crawford wears throughout the film, noting: "If I seem to bear upon these points it is only because I was so stunned by the magnificence of it all I could scarcely pay attention to the brilliant story which was being unfolded."[50] Despite his sarcasm regarding the film's "brilliant story," Forsythe notes how spectacle can deflect the critic's attention away from even the most banal of romance plots.[51]

As much as Forsythe wants to reject the film as trash, he willingly admits that its spectacle had a strong affect on him: "This is where madness sets in; this is where the movie reviewer ceases to be a critic and becomes an adjunct of Metro-Goldwyn-Mayer despite the earlier granite-like quality of his intellect."[52] To admit the allure of spectacle was to play unwittingly into the Hollywood ideology that Left film criticism initially set out either to critique or to improve. If anything, many U.S. Left film critics' harsh responses to spectacle indicated their desire to distance themselves from both their own attraction to such films and the type of mainstream film criticism that served as nothing more than Hollywood public relations. Furthermore, their silence regarding personal issues might not have been just a political strategy, but also a way of effacing the embarrassing contradictions that can arise between personal feelings and political beliefs whenever one grapples with the nebulous terrains of art and popular culture.

Despite most Left film critics' overt rejection of spectacle and its effects on gender identities, a few recognized the complexities that could arise from this cultural moment. As mentioned in Chapter Two, Lewis Jacobs cites the Jazz Age films of the 1920s as indicating how postwar prosperity brought about a significant change in the representation of women: "Thus began that remarkable series of jazz-age pictures exemplified in De Mille's works, which, speaking for the hedonism of a nation on the wave of prosperity, helped to set new styles in social behavior and reflected the new standards of living," adding, "The mockery of ethics, of the old 'inner goodness' of the film heroes and heroines, was paralleled by the new regard for material things."[53] One of the positive outcomes of materialism and the problematization of older moral values was the characterization of women as more independent and better able to express their desires than before, especially in films that showed marriage as confining women's actions. Jacobs emphasizes how "the Cinderella tradition of feminine modesty, in which woman is a vassal-in-waiting, was thus supplanted by the post-Ibsen concept of a 'devastating,' aggressive creature, attractive, smart, seductive, independent, daring, fast."[54] Jacobs rightly notes how women's links with consumerism allowed them to act in masculine ways that were once deemed inappropriate. Although consumerism mainly allowed women to only act in more masculine ways (rather than challenging the masculine altogether), it still provided a wider range of female agency than had previously been available. One can sense a feeling of admiration in Jacobs's description of the "new woman" in film, but her very presence led to the troubling conclusion that consumer culture was not as completely debilitating as most Left critics would have had it—that there was a potentially liberating impulse for women within consumer capitalism, even though it created further class stratification and commodified people.

But for the most part, Left film critics ignored any liberatory impulse that consumerism provided for women. Their implicit dependence upon a male gaze foreclosed their ability to recognize that establishing a progressive film culture required the historicizing of gender on its own terms. Women's desires were considered, at best, as resulting from a fully commodified perspective, which Left film theory and criticism was attempting to overthrow.

Furthermore, U.S. Left film critics' male gaze marginalized critical representations of women that did not fit into this commodified model. *La Marseillaise* offers a remarkable instance of women's new revolutionary role as well as the unjustified male anxieties that accompanied it. The film provides an image of a strong revolutionary leader, Louise Vauclair (Jenny Hélia). Among other things, she addresses the revolutionary assembly of the Club of Friends of the Constitution. The first shot is of the club's sign. We hear her introduce herself by giving an account of how her lover's death was the result of betrayal by fellow revolutionaries. As she speaks, the camera pans nearly 360 degrees to show the mostly male audience hanging on her words. Tellingly, the shot stops on the upper balcony, where women are watching her, suggesting her idealized status for them. Renoir pans farther, separating Vauclair's voice from her body, implying

Louise Vauclair (Jenny Hélia) in La Marseillaise, *showing that women can be revolutionaries—a fact overlooked by U.S. Left film critics.*

its transcendence as it unites audience and speaker. Her speech becomes less personal as she discusses the ideals of the revolution. In a medium close shot, she speaks with authority, and the crowd responds positively. Eventually, a man stands up and asks the male audience members, "Is it a woman's place to say such things on the tribune?" The female balcony yells, "Yes," forcing him to temporarily look their way. He then addresses his male colleagues again, "I say a woman's place is in the home." But another male revolutionary responds, "Your place is in the galleys." Vauclair, seemingly unperturbed by the interruption, continues with her speech. Significantly, the man who questions women's public role also denounces Robespierre at the end of her speech, which enrages most of the revolutionaries. By associating the man with a rejection of the revolution's most radical leader, Renoir exposes how such misogyny was tied to a political conservatism that ultimately could not benefit the revolution.

The scene asks for a reappraisal of the film's earlier misogynistic tendencies. The film is, finally, not so much opposed to women's independence as opposed to women who endorse a patriarchal and commodified ideology. Women who want to enslave themselves in the realm of the domestic without regard to public issues and social change are hopelessly compromised, as are women who engage in capitalist enterprise. Yet the film praises a woman like Vauclair who truly understands the revolution's principles and possesses the fortitude to speak before the club. Granted, such appraisal is done by valorizing the public sphere over the domestic, but the film's acknowledgment of women's rights as being important to social revolution is more sophisticated than U.S. Left film critics were able to identify. Although the film problematically subsumes gender to class issues, as was common of the historical male Left, it also acknowledges how revolutionary practices had to problematize more traditional notions of gendered spheres and identities; it is this latter point that U.S. Left film critics consistently missed by associating all stereotypically "unfeminine" representations and desires of women with the debased processes of consumerism and a commodified ethos.

Because of such an outlook, one can begin to see why the historical costume drama would pose such a threat to U.S. Left film critics. First of all, most of these films provided strong female characters for female audience members to identify with. Left critics were well aware that the primary audience for most Hollywood films was women. Margaret Thorp writes: "It is really that solid citizen's wife who commands the respectful attention of the industry."[55] She understands that women identified with such films, for they provided female viewers with a sense of fulfillment that they lacked in their own lives: "In the movies a wife finds it quite worth while to get into a new evening frock for a *tête-à-tête* dinner at home because her husband is sure, by dessert time at least, to take her hand across the intimately small and convenient table and say, 'Darling, you get lovelier every day.'"[56] Similarly, Sarah Berry quotes a press book to show how historical costume dramas appealed to women who desired to escape from the domestic confines of the home: "To the housewife of only yesterday who believed that 'woman's place is in the home' these famous and powerful women monarchs were strange people in history books . . . Then something happened . . . They battled their way into the professions, business and politics. They swept aside the old stigmas against actresses, and they set up screen and stage stars as women of ideals and purpose."[57]

Furthermore, many of the historical costume dramas exposed men as weak and effeminate. King Louis XVI in *Marie Antoinette* is a bumbling idiot, suspected of impotency. Lord Darnley in *Mary of Scotland* wears lipstick and earrings and speaks in a high register. Upon first visiting the queen, he comments to her maids that they are "four pretty wenches." One replies, "Five, now that you're here, my lord." And the grand duke in *The*

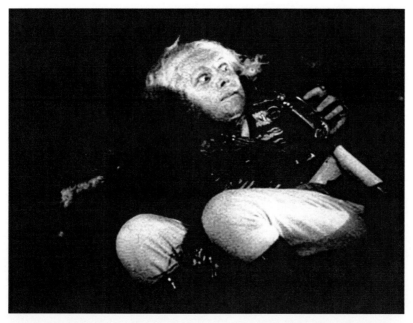

Grand Duke Peter (Sam Jaffe) as an impotent imbecile in Josef von Sternberg's
The Scarlet Empress *(1934). This image of damaged masculinity disturbed U.S.
Left film critics.*

Scarlet Empress is portrayed as an imbecile who plays with toy soldiers and
is dominated by his mother. By destabilizing stereotypical gender roles,
the Depression-era historical costume drama touched upon male Left film
critics' fears that their own gender positions were under attack. As a result, their eventual praise of the male-centered biopic and selective reading of *Juarez* as an ideal embodiment of the techniques used in Renoir's *La
Marseillaise* were symptomatic of the sexist assumptions that had guided
their analysis of historical films ever since Harry Alan Potamkin's praise
of *The Passion of Jean of Arc.*

A NEW DIRECTION: THE BIOPIC AS
HISTORICAL RECOVERY

For many U.S. Left film critics, the rise of the biopic by the mid-1930s
served as the ideal corrective to the historical costume drama. Here was a
set of films that prided themselves on historical research, dealt with broad,
liberal social content, minimized star power for character development,
and centered on powerful men rather than women. Although Twentieth

Century–Fox rivaled Warner Bros. in the output of biopics during the 1930s, U.S. Left film critics emphasized Warner Bros.' films more in their columns because of Warners' clear commitment to social issues in earlier films like *I Am a Fugitive from a Chain Gang* (1932), *Five Star Final* (1931), and *Massacre* (1934), as well as its current commitment, fostered by such liberal employees as John Wesley, Robert Rossen, Howard Koch, John Bright, James Cagney, Edward G. Robinson, Paul Muni, Sylvia Sidney, Karen Morley, Michael Curtiz, Mervyn LeRoy, Lloyd Bacon, and William Wellman. Warners initiated its biopic success with *Disraeli* (1929), starring George Arlis, which won great acclaim from many mainstream critics. But it was only with the release of biopics such as *The Story of Louis Pasteur* (1936) and *The Life of Emile Zola* (1937) that Left film critics and film groups began to take note of the biopic, largely because of the combination of Paul Muni's acting and William Dieterle's direction.

U.S. Left film critics' belief that the biopic's growing prestige was a response to the Left's collective pressure serves as an important addendum to how the biopic has been typically historicized. Thomas Elsaesser has suggested that Warners turned to the biopic as a response to the conservative mandates of the 1934 Production Code. By replacing contemporary social realism with earlier-period historical accuracy, "the bio-pic suggests that the call for censorship was answered not so much by internalization and self-censorship, but by a sort of textual displacement of exhibition values (realism to authenticity; sex to European culture and sophistication; domestic and social issues to world politics)."[58]

But U.S. Popular Front film criticism reveals how the biopic was seen also as a response to progressives' growing strength. In 1937, Peter Ellis observed, in terms similar to Elsaesser's, the differences between Warners' earlier social films and its more recent biopics. According to Ellis, Warners once specialized in "headline" films such as *I Am a Fugitive from a Chain Gang* (1933) and *They Won't Forget* (1937).[59] They were all "muck-racking films. That is good, for we need that type of film. They [were], in a sense, reformist and [told] their story through the process of individual development."[60] However, with the appearance of *The Life of Emile Zola*, the studio inaugurated "a new era in the film industry. For the first time a commercial producer has given us a film with a broad political idea" in its denunciation of war and fascism.[61] Therefore, the textual displacement that Elsaesser sees operating in Warners' biopics as a result of censorship was interpreted by U.S. Left film critics as a political advance: the replacement of films that once focused on individuated stories of domestic hardship with ones that were more politically global in scope and critique, and that resonated with the critics' Popular Front, antifascist stance.

The Muni-Dieterle biopic trilogy—*The Story of Louis Pasteur* (1936), *The Life of Emile Zola* (1937), and *Juarez* (1939)—found particular favor with Left film critics. Not only did the films feature a progressive social agenda and characterizations that challenged many Hollywood norms, but they were also made by people who were clearly sympathetic to Left causes. Paul Muni had already been praised by Left film critics for his work in *I Am a Fugitive from a Chain Gang*.[62] And despite the overall conservative tenor of *Black Fury* (1935), many critics felt that Muni attempted a sympathetic portrait of a miner.[63] Muni has been described by film historian Nick Roddick as "Warners' social conscience actor *par excellence*," since he would not do films that he felt did not address some significant issue, and when he agreed to do such films, he was involved in preproduction script development and production decisions.[64] But it was Dieterle, more than Muni, whom Left film critics really valued.

Dieterle was virtually unknown by Left film critics until he teamed up with Muni on their first film, *Dr. Socrates* (1935). *The Story of Louis Pasteur*, though occasionally praised by Left critics, was generally ignored.[65] *The Life of Emile Zola*, however, received unanimous praise from the Left press for its antifascist stance. Associated Film Audiences wrote to Harry Warner: "*Zola* we believe to be one of the most outstanding pictures with a social theme yet produced by the U.S. film industry. In these times of social unrest and intolerance, any motion picture that speaks out as clearly as *Zola* for social justice is to be commended. Taking a historical incident, it points to a message for today."[66] David Platt claimed: "For the first time Hollywood has desired to give us an historical film that is unmistakably anti-war, anti-fascist all along the line."[67] Peter Ellis wrote: "*Zola*'s fight is indicative of the entire anti-fascist front."[68] The film won three Academy Awards, including those for best picture and best screenplay, and was nominated for another six, including best actor, best direction, and best musical score.[69] Here was a film that could bridge popularity and intelligence, profit and innovation. U.S. Left film critics felt that it showed producers that they could take a risk on a genre that had long been suspect. Margaret Thorp quotes a small-town Wisconsin exhibitor who was pleased to discover "that even the lower classes [that normally reject intellectual fare] enjoyed it."[70]

By 1938, Dieterle had become something of a superstar for U.S. Left film critics. He was actively involved with the Hollywood Anti-Nazi

League, and he cofounded the European Film Fund in October 1939 in order to assist German refugees.[71] His 1938 film *Blockade* not only represented a daring attempt to bring the Spanish Civil War to Hollywood screens, but also fostered wide debate about Hollywood's ability to produce contemporary political films.[72] The *New Masses* reported on his 1937 trip to the Soviet Union and his desire to do a biopic on Karl Marx.[73] Gordon Cassons's observation in the *Daily Worker* was emblematic of U.S. Left film critics' general attitude toward Dieterle: "[He] embodied all that was desirable in a progressive, creative director."[74]

Therefore, U.S. Left film critics held high expectations for Dieterle's next film, *Juarez*. The film was originally conceived as a historical costume drama centered on the doomed love of Empress Carlotta (Bette Davis) and Emperor Maximilian (Brian Aherne), but when Muni became involved in the project, *Juarez* was transformed into a biopic about Indian president Benito Juárez (Paul Muni) and his fight against the French puppet monarchy imposed on Mexico.[75] As a result, the film possesses contradictory impulses both to develop a love story and to chart a political struggle. However, anyone reading U.S. Left film critics' accounts of the film would not be aware of this fact.

Juarez, STARS, AND SCAPEGOATS

As in their responses to *The Life of Emile Zola*, U.S. Left film critics praised *Juarez*'s focus on contemporary antifascist issues like the defense of democracy.[76] James Dugan wrote in the *New Masses* that "as a political event *Juarez* is a proud and heartening thing. When it speaks truthfully on Mexican history it gets to the heart of the Hispano-U.S. relations—Spain today; Cardenas, the true son of Juarez; foreign imperialism in Latin America, in fact the whole problem of rapprochement with Mexico and South America."[77] Just as *La Marseillaise* connected the issues of the French Revolution with those of the Popular Front, *Juarez* linked the struggle for national sovereignty in Mexico in the nineteenth century with its desire for economic sovereignty in the 1930s. The film's focus on Juárez's fight against the political encroachment of France allowed Left film critics to draw connections with Mexican president Lázaro Cárdenas's expropriation of U.S.-based oil companies. Both leaders eventually removed foreign occupying powers from Mexico in order to grant the nation political and economic sovereignty.[78]

From the opening of the film, the editing of *Juarez* announces that this is a film about ideas as much as character. Similar to how Renoir used panning and mise-en-scène to emphasize the collective will of the people as the embodiment of the French Revolution, Dieterle combined Eisensteinian montage with a carefully arranged mise-en-scène to indicate the film's narrative focus on the Mexican people. The film begins with an over-the-shoulder medium shot of Juárez, whose face is not visible, placing a blank sheet of paper on his desk. A close-up shows Juarez's hand writing a proclamation against the new monarchy. A medium shot pans left to Juárez's officers entering the room. A youthful Porfirio Díaz (John Garfield) reads Juarez's proclamation. The lighting illuminates Díaz and the other men but leaves Juarez in darkness, causing his figure to blend in with the people surrounding him. After Díaz finishes reading and the officers approve, a close-up follows of Juarez signing his name to the proclamation, establishing the connection between Juárez's word, the people's approval and action, and the final official signature to transform the proclamation into law. The revolution is dependent on the interaction between the heroic individual and the people. Dieterle, from this opening scene, establishes the film's desire to balance characters with context, and ideas with action. James Dugan observed as much in his *New Masses* review of the film: "Movie habit discerns history in the persons of great men, following the dictum of [Thomas] Carlyle, and when first the movies bring us issues as much as men, the dramatic problem is highly involved. Ill-equipped movie audiences, never expected to lend themselves to this kind of probing under the surfaces, must go to this picture with new eyes."[79]

Further undermining a top-down notion of revolution is the film's populist stance. Juárez learns as much from the people as the people learn from him. Like *La Marseillaise,* which shows how revolutionary leaders emerge from the people themselves, *Juarez* portrays its leader as a man of the people. When trying to construct a military plan against Maximilian, Juárez is introduced to a shepherd named Pepe (Manuel Díaz). Juárez mentions his common origins and asks how Pepe's flock has fared. Pepe replies, "Not so good," since a timber wolf repeatedly attacked his sheep. He explains that, initially, each time a dog would attack, the wolf would bite back. But finally the dogs encircled the wolf, realizing that the wolf would run after the attacking dog. As one dog was chased, another would attack the wolf's flank until they could all close in on the kill. Juárez reflects upon this strategy and replies, "Yes, Pepe, that is the right way to fight the wolf." He then employs the dog-and-wolf strategy against the monarchy's military. Juárez's military strategy is linked to the people, suggesting that both revolutionary thought and action are natural outgrowths of the people and land. Although Juárez is the ultimate arbiter on such matters, his decisions are dependent upon his intimacy with the people.

The film contrasts Juárez's populist outlook by negatively linking Maximilian and Carlotta to spectacle. Pictures of Carlotta dominate the palace's mise-en-scène. Another scene begins with a close-up of Maximilian in a regal cape. The camera pulls back and pans left to expose this image as Maximilian's reflection in a mirror as he gives orders to his generals on how to tailor his cape properly. Spectacle and deception define the monarchy. In another sequence, Juárez's men state that Maximilian changes his clothes four times a day. They also claim that the Indians mistake Maximilian for the white god, Quetzalcóatl, whom Cortés was mistaken for during the conquest, revealing the common imperialism and violence that underlay both regimes. Juárez replies that his men "must strip the cloak of godliness from him [Maximilian] and show him to the Mexican people for what he really is": a dictator. Unlike Juárez, who dresses simply in all black, Maximilian and Carlotta dress extravagantly—as if their dress itself is designed to obfuscate their unjust rule. Juárez's lighting is often high key in a realistic and down-to-earth style. Carlotta, on the other hand, is often filmed in soft focus, emphasizing her aesthetic beauty, unreality, and deception. It is interesting that no Left film critics noticed the film's internal critique of spectacle. These critics stated often enough how spectacle is concerned only with appearance and superficial issues. *Juarez* provides countless examples linking spectacle explicitly to superficiality and injustice. Were U.S. Left film critics too concerned with distancing the film from the costume drama to notice such elements, or did they ignore such elements because any positive acknowledgment would have required a reevaluation of the generally dismissed genre? It is difficult to tell.

One thing that U.S. Left film critics did notice was that like *La Marseillaise, Juarez* offered complex characterizations because of how it revised its use of stars. Dieterle had been critiqued earlier by Left film critics for his simplified characterizations in *The Story of Louis Pasteur* (1936). Peter Ellis asked: "Why the excessive contrasts in characterization, making Pasteur a Messiah and his colleagues inhuman and wooden villains?"[80] Instead of simply idealizing the man as a scientific innovator, Ellis felt that the film should have dealt with Pasteur's arrogance and conservatism, since "this full complexity of the man [would have] provided the material for a much higher and more dramatic film than the present product."[81] With *Juarez,* however, U.S. Left film critics felt that Dieterle had learned his lesson. James Dugan wrote that the film's stars "are scattered throughout a picture in enforcedly small footage."[82] Unlike most star-studded films, in which the spectacular presence of the stars dominates the film's narrative and ideas, Dugan felt that the stars in *Juarez* "are fitted into a real story, worthy of them."[83] He went on to note that "movies have accustomed us to black and white villains and heroes. Here the nominal characteristics are reversed: Juarez is cold and ugly, the emperor warm and handsome, and both roles are lighted up with profound psychological understanding. Benito Juarez is democracy incarnate and the Hapsburg is a kind of exception to monarchy."[84] Yet Dugan's final sentence reveals one of the central problems with the film: Juárez seems more like the incarnation of the principle of democracy than a rounded character, whereas Maximilian seems more like a person than a mere symbol of monarchy.

Maximilian is humanized because of his intimate relationship with Carlotta, whereas Juárez seems close to no one and yet everyone. Although Juárez is supposed to love "the people," he always seems remote, too caught up in his principles to notice those around him. Maximilian, on the other hand, attempts to maintain a close relationship with Carlotta as the revolution threatens their happiness. As Leger Grindon observes: "The film centers on European royalty victimized by politics through the agency of Juarez, a national savior, but also a stern, superhuman figure who destroys romance."[85] The film thus emulates a similar structure found at work within *Marie Antoinette* and other costume dramas that pit political revolution against its central couple's romantic happiness.

Left film critics were aware of the film's imbalance at the time, but rather than focusing on how the love story is set in opposition to Juárez's political fight, they saw the film as marked by opposing narratives about men: Maximilian versus Juárez. James Dugan wrote: "The picture is out of balance. To put it bluntly, Maximilian almost wins" by being given undue sympathy, beyond that accorded Juárez.[86] Erased from this account is the importance of Carlotta in creating sympathy for Maximilian. In a relationship typical of the historical-costume-drama formula, the weak leader Maximilian is under Carlotta's thumb. She directs his actions and ambitions. From the very beginning of the film, Carlotta worries about her influence upon Maximilian. She tells him, "But you must never let my own opinions influence your own best judgment." Yet they do, finally causing her to confess, "It was I who said accept the crown. It was I who said don't abdicate. I alone am responsible, and I will help you now" by going back to France to demand from Louis-Napoléon military support to conquer Juárez's troops.

But by making Maximilian subservient to her will, Carlotta takes all the blame for Maximilian's political misjudgment. She becomes the displaced site of male culpability and failure. This is similar to how *La Marseillaise* creates sympathy for Louis XVI by making Marie Antoinette the dominating force and thus the figure responsible for a weak king's decisions. As Leger Grindon writes: "The queen, identified as a subversive foreigner whose power over her husband threatens national unity, is the chief enemy of the Revolution."[87] While James Dugan ignores how blame is displaced upon Carlotta in *Juarez*, he obliquely acknowledges this dynamic at work in Renoir's film: "Lise Delamore [*sic*] as Marie Antoinette is enough to uncurl Norma Shearer's hair in her portrayal of the beautiful, ignorant, and vain Austrian."[88] Unmentioned, however, is how Delamare's role serves as a scapegoat for the king's ill-designed policies. By focusing blame on a strong spouse, both Dugan and the films suggest that monstrous political decisions arise more from "imbalanced" domestic relationships than from the hierarchal and unjust structures of patriarchal rule.

U.S. Left film critics' analyses of *Juarez* encapsulated their general stance toward all late-1930s progressive Hollywood historical films: emphasize the relations between form and antifascist themes while ignoring gender issues. As a final example, we can see this dynamic at work in a review of *Abe Lincoln in Illinois* (1940). James Dugan notes somewhat hyperbolically that the movie was "not filmic in its conception, but teaches the movie audience as the best and most explicit political film made in this country."[89] He particularly highlights one of Lincoln's speeches: "This country with its institutions belongs to the people who inhabit it. Whenever they shall grow weary of the existing government they can exercise their constitutional right to amend it or their revolutionary right to dismember and overthrow it."[90]

However, once again overlooked is how the film positions Mary Todd (Ruth Gordon), the future wife of Lincoln (Raymond Massey), as the embodiment of calculating and heartless political ambition. She incarnates Lincoln's repressed political desires. Both attracted and repulsed by Todd, Lincoln finally confesses to a friend, "I have to tell her I have hatred for her eternal ambition. That I don't want to be ridden and driven onward and upward through life with her whip dashing me and her spurs digging into me." But his friend calls Lincoln's bluff, "You're not abandoning Miss Mary Todd. No, you're only using her as a living sacrifice, offering her up in the hope that you'll gain forgiveness for your failure to do your own great duty," which requires those very aspects of her personality that he does not want to recognize in himself. *Abe Lincoln in Illinois* remains unique among historical biopics in how it draws attention to the genre's tendency to make women function as "living sacrifices" for male deficiencies and desires. Yet Dugan only vaguely comments that "Ruth Gordon as the ambitious shrew, Mary Todd Lincoln, contributes much to the unusual picture of a great man's family life," thus brushing aside the gender insights that the film had to offer by instead primarily focusing upon the "great man" rather than on "the ambitious shrew."[91] In *Juarez*, Carlotta functions in the very same way for Maximilian—though not one U.S. Left film critic even mentioned that the film portrays Maximilian as an extremely weak man, an item that would have strengthened their case for the film's liberal sympathies for Juárez and revolution, but that would also have drawn gender to the forefront of their analyses.

One possible answer for Left film critics' silence on Maximilian's weakness is that their gender loyalty and fears trumped their gender and class analysis. The film, time and again, emphasizes Maximilian's weakness before Carlotta. In many scenes of Maximilian speaking with his political ministers, an enormous painting of Carlotta, dead center in the frame, dominates the shot, suggesting that even when she is not physically present, her influence dominates Maximilian's thoughts and actions, which, as mentioned earlier, the narrative underlines.

Carlotta's power serves as an interesting contrast to Davis's own real-life battle with Warners over her career. Davis for years pushed for complex, strong female roles. But Warners failed to capitalize on Davis's desires, instead placing her in weak, formulaic, second-rate roles. Finally, after Warners refused to let her play the lead in John Ford's RKO production *Mary, Queen of Scots,* a role that she highly valued, Davis refused to appear in any Warners pictures until her status at the studio improved. Davis sued Warners and stayed out of pictures for nearly a year. Although she lost her suit, Warners began offering her roles that she desired. The first role she received when she returned to Warners was Mary Dwight in the female-centered gangster picture *Marked Woman* (1937). Shortly thereafter, Warners purchased the rights to a property that Davis coveted, *Jezebel* (1938), for which she won her second Oscar.[92]

All this backstory, which was fairly well known at the time by film critics, was conveniently overlooked by James Dugan. Here was an actress fighting hard against the studio hierarchy for the very type of character development that Left film critics desired but failed to notice when women were advancing their program. Tellingly, Dugan mentions Bette Davis's performance only at her character's weakest moment: her descent into madness at the end of the film. Dugan notes: "Bette Davis has a virtuoso opportunity in Carlotta and she wrings every effect from it: the mad scene in Louis Napoleon's palace is fearfully dramatic business, handled with inspiration by William Dieterle."[93] Notice how Dugan situates Davis's performance within Dieterle's handling, thus deemphasizing Davis's acting while highlighting it, and totally effacing her struggle to obtain powerful roles.

Carlotta's descent into madness can be seen as the film's narrative attempt to punish this strong female character's (and star's) transgression of male control. Before going insane, she bursts into Louis-Napoléon's conference room. Accusing him of setting up Maximilian as a patsy for his own ambitions, she yells, "A bourgeois Napoléon: a charlatan. A murderer. A murderer," before passing out. But even after going insane, Carlotta remains a perceptive character who detects the ruse behind Louis-Napoléon's rule, while her husband remains oblivious of such political realities. With a vacant stare, Carlotta tells a prince that "they want to kill me. People think that he is emperor because he wears a crown on his head. But I know better. He hates mankind. His purpose is to debase humanity, to rob men of their godliness until they turn against one another and destroy themselves like beasts." Unlike her husband, who believes to the end in the justice of monarchical power, Carlotta eventually recognizes the corruption at the heart of Louis-Napoléon's regime. She comes to a political awakening while her husband does not, and offers a stronger criticism of the emperor than any other character in the film. Despite the film's conservative tendency to demonize Carlotta throughout, its ending implies that she nonetheless was the true heir to power rather than her husband: she understood how power operates, whereas her husband was lost in abstract monarchical principles that had very little to do with the daily demands of ruling a kingdom.

Two parallel scenes at the end of the film indicate that Carlotta, not Maximilian, was Juárez's true adversary. Before Maximilian is executed, Carlotta, captured in long shot, sits in a chair on the right side of the frame. Through an enormous window to her left, light descends onto her through the room's dust. The low lighting suggests both mystery and madness as she leaves her chair, goes to the window, and calls out to Maximilian as if provided with a premonition of his execution. After Maximilian's death, Juárez is seen in long shot in a chapel. A window to the right filters light onto him as he slowly walks to the altar to ask forgiveness for having executed Maximilian. The reversal of light from Carlotta's scene implies that Juárez is on the right side, whereas Carlotta is in the wrong. But the parallel mise-en-scènes of the episodes also suggest how these opposites meet: the two figures both posses intimate knowledge of how political power works; they both transform their political ideals into reality; and they both realize that Maximilian was nothing but a pawn in an international political game.

Finally, both characters come to a fuller knowledge of problems attending their different beliefs about government: Carlotta realizes the corruption of the monarchy under Louis-Napoléon; Juárez understands how his adherence to democratic principles nonetheless forced him to put to death a man who ultimately did not deserve to die. In the film's recognition of Carlotta's intelligence and the rightness of Juarez's fight for democracy, we see how *Juarez* is pulled between costume drama and biopic. But the film's dual impulses tend to make Juárez's victory, at best, bittersweet, and Carlotta's political insight comes only after her character is demonized for the first two-thirds of the film.

CONCLUSION

One of the most interesting conclusions to be drawn from U.S. Left film critics' analyses of *Juarez* is that they were actually very far from being too critical of Hollywood films; indeed, they were not critical enough. Although they pointed to some of the film's flaws, their critiques stopped short of recognizing how the inclusion of progressive content in commercial films was both hindered and assisted by conservative Hollywood genres like the historical costume drama. By wanting to claim *Juarez* as an ideal progressive Hollywood film, U.S. Left film critics minimized the film's conflicted political impulses in favor of clear and uncomplicated progressive readings. With its liberal sympathies, *Juarez* might have helped advance a progressive political project, but it seems more interesting to a contemporary film historian for its hybrid attempt to unite melodrama with a progressive politics, romance with social action, "bourgeois," individual characterization with social commentary—in essence, all the elements of a biopic with those of a historical costume drama. Although U.S. Left film critics had from the mid-1930s advocated that a progressive political agenda be fused with commercial cinematic conventions, they failed to note the interesting results and contradictions that emerged when such a project was enacted in a film like *Juarez*.

By the late 1930s, Jean Renoir's films were serving as models from which U.S. Left film critics began formulating an alternative socio-aesthetic framework to montage. Although somewhat ill equipped to define Renoir's innovative stylistic techniques, Left critics used close film analysis to begin identifying some key ways in which these techniques offered the sort of dialectical, totalistic vision that they had been advocating since their original discussions of montage theory. This provided them with a sophisticated understanding of how commercial films might be inflected in progressive directions.

At the same time, U.S. Left film critics' implicit theoretical reliance upon a male gaze once again foreclosed their ability to note how female-centered genres could assist their goal of creating a progressive film culture, or how Left directors like Renoir were exploring the necessity of challenging traditional gender roles if progressive change were to take place. U.S. Left film criticism steadfastly resisted a reevaluation of its problematic gender assumptions, which had haunted it since its origins and which would continue into the 1940s as critics focused on other male-centered genres and styles like the war film, the boxing film, and film noir. Seeing gender mainly as a metaphor, if at all, and historical costume dramas as examples of reactionary spectacular excess, Left film criticism failed to acknowledge the crucial ways in which gender identities were taking on new configurations around them. As a result, U.S. Left film criticism held a contradictory ideological position: a utopian hope to create progressive films that would allow audiences to envision themselves in egalitarian and collectively empowering ways, and a reactionary desire to hold on to older structures of male privilege, which the Depression, the historical costume drama, and consumer culture were challenging.

Conclusion

FRAGMENTS OF THE FUTURE

By the late 1930s, the U.S. Popular Front had begun to splinter. The 1936 Moscow Trials opened a rift in the historical Left between Trotskyites and Stalinists. Although the trials were later shown to have been horrifying frame-ups that led to the executions of many participants in the Russian Revolution, U.S. Left writers at the time were unclear about their exact meaning. In 1937, John Dewey headed a commission that traveled to Mexico, where Trotsky was in political asylum, to investigate treasonous allegations Stalin had leveled against Trotsky. The commission found Trotsky innocent.[1]

The Trotskyite and Stalinist division served as a major impetus behind the creation of the anti-Stalinist Left, which adhered to some Marxist principles but rejected its more radical tenets. Philip Rahv, Williams Phillips, Clement Greenberg, and Dwight Macdonald were some of its key figures. Together they relaunched the *Partisan Review* in 1937 as its flagship journal. In its pages, anti-Stalinists recast the 1930s U.S. Left as nothing more than an assembly of vulgar and reactionary Marxists. In an effort to distance themselves from their previous radical politics, the anti-Stalinist Left derided the organizations they once belonged to and the beliefs that they had once held dear. As the Cold War heated up, the myths they conjured up about the 1930s U.S. Left ossified into the dry husks of unsubstantiated fact, bearing little resemblance to the rich complexities of the actual cultural moment.[2]

A perfect example of how the anti-Stalinist Left refashioned older Left concepts into a conservative framework can be seen in their attitude toward kitsch. Clement Greenberg's essay "Avant-Garde and Kitsch" (1939) offers a dramatic contrast to Hanns Sachs's 1932 *Close Up* essay on the same subject, which is discussed in Chapter One. Although Greenberg's essay has been canonized as a theoretical breakthrough that established the boundaries between a high-art, avant-garde tradition and the supposed dreck of mass art facilitated by modernization, the context of its emergence has often been effaced.

A year and a half before Greenberg's piece appeared, Dwight Macdonald wrote a three-part series concerning the recent commercialization of Soviet cinema. Macdonald claims that with the arrival of Stalin's totalitarianism, Russian cinema metamorphosed from a challenging and innovative experimental form to a standardized commercial product indistinguishable from Hollywood films.[3] The Soviet regime rejected the avant-garde, according to Macdonald, because it did not want films that stimulated its populace's critical thought and encouraged internationalism, which could challenge Stalin's absolutist reign. Macdonald holds that the Soviet populace was being subtly conditioned to desire banal and standardized films. He asserts that if audiences desire to see these films, "it is largely because they have been conditioned to shun 'formalism' and to admire 'socialist realism.'"[4] Although Macdonald holds a rather passive view of Soviet spectators, which would most likely trouble contemporary film scholars, Greenberg felt that Macdonald attributed too much autonomy to the Soviet masses and wrote "Avant-Garde and Kitsch" in response.

For Greenberg, the kitsch found in Soviet films and international cinema was not the result of a repressive political regime's transformation of art into an opiate for the masses, but a direct result of the masses' desire for mindless entertainment. The problems with Soviet film, according to Greenberg, were due not to Stalin's cultural mandates, but to Stalin giving the masses precisely what they wanted: kitsch.[5] Greenberg believes that Macdonald's and other Left critics' desire to harness socialism for cultural uplift was a bankrupt proposition, since such a project inevitably would never improve the masses' tastes but would instead lead to the ultimate degradation of the avant-garde tradition as it became mired in the general populace's regressive sensibilities.[6]

The avant-garde, for Greenberg, was the only remaining high-art realm free from mass commodification. His essay is a plea to use socialism not for the masses, but to preserve the cultural sanctity of an apolitical avant-garde. As Andrew Ross observes in *No Respect: Intellectuals and Popular Culture,* a fear of contagion permeates Greenberg's essay. Kitsch symbolizes a virus that destroys the distinction between the realms of high and low art. The cultural critic must endlessly fight against the seemingly inevitable commodification that intrudes upon once-autonomous realms of art when the barbarities of modernization and democracy seize control.[7]

Underlying Greenberg's argument is the assumption that there once were clear lines of demarcation between high and low art. But as this book has demonstrated, these lines were far from apparent to early-1930s U.S.

Left film theorists and critics. Such distinctions were instituted by Greenberg and other writers at the *Partisan Review* in order to force earlier cultural moments into a framework that sheared off their historical specificity and effaced the reactionary and antidemocratic spirit of anti-Stalinist Left revisionist criticism. For example, if we glance back at Hanns Sachs's essay, we see that unlike Greenberg, he does not view kitsch as a powerful contagion that threatens to wipe out progressive art. Kitsch, for Sachs, is not the endgame of industrialization, but only a limiting style that can be found in all art of every age. Sachs asserts that "kitsch no more finds a permanent resting place in its age than it does in the soul of the individual," because it never really affects the spectator strongly enough to make a lasting impression.[8] It is the ever-disposable commodity. As soon as it is created, it becomes outdated. Kitsch cannot encroach on more innovative artistic styles because it does not possess the integrity to do so. Sachs's hopeful outlook strongly contrasts with Greenberg's fear of both modernization and democracy.[9] For Greenberg, kitsch's abundance is the result of the masses' demand for it. Kitsch, for Sachs, is only a style used to limit spectators by inhibiting complex emotions and perspectives—an approach that Dwight Macdonald similarly advocates in his essay.

The fact that Greenberg's notion of kitsch has prevailed over Sachs's in the historical record is more representative of the politically reactionary state of contemporary cultural scholarship and its lack of historical perspective than the inherent merits of one theory over the other. Yet some scholars of the historical Left, like Michael Denning, Paula Rabinowitz, and Robin D. G. Kelley, have plunged into the archives and primary sources and excavated beneath the tundra of Cold War histories to expose a much more vibrant and complex Left culture than has previously been portrayed. This book has followed similar lines of approach.

Another event that provoked the dissolution of the U.S. Popular Front was the Nazi-Soviet Pact of August 24, 1939. Suddenly, the communists reneged on their antifascist stance, casting themselves (briefly) as isolationists. Dumbfounded by this jarring reversal of positions, many fellow travelers felt betrayed by their comrades who adopted this new line. Antifascism had served as the lynchpin holding the Popular Front together. As Chapter Three shows, antifascism provided a strong metaphor with which critics could address and compare domestic and international oppression while eliding the sorts of divisive class issues that had previously troubled transracial political alliances. Without its antifascist stance, the Popular Front was left reeling.[10]

At the same time, Hollywood was coming under increasing investigation and attack by anticommunists. In September 1938, Martin Dies, a House Democrat, announced his intent to investigate communist infiltration of the major film studios. Similarly, in 1941, Jack Tenney, chairman of the Joint Fact-Finding Committee on Un-American Activities of the California legislature, launched another commission to investigate "enemy aliens in the film industry."[11] Although both investigations yielded no conclusive proof of communist subversion, they indicated a growing conservative tide that would swell after Roosevelt's death and the conclusion of World War II, and crash upon the studios during the House Un-American Activities Committee hearings of October 1947.

Despite the increasing problems concerning the U.S. Popular Front and the historical Left in general, U.S. Left film critics maintained their focus on film content concerning race, antifascism, and the working class. They critiqued the racist revisionism of David Selznick's *Gone with the Wind* (1939) and celebrated *Confessions of a Nazi Spy*'s (1939), an exposé of the Nazi bund.[12] They praised John Ford's adaptation of John Steinbeck's *The Grapes of Wrath* (1940) for highlighting the plight of migrant laborers.[13]

Paul Buhle and Dave Wagner in *Radical Hollywood* have provided invaluable information about how U.S. Left film theory and criticism reconfigured itself during and after World War II. They note that the 1941 League of American Writers Congress foregrounded screenwriting by drawing together Left film workers like John Howard Lawson, Paul Jarrico, John Bright, and Paul Strand.[14] Furthermore, U.S. Left film theory and criticism became more integrated with universities, represented by UCLA's sponsorship of the *Hollywood Quarterly* (1945–1950), which introduced readers to a wide variety of writers like Lewis Jacobs, Abraham Polonsky, Theodor Adorno, and Siegfried Kracauer. The *Hollywood Quarterly* served as the locus for film theory in the 1940s, just as *Close Up* and *Experimental Cinema* did during the late 1920s and early 1930s.

Future scholarship needs to theoretically bridge 1930s and 1940s U.S. Left film theory and criticism in order to identify their points of contact, development, and divergence. How, for example, did critics and screenwriters who focused on film noir in the 1940s redeploy a sexist male gaze that prioritized male-centered genres over female-centered ones? How did the outlook of writers like Lewis Jacobs and Seymour Stern, whose work stretches across decades, change and why? Such questions demand not only a conceptualization that spans decades, but also a much more systematic and thorough analysis of U.S. Left film theory and criticism within specific periods.

Also, more work needs to be done in tracing the transnational links between international Left aesthetic debates. For example, positions taken by U.S. Left film theorists and critics generally resonated with the debates on realism conducted by Theodor Adorno, Walter Benjamin, Ernst Bloch, Bertolt Brecht, and Georg Lukács in Germany. On one level, Left film theorists' and critics' focus on radical montage during the early part of the 1930s adhered to a Brechtian-Benjaminian position that viewed film as a central medium in reconfiguring the fragmented world into a more totalistic framework. On another level, Left film theorists' and critics' focus on totality resonated with Lukács's similar theoretical focus rather than with that of Brecht and Benjamin, who considered the concept overly reductive. As a result, this early phase of U.S. Left film theory and criticism incorporated opposing tendencies of the German debates.

Similarly, U.S. Left film critics' Popular Front orientation by middecade can be considered an even more explicit link with Lukács in its prioritization of linear narrative and character development to draw together the individual and his or her social environment into dialectical tension through a totalistic framework. Yet at the same time, they celebrated Renoir not for his realist tendencies but for being an innovative modernist director who employed mise-en-scène and the long take for progressive ends. These critics weren't pining over a nineteenth-century form, as Lukács was, but were instead searching for emerging developments in cinematic form that could be aligned with classical Hollywood narratives and a Left outlook.

Finally, U.S. Left film theorists' and critics' concern with altering viewers' modes of reception by providing discussions after screenings, advocating audience organizations, and using their writing to foster critical spectatorship speaks to Brecht's own practices of breaking the fourth wall, utilizing nontraditional theatrical spaces, and talking to audiences. Both were aware of how modes of reception must be redefined if cultural forms and modes of production are to be radicalized. Practices of cultural consumption, in other words, are inextricably intertwined with specific socio-aesthetic forms. A circuit exists between producer and consumer. If one is to change, then so must the other. A critically engaged spectator must supplant the bourgeois consumer of yesteryear.

This is not to claim that there was a direct link between U.S. Left film theory and criticism and the German realist debates. My research shows that U.S. film theorists and critics were largely unaware of the writings of Adorno, Bloch, and Benjamin during the early to mid 1930s—Brecht and Lukács were the sole exceptions. Instead, these transnational links need to be sketched so that Left cultural scholarship might better identify and theorize an extremely rich body of work that has only recently been recognized.

Overall, as Michael Denning points out, 1930s U.S. Left film theorists and critics "wrote the first serious studies of the popular arts in the United States . . . They were the first to develop a lasting film criticism and history in journals like *Experimental Cinema, Filmfront,* and *Hollywood Quarterly,* and in the work of figures like Harry Potamkin, the young proletarian critic who died at the age of thirty-three in 1933, Lewis Jacobs, whose *The Rise of the American Film* (1939) was the first major history of film, and Jay Leyda, the translator and editor of Eisenstein's writings on film."[15]

Furthermore, for better or worse, U.S. Left film theory and criticism unconsciously structures much contemporary film history and theory. As mentioned in Chapter Three, it undergirds many contemporary accounts of Fritz Lang's *Fury.* Sadly, its celebration of masculine aesthetic forms and media at the expense of female-centered, "feminine" ones carries over into much contemporary film theory and new-media debates.[16] Many of its concerns returned like specters from a forgotten time in the pages of *Screen, Jump Cut, Cahiers du Cinema,* and *Positif* during the 1960s and 1970s—which is not entirely surprising, since many of these later debates were spurred by an exploration of the foundational texts of montage theory.

Depression-era U.S. Left film theory and criticism marked the first sustained body of ideological film analysis written in the United States. As Tom Brandon succinctly put it:

> The most consciously probing concern with film at the time was found in the Left and Communist press. These publications strove to formulate answers to film problems on both levels [of aesthetics and ideology]. The consolidation of the talkies coincided with the opening of the Thirties, and also with the onset of the Great Depression, and against that background the progressive press was to come to the fore as the arena of film comment. Indeed, the equation between aesthetic concerns and social goals was to be the principal thesis/antithesis of the film dialectic of the 1930s.[17]

The reason that it deserves further attention is because many of the problems that define this body of work still haunt us. To dismiss it as vulgar is not only a form of intellectual arrogance that forecloses our ability to adequately theorize the cultural matrices of the past, but also an implicit form of political resignation that rejects the study of radical film culture as somehow irrelevant to present concerns.

This study, in essence, offers an intricate sketch of a moment in time when international and U.S. Left filmmakers, theorists, and critics imagined a film culture that was politically Left, modernist, and popular. Although this body of work possesses some severe limitations, it also reveals significant theoretical breakthroughs. I have tried neither to glamorize nor demonize 1930s U.S. Left film theorists and critics, but instead to trace some of the contours of their writings so that we might better understand their and our own theoretical insights about film, politics, mass culture, and gender. Ultimately, I hope that this study represents a moment of contact between past and present theoretical and political concerns. After all, as Walter Benjamin wrote, historical understanding is "the afterlife of that which has been understood and whose pulse can be traced in the present."[18]

But like all attempts to create links between the past and present, this one is filtered through my own psyche and the ideological constraints of the present moment. As Marxism never fails to remind us, there is no unmediated access to history. But at the same time, one must not relinquish the search. The desire to know a moment in history, even if always at some remove, represents not only an intellectual paradox but also an ontological one. I am reminded of a particularly moving scene from Queen Christina. Christina (Garbo) pretends to be a male attendant instead of a queen at the remote lodge where she meets Prince Antonio (John Gilbert) of Spain. After Antonio discovers that she is a woman and they enjoy a night of sex and romance, she slowly circles the room they share, taking in each of its objects through sight, smell, touch, and taste. Her desire to connect with the moment's underlying reality is both beautiful and tragic: beautiful in that she takes such care to notice the most minuscule details surrounding each object, yet tragic in that no matter how much she observes and records, it will never be enough to recover the experience. The fleetingness of the moment is suggested when she sees Antonio's reflection in a mirror. She at first smiles back to him, but gradually frowns, as if realizing the mirror's symbolism: reality has already slipped into representation. The tragedy of the scene is heightened because both Christina and the viewer realize that she must soon return to her role as queen and all the responsibilities that it entails. The scene expresses a utopian desire to step outside one's social confines in order to experience a reality that one normally never has access to.

This scene somewhat parallels the politically engaged scholar's own desires: to be able to step outside one's own limited ideological and historical confines in order to experience and know a moment that is utterly alien yet engaging, a moment that can perhaps redirect us toward more open and better futures. Yet, like Christina, all we can do is observe the surface of things because the moment itself has already long since passed. Terry Eagleton notes how history itself operates in an identical manner: "History is 'present' in the text in the form of a double-absence. The text takes as its object, not the real, but certain significations by which the real itself lives—significations which are themselves the product of its partial abolition."[19]

Whether one wants to look at the matter theoretically, as Eagleton does, or tragically, as Christina does, our desire to know and reexperience that which escapes us is nonetheless valuable, since it opens up previously in-accessible avenues of thought and actions. These pursuits help us not only see more clearly where we are currently located, but also notice its contin-gency—along with our ability to alter our situations for the better. I hope that this work has the subtlety of Christina's touch to open up at least one or two such avenues for future study.

Notes

INTRODUCTION

The letter from Tom Brandon quoted in the epigraph is in file D40, Tom Brandon Archives, Film Studies Center, Museum of Modern Art, New York (hereafter cited as Tom Brandon Archives).

1. As of 2010, only a relatively small amount of work had been conducted regarding U.S. Left film criticism, and a majority of the studies appeared more than two decades ago. See Myron Osborn Lounsbury, *The Origins of American Film Criticism, 1909-1939;* William Alexander, *Film on the Left: American Documentary Film from 1931 to 1942;* Russell Campbell, *Cinema Strikes Back: Radical Filmmaking in the United States, 1930-1942;* and Anna Everett, *Returning the Gaze: A Genealogy of Black Film Criticism, 1909-1949.*

2. Rohama Lee, "World Cinema: The Brandon Story," *Film News* 28, no. 3 (1971): 18.

3. Ibid., 17-21, 27.

4. Tom Brandon, unpublished MS, file D43, 76a, Tom Brandon Archives.

5. Ibid., 79.

6. Hurwitz is quoted in Tom Brandon to members of the New York Film and Photo League, September 4, 1974, file D40, Tom Brandon Archives.

7. Ibid.

8. Fredric Jameson, *The Political Unconscious: Narrative as a Socially Symbolic Act,* 35.

9. Ibid., 29-30, 81.

10. Ibid., 40.

11. Michael Denning, *Culture in the Age of Three Worlds,* 120.

12. Walter Benjamin, "Eduard Fuchs: Collector and Historian," 227.

13. Ibid., 233. Raymond Williams develops this notion well in his discussion of the dominant, residual, and emergent (*Marxism and Literature,* 121-127).

14. Walter Benjamin, "Theses on the Philosophy of History," 255.

15. Ibid., 262-263.

16. Ibid., 255.

17. Brandon, unpublished MS, file D43, 6.

18. Ibid.

19. Andrew Ross, *No Respect: Intellectuals and Popular Culture*, 4–5.

20. Benjamin, "Philosophy of History," 255.

21. The scholarship regarding modernity's effects upon U.S. culture is too vast to fully document here. For some of the most outstanding contributions, see Alan Trachtenberg, *The Incorporation of America: Culture and Society in the Gilded Age*; Kathy Peiss, *Cheap Amusements: Working Women and Leisure in Turn-of-the-Century New York*; William Leach, *Land of Desire: Merchants, Power, and the Rise of a New American Culture*; Lauren Rabinovitz, *For the Love of Pleasure: Women, Movies, and Culture in Turn-of-the-Century Chicago*; Nan Enstad, *Ladies of Labor, Girls of Adventure: Working Women, Popular Culture, and Labor Politics at the Turn of the Twentieth Century*; and Ben Singer, *Melodrama and Modernity: Early Sensational Cinema and Its Contexts*.

22. See Haidee Wasson, *Museum Movies: The Museum of Modern Art and the Birth of Art Cinema*; Dana Polan, *Scenes of Instruction: The Beginnings of the U.S. Study of Film*; Greg Taylor, *Artists in the Audience: Cults, Camp, and American Film Criticism*; Peter Decherney, *Hollywood and the Culture Elite: How the Movies Became American*; and Raymond J. Haberski, Jr., *"It's Only a Movie": Films and Critics in American Culture*.

23. Wasson, *Museum Movies*, 13.

24. In addition to Wasson, *Museum Movies*; Polan, *Scenes of Instruction*; and Decherney, *Hollywood and the Culture Elite*; see Anne Morey, *Hollywood Outsiders: The Adaptation of the Film Industry, 1913-1934*, Gregory D. Black, *Hollywood Censored: Morality Codes, Catholics, and the Movies*; and Lea Jacobs, *The Wages of Sin: Censorship and the Fallen Woman Film, 1928-1942*.

25. Brandon, unpublished MS, file D43, 29–30.

26. Sylvia Harvey, *May '68 and Film Culture*, 24.

27. U.S. Left film theory and criticism supports Lee Grieveson and Haidee Wasson's claim that "the twin poles of sociopolitical critique and aesthetic analysis that constitute standard maps of the discipline [of film studies] have in fact played themselves out in various ways across a long history of studying cinema" ("The Academy and Motion Pictures," xvi). I would further add that the 1930s represent the first convergence of these two tendencies for radical political purposes in the United States.

28. Walter Benjamin, "The Author as Producer," 229.

29. Brandon, unpublished MS, file D43, 59b.

30. Miriam Hansen, "The Mass Production of the Senses: Classical Cinema as Vernacular Modernism," 337.

31. David Bordwell, Janet Staiger, and Kristin Thompson, *The Classical Hollywood Cinema: Film Style and Mode of Production to 1960*, 311–312.

32. Some important sources regarding Hollywood unionization are Murray Ross, *Stars and Strikes: Unionization of Hollywood*; Nancy Lynn Schwartz, *The Hollywood Writers' Wars*; and Gerald Horne, *Class Struggle in Hollywood, 1930-1950: Moguls, Mobsters, Stars, Reds, and Trade Unionists*.

33. Hansen, "Mass Production of the Senses," 341.

34. Robert Sklar, *Movie-Made America: A Cultural History of American Movies*, 162.

35. For the argument that Wall Street bankers straitjacketed Hollywood, see Lewis Jacobs, *The Rise of American Film: A Critical History*, and Colin Shindler, *Hollywood in Crisis: Cinema and American Society, 1929-1939*.

36. Thomas Schatz's book *The Genius of the System: Hollywood Filmmaking in the Studio Era* is particularly informative about how producers used their intimate knowledge of the film industry to manipulate Wall Street, continue turning out high-cost productions, maintain their lofty salaries, and impose many of their general whims.

37. Although Fitzgerald has often been classified as an apolitical figure, Ring Lardner, Jr., and others insisted that "Scott thought of himself as quite a communist" at the time he wrote the novel (quoted in Nancy Schwartz, *Writers' Wars*, 145). Supposedly rejected for membership in the Communist Party because of his excessive drinking, Fitzgerald remained politically progressive, and his fear of and fascination with Hollywood was shared by many other progressive filmmakers, scriptwriters, and critics of the time.

38. Fitzgerald, *The Last Tycoon*, 58.

39. Ibid., 48.

40. William Dieterle, "Will Hollywood Give Up Intelligence?" *Liberty* 7 (December 1940): 30.

41. Ibid., 31.

42. Matthew Bernstein, *Walter Wanger: Hollywood Independent*, 23.

43. Ibid., 37.

44. Ibid., 85.

45. James Dugan, "Movies," *New Masses*, August 2, 1938, 30.

46. Bernstein, *Walter Wanger*, 140. For more information regarding *Blockade* and the U.S. cultural Left, see Greg M. Smith, "Blocking *Blockade*: Partisan Protest, Popular Debate, and Encapsulated Texts," *Cinema Journal* 36, no. 1 (Fall 1996): 18-38.

47. Schatz, *Genius of the System*, 135.

48. Ibid., 141.

49. Ibid., 142-148.

50. Leo C. Rosten, *Hollywood: The Movie Colony, the Movie Makers*, 174-175.

51. Michael E. Birdwell, *Celluloid Soldiers: Warner Bros.'s Campaign against Nazism*, 19, 29.

52. Rosten, *Hollywood*, 154.

53. For more information regarding the Left's involvement within Hollywood, see Saverio Giovacchini, *Hollywood Modernism: Film and Politics in the Age of the New Deal*; Nancy Schwartz, *Writers' Wars*; and Larry Ceplair and Steven Englund, *The Inquisition in Hollywood: Politics in the Film Community, 1930-1960*.

54. For more information regarding the connections between Left Holly-

wood filmmakers and those in the avant-garde and documentary communities, see Jan-Christopher Horak, ed., *Lovers of Cinema: The First American Film Avant-Garde, 1919-1945.*

55. Brandon, unpublished MS, file D43, 11.

56. Giovacchini, *Hollywood Modernism,* 83.

57. Neal Gabler, *An Empire of Their Own: How the Jews Invented Hollywood,* 328.

58. Ibid., 329.

59. Giovacchini, *Hollywood Modernism,* 84.

60. Ibid., 85.

61. Ibid., 86.

62. Margaret Farrand Thorp, *America at the Movies,* 149. Mooney was a labor leader framed for the death of ten people during a bomb explosion in 1916. He remained in jail for more than twenty years. The Salinas strike was a month-long strike by lettuce workers for higher wages. This strike was a part of the 1933-1934 California farm strikes, which involved up to 50,000 workers (Watkins, *The Great Depression: America in the 1930s,* 199).

63. Joseph North, "The New Hollywood," *New Masses,* July 11, 1939, 14.

64. Michael Denning, *The Cultural Front: The Laboring of American Culture in the Twentieth Century,* 88-89.

65. Ibid., 89; Nancy Schwartz, *Writers' Wars,* 188.

66. Ceplair and Englund, *Inquisition in Hollywood,* 18.

67. Denning, *Cultural Front,* 89. The Popular Front represented a change in Communist Party ideology away from a radical anticapitalist stance to a more moderate political approach in working with bourgeois nations against fascism. This change in outlook was initiated in 1935 during the Seventh Congress of the Communist International.

68. Quoted in Nancy Schwartz, *Writers' Wars,* 67.

69. North, "New Hollywood," 14.

70. Jacobs, *Rise of American Film,* 420.

71. Joseph North, "Renaissance in Hollywood?" *New Masses,* July 4, 1939, 4.

72. Jan-Christopher Horak, "The First American Film Avant-Garde, 1919-1945," in Horak, *Lovers of Cinema,* 20.

73. Robert Forsythe, "In a Burst of Fury," *New Masses,* September 25, 1934, 30.

74. North, "Renaissance in Hollywood?" 4.

75. See Irving Lerner, "Glorified Horse Opera," *New Masses,* June 12, 1934, 29-30; Edwin Locke, "John Ford's *The Grapes of Wrath,*" 316-323; and Brandon, unpublished MS, file D55, 1-6, Tom Brandon Archives.

76. For a more thorough account of the Production Code Administration during the 1930s, see Lea Jacobs, *Wages of Sin;* and Black, *Hollywood Censored.*

77. Alexander, *Film on the Left,* 113.

78. Brandon, unpublished MS, file D43, 6-7.

79. Alexander, *Film on the Left,* 113; Brandon, unpublished MS, file D48, 7, Tom Brandon Archives.

80. *Films for Democracy* (pamphlet), 3, file L234, Tom Brandon Archives; "Group Plans Films to Aid Democracy," *New York Times,* November 15, 1938.

81. Brandon, unpublished MS, file D48, 17.

82. Ibid.

83. Ibid., 17–18.

84. Ibid., 18.

85. Ibid.

86. Ibid.

87. Ibid., 19.

88. Quoted in ibid., 20.

89. Ibid., 22.

90. Ibid., 35.

91. Brandon, unpublished MS, file D43, 35.

92. Thorp, *America at the Movies,* 277.

93. Clifford Howard, "The Coming Revolution," *Close Up* 8, no. 3 (September 1931): 218.

94. Clifford Howard, "American Tendencies," *Close Up* 9, no. 4 (December 1932): 286.

95. Lewis Jacobs, *Rise of the American Film,* 424.

96. Ibid.

97. Frank Daugherty, "Paul Green in Hollywood," *Close Up* 9, no. 2 (June 1932): 83.

98. Some recent film historians acknowledge that the early thirties provided a brief rupture in Hollywood screen content because of the devastating impact the Depression had on studio incomes. As Colin Schindler asserts, "In its attempts to give the customers what they seemed now to want, Hollywood started to make movies which portrayed American society in flux" (*Hollywood in Crisis: Cinema and American Society, 1929–1939,* 17). But it is often assumed that because the Depression lessened significantly after 1934 and the Production Code was strongly enforced, a majority of screen content was renormalized. But rather than using the theoretically imprecise term "renormalization," I support Thomas Elsaesser's view that the newly enforced Production Code offered a type of textual displacement in regard to political subject matter: historical narratives supplanted contemporary "realist" pictures; European and Latin American nations replaced the United States as a setting; individual narratives expanded into allegorical tales about a people. See Thomas Elsaesser, "Film as Social History: The Dieterle/Warner Brothers Bio-pic," *Wide Angle* 8, no. 2 (1986): 23–24. This is similarly reinforced by Lea Jacobs's scholarship on censorship, which sees more textual ambiguity at work in regard to sexual themes after 1934. Overall, this study argues for a more sophisticated understanding of how both economic and political factors affected Hollywood than is often assumed. Although the economic instability of the early

thirties might have led to more controversial film content, it certainly did not yield more political power to progressives within Hollywood. One need only note the repression Hollywood invoked against Upton Sinclair and his supporters during his 1934 gubernatorial campaign to observe the disempowered position progressives within Hollywood held at the time. Yet as the Depression's economic effects lessened in the later thirties, progressivism both within and outside of Hollywood gained greater organization and power. Although the studios found themselves in a better economic position, many groups were agitating for more-sophisticated and more-political films. The Production Code's limited success in obscuring sexual content might not be solely due to its enforcers' puritanical stance but also to various progressive groups' failure to address the need for cinema to present a more sophisticated understanding of sexuality. Because sexuality barely registered on progressive filmmakers' and critics' theories about film, the Production Code censored sexuality more freely than the overtly political content found in films such as *One Third of a Nation* (1939), *Confessions of a Nazi Spy* (1939), and *They Won't Forget* (1937). To assume that all film content was effectively censored after 1934 is to believe that countless progressives' faith in Hollywood was nothing but a mass delusion. Rather than seeing the code simply as an arbitrator of film content, one must acknowledge how progressive critics and filmmakers continually challenged some aspects of the code throughout the 1930s. Although the code limited the political content of film, critics addressed not only these limits but also alternative ways in which some content still managed to seep through the code.

99. North, "Renaissance in Hollywood?" 4.

100. Thorp, *America at the Movies*, 23.

101. Paul Buhle and Dave Wagner, *Radical Hollywood: The Untold Story behind America's Favorite Movies*, 72–89; Haberski, *"It's Only a Movie"*; John Bodnar, *Blue-Collar Hollywood: Liberalism, Democracy, and Working People in American Film*; and Paul R. Gorman, *Left Intellectuals and Popular Culture in Twentieth-Century America*.

102. Denning, *Cultural Front*, xvii. For an example of this morality tale, see Daniel Aaron, *Writers on the Left: Episodes in American Literary Communism*, and Walter B. Rideout, *The Radical Novel in the United States, 1900–1954*.

103. Malcolm Sylvers, "Popular Front," 591–595.

104. Alan Wald, *The New York Intellectuals: The Rise and Decline of the Anti-Stalinist Left from the 1930s to the 1980s*; Wald, *Exiles from a Future Time: The Forging of the Mid-Twentieth Century Literary Left*; Wald, *Trinity of Passion: The Literary Left and the Antifascist Crusade*; Robin D. G. Kelley, *Hammer and Hoe: Alabama Communists during the Great Depression*; Kelley, *Race Rebels: Culture, Politics, and the Black Working Class*; Kelley, *Freedom Dreams: The Black Radical Imagination*; Cary Nelson, *Repression and Recovery: Modern American Poetry and the Politics of Cultural Memory, 1910–1945*; Bill Mullen and Sherry Linkon, eds., *Radical Revisions: Rereading 1930s Culture*; Paula Rabinowitz, *Labor and*

Desire; Rabinowitz, *They Must Be Represented: The Politics of Documentary*; and Barbara Foley, *Spectres of 1919: Class and Nation in the Making of the New Negro*.

105. Denning, *Cultural Front*, 5.

106. Antonio Gramsci, *Selections from the Prison Notebooks*, 366.

107. Denning, *Cultural Front*, 22.

108. Ibid., 6.

109. Williams, *Marxism and Literature*, 117.

110. Ibid., 119.

111. See Alexander, *Film on the Left*; and Campbell, *Cinema Strikes Back*.

112. Brandon, unpublished MS, file D43, 24.

113. Ibid., 37.

114. Lounsbury, *Origins of American Film Criticism*, 462.

115. Lewis Jacobs, interviewed by Tom Brandon, file J185, 5–6, Tom Brandon Archives.

116. Everett, *Returning the Gaze*, 255.

117. Ella Shohat and Robert Stam, *Unthinking Eurocentrism: Multiculturalism and the Media*, 341.

118. Lewis Jacobs, interview, 2.

119. Lounsbury, *Origins of American Film Criticism*, 134, 135.

120. Anne Friedberg, "Introduction: Reading *Close Up*, 1927–1933," 4.

121. Wasson, *Museum Movies*, 73.

122. See Fredric Jameson, *A Singular Modernity: Essay on the Ontology of the Present*; Miriam Bratu Hansen, "America, Paris, and the Alps: Kracauer (and Benjamin) on Cinema and Modernity"; Wasson, *Museum Movies*; and Singer, *Melodrama and Modernity*.

123. Jameson, *Singular Modernity*, 134–135.

124. Hansen, "America, Paris, and the Alps," 365.

125. Brandon, unpublished MS, file D43, 10.

126. Buhle and Wagner, *Radical Hollywood*, 76.

127. Campbell, *Cinema Strikes Back*, 27–28.

128. See Rabinowitz, *Labor and Desire*; Rabinowitz, *They Must Be Represented*; Enstad, *Ladies of Labor*; Constance Coiner, *Better Red: The Writing and Resistance of Tillie Olsen and Meridel Le Sueur*; and Barbara Foley, *Radical Representations: Politics and Form in U.S. Proletarian Fiction, 1929–1941*.

129. Janet Staiger, *Bad Women: Regulating Sexuality in Early American Cinema*, 28.

130. See Enstad, *Ladies of Labor*; Lauren Rabinovitz, *For the Love of Pleasure: Women, Movies, and Culture in Turn-of-the-Century Chicago*; Peiss, *Cheap Amusements*; Miriam Hansen, *Babel and Babylon: Spectatorship in American Silent Film*; and Anne Friedberg, *Window Shopping: Cinema and the Postmodern*.

131. Rabinowitz, *Love of Pleasure*, 138.

132. Michael Kimmel, *Manhood in America: A Cultural History*, 193.

133. David M. Lugowski, "Queering the (New) Deal: Lesbian and Gay Representations and the Depression-Era Cultural Politics of Hollywood's Production Code," *Cinema Journal* 38, no. 2 (Winter 1999): 12.

134. Barbara Melosh, *Engendering Culture: Manhood and Womanhood in New Deal Public Art and Theater*, 4.

135. Kelley, *Race Rebels*, 114.

136. Rabinowitz, *Labor and Desire*, 8.

137. Rabinovitz, *Love of Pleasure*, 181.

138. See Robert Forsythe, "Mae West: A Treatise on Decay," *New Masses*, October 9, 1934, 29; David Lugowski, "'A Treatise on Decay': Liberal and Leftist Critics and Their Queer Readings of Depression-Era U.S. Film."

139. Patrice Petro, "Mass Culture and the Feminine: The 'Place' of Television in Film Studies," 578.

140. Fredric Jameson, "Reification and Utopia in Mass Culture," 142.

141. Jane Gaines, "Dream/Factory," 107–108.

142. Brandon, unpublished MS, file D46, 7, Tom Brandon Archives.

CHAPTER ONE

1. Ben Singer, "Modernity, Hyperstimulus, and the Rise of Popular Sensationalism," 74; see also Singer, *Melodrama and Modernity*.

2. Henry Adams, *The Education of Henry Adams*, 501.

3. Ibid., 499.

4. Georg Lukács, "What Is Orthodox Marxism?" 12–13.

5. Lukács, on the other hand, assigns realist literature as the primary aesthetic form for creating a dialectical, totalistic vision between the individual and his or her environment, dismissing much of modernism as an atomized, hyperindividualistic vision symptomatic of the reified processes of modernity and late capitalism; see Georg Lukács, "The Ideology of Modernism."

6. Bodnar, *Blue-Collar Hollywood*, 47.

7. Ibid., 47–48.

8. Campbell, *Cinema Strikes Back*, 27.

9. Ibid., 28.

10. For more information regarding the realism debates of the 1930s concerning Brecht, Lukács, Adorno, Benjamin, and Block, see Theodor Adorno, Walter Benjamin, Ernst Bloch, Bertolt Brecht, and Georg Lukács, *Aesthetics and Politics: The Key Texts of the Classic Debate within German Marxism*; Eugene Lunn, *Marxism and Modernism: An Historical Study of Lukács, Brecht, Benjamin and Adorno*; Susan Buck-Morss, *The Origins of Negative Dialectics: Theodor W. Adorno, Walter Benjamin, and the Frankfurt Institute*; and David Midgley, "Communism and the Avant-Garde: The Case of Georg Lukács."

11. See Jameson, *Singular Modernity*; Rabinowitz, *They Must Be Represented*;

Giovacchini, *Hollywood Modernism;* Nelson, *Repression and Recovery;* Denning, *Cultural Front;* and William J. Maxwell, *New Negro, Old Left: African-American Writing and Communism between the Wars.*

12. Denning, *Cultural Front,* 118.

13. Ibid.

14. Ibid., 122.

15. Lewis Jacobs, interview, file J185, 2, Tom Brandon Archives.

16. Brandon, unpublished MS, file D43, 22B–37, Tom Brandon Archives.

17. Ibid, 4.

18. Everett, *Returning the Gaze,* 12–58, 107–178.

19. Brandon, unpublished MS, file D43, 21–26. Willi Muenzenberg, "Capture the Film!" *Daily Worker,* July 23, 1925, 3; "The Picture and The Film in the Revolutionary Moment," *Daily Worker,* August 15, 1925, Supplement 4; "The Role of Moving Pictures in the Labor Movement," *Daily Worker,* September 1, 1925, 6; "The Presentation of Proletarian Films," *Daily Worker,* September 26, 1925, Supplement 1; "The Film Activity of the IWA," *Daily Worker,* October 10, 1925, Supplement 1.

20. Friedberg, "Introduction: Reading *Close Up,* 1927–1933," 9–10.

21. George Amberg, introduction to *Experimental Cinema, 1930-1934,* iv.

22. Harry Alan Potamkin, "Film Novitiates," *Close Up* 7, no. 5 (November 1930): 318–319.

23. Brandon, unpublished MS, file D43, 20.

24. David Peck, "New Masses," 527.

25. My view of the increasingly moderate stance taken by the *New Masses* film critics is at variance with prior film and historical scholarship, which assumes that the editorial changes at the journal reflected changes in Soviet policy, which supposedly controlled the journal's editorial policies, rather than an autonomous development by the journal's contributors and editorial board. For example, Paul Buhle and Dave Wagner claim that *New Masses*'s film critics often viewed Hollywood as the enemy, "at least until a bureaucratic turn confirmed in far-off Moscow would give the *New Masses* and radicals entrée into the movies and a renaissance in a middle-class life" (*Radical Hollywood,* 74). Rather than examine the film debates that engaged *New Masses* film critics and the political events within the United States that influenced their critical positions, Buhle and Wagner decontextualize U.S. film theory of the 1930s by raising the specter of "Soviet control," which supposedly had a stranglehold on this journal and most leftists affiliated with it.

26. Forsythe, "In a Burst of Fury," 30.

27. Brandon, unpublished MS, file D46, 9.

28. Tom Brandon, "Who Are the Forces behind the Legion of Decency Drive?" *Daily Worker,* August 17, 18, 20, and 21, 1934; Sergei Eisenstein, "My Theme is Patriotism," *Daily Worker,* April 1, 1939.

29. "Film and Photo League Begins Movie School," *Daily Worker,* October 12,

1935; Dorothy Parker, "On Movie Writers and the 'Want-to-be-Alone' Spirits," *Daily Worker*, August 8, 1937; "American League Mobilizes to Picket Lowes Theatres against *Riff-Raff* Showing," *Daily Worker*, February 27, 1936.

30. Aaron, *Writers on the Left*, 25–26.

31. Alexander, *Film on the Left*, 41–64; Campbell, *Cinema Strikes Back*, 115–144.

32. John Howard Lawson, letter, *Filmfront* no. 4 (February 15, 1935): 16.

33. Lawrence H. Schwartz offers compelling evidence that the CPUSA never developed a coherent sociocultural agenda: "The real tragedy in the cultural work of the CPUSA in the 1930s was not, as is usually argued, the intrusion of politics into literature; it was that the Party did *not* develop a more fully conscious political program for art. The more the revolutionary Communist line was submerged in the later half of the decade, the bigger, and on the surface successful, the popular front became. The Party decided it was not practical to raise a sharp revolutionary line while fighting fascism and building mass organizations" (*Marxism and Culture: The CPUSA and Aesthetics in the 1930s*, 5).

34. See V. I. Pudovkin, *Film Technique and Film Acting: The Cinema Writings of V. I. Pudovkin*; Sergei Eisenstein, *Film Form: Essays in Film Theory*; Eisenstein, *The Film Sense*; Eisenstein, *The Eisenstein Reader*; and Dziga Vertov, *Kino-Eye: The Writings of Dziga Vertov*.

35. Lewis Jacobs, *Rise of the American Film*, 313.

36. Myron Osborn Lounsbury, *Origins of American Film Criticism*, 226.

37. Lewis Jacobs, *Rise of the American Film*, 322–323.

38. The "kino-eye" is Dziga Vertov's term for film's ability to disregard all prior bourgeois forms by creating absolutely new methods of perception. The "kino-fist" is Eisenstein's critique of Vertov. Eisenstein instead claims that cinema must use the bourgeois aesthetic tradition in new ways within film. Disregarding this tradition leads to oversimplified and unstructured films. For a well-stated, concise summary of these directors' positions, see Judith Mayne, *Kino and The Woman Question*, 17–21.

39. Hanns Sachs, "Film Psychology"; Sachs, "Kitsch," *Close Up* 9, no. 3 (Sept. 1932): 200–205.

40. Clement Greenberg, "Avant-Garde and Kitsch," *Partisan Review* 5, no. 5 (Fall 1939): 34–49. For an excellent contextualization of Greenberg's piece, see Andrew Ross, *No Respect*, 43–47.

41. Sachs, "Kitsch," 201.

42. Ibid., 202.

43. Ibid., 204.

44. Sachs, "Film Psychology," 251.

45. Ibid., 252.

46. Ibid.

47. Sachs's links between psychoanalysis and cinema strongly resonate with Walter Benjamin's own insights concerning the "unconscious optics" of cinema in

"The Work of Art in the Age of Mechanical Reproduction." Devices such as the close-up and slow motion, according to Benjamin, reveal "entirely new structural formations of the subject" (236). Film, in general, bursts apart our reified perceptions into "unconscious optics as does psychoanalysis to unconscious impulses" (237). Contrary to accounts that champion Benjamin as the sole originator of this concept, it seems much more likely that his explanation was in part derived from earlier debates that offered similar, though less nuanced, observations. Needless to say, much more work needs to be done on situating Benjamin and other members of the Frankfurt School in relation to international socio-aesthetic debates regarding film.

48. Peter Wollen's "The Two Avant-Gardes" is often considered the main perpetrator in overemphasizing the differences between the politicized Soviet montage filmmakers and the painterly, European avant-garde filmmakers of the 1920s. Although Wollen, at times, overexaggerates the differences between the two groups, he acknowledges certain similarities between them, too, such as their editing styles (173). The main problem with Wollen's article comes not in its argumentation but in its later interpretation by scholars as a historical argument rather than a theoretical one. Much of what Wollen claims is still theoretically useful to film studies, but one must not assume that Wollen's interpretation of the 1920s avant-garde in any way resembles the way in which the directors at the time regarded their works. Wollen's heavy reliance on poststructural assumptions about signification should clearly serve as a red flag to the unwary scholar that the essay is reinterpreting the 1920s in relation to 1970s film trends, not examining the distinctness of the 1920s theories themselves.

49. Zygmunt Tonecky, "The Preliminary of Film Art," *Close Up* 8, no. 3 (Sept. 1931): 196.

50. Ibid., 194.

51. Ibid., 196.

52. Ibid., 198.

53. Ibid., 199.

54. Joseph Gollomb, "The New Movie," *Daily Worker*, March 29, 1936.

55. It is also worth pointing out that Gollomb's article appeared at the height of the Soviet Communist Party's rejection of formalist films. This suggests that the cultural reviewers of the *Daily Worker* had more latitude than its political correspondents, and reinforces Lawrence H. Schwartz's observation that the Communist Party had no coherent cultural strategy or program (*Marxism and Culture*, 9).

56. Once again, this discussion resonates with Walter Benjamin's focus on "aura" in "The Work of Art in the Age of Mechanical Reproduction." Benjamin's central claim—that mechanical reproduction, and cinema in particular, destroys the "aura" of the work of art—seems related to Tonecky's focus on abstract films' ability to decontextualize objects from their surroundings. Although Benjamin is speaking about a new cultural mode of production, whereas Tonecky is addressing a specific cinematic style, they are both concerned with the ideologically lib-

erating effects produced by cinematic defamiliarization. Both writers emphasize a "shattering of tradition" that could unshackle objects, people, and events from ritualized ways of seeing and acting.

57. Maya Deren, "Cinematography: The Creative Use of Reality."

58. Friedberg, "Introduction: *Borderline* and the POOL Films," 218.

59. Ibid., 219–220.

60. Sergei Eisenstein, "The Filmic Fourth Dimension," 66.

61. Ibid., 67.

62. Ibid., 71.

63. Kenneth Macpherson, "As Is," 236–237.

64. H.D., "*Borderline:* A POOL Film with Paul Robeson," 232.

65. Ibid., 234.

66. Sergei Eisenstein, W. I. Pudowkin, and G. V. Alexandroff, "The Sound Film: A Statement from U.S.S.R.," 83–84.

67. Seymour Stern, "Cinema Notes of the Quarter," *Left* 1, no. 2 (Summer–Autumn 1931): 79.

68. Harry Alan Potamkin, "First Films," 145.

69. Harry Alan Potamkin, "'A' in the Art of the Movie and Kino," *New Masses,* December 1929, 14.

70. David Platt, "Focus and Mechanism," *Experimental Cinema* 1, no. 2 (February 1930): 2.

71. B. G. Braver-Mann, "Josef Von Sternberg," *Experimental Cinema* 1, no. 5 (February 1934): 18.

72. Leo Hurwitz, "One Man's Voyage: Ideas and Films in the 1930s," 275.

73. William Troy, "Collectivism More or Less," *Nation,* October 24, 1934, 488.

74. B. G. Braver-Mann, "Vidor and Evasion," *Experimental Cinema* 1, no. 3 (February 1931): 26.

75. Walter Benjamin, "On Some Motifs in Baudelaire," 158–159.

76. Braver-Mann, "Vidor and Evasion," 26.

77. Harry Alan Potamkin, "Novel into Film: A Case Study of Current Practice," 196. To give Vidor credit, the ending is far from being the cliché that Potamkin suggests. The children's song contains such repetitive lyrics as "the farmer kills the wife" and "the wife kills the child, hi-ho the Derry-O, the wife kills the child," suggesting the cyclic and repetitive violence that family life inflicts upon its members, as we have just seen throughout the film. Despite Rose's affirmation that she will come back to Sam after they both get older and establish themselves, the children's song not only takes the focus away from Rose and Sam by situating their lives into a larger context of familial violence but also indicates that their own future together might perpetuate this bleak existence.

78. Stern, "Cinema Notes of the Quarter," 78.

79. Alexander Bakshy, "Street Scene," *Nation,* September 16, 1931, 290.

80. Raymond Durgnat and Scott Simmon, *King Vidor, American,* 119.

81. Ibid., 123.

82. Unbeknownst to critics at the time, the preproduction debates between Vidor and Elmer Rice, the playwright and screenwriter of *Street Scene*, support the critics' assumptions that Vidor was attempting to suppress the social implications within his film. Despite Rice's insistence that *Street Scene* investigate the conditions that create tenement life, Vidor penciled in his script, "It is not our surroundings that defeat us" (Durgnat and Simmon, *Vidor*, 119).

83. Ibid., 122.

84. Ibid.

85. Braver-Mann, "Josef von Sternberg," 20.

86. Ibid., 18.

87. Ibid.

88. Ibid.

89. See Judith Mayne, "Marlene Dietrich, *The Blue Angel*, and Female Performance."

90. Braver-Mann, "Josef von Sternberg," 18.

91. Sachs, "Kitsch," 203.

92. See Laura Mulvey, "Visual Pleasure and Narrative Cinema."

93. Gaylyn Studlar, *In the Realm of Pleasure: Von Sternberg, Dietrich, and the Masochistic Aesthetic*, 160.

94. Ibid., 48.

95. Laura Marcus, "Introduction to Part 4," 150.

96. Dorothy Richardson, "Continuous Performance," 160.

97. Richardson's account shows that Kathy Peiss's observation in *Cheap Amusements* about the cinema offering working-class women and girls a newly found sanctuary to meet and bond was also true in Britain.

98. Dorothy Richardson, "The Cinema in the Slums," 181.

99. Dorothy Richardson, "The Cinema in Arcady," 185.

100. Benjamin, "Work of Art," 225.

101. Ibid., 240.

102. Hansen, "Mass Production of the Senses," 341–342.

103. Dorothy Richardson, "This Spoon-Fed Generation?" 203, 204.

104. Dorothy Richardson, "Narcissus," 202–203.

105. Ibid., 202.

106. Ibid.

107. Ibid.

108. Dorothy Richardson, "The Thoroughly Popular Film," 178.

109. Ibid., 179.

110. Jameson, "Reification and Utopia," 142.

111. Gaines, "Dream/Factory," 108.

112. Dorothy Richardson, "The Film Gone Male," 205–206.

113. Ibid., 206.

114. Ibid.

CHAPTER TWO

1. See Sergei Eisenstein, "The Fourth Dimension of Cinema."

2. Vladimir Nizhny, *Lessons With Eisenstein*, 19–62, 93–139; Jacques Aumont, *Montage Eisenstein*, 135–137, 154–156; David Bordwell, *The Cinema of Eisenstein*, 141–145.

3. See Deborah Rosenfelt, "From the Thirties: Tillie Olsen and the Radical Tradition"; Rabinowitz, *Labor and Desire;* Rabinowitz, *They Must Be Represented;* and Enstad, *Ladies of Labor.*

4. Sergei Eisenstein, "An American Tragedy." *Close Up* 10, no. 2 (June 1933): 121.

5. Ibid., 116.

6. Harry Alan Potamkin, "Film Problems of Soviet Russia," 312.

7. Potamkin, "Novel into Film," 195.

8. Seymour Stern, "Eisenstein in Mexico," *Experimental Cinema*, February 1931, 22.

9. Adolfo Best-Maugard, "Mexico into Cinema," *Theatre Arts Monthly* 16, no. 11 (1932): 926–927.

10. See Marie Seton, *Sergei M. Eisenstein;* and Harry M. Geduld and Ronald Gottesman, *Sergei Eisenstein and Upton Sinclair: The Making and Unmaking of "Que Viva Mexico!"* for further information about the problems with finishing *¡Que Viva México!* Seton's work sides with Eisenstein, while Geduld and Gottesman's work sympathizes more with Upton Sinclair. See also Masha Salazkina, *In Excess: Eisenstein's México.*

11. Seymour Stern, "Hollywood and Montage," *Experimental Cinema*, February 1933, 49.

12. Ibid., 52.

13. Ibid., 51.

14. Ibid., 49.

15. Sergei Eisenstein, "First Outline of *Que Viva Mexico!*" 251.

16. Geduld and Gottesman, *Eisenstein and Sinclair*, 127–128.

17. Seton, *Sergei M. Eisenstein*, 265.

18. See Stern, "Eisenstein in Mexico," 22; Best-Maugard, "Mexico Into Cinema"; Agustin Aragón Leiva, "Eisenstein's Film on Mexico," *Experimental Cinema*, February 1933, 5–6; Morris Helprin, "*Que Viva Mexico!*" *Experimental Cinema*, February 1933, 13–14; *Experimental Cinema* editors, "Manifesto on Eisenstein's Mexican Film," *Close Up* 10, no. 2 (June 1933): 210–212; Herman G. Weinberg, "The 'Lesser' of Two Evils," *Modern Monthly* 7, no. 5 (June 1933): 299–301, 311; William Troy, "The Eisenstein Muddle," *Nation*, July 19, 1933, 83–84; Seymour Stern, "Second Manifesto by the Editors of *Experimental Cinema*," *Close Up* 10, no. 2 (September 1933): 248–254; Sam Brody and Tom Brandon, "A Mexican Trailer," *New Masses*, September 1933, 28; Seymour Stern, "The Greatest Thing Done on This Side of the Atlantic," *Modern Monthly* 7, no. 9 (October 1933): 525–

532; William Troy, "Selections from Eisenstein," *Nation,* October 4, 1933, 391–392; Pare Lorentz, "*Thunder over Mexico*"; George W. Hesse, "The Cine Analyst," *Personal Movies,* November 15, 1933, 268, 285; Upton Sinclair, "*Thunder over Mexico: Mr. Upton Sinclair Defends Himself,*" *Close Up* 10, no. 4 (December 1933): 361–363; Sam Brody (as "Lens"), "Flashes and Close Ups," *Daily Worker,* January 18, 1934, 5; Workers Film and Photo League, "The Thunder Dies," *New Masses,* January 22, 1934, 21; Lerner, "Glorified Horse Opera"; Marie Seton, review of *Thunder over Mexico, Film Art,* Spring 1934, 21–22; *Film Art,* untitled review of *Thunder over Mexico,* Spring 1934, 36; Seymour Stern, "Introduction to *Que Viva Mexico!*" *Experimental Cinema,* February 1934, 3–4; Sergei Eisenstein and V. G. Alexandroff, "Synopsis for *Que Viva Mexico!*" *Experimental Cinema,* February 1934, 5–13; *Experimental Cinema* editors, "Manifesto on *Que Viva Mexico!*" *Experimental Cinema,* February 1934, 14.

19. *Experimental Cinema* editors, "Manifesto on Eisenstein's Mexican Film," 211.

20. Troy, "Eisenstein Muddle," 84.

21. Brody and Brandon, "Mexican Trailer," 28.

22. Ibid., 28.

23. Troy, "Selections from Eisenstein," 391. It is interesting to note also that Troy was one of the first film critics to note the sadistic impulses in Eisenstein. His insight was likely aided by *¡Que Viva México!* remaining one of Eisenstein's most sadomasochistic films (peons trampled to death by horses, cacti lashed to characters' bare backs, point-of-view shots from a bull about to be killed by a matador) and also by *Thunder over Mexico*'s lack of thematic development, which drew more attention to the film's spectacular sadistic nature. Not that earlier Eisenstein films had lacked examples of sadism—for example, the hanging of a worker, the dropping of a baby off a balcony, the slaughter of a bull, and the mass murder of workers in *Strike;* the Odessa steps sequence in *Battleship Potemkin;* and the stabbing to death of a Bolshevik with umbrellas in *October.* A focus on sadism would eventually take on particular importance in gay readings of Eisenstein's films. See, for example, Tyler Parker, *Screening the Sexes: Homosexuality in the Movies;* Harry M. Benshoff, "Homoerotic Iconography and Anti-Catholic Marxism: Proto-Feminist Discourse in Sergei M. Eisenstein's *Que Viva Mexico!*"; Thomas Waugh, "A Fag-Spotters Guide to Eisenstein"; and Al LaValley, "Maintaining, Blurring, and Transcending Gender Lines in Eisenstein."

24. Troy, "Selections from Eisenstein," 392.

25. *Experimental Cinema* editors, "Manifesto on Eisenstein's Mexican Film," 211.

26. Stern, "Second Manifesto," 251.

27. Brody and Brandon, "Mexican Trailer," 28.

28. Troy, "Selections from Eisenstein," 391.

29. *Experimental Cinema* editors, "Manifesto on Eisenstein's Mexican Film," 211.

30. Quoted in Brody and Brandon, "Mexican Trailer," 28.

31. Weinberg, "'Lesser' of Two Evils," 300.

32. Brody and Brandon, "Mexican Trailer," 28.

33. Although all contemporary film historians of Soviet cinema note how Eisenstein was forced to recut *October* when Stalin took power in order to rid the film of all references to Trotsky, most 1930s U.S. Left film critics either did not know this or knew of it only as a rumor.

34. Harry Alan Potamkin, "Eisenstein and the Theory of Cinema," 440.

35. Ibid.

36. Troy, "Selections from Eisenstein," 392.

37. Ibid.

38. Potamkin, "Eisenstein and Cinema," 444.

39. Ian Christie, introduction to *Eisenstein Rediscovered*, 8–9.

40. Ibid., 4–14.

41. Ibid., 5–6.

42. Ibid., 8.

43. Benshoff, "Homoerotic Iconography," 16.

44. Ibid.

45. Marie Seton offered her own reconstruction of the film with *A Time in the Sun* (1939), which takes a much more conservative stance toward gender, race, and religion than the Alexandrov version; she maintains a rather patronizing view of women and indigenous peoples and minimizes criticisms of the latter. I don't prioritize Seton's film in my analysis of *¡Que Viva México!* for several reasons: her distance from any involvement with the original project, her unfamiliarity with Mexico, and the difference between her cultural assumptions as an American and those of the original Russian filmmakers. In addition, the rough cut of the film was to be previewed at the Academy of Motion Picture Arts and Sciences in Hollywood for many of the people who had denied distribution to *¡Que Viva México!* leading one to believe that Seton's reconstruction must have had a somewhat limited representation of radical political themes. That said, however, I must acknowledge that *A Time in the Sun* serves as an interesting study of how Eisenstein's Mexican footage can be edited in less radical ways than I am suggesting for this essay.

46. The Russian director Oleg Kovalov made his own very loose reconstruction of the film during the 1990s, *Sergei Eisenstein: Mexican Fantasy* (1998). It doesn't attempt to follow Eisenstein's intended structure, but the extra footage it provides for the "Maguey" and "Fiesta" episodes cannot be seen in any other version of the film.

47. Stern, "Greatest Thing," 592.

48. Tom Brandon, interviewed by Irving Lerner, September 3, 1974, File J193, 21–22, Tom Brandon Archives.

49. Sergei Eisenstein, "The Cinematographic Principle and the Ideogram," 128.

50. Sergei Eisenstein, "Perspectives," 44.

51. Eisenstein, "Fourth Dimension," 112–113.

52. Best-Maugard, "Mexico into Cinema," 933.

53. Lorentz, "*Thunder over Mexico*," 119.

54. Rosamund Bartlett, "The Circle and the Line: Eisenstein, Florensky, and Russian Orthodoxy"; and Mikael Enckell, "A Study in Scarlet."

55. Seton, *Sergei M. Eisenstein*, 109.

56. One could argue that Boris Shumyatsky rejected Eisenstein's next film, *Bezhin Meadow*, mainly because the film employed the sort of blatant religious symbolism of Christ's suffering that Eisenstein had begun exploring in *¡Que Viva México!* Gwen Seiler, who visited Eisenstein during the making of *Bezhin Meadow*, summarized the film as comprising "the Christ story plus the religious ecstasy of the Mexicans [that Eisenstein experienced while filming *¡Que Viva México!*]" (quoted in Seton, *Sergei M. Eisenstein*, 363).

57. Sergei Eisenstein, "Cinematography with Tears," *Close Up* 10, no. 1 (March 1933): 3–17.

58. Forsythe, "Burst of Fury."

59. Lawson, letter to the editor, *Filmfront*, February 15, 1934, 16.

60. This latter point is intended to further Judith Mayne's work in *Kino and the Woman Question*, in which she initiated a "dialogue between the woman question and cinematic narrative. Such a dialogue involves the exploration of how Soviet film narrative turns, ideologically and aesthetically, on the representation of woman, and of how the woman question is concerned, centrally and vitally, with questions of narrative" (15). Although Mayne focuses on silent cinema, her observations are still germane to an analysis of *¡Que Viva México!* And her observation that the changes in women's lives during the Russian Revolution have been barely explored in relation to Soviet cinema still holds true for much recent scholarship on Russian cinema (14). Therefore, I consider it important to explore how *¡Que Viva México!* may hold residual elements concerning the woman question in its structure.

61. Eisenstein and Alexandroff, "Synopsis for *Que Viva Mexico!*" 7.

62. Leyda's version, even more tellingly, locates this conquest imagery at the end of "Maguey," making the symbolic link of the upside-down U in the two different contexts even more apparent. Eisenstsein's scenario, in which "Fiesta" follows "Maguey," suggests that the conquest imagery was supposed to make up the former. Yet in Alexandrov's version, "Maguey" follows "Fiesta"; therefore, Leyda's footage might represent the transition between episodes found in Eisenstein's scenario.

63. It is worth noting how this critique of the family seems to offer a visual representation of the very same critique that the Bolsheviks endorsed immediately after the revolution. Historian Gail Warshofsky Lapidus claims that the Bolsheviks initially did not view the family "as a bulwark of freedom and self-fulfillment but as a significant locus of exploitation, oppression, and humiliation" (*Women*

in Soviet Society: Equality, Development, and Social Change, 82). In 1919, Lenin proclaimed that "petty housework crushes, strangles, stultifies and degrades [the wife], chains her to the kitchen and nursery, and she wastes her labour on barbarously unproductive, petty, nerve-racking, stultifying and crushing drudgery" (quoted in Richard Stites, *The Women's Liberation Movement in Russia: Feminism, Nihilism, and Bolshevism, 1860–1930,* 378). One could argue also that Eisenstein's gay or bisexual background made him particularly critical of the heterosexual family, which is noticeable either for its absence (in *Battleship Potemkin, October,* and *Alexander Nevsky*) or for its dysfunctional and sometimes psychopathic role (in *iQue Viva México! Bezhin Meadow,* and *Ivan the Terrible, Parts I and II*).

64. Jane Gaines, "Can We Enjoy Alternative Pleasure?" 79.

65. Benshoff, "Homoerotic Iconography," 14.

66. Ibid.

67. Ibid., 14–15.

68. Ibid., 14.

69. Philip Rosen has suggested that Engels rather than Marx was a central influence on Eisenstein's filmmaking and theorizing. *iQue Viva México!* might mark one of the most explicit ways in which Engels inflected his work (Philip Rosen, "Eisenstein's Marxism, Marxism's Eisenstein").

70. Frederick Engels, *The Origins of the Family, Private Property, and the State,* 77.

71. Mayne, *Kino and the Woman Question,* 26; Mary Buckley, "Soviet Interpretations of the Woman Question," 34; and Stites, 392–406.

72. Benshoff, "Homoerotic Iconography," 9–10.

73. Lapidus, *Women in Soviet Society,* 95–122; Stites, *Women's Liberation in Russia,* 406–416.

74. Abram Room's 1927 film *Third Meshchanskaia Street (Bed and Sofa)* serves as an interesting contrast to "Sanduga" in the way that it explicitly investigates women's "double burden" and criticizes men for not helping with domestic chores. But the film's rather sophisticated and all too realistic representations of gender issues and domestic labor led it to be almost unanimously denounced within the Soviet Union, suggesting that the male film critics reviewing the film didn't enjoy being reminded about the failure to achieve women's equality. See Denise J. Youngblood, *Soviet Cinema in the Silent Era, 1918–1936,* 119–124.

75. Engels, *Origins of the Family,* 145.

76. Eisenstein and Alexandroff, "Synopsis for *Que Viva Mexico!*" 7.

77. Benshoff, 15.

78. Lapidus, 73; Buckley, 37–38.

79. Eisenstein and Alexandroff, "Synopsis for *Que Viva Mexico!*" 12.

80. LaValley, "Maintaining, Blurring, and Transcending," 53.

81. Ibid., 56–61.

82. Ibid., 56, 59–60. LaValley also makes an interesting observation on

"Fiesta" in *¡Que Viva México!*: "In David Laceaga, the young bullfighter, the film reveals little of the machismo that traditionally surrounds bullfighting, but concentrates instead on the elaborate almost feminine ritual of his dress, his parading into the ring like a dancer, and the extraordinary beauty of his near-deathly dance with the bull" (60–61). Leyda's reconstruction of the film particularly emphasizes Eisenstein's fascination with Laceaga's *paso mariposa* (butterfly pass) in luring the bull to its death. Thousands of feet of film were used to record Laceaga's balletic actions.

83. Eisenstein and Alexandroff, "Synopsis for *Que Viva Mexico!*" 12.

84. Kaja Silverman, *The Threshold of the Visible World*, 90–93.

85. LaValley, "Maintaining, Blurring, and Transcending," 62; Bordwell, *Cinema of Eisenstein*, 194; Aumont, *Montage Eisenstein*, 50–61; Håkan Lövgren, "Trauma and Ecstasy: Aesthetic Compounds in Dr. Eisenstein's Laboratory"; and Bartlett, "Circle and Line," 73.

86. Sergei Eisenstein, *Beyond the Stars: The Memoirs of Sergei Eisenstein*, 421.

87. Octavio Paz, *The Labyrinth of Solitude, and Other Writings*, 57. For the political potentialities opened up by the space of carnival, see Mikhail Bakhtin, *Rabelais and His World*.

88. Similarly, montage provides an identical operation. By harnessing mundane material and reconstructing it in new ways, film allows spectators to see the revolutionary potential that structures their own lives but that they have been ideologically positioned to largely ignore. Eisenstein believed that it was the cinema's job to offer spectators a glimpse of the social totality so that they could observe how the ossified categories organizing their daily lives and actions were merely tentative constructions that only seemed universal because of the enormous efforts made by the ruling class to maintain such illusions.

89. *Experimental Cinema* editors, "Manifesto on *Que Viva Mexico!*," 14.

90. See Grace Hutchins, "Feminists and the Left Wing," *New Masses*, November 20, 1934, 14–15; Meridel Le Sueur, "Women on the Breadlines," *New Masses*, January 1932, 5–7, and "I Was Marching," *New Masses*, September 18, 1934, 16–18; Martha Millet, "Last Night," *New Masses*, June 19, 1934, 17; Rebecca Pitts, "Women and Communism," *New Masses*, February 19, 1935, 14–18; and Mary Heaton Vorse, "Lauren Gilfillan's Education," *New Masses*, April 10, 1934, 16.

91. See Ella Winter, "Woman Freed."

92. Grace Hutchins, "Women under Capitalism."

93. Le Sueur, "Women on the Breadlines" and "Women Are Hungry."

94. Paula Rabinowitz, "Women and U.S. Literary Radicalism," 8.

95. Pitts, "Women and Communism," 15.

96. Ibid.

97. Ibid., 16.

98. Ibid., 15.

99. Ibid., 18.

100. Ibid.

101. Agnes Smedley, *Daughter of Earth*; Grace Lumpkin, *To Make My Bread*; and Tillie Olsen, *Yonnondio: From the Thirties*.

102. Helprin, "*Que Viva Mexico!*" 14.

103. Ibid.

104. Ibid.

105. Ibid., 13.

106. Ibid., 14.

107. Rabinowitz, *Labor and Desire*, 4.

108. Ibid., 8.

109. Seton, *Sergei M. Eisenstein*, 507.

110. Stern, "Greatest Thing," 528.

111. Rabinowitz, *They Must Be Represented*, 67.

112. Stern, "Greatest Thing," 525; *Experimental Cinema* editors, "Manifesto on Eisenstein's Mexican Film," 211.

113. Weinberg, "'Lesser' of Two Evils," 299.

114. Ibid.

115. Peiss, *Cheap Amusements*; Janet Staiger, *Bad Women*; Enstad, *Ladies of Labor*; and Shelley Stamp, *Movie-Struck Girls: Women and Motion Picture Culture after the Nickelodeon*. See also Hansen, *Babel and Babylon*; Friedberg, *Window Shopping*; and Rabinovitz, *For the Love of Pleasure*.

116. Sarah Berry, *Screen Style: Fashion and Femininity in 1930s Hollywood*, xix.

117. Jacobs, *Rise of the American Film*, 410.

118. The quotation is from Peiss, *Cheap Amusements*, 6; see also Enstad, *Ladies of Labor*, 17–47.

119. Hansen, *Babel and Babylon*, 117.

120. Mike Gold, "Movie Madness and the Child," *Daily Worker*, May 11, 1937, 7.

121. Ibid.

122. Forsythe, "Mae West," 29.

123. Ibid.

124. Lugowski, "Queering the (New) Deal," 12.

125. For a critique of the homophobia found in this particular article, see David Lugowski, "'A Treatise on Decay.'"

126. Herman Weinberg, letter to the editor, *Modern Monthly*, July 1933, 373.

127. Stern, "Greatest Thing," 531.

128. James Goodwin, *Eisenstein, Cinema, and History*, 139–155.

129. Geduld and Gottesman, *Eisenstein and Sinclair*, 194, 211.

130. Weinberg, "'Lesser' of Two Evils," 301.

131. This change in Soviet film production is most explicitly noted in Dwight Macdonald's three-part essay "The Soviet Cinema: 1930–1938," which he wrote for the *Partisan Review* in 1938–1939.

132. Leo Hurwitz, "Survey of Workers Films," *New Theatre*, October 1934, 27.

133. Leo Hurwitz and Ralph Steiner, "A New Approach to Film Making," *New Theatre,* September 1935, 22.

134. Ibid.

135. Ibid.

136. Ibid.

137. Ibid.

138. See Robert Forythe, "*Chapayev* Is Here," *New Masses,* January 22, 1933, 29–30; Forsythe, "The British are Coming, Boom!" *New Masses,* January 29, 1935, 29–30; Denis Johnston, review of *Chapayev, Film Art* 2, no. 6 (Autumn 1935): 78, 81; David Platt, review of *Chapayev, Filmfront,* January 28, 1935, 17–18.

139. Sergei Eisenstein, "The New Soviet Cinema," *New Theatre,* January 1935, 21.

140. Ibid.

141. Ibid.

142. See William Alexander's *Film on the Left* and Russell Campbell's *Cinema Strikes Back* for thorough accounts of the creation of NYKino and Frontier Films.

CHAPTER THREE

1. Lawson, letter to the editor, *Filmfront,* February 15, 1935, 16.

2. Ibid.

3. Sylvers, "Popular Front."

4. Ceplair and Englund, *Inquisition in Hollywood,* 98.

5. Denning, *Culture in Three Worlds,* 9.

6. Lounsbury, *Origins of American Film Criticism,* 462.

7. Christopher Waldrep, *The Many Faces of Judge Lynch: Extralegal Violence and Punishment in America,* 10.

8. For some statistics on the number of lynching victims, see W. Fitzhugh Brundage, *Lynching in the New South: Georgia and Virginia, 1880–1930.*

9. Ibid., 98–110.

10. Amy Helene Kirschke, *Art in Crisis,* 56.

11. George Hutchinson, *The Harlem Renaissance in Black and White,* 143.

12. Foley, *Spectres of 1919,* 41.

13. Ibid, 51.

14. Everett, *Returning the Gaze,* 103–104.

15. Ibid., 96–99.

16. For more information regarding Micheaux's background, see Pearl Boswer, Jane Gaines, and Charles Musser, eds. *Oscar Micheaux and His Circle: African-American Filmmaking and Race Cinema of the Silent Era;* Pearl Bowser and Louise Spence, *Writing Himself into History: Oscar Micheaux, His Silent Films, and His Audiences;* J. Ronald Green, *Straight Lick: The Cinema of Oscar Micheaux;* J. Ronald Green, *With a Crooked Stick: The Films of Oscar Micheaux;* Jane Gaines, *Fire and Desire: Mixed-Race Movies in the Silent Era;* Patrick McGilligan, *Oscar*

Micheaux, the Great and Only: The Life of America's First Great Black Filmmaker; Thomas Cripps, *Slow Fade to Black: The Negro in American Film, 1900-1942;* Cedric J. Robinson, *Forgeries of Memory and Meaning: Blacks and the Regimes of Race in American Theater and Film before World War II;* and Matthew H. Bernstein, *Screening a Lynching: The Leo Frank Case on Film and Television.*

17. Robinson, *Forgeries of Memory and Meaning,* xiv.

18. Gaines, *Fire and Desire,* 185–218.

19. Charlene Regester, "The African-American Press and Race Movies, 1909-1929," 37.

20. Robinson, *Forgeries of Memory and Meaning,* 271.

21. Ibid., 74.

22. Ibid., 77–78.

23. Kelley, *Race Rebels,* 107.

24. Mark Solomon, *The Cry was Unity: Communists and African Americans, 1917-1936,* 52.

25. Kelley, *Race Rebels,* 109.

26. Ibid., 110.

27. Suzanne Sowinska, "Writing across the Color Line: White Women Writers and the 'Negro Question' in the Gastonia Novels," 121.

28. Ibid., 122.

29. Maxwell, *New Negro, Old Left,* 133.

30. Dan T. Carter, *Scottsboro: A Tragedy of the American South,* 137.

31. Ibid., 138.

32. Ibid.

33. For more detailed accounts of the Scottsboro Boys, see Carter, *Scottsboro,* and James Goodwin, *Stories of Scottsboro.*

34. Carter, *Scottsboro,* 57.

35. Kelley, *Hammer and Hoe,* 91.

36. Kelley, *Race Rebels,* 124.

37. Quoted in Carter, *Scottsboro,* 85.

38. For more information on Potamkin, see Lewis Jacobs's introduction to *The Compound Cinema: The Film Writings of Harry Alan Potamkin;* and Dudley Andrews, "Harry Alan Potamkin," *Film Comment* (March 1974): 55–57.

39. Harry Alan Potamkin, "The Aframerican Cinema," *Close Up* 5, no. 2 (August 1929): 109.

40. Ibid., 115.

41. It should also be noted that at this point in his career, Potamkin essentialized all nationalities. Myron Lounsbury explains: "The cultural traditions of each nation, Potamkin suggested, prescribed the proper subject matter for film expression" (*Origins of American Film Criticism,* 280). Potamkin believed that "if a nation or race remained true to its folk art, it would quite naturally discover meaningful form or structure within its aesthetic tradition" (283). I am not claiming that this justifies Potamkin's essentialization of African Americans, but that it reveals

how this essentialism pervaded Potamkin's entire understanding of ethnicities and nationalities.

42. Potamkin, "Aframerican Cinema," 111.

43. Ibid., 110.

44. H.D., "*Borderline*," 224.

45. Kenneth Macpherson, "As Is," *Close Up* 5, no. 2 (August 1929): 89–90.

46. Sam Brody, "On a Theory of Sources," *Experimental Cinema*, February 1931, 23.

47. Ibid., 24.

48. Ibid.

49. Ibid.

50. Ibid., 23.

51. Ibid., 24.

52. Ibid.

53. Ibid.

54. Harry Alan Potamkin, "Lost Paradise: *Tabu*," *Creative Art* 8 (June 1931): 462, 463.

55. Ibid., 463.

56. Ibid.

57. Ibid.

58. Ibid.

59. Geraldyn Dismond, "The Negro Actor and the American Movies," *Close Up* 5, no. 2 (August 1929): 96–97.

60. Robert Stebbins, "Hollywood's Imitation of Life," *New Theatre*, July 1935, 8.

61. Harry Alan Potamkin, "The Eyes of the Movie," 249.

62. Ibid.

63. Solomon, *Cry Was Unity*, 174; Cripps, *Slow Fade to Black*, 212.

64. "Soviet Seeks Negroes to Make Film of Conditions Here," *New York Amsterdam News*, March 9, 1932.

65. Cripps, *Slow Fade to Black*, 213.

66. "Withdrawal of Russian Plan for Movie on Race Issue 'Strands' 22 US Negroes," *Atlanta Daily World*, August 16, 1932.

67. "All that Glitters," *New York Amsterdam News*, October 5, 1932, 6.

68. "Russian Negro Film Is Finally Banned," *Atlanta Daily World*, October 5, 1932, 1a.

69. Louise Thompson, "The Soviet Film," *Crisis*, February 1937, 37.

70. Ibid., 37, 46.

71. Ibid., 46.

72. Everett, *Returning the Gaze*, 265.

73. "Negro Editors on Communism: A Symposium of the American Negro Press," *Crisis*, May 1932, 155.

74. Ibid., 156.

75. Ibid.

76. W.E.B. Du Bois, "Postscript," *Crisis,* June 1932, 190.

77. Cedric J. Robinson, *Black Marxism: The Making of the Black Radical Tradition,* 207.

78. W.E.B. Du Bois, "Marxism and the Negro Problem," *Crisis,* May 1933, 103.

79. Ibid., 103–104.

80. Ibid., 104.

81. Ibid.

82. See David R. Roediger, *The Wages of Whiteness: Race and the Making of the American Working Class,* chapter 1.

83. Du Bois, "Marxism," 104.

84. Ibid., 103.

85. Ibid.

86. Ibid.

87. Ibid.

88. Harold Preece, "Fascism and the Negro," *Crisis,* December 1934, 355.

89. Jacob J. Weinstein, "The Negro and the Jew," *Crisis,* July 1934, 197–198.

90. Bruce M. Tyler, *From Harlem to Hollywood: The Struggle for Racial and Cultural Democracy, 1920–1943,* 49.

91. Ibid.

92. David H. Pierce, "Fascism and the Negro," *Crisis,* April 1935, 107. In *Working toward Whiteness: How America's Immigrants Became White,* David R. Roediger observes how New Deal policies and the industrial unionism of the 1930s were responsible for federally instituting a racial divide that categorized numerous immigrants as white while systematically excluding blacks, Mexicans, Japanese, and several other groups from the benefits of that classification.

93. The following list represents only a cross-section of the innumerable articles on fascism published in the *New Masses:* David Ramsey, "A New Deal in Trusts," January 9, 1934, 17–18; John Strachey, "Fascism in America," January 2, 1934, 8, 10; James King, "Mrs. Roosevelt Will Not Speak," May 28, 1935, 9–12; Joseph Freeman, "'Fortune' and the Jews: Anti-Semitism in America Today," February 4, 1936, 9–12; John L. Spivak, "Wall Street's Conspiracy: Testimony that the Dickstein Committee Suppressed," January 29, 1935, 9–15, and February 5, 1935, 10–15; Spivak, "Plotting the American Pogroms," October 2, 1934, 9–13; October 9, 1934, 9–13; October 16, 1934, 9–12; October 23, 1934, 10–13; October 30, 1934, 9–13; November 6, 1934, 9–12; November 13, 1934, 8–11; November 20, 1934, 9–13; November 27, 1934, 10–12.

94. A. B. Magil and Henry Stevens, *The Perils of Fascism: The Crisis of American Democracy,* 218.

95. Ibid., 219.

96. Ibid., 219–220.

97. William Pickins, "Why the Negro Must Be Anti-Fascist," *New Masses*, May 30, 1939, 11.

98. Ibid.

99. Kirschke, *Art in Crisis*, 108.

100. Ibid.

101. Ibid., 110.

102. Ibid.

103. Brandon, unpublished MS, file D43, 29–30, Tom Brandon Archives.

104. Quoted in Everett, *Returning the Gaze*, 255.

105. Ibid., 256.

106. Quoted in Ibid., 260.

107. Ibid., 258.

108. L.E.H., "Hollywood Letter: Role of the Negro in American Films," *Daily Worker*, August 14, 1933, 7.

109. Ibid. For a thorough analysis of the international pressure on Hollywood to mitigate its racist stereotypes of non-Americans, see Ruth Vasey, *The World according to Hollywood, 1918–1939*.

110. Tyler, *From Harlem to Hollywood*, 39.

111. Everett, *Returning the Gaze*, 265.

112. For a detailed study of the transformation of the book *Trader Horn* into its film version, see Robinson, *Forgeries of Memory and Meaning*.

113. Miller, "Uncle Tom in Hollywood," 329.

114. Ibid.

115. Miller's observation uncannily anticipates Frantz Fanon's similar experience of watching *Tarzan* in the Antilles, where an all-black audience identified with Tarzan against the tribesmen (*Black Skin, White Masks*, 152–153). Furthermore, *Trader Horn* plays a central role in Richard Wright's novel *Native Son*. While watching the film, Bigger Thomas unconsciously identifies with the African tribesmen, "hearing the roll of tom-toms and the screams of black men and women dancing free and wild, men and women who were adjusted to their soil and at home in their world, secure from fear and hysteria" (Wright, *Native Son*, 37–38). It is significant that Thomas can only unconsciously identify with the utopian impulses symbolized by the native community, since the film's explicit narrative structure attempts to demonize them. Wright draws attention to how a spectator's psychic economy might pull like an undertow against cinematic narrative—a fact often lost on film theorists and historians. There is a significant need for film theorists and historians to further explore how literature has supplemented subtle notions of film viewing if they are to reconceptualize past and present modes of spectatorship.

116. Miller, "Uncle Tom in Hollywood," 336.

117. Ibid., 329.

118. Ibid.

119. Ibid., 336.

120. Ibid.

121. Ibid.

122. Ibid.

123. Lotte Eisner, *Fritz Lang*; Paul M. Jensen, *The Cinema of Fritz Lang*; Robert A. Armour, *Fritz Lang*; Nick Smedley, "Fritz Lang's Trilogy: The Rise and Fall of a European Social Commentator," *Film History* 5 (1993): 1–21.

124. Jensen, *Cinema of Lang*, 113–128; Nick Smedley, "Fritz Lang's Trilogy."

125. D.W.C., "Fritz Lang Bows to Mammon," *New York Times*, June 14, 1936.

126. Ibid.

127. Peter Bogdanovich, *Fritz Lang in America*, 32.

128. Ibid.

129. Barbara Mennel, "White Law and the Missing Black Body in Fritz Lang's *Fury*," *Quarterly Review of Film and Video* 20, no. 3 (January 2003): 217.

130. Patrick McGilligan, *Fritz Lang: The Nature of the Beast*, 227–228.

131. Fritz Lang, "The Viennese Night: A Fritz Lang Confession, Parts One and Two," 63.

132. Fritz Lang, "Interview with Fritz Lang," by Charles Higham and Joel Greenberg, 119.

133. Anthony Kaes, "A Stranger in the House: Fritz Lang's *Fury* and the Cinema of Exile," *New German Critique* 89 (Summer/Spring 2003): 57.

134. Denning, *Cultural Front*, 123–136.

135. Ibid., 134.

136. Giovacchini, *Hollywood Modernism*, 66.

137. Martin Rubin, "The Crowd, the Collective, and the Chorus: Busby Berkeley and the New Deal," 83.

138. Tom Gunning, *The Films of Fritz Lang: Allegories of Vision and Modernity*, 225.

139. Leo Braudy, *The World in a Frame: What We See in Films*, 48; Andrew Sarris, *The American Cinema: Directors and Directions, 1929–1968*.

140. Louis J. Budd, "The American Background," 27–31.

141. Ibid., 43.

142. Ibid.

143. It is worth noting here the similarities between Lang's analysis of the fascist tendencies in American culture and Adorno and Horkheimer's observations in *Dialectic of Enlightenment: Philosophical Fragments*. Although Lang's naturalistic outlook could not be more opposed to Adorno and Horkheimer's Marxist perspective, the fact that they both saw certain fascist tendencies at work in American culture deserves study in itself.

144. R.O., "Reviewer Acclaims New Film: Calls *Fury* Worthy Indictment of Mob Violence in U.S.," *New York Amsterdam News*, June 13, 1936.

145. Kenneth Fearing, "The Screen: *Fury*—Anti-Lynch Film," *New Masses*, June 16, 1936, 28.

146. John L. Spivak, "Who Backs the Black Legion?" *New Masses*, June 16, 1936, 9–10; Birdwell, *Celluloid Soldiers*, 46.

147. Spivak, "Who Backs the Black Legion?" 9.

148. Benjamin, "Philosophy of History," 262.

149. Ibid., 263.

150. Advertisement for *Fury, New Theatre*, July 1936, page unknown, file P320, Tom Brandon Archives.

151. Ben Davis, Jr., "Film Indictment of Lynching," *Daily Worker*, June 9, 1936, 7.

152. Ibid.

153. Ibid.

154. R.O., "Reviewer Acclaims New Film," 8.

155. Ibid.

156. Ibid.

157. Ibid.

158. Ibid.

159. The drawing initially appeared in the *New Yorker*, September 8, 1934.

160. Robert D'Attilio, "Sacco-Vanzetti Case," 669.

161. Davis, "Film Indictment of Lynching," 7.

162. Robert Stebbins, "Fritz Lang and *Fury*," *New Theatre*, July 1936, 11.

163. Ibid.

164. Davis, "Film Indictment of Lynching," 7.

165. Otis Ferguson, "Hollywood's Half a Loaf," *New Republic*, June 10, 1936, 130.

166. Fearing, "*Fury*—Anti-Lynch Film," 28.

167. R.O., "Reviewer Acclaims New Film," 8.

168. Ibid.

169. Ibid.

170. Ibid. Shohat and Stam, *Unthinking Eurocentrism*, 35.

171. See bell hooks, "The Oppositional Gaze"; Manthia Diawara, "Black Spectatorship: Problems of Identification and Resistance"; and Gaines, *Fire and Desire*, 24–51.

172. Potamkin, "Eyes of the Movie," 249.

173. "Star of Lynching Story Gets Membership on Honor Roll," *Chicago Defender*, January 2, 1937.

174. Frank S. Nugent, "*Fury*, a Dramatic Indictment of Lynch Law, Opens at Capitol," *New York Times*, June 6, 1936.

175. Gunning, *Films of Lang*, 218.

176. Ibid., 221.

177. Jensen, *Cinema of Lang*, 117.

178. McGilligan, *Fritz Lang*, 226.

179. Fearing, "*Fury*—Anti-Lynch Film," 28.

180. Ibid. Both Cedric J. Robinson and Anna Everett have rightly criticized

the myth that the southern box office served as a geographically isolated alibi for Hollywood racism. For more information, see Robinson, *Forgeries of Memory and Meaning*, 88–90, and Everett, *Returning the Gaze*, 299–303.

181. Stebbins, "Fritz Lang and *Fury*," 11.

182. Robert Geroux, "Unsettled Accounts," *Nation*, June 24, 1936, 821.

183. Ferguson, "Hollywood's Half a Loaf," 130.

184. Fearing, "*Fury*—Anti-Lynch Film," 28.

185. Peter Ellis, "Sights and Sounds," *New Masses*, July 20, 1937, 28.

186. David Platt, "*They Won't Forget* Rivals *Fury* in Social Content," *Daily Worker*, May 21, 1937, 7.

187. Ibid.

188. Ibid. Much of this understatement can be attributed to the Production Code Administration's intense scrutiny of *They Won't Forget* after it was criticized for approving *Fury*'s explicit representations of mob violence. For more information regarding the censorship of *They Won't Forget*, see Bernstein, *Screening a Lynching*.

189. Interestingly enough, Left film critics had nothing to say about Oscar Micheaux's two films concerning the lynching of Leo Frank, *Lem Hawkins' Confession* (1935) and *Murder in Harlem* (1936). Although one cannot exactly determine the reasons for the films' absence from their columns, I suspect that Left film critics either were unaware of the films or did not want to risk resurrecting the tensions between blacks and Jews that the Frank case embodied, especially at a time when the historical Left was attempting to overcome such racial and ethnic divides. For more information regarding these two films, see Bernstein, *Screening a Lynching*.

190. Stebbins, "Fritz Lang and *Fury*," 11.

191. Ferguson, "Hollywood's Half a Loaf," 131.

192. Advertisement for *Fury*, *New Theatre*, July 1936.

193. "Anti-Lynch Film Order of Day in Hollywood," *Atlanta Daily World*, January 25, 1937.

194. Ibid.

195. "MGM Movie *Fury* Seen as Excellent Anti-Lynch Film," *Chicago Defender*, June 20, 1936.

196. Davis, "Film Indictment of Lynching," 7.

197. Ibid.

198. New Film Alliance, pamphlet, 1, file L234, Tom Brandon Archives.

199. Ibid., 2.

200. "Masses Form Film Alliance," *Daily Worker*, February 9, 1937.

201. David Platt, "Progressive Films Take over Silver Screen of Hollywood," *Daily Worker*, August 29, 1937, 10.

202. Quoted in Tyler, *From Harlem to Hollywood*, 45.

203. Ceplair and Englund, *Inquisition in Hollywood*, 104.

204. Giovacchini, *Hollywood Modernism*, 83.

205. Platt, "Progressive Films," 10.

206. Ibid.

207. Films for Democracy, newsletter, file L234, Tom Brandon Archives.

208. Edgar Dale, "The Movies and Race Relations," *Crisis*, October 1937, 296.

209. Ibid.

210. Quoted in ibid., 315.

211. Harry Alan Potamkin, "The Year of the Eclipse," 205.

212. Bogdanovich, *Lang in America*, 30–31.

213. Judith Mayne, *The Woman at the Keyhole: Feminism and Women's Cinema*, 43.

214. Carolyn Kay Steedman, *Landscape for a Good Woman: A Story of Two Lives*, 123.

215. Ibid.

216. June Howard, *Form and History in American Literary Naturalism*, 95–96.

217. For a critique of the New Woman, see Mary Ann Doane, "The Economy of Desire: The Commodity Form in/of the Cinema." For a more postmodern approach, see Lori Landay, "The Flapper Film: Comedy, Dance, and Jazz Age Kinaesthetic."

218. Nugent, "*Fury*," 21.

219. Ferguson, "Hollywood's Half a Loaf," 130.

220. *Fury* advertisement, *New York Times*, June 4, 1936.

221. McGilligan, *Fritz Lang*, 226.

222. Mennel, "White Law and Black Body," 214.

223. Ibid.

224. Rubin, "Crowd, Collective, and Chorus," 75.

225. A more recent example of a woman serving as a distraction from male trauma and hysteria occurs in *Night of the Living Dead* (1968). Like Katherine, Barbara (Judith O'Dea) remains catatonic for a majority of the film. The utter ridiculousness of Barbara's state—lifelessly propped in the living room with her mouth agape—diverts the viewer's focus from the male hysteria of Ben (Duane Jones), Harry (Karl Hardman), and Tom (Keith Wayne).

226. Gunning, *Films of Lang*, 214.

227. Kaja Silverman, "Dis-Embodying the Female Voice," 312.

228. Ibid., 313.

CHAPTER FOUR

1. Seymour Stern, "The Bankruptcy of Cinema as Art," 133.

2. Thorp, *America at the Movies*, 19.

3. See Clayton R. Koppes and Gregory D. Black, *Hollywood Goes to War: How Politics, Profits and Propaganda Shaped World War II*, and Buhle and Wagner, *Radical Hollywood*.

4. Although U.S. Left film critics had been championing the Soviets' ability

to offer better character-based histories since the appearance of *Chapayev* (1934) and *The Youth of Maxim* (1934), they could not foresee these films having an impact on Hollywood filmmaking.

5. William Dieterle, "From Hollywood to the USSR," *Daily Worker*, January 18, 1938, clipping in file O287, Tom Brandon Archives.

6. Harry Alan Potamkin, "Carl Dreyer's *The Passion of Jeanne D'Arc*," 166.

7. Ibid.

8. H.D., *"Joan of Arc,"* 131. Telisila (or Telisilla) was an ancient Greek poet of Argos who dressed herself in male armor and led a group of women in repelling an attack by Sparta.

9. Ibid., 132.

10. Ibid.

11. Irving Lerner, "The Screen," *New Masses*, January 16, 1934, 30.

12. Ibid. One can't help noticing the misogynistic and homophobic stance that informs Lerner's description of Queen Christina as "ugly, sickly, and sexually abnormal." This is a far from isolated incident. All too often, male U.S. Left film critics used a famous woman as a metonymic effigy for all the ills of society, usually citing her looks and nonheterosexual behavior as damning evidence of the decadence her privileged class represents. For a particularly acute example of this, see Forsythe, "Mae West: A Treatise on Decay."

13. Lerner, "The Screen."

14. Peter Ellis, "The Screen: Verona Comes to Hollywood," *New Masses*, September 1, 1936, 29.

15. William Troy, "Russia a la Mode," *Nation*, October 3, 1934, 392.

16. Braver-Mann, "Josef von Sternberg," 18, 19.

17. See Christopher Faulkner, *The Social Cinema of Jean Renoir*; Martin O'Shaughnessy, *Jean Renoir*; and Jonathan Buschbaum, *Cinema Engagé: Film in the Popular Front*.

18. James Dugan, "Renoir's Great War Film," *New Masses*, September 27, 1938, 29.

19. Ibid., 28.

20. André Bazin, *Jean Renoir*, 80.

21. Jean Renoir, *My Life and My Films*, 132–133.

22. James Dugan, "A Year off My Life," *New Masses*, January 3, 1939, 29.

23. Richard Rene Plant, "Jean Renoir," *Theatre Arts Monthly* 23, no. 6 (1939): 431.

24. Dugan, "A Year off My Life," 29.

25. Plant, "Jean Renoir," 432.

26. Dugan, "A Year off My Life," 29.

27. Ibid.

28. Bazin, *Jean Renoir*, 85.

29. André Bazin, "The Evolution of the Language of Cinema," 156.

30. Faulkner, *Social Cinema of Renoir*, 50.

31. Barbara Stavis, "Sights and Sounds: French Social Films," *New Masses,* May 2, 1939, 28.

32. Peter Kramer, "Post-classical Hollywood," 291.

33. For an excellent account of the film's production, see Dudley Andrews and Steven Ungar, *Popular Front Paris and the Poetics of Culture,* 146.

34. Stavis, "French Social Films," 28.

35. Ibid.

36. James Dugan, "Allons, Enfants," *New Masses,* November 21, 1939, 28.

37. Guy Debord, *The Society of the Spectacle,* 49.

38. James Dugan, "Movies," August 30, 1938, 30.

39. Ibid.

40. Andrews and Ungar, *Popular Front Paris,* 157.

41. Dugan, "Allons, Enfants," 28.

42. Ibid.

43. Dugan, "Movies," August 30, 1938, 30.

44. Lauren Adams, "The New Film: Queen and Lover," *Daily Worker,* August 1, 1936, 7.

45. Dugan, "Allons, Enfants," 28–29. Despite Dugan's initial claim about "the status of women" within the film, his article doesn't elaborate on this point.

46. Plant, "Jean Renoir," 435.

47. Leger Grindon, *Shadows of the Past: Studies in the Historical Fiction Film,* 62.

48. Forsythe, "Burst of Fury," 29.

49. Ibid.

50. Ibid.

51. Jane Gaines makes a similar point: "Adrian's whimsical design for design's sake often conflicted, then, with the costumer's code as it adhered to the laws of continuity cinema" ("The *Queen Christina* Tie-Ups: Convergence of Show Window and Screen," *Quarterly Review of Film and Video* 11, no. 1 [1989]: 40). Stylistic codes trumped narrative codes, which is exactly what Forsythe was grappling with in his article.

52. Ibid.

53. Lewis Jacobs, *Rise of the American Film,* 405, 407.

54. Ibid., 411.

55. Thorp, *America at the Movies,* 5.

56. Ibid., 6.

57. Berry, *Screen Style,* 82.

58. Elsaesser, "Film History as Social History," 23–24.

59. Peter Ellis, "Sights and Sounds," *New Masses,* August 17, 1937, 29.

60. Ibid.

61. Ibid.

62. Potamkin, "Year of the Eclipse"; Harry Alan Potamkin, "The Ritual of the Movies."

63. William Troy, "Half a Loaf," *Nation*, April 24, 1935, 491–492.

64. Nick Roddick, *A New Deal in Entertainment: Warner Brothers in the 1930s*, 184.

65. Peter Ellis, "The Screen," *New Masses* February 5, 1936, 30.

66. "Associated Film Audiences Praise Warner's *Zola* Film," *Daily Worker*, July 27, 1937.

67. David Platt, "*Life of Emile Zola* Is Brilliant Biography and Social Document," *Daily Worker*, August 14, 1937, 7.

68. Ellis, "Sights and Sounds," August 17, 1937, 29.

69. Roddick, *New Deal in Entertainment*, 266.

70. Thorp, *America at the Movies*, 23.

71. Giovacchini, *Hollywood Modernism*, 87; and John Russell Taylor, *Strangers in Paradise: The Hollywood Émigrés, 1933–1950*, 146–147.

72. See John Howard Lawson, "Banning of *Blockade* Threatens Freedom of the Screen in America," *Theatre Arts Committee*, July 1938, 5; James Dugan, "Movies," *New Masses*, August 2, 1938, 30–31; and Alfred O'Malley, "*Blockade*," *Daily Worker*, n.d., 9. For a historical contextualization of the debates on *Blockade*, see Bernstein, *Walter Wanger*, 129–150, and Smith, "Blocking *Blockade*."

73. Peter Ellis, "Sights and Sounds," *New Masses*, October 5, 1937, 29.

74. Gordon Cassons, "Put Real Life into Our Films," *Daily Worker*, unknown date, 1938, 3 (clipping in box O287, Tom Brandon Archives).

75. Roddick, *New Deal in Entertainment*, 191.

76. Again, like *The Life of Emile Zola*, *Juarez* had a production team of antifascist German exiles who strongly influenced the film's antifascist stance: producer Henry Blanke, playwright Franz Werfel, screenwriter Wolfgang Reinhardt, and composer Erich Wolfgang Korngold.

77. James Dugan, "Hollywood's Greatest Films," *New Masses*, May 9, 1939, 27.

78. Additionally, Nick Roddick has discovered that Cardenas sent Jack Warner a telegram wishing him luck during the film's premiere (*New Deal in Entertainment*, 194).

79. Ibid.

80. Peter Ellis, "The Screen: *The Story of Louis Pasteur*," *New Masses*, February 25, 1936, 30.

81. Ibid.

82. James Dugan, "Making the Social Film," *New Masses*, May 23, 1939, 28.

83. Ibid.

84. Dugan, "Hollywood's Greatest Films," 27.

85. Grindon, *Shadows on the Past*, 13.

86. Dugan, "Making the Social Film," 28.

87. Grindon, *Shadows on the Past*, 52.

88. Dugan, "Allons, Enfants," 29.

89. James Dugan, "Lincoln for President!" *New Masses*, March 12, 1940, 28.

90. Quoted in ibid.

91. Ibid.

92. Thomas Schatz, *The Genius of the System: Hollywood Filmmaking in the Studio Era*, 218–220.

93. Dugan, "Hollywood's Greatest Films," 28.

CONCLUSION

1. For more information on the Moscow Trials, see Wald, *New York Intellectuals*, 128–163.

2. For an excellent account of the *Partisan Review*, see James F. Murphy, *The Proletarian Moment: The Controversy over Leftism in Literature*.

3. Dwight Macdonald, "The Soviet Cinema: 1930–1938, Part II," *Partisan Review*, August–September 1938, 54–58.

4. Dwight Macdonald, "Soviet Society and Its Cinema," *Partisan Review*, Winter 1939, 88.

5. Greenberg, "Avant-Garde and Kitsch," 41.

6. Ibid., 47.

7. Andrew Ross, *No Respect*, 43–45.

8. Sachs, "Kitsch," 205.

9. Andrew Ross, *No Respect*, 45.

10. For more information, see Ceplair and Englund, *Inquisition in Hollywood*; and Harvey Klehr, *The Heyday of American Communism: The Depression Decade*.

11. Ceplair and Englund, *Inquisition in Hollywood*, 158.

12. Albert Maltz, "Four Millions Dollars Worth of Wind," 324–327; James Dugan, "G'wan with the Wind," *New Masses*, January 2, 1940, 29–30; Dugan, "Facts on the Wind," *New Masses*, January 23, 1940, 28–30; Dugan, "Reconstruction and *GWTW*," *New Masses*, January 30, 1940; Jack Weatherwax, "Hollywood Says *Confessions of a Nazi Spy* Will be a Powerful Expose Film," *Daily Worker*, April 14, 1939, 7; Stephen Peabody, "Inquiring Reporter Learns Why Film Crowd Cheers *Confessions of a Nazi Spy*," *Daily Worker*, May 5, 1939, 7; Harrow, "Public Demands Hollywood Make More Anti-Nazi Films," *Daily Worker* July 5, 1939, 7.

13. Edwin Locke, "John Ford's *The Grapes of Wrath*"; James Dugan, "The Great American Film," *New Masses*, February 6, 1940, 28–30; Dugan, "Of Mice and Men," *New Masses*, March 5, 1940, 29–30; Pare Lorentz, "*The Grapes of Wrath*," *Lorentz on Film*, 183–186.

14. Buhle and Wagner, *Radical Hollywood*, 277–282.

15. Denning, *Cultural Front*, 455.

16. See Petro, "Mass Culture and the Feminine"; and Tania Modleski, "Femininity as Mas[s]querade: A Feminist Approach to Mass Culture."

17. Brandon, unpublished MS, file D43, 15, Tom Brandon Archives.

18. Benjamin, "Eduard Fuchs," 227.

19. Terry Eagleton, *Criticism and Ideology*, 72.

Bibliography

Aaron, Daniel. *Writers on the Left: Episodes in American Literary Communism.* New York: Columbia Univ. Press, 1992 ed.

Adams, Henry. *The Education of Henry Adams.* New York: Modern Library, 1918.

Adams, Lauren. "The New Film: Queen and Lover." *Daily Worker,* August 1, 1936.

Adorno, Theodor, Walter Benjamin, Ernst Bloch, Bertolt Brecht, and Georg Lukács. *Aesthetics and Politics: The Key Texts of the Classic Debate within German Marxism.* New York: Verso, 1977.

Alexander, William. *Film on the Left: American Documentary Film from 1931 to 1942.* Princeton, N.J.: Princeton Univ. Press, 1981.

Amberg, George. *Experimental Cinema.* New York: Arno, 1969.

Andrews, Dudley. "Harry Alan Potamkin." *Film Comment,* March 1974, 55–57.

Andrews, Dudley, and Steven Ungar. *Popular Front Paris and the Poetics of Culture.* Cambridge, Mass.: Harvard Univ. Press, 2005.

Aragón Leiva, Agustin. "Eisenstein's Film on Mexico." *Experimental Cinema,* February 1933, 5–6.

Armour, Robert A. *Fritz Lang.* Boston: Twayne, 1978.

Atlanta Daily World, "Anti-Lynch Film Order of the Day," January 25, 1937.

———, "Russian Negro Film is Finally Banned," October 5, 1932.

———, "Withdrawal of Russian Plan for Movie on Race Issue 'Strands' 22 U.S. Negroes," August 16, 1932.

Aumont, Jacques. *Montage Eisenstein.* Translated by Lee Hildreth, Constance Penley, and Andrew Ross. Bloomington: Indiana Univ. Press, 1987.

Bakhtin, Mikhail. *Rabelais and His World.* Translated by Hélène Iswolsky. Bloomington: Indiana Univ. Press, 1984.

Bakshy, Alexander. "Street Scene." *Nation,* September 16, 1931, 290.

Bartlett, Rosamund. "The Circle and the Line: Eisenstein, Florensky, and Russian Orthodoxy." In LaValley and Scherr, *Eisenstein at 100,* 65–76.

Bazin, André. "The Evolution of the Language of Cinema." In Mast, Cohen, and Braudy, *Film Theory and Criticism,* 155–167.

———. *Jean Renoir.* Translated by W. W. Halsey II and William H. Simon. Edited by Francois Truffaut. New York: Dell, 1973.

Belton, John, ed. *Movies and Mass Culture.* New Brunswick, N.J.: Rutgers Univ. Press, 1996.

Benjamin, Walter. "The Author as Producer." In *Reflections*, 220–238. Translated by Edmund Jephcott. New York: Schocken, 1978.

———. "Eduard Fuchs: Collector and Historian." In *The Essential Frankfurt School Reader*, edited by Andrew Arato and Eike Gebhardt, 225–253. New York: Continuum, 1997.

———. *Illuminations: Essays and Reflections*. Edited by Hannah Arendt. New York: Schocken, 1968.

———. "On Some Motifs in Baudelaire." In *Illuminations*, 155–200.

———. "Theses on the Philosophy of History." In *Illuminations*, 253–264.

———. "The Work of Art in the Age of Mechanical Reproduction." In *Illuminations*, 217–251.

Benshoff, Harry M. "Homoerotic Iconography and Anti-Catholic Marxism: Proto-Feminist Discourse in Sergei M. Eisenstein's *Que Viva Mexico!*" *Spectator* 11, no. 1 (Fall 1990): 6–17.

Bergan, Ronald. *Sergei Eisenstein: A Life in Conflict*. London: Warner, 1997.

Bergman, Andrew. *We're in The Money: Depression America and Its Films*. New York: Harper Torchbooks, 1971.

Bernstein, Matthew. *Screening a Lynching: The Leo Frank Case on Film and Television*. Athens: Univ. of Georgia Press, 2009.

———. *Walter Wanger: Hollywood Independent*. Berkeley and Los Angeles: Univ. of California Press, 1994.

Berry, Sarah. *Screen Style: Fashion and Femininity in 1930s Hollywood*. Minneapolis: Univ. of Minnesota Press, 2000.

Best-Maugard, Adolfo. "Mexico into Cinema." *Theatre Arts Monthly* 16, no. 11 (1932): 926–933.

Birdwell, Michael E. *Celluloid Soldiers: Warner Bros.'s Campaign against Nazism*. New York: New York Univ. Press, 1999.

Black, Gregory. *Hollywood Censored: Morality Codes, Catholics, and the Movies*. Cambridge: Cambridge Univ. Press, 1994.

Bodnar, John. *Blue-Collar Hollywood: Liberalism, Democracy, and Working People in American Film*. Baltimore: Johns Hopkins Univ. Press, 2003.

Bogdanovich, Peter. *Fritz Lang in America*. New York: Praeger, 1967.

Bordwell, David. *The Cinema of Eisenstein*. Cambridge, Mass.: Harvard Univ. Press, 1993.

Bordwell, David, Janet Staiger, and Kristin Thompson. *The Classical Hollywood Cinema: Film Style and Mode of Production to 1960*. New York: Columbia Univ. Press, 1985.

Bowser, Pearl, Jane Gaines, and Charles Musser, eds. *Oscar Micheaux and His Circle: African-American Filmmaking and Race Cinema of the Silent Era*. Bloomington: Indiana Univ. Press, 2001.

Bowser, Pearl, and Louise Spence. *Writing Himself into History: Oscar Micheaux, His Silent Films, and His Audiences*. New Brunswick, N.J.: Rutgers Univ. Press, 2000.

Brandon, Tom. "Who Are the Forces behind the Legion of Decency Drive?" *Daily Worker,* August 17, 18, 20, and 21, 1934.

Braudy, Leo. *The World in a Frame: What We See in Films.* Garden City, N.Y.: Anchor Doubleday, 1977.

Braver-Mann, B.G. "Josef von Sternberg." *Experimental Cinema,* February 1934, 17–21.

———. "Vidor and Evasion." *Experimental Cinema,* February 1931, 26–29.

Brody, Sam (as "Lens"). "Flashes and Close Ups." *Daily Worker,* January 18, 1934, 5.

———. "On a Theory of Sources." *Experimental Cinema,* February 1931, 23–25.

Brody, Sam, and Tom Brandon. "A Mexican Trailer." *New Masses,* September 1933, 28.

Brundage, Fitzhugh W. *Lynching in the New South: Georgia and Virginia, 1880–1930.* Urbana: Univ. of Illinois Press, 1993.

Buckley, Mary. "Soviet Interpretations of the Woman Question." In *Soviet Sisterhood: British Feminists on Women in the U.S.S.R.,* edited by Barbara Holland, 24–53. London: Fourth Estate, 1985.

Buck-Morss, Susan. *The Origins of Negative Dialectics: Theodor W. Adorno, Walter Benjamin, and the Frankfurt Institute.* New York: Free Press, 1977.

Budd, Lewis J. "The American Background." In *American Realism and Naturalism: Howells to London,* edited by Donald Pizer, 21–46. Cambridge: Cambridge Univ. Press, 1995.

Buhle, Mari Jo, Paul Buhle, and Dan Georgakas, eds. *Encyclopedia of the American Left.* Urbana: Univ. of Illinois Press, 1990.

Buhle, Paul, and Dave Wagner. *Radical Hollywood: The Untold Story Behind America's Favorite Movies.* New York: New Press, 2002.

Bulgakowa, Oksana. *Sergei Eisenstein: A Biography.* San Francisco: Potemkin Press, 2002.

Buschbaum, Jonathan. *Cinema Engagé: Film in the Popular Front.* Urbana: Univ. of Illinois Press, 1988.

Campbell, Russell. *Cinema Strikes Back: Radical Filmmaking in the United States, 1930–1942.* Ann Arbor, Mich.: UMI Research Press, 1982.

Carter, Dan. *Scottsboro: A Tragedy of the American South.* Baton Rouge: Louisiana State Univ. Press, 1979.

Cassons, Gordon. "Put Real Life into Our Films." *Daily Worker,* 1938.

Ceplair, Larry, and Steven Englund. *The Inquisition in Hollywood: Politics in the Film Community, 1930–1960.* Urbana: Univ. of Illinois Press, 2003 ed.

Chicago Defender, "MGM Movie *Fury* Seen as Excellent Anti-Lynch Film," June 20, 1936.

———, "Star of Lynching Story Gets Membership on Honor Roll," January 2, 1937.

Christie, Ian, and Richard Taylor, eds. *Eisenstein Rediscovered.* London and New York: Routledge, 1993.

Coiner, Constance. *Better Red: The Writing and Resistance of Tillie Olsen and Meridel Le Sueur.* Urbana: Univ. of Illinois Press, 1998.

Cripps, Thomas. *Slow Fade to Black: The Negro in American Film, 1900-1942.* Oxford: Oxford Univ. Press, 1977.

Crisis. "Negro Editors on Communism: A Symposium of the American Negro Press." April 1932, 117, 119; May 1932, 154, 156.

Daily Worker, "American League Mobilizes to Picket Lowes Theatres against *Riff-Raff* Showing," February 27, 1936.

———, "Associated Film Audiences Praise Warner's *Zola* Film," July 27, 1937.

———, "Film and Photo League Begins Movie School," October 12, 1935.

———, "Masses Form Film Alliance," February 9, 1937.

Dale, Edgar. "The Movies and Race Relations." *Crisis,* October 1937, 294-296, 315-316.

D'Attilio, Robert. "Sacco-Vanzetti Case." In Buhle, Buhle, and Georgakas, *Encyclopedia of the American Left,* 667-670.

Daugherty, Frank. "Paul Green in Hollywood." *Close Up* 9, no. 2 (June 1932): 81-86.

Davis Jr., Ben. "Film Indictment of Lynching." *Daily Worker,* June 9, 1936.

Debord, Guy. *The Society of the Spectacle.* Detroit: Black and Red, 1983.

Decherney, Peter. *Hollywood and the Culture Elite: How the Movies Became American.* New York: Columbia Univ. Press, 2005.

Denning, Michael. *The Cultural Front: The Laboring of American Culture in the Twentieth Century.* London: Verso, 1997.

———. *Culture in the Age of Three Worlds.* London: Verso, 2004.

Deren, Maya. "Cinematography: The Creative Use of Reality." In Mast, Cohen, and Braudy, *Film Theory and Criticism,* 66-68.

Diawara, Manthia. "Black Spectatorship: Problems of Identification and Resistance." In *Black American Cinema,* 211-220. New York: Routledge, 1993.

Dieterle, William. "From Hollywood to the USSR." *Daily Worker,* January 18, 1938.

———. "Will Hollywood Give Up Intelligence?" *Liberty* 7 (December 1940): 29-31.

Dismond, Geraldyn. "The Negro Actor and the American Movies." *Close Up* 5, no. 2 (August 1929): 96-97.

Doane, Mary Ann. "The Economy of Desire: The Commodity Form in/of the Cinema." In Belton, *Movies and Mass Culture,* 119-134.

Donald, James, Anne Friedberg, and Laura Marcus, eds. *"Close Up," 1927-1933: Cinema and Modernism.* Princeton, New Jersey: Princeton University Press, 1998:

Du Bois, W. E. B. "Marxism and the Negro Problem." *Crisis,* May 1933, 103-104, 118.

———. "Postscript." *Crisis,* June 1932, 190.

Dugan, James. "Allons, Enfants . . ." *New Masses,* November 21, 1939, 28-30.

———. "Facts on the Wind." *New Masses,* January 23, 1940, 28-30.

———. "The Great American Film." *New Masses,* February 6, 1940, 28–30.

———. "G'wan with the Wind." *New Masses,* January 2, 1940, 29–30.

———. "Hollywood's Greatest Films." *New Masses,* May 9, 1939, 27–29.

———. "Lincoln for President!" *New Masses,* March 12, 1940, 28.

———. "Making the Social Film." *New Masses,* May 23, 1939, 28–30.

———. "Movies." *New Masses,* August 2, 1938, 30–31.

———. "Movies." *New Masses,* August 30, 1938, 30–31.

———. "Of Mice and Men." *New Masses,* March 5, 1940, 29–30.

———. "Reconstruction and *GWTW.*" *New Masses,* January 30, 1940, 28–30.

———. "Renoir's Great War Film." *New Masses,* September 27, 1938, 28–30.

———. "A Year off My Life." *New Masses,* January 3, 1939, 29–31.

Durgnat, Raymond, and Scott Simmon. *King Vidor, American.* Berkeley and Los Angeles: Univ. of California Press, 1988.

D.W.C. "Fritz Lang Bows to Mammon." *New York Times,* June 14, 1936.

Dyer, Richard. *Stars.* London: BFI, 1998.

Eagleton, Terry. *Criticism and Ideology.* London: Verso, 2006.

Eckert, Charles. "The Carole Lombard in Macy's Windows." In Belton, *Movies and Mass Culture,* 95–118.

Eisenstein, Sergei. "An American Tragedy." *Close Up* 10, no. 2 (June 1933): 109–124.

———. *Beyond the Stars: The Memoirs of Sergei Eisenstein.* Translated by William Powell. London: BFI, 1995.

———. "The Cinematographic Principle and the Ideogram." In Mast, Cohen, and Braudy, *Film Theory and Criticism,* 127–138.

———. "Cinematography with Tears." *Close Up* 10, no. 1 (March 1933): 3–17.

———. *The Eisenstein Reader.* Edited by Richard Taylor. London: BFI, 1998.

———. *Film Form: Essays in Film Theory.* Edited and translated by Jay Leyda. New York: Harcourt, Brace, and World, 1949.

———. "The Filmic Fourth Dimension." In *Film Form: Essays in Film Theory,* 64–71.

———. *The Film Sense.* Edited and translated by Jay Leyda. New York: Harcourt, Brace, and World, 1947.

———. "First Outline of *Que Viva Mexico!*" In *The Film Sense,* 251–255.

———. "The Fourth Dimension in Cinema." In *The Eisenstein Reader,* edited by Richard Taylor, 111–123. London: BFI, 1998.

———. "My Theme is Patriotism." *Daily Worker,* April 1, 1939.

———. "The New Soviet Cinema." *New Theatre,* January 1935, 9, 21.

———. "Perspectives." In *Film Essays,* edited by Jay Leyda, 35–47. New York: Praeger, 1970.

———. *Writings, 1922–1934.* Edited by Richard Taylor. London: BFI, 1988.

Eisenstein, Sergei, and V. G. Alexandroff. "Synopsis for *Que Viva Mexico!*" *Experimental Cinema,* February 1934, 5–13.

Eisenstein, Sergei, W. I. Pudowkin, and G. V. Alexandroff. "The Sound Film:

A Statement from U.S.S.R." In Donald, Friedberg, and Marcus, *"Close Up,"* *1927–1933*, 83–84.

Eisner, Lotte. *Fritz Lang*. London: Da Capo, 1976.

Ellis, Peter. "The Screen." *New Masses*, February 5, 1936, 30.

———. "The Screen: *The Story of Louis Pasteur*." *New Masses*, February 25, 1936, 30.

———. "The Screen: Verona Comes to Hollywood." *New Masses*, September 1, 1936, 29.

———. "Sights and Sounds." *New Masses*, July 20, 1937, 28.

———. "Sights and Sounds." *New Masses*, August 17, 1937, 29.

———. "Sights and Sounds." *New Masses*, October 5, 1937, 29.

Elsaesser, Thomas. "Film History as Social History: The Dieterle/Warner Brothers Bio-pic." *Wide Angle* 8, no. 2 (1986): 15–31.

Enckell, Mikael. "A Study in Scarlet." In Kleberg and Lövgren, *Eisenstein Revisited*, 113–131.

Engels, Frederick. *The Origins of the Family, Private Property, and the State*. New York: Pathfinder, 1972.

Enstad, Nan. *Ladies of Labor, Girls of Adventure: Working Women, Popular Culture, and Labor Politics at the Turn of the Twentieth Century*. New York: Columbia Univ. Press, 1999.

Erens, Patricia, ed. *Issues in Feminist Film Theory*. Bloomington: Indiana Univ. Press, 1990:

Everett, Anna. *Returning the Gaze: A Genealogy of Black Film Criticism, 1909–1949*. Durham, N.C.: Duke Univ. Press, 2001.

Experimental Cinema editors. "Manifesto on Eisenstein's Mexican Film." *Close Up* 10, no. 2 (June 1933): 210–212.

———. "Manifesto on *Que Viva Mexico!*" *Experimental Cinema*, February 1934, 14.

———. "Statement." *Experimental Cinema*, February 1931, 3.

Fanon, Frantz. *Black Skin, White Masks*. New York: Grove, 1967.

Faulkner, Christopher. *The Social Cinema of Jean Renoir*. Princeton, N.J.: Princeton Univ. Press, 1986.

Fearing, Kenneth. "The Screen: *Fury*—Anti-Lynch Film." *New Masses*, June 16, 1936, 28.

Ferguson, Otis. "Hollywood's Half a Loaf." *New Republic*, June 10, 1936, 130.

Film Art. Untitled article. Spring 1934, 21–22.

Fitzgerald, F. Scott. *The Last Tycoon*. New York: Collier, 1941.

Foley, Barbara. *Radical Representations: Politics and Form in U.S. Proletarian Fiction, 1929–1941*. Durham, N.C.: Duke Univ. Press, 1993.

———. *Spectres of 1919: Class and Nation in the Making of the New Negro*. Urbana: Univ. of Illinois Press, 2003.

Forsythe, Robert. "The British Are Coming, Boom!" *New Masses*, January 29, 1935, 29–30.

———. "*Chapayev* Is Here." *New Masses,* January 22, 1933, 29–30.

———. "In a Burst of Fury." *New Masses,* September 25, 1934, 29–30.

———. "Mae West: A Treatise on Decay." *New Masses,* October 9, 1934, 29.

Freeman, Joseph. "'Fortune' and the Jews: Anti-Semitism in America Today." *New Masses,* February 4, 1936, 9–12.

Friedberg, Anne. "Introduction: *Borderline* and the POOL Films." In Donald, Friedberg, and Marcus, "*Close Up,*" *1927–1933,* 212–220.

———. "Introduction: Reading *Close Up, 1927–1933.*" In Donald, Friedberg, and Marcus, "*Close Up,*" *1927–1933,* 1–26.

———. *Window Shopping: Cinema and the Postmodern.* Berkeley and Los Angeles: Univ. of California Press, 1993.

Gabler, Neal. *An Empire of Their Own: How the Jews Invented Hollywood.* New York: Anchor, 1988.

Gaines, Jane. "Can We Enjoy Alternative Pleasure?" In Erens, *Issues in Feminist Film Criticism,* 75–92.

———. "Dream/Factory." In *Reinventing Film Studies,* edited by Christine Gledhill and Linda Williams, 100–113. London: Arnold, 2000.

———. *Fire and Desire: Mixed-Race Movies in the Silent Era.* Chicago: Univ. of Chicago Press, 2001.

———. "The *Queen Christina* Tie-Ups: Convergence of Show Window and Screen." *Quarterly Review of Film and Video* 11, no. 1 (1989): 35–60.

Geduld, Harry M., and Ronald Gottesman. *Sergei Eisenstein and Upton Sinclair: The Making and Unmaking of "Que Viva Mexico!"* Bloomington: Indiana Univ. Press, 1970.

Geroux, Robert. "Unsettled Accounts." *Nation,* June 24, 1936, 821.

Giovacchini, Saverio. *Hollywood Modernism: Film and Politics in the Age of the New Deal.* Philadelphia: Temple Univ. Press, 2001.

Gold, Mike. "Movie Madness and the Child." *Daily Worker,* May 11, 1937.

Gollomb, Joseph. "The New Movie." *Daily Worker,* March 29, 1936.

Goodwin, James. *Eisenstein, Cinema, and History.* Urbana: Univ. of Illinois Press, 1993.

———. *Stories of Scottsboro.* New York: Vintage, 1994.

Gorman, Paul R. *Left Intellectuals and Popular Culture in Twentieth-Century America.* Chapel Hill: Univ. of North Carolina Press, 1996.

Gramsci, Antonio. *Selections from the Prison Notebooks.* Edited and translated by Quintin Hoare and Geoffrey Nowell Smith. New York: International Publishers, 1971.

Green, J. Ronald. *Straight Lick: The Cinema of Oscar Micheaux.* Bloomington: Indiana Univ. Press, 2000.

———. *With a Crooked Stick.* Bloomington: Indiana Univ. Press, 2004.

Greenberg, Clement. "Avant-Garde and Kitsch." *Partisan Review* 5, no. 5 (Fall 1939): 34–49.

Grieveson, Lee, and Haidee Wasson. "The Academy and Motion Pictures." In *In-*

venting Film Studies, edited by Lee Grieveson and Haidee Wasson, xi–xxxii. Durham: Duke Univ. Press, 2008.

Grindon, Leger. *Shadows on the Past: Studies in the Historical Fiction Film.* Philadelphia: Temple Univ. Press, 1994.

Gunning, Tom. *The Films of Fritz Lang: Allegories of Vision and Modernity.* London: BFI, 2000.

H.D. "Beauty." In Donald, Friedberg, and Marcus, *"Close Up,"* 1927–1933, 105–109.

———. *"Borderline:* A POOL Film with Paul Robeson." In Donald, Friedberg, and Marcus, *"Close Up,"* 1927–1933, 221–236.

———. *"Joan of Arc."* In Donald, Friedberg, and Marcus, *"Close Up,"* 1927–1933, 130–133.

Haberski, Raymond J., Jr. *"It's Only a Movie": Films and Critics in American Culture.* Lexington: Univ. Press of Kentucky, 2001.

Hansen, Miriam Bratu. "America, Paris, the Alps: Kracauer (and Benjamin) on Cinema and Modernity." In *Cinema and the Invention of Modern Life,* edited by Leo Charney and Vanessa R. Schwartz, 362–402. Berkeley and Los Angeles: Univ. of California Press, 1995.

———. *Babel and Babylon: Spectatorship in American Silent Film.* Cambridge, Mass.: Harvard Univ. Press, 1991.

———. "The Mass Production of the Senses: Classical Cinema as Vernacular Modernism." In *Reinventing Film Studies,* edited by Christine Gledhill and Linda Williams, 332–350. London: Arnold, 2000.

Harvey, Sylvia. *May '68 and Film Culture.* London: BFI, 1980.

Haskell, Frank. *"Marie Antoinette* Is a Lavish Distortion of French Revolution." *Daily Worker,* n.d.

Helprin, Morris. *"Que Viva Mexico!" Experimental Cinema,* February 1933, 13–14.

Hesse, George W. "The Cine Analyst." *Personal Movies,* November 15, 1933, 268, 285.

hooks, bell. "The Oppositional Gaze." In *Black Looks: Race and Representation,* 115–131. Boston: South End, 1992.

Horak, Jan-Christopher. *Lovers of Cinema: The First American Film Avant-Garde, 1919–1945.* Madison: Univ. of Wisconsin Press, 1995.

Horne, Gerald. *Class Struggle in Hollywood, 1930–1950: Moguls, Mobsters, Stars, Reds, and Trade Unionists.* Austin: Univ. of Texas Press, 2001.

Howard, Clifford. "American Tendencies." *Close Up* 9, no. 4 (December 1932): 285–286.

———. "The Coming Revolution." *Close Up* 8, no. 3 (September 1931): 214–218.

Howard, June. *Form and History in American Literary Naturalism.* Chapel Hill: Univ. of North Carolina Press, 1985.

Hurwitz, Leo. "One's Man Voyage: Ideas and Films in the 1930s." In Platt, *Celluloid Power,* 261–281.

———. "Survey of Workers Films." *New Theatre,* October 1934, 27–28.

Hurwitz, Leo, and Ralph Steiner. "A New Approach to Film Making." *New Theatre,* September 1935, 22–23.

Hutchins, Grace. "Feminists and the Left Wing." *New Masses,* November 20, 1934, 14–15.

———. "Women under Capitalism." In Nekola and Rabinowitz, *Writing Red,* 329–334.

Hutchinson, George. *The Harlem Renaissance in Black and White.* Cambridge, Mass.: Harvard Univ. Press, 1995.

Jacobs, Lea. *The Wages of Sin: Censorship and the Fallen Woman Film, 1928–1942.* Berkeley and Los Angeles: Univ. of California Press, 1995.

Jacobs, Lewis. *The Rise of the American Film: A Critical History.* New York: Teachers College Press, 1967.

Jameson, Fredric. *The Political Unconscious: Narrative as a Socially Symbolic Act.* Ithaca, N.Y.: Cornell Univ. Press, 1981.

———. "Reification and Utopia in Mass Culture." In *The Jameson Reader,* edited by Michael Hardt and Kathi Weeks, 123–148. Oxford: Blackwell, 2000.

———. *A Singular Modernity: Essays on the Ontology of the Present.* New York: Verso, 2002.

Jensen, Paul M. *The Cinema of Fritz Lang.* New York: International Film Guide Series, 1969.

Johnston, Denis. Review of *Chapayev. Film Art* 2, no. 6 (Autumn 1935): 78, 81.

Kaes, Anthony. "A Stranger in the House: Fritz Lang's *Fury* and the Cinema of Exile." *New German Critique* 89 (Summer–Spring 2003), 33–58.

Kaplan, E. Ann. "Classical Hollywood Film and Melodrama." In *The Oxford Guide to Film Studies,* edited by John Hill and Pamela Church Gibson, 272–282. New York: Oxford Univ. Press, 1998.

Kelley, Robin D.G. *Freedom Dreams: The Black Radical Imagination.* Boston: Beacon, 2002.

———. *Hammer and Hoe: Alabama Communists during the Great Depression.* Chapel Hill: Univ. of North Carolina Press, 1990.

———. *Race Rebels: Culture, Politics, and the Black Working Class.* New York: Free Press, 1994.

Kimmel, Michael. *Manhood in America: A Cultural History.* New York: Free Press, 1996.

King, James. "Mrs. Roosevelt Will Not Speak." *New Masses,* May 28, 1935, 9–12.

Kirschke, Amy Helene. *Art in Crisis.* Bloomington: Indiana Univ. Press, 2007.

Kleberg, Lars, and Håkan Lövgren, eds. *Eisenstein Revisited: A Collection of Essays.* Stockholm: Almqvist and Wiksell, 1987.

Klehr, Harvey. *The Heyday of American Communism: The Depression Decade.* New York: Basic Books, 1984.

Koppes, Clayton R., and Gregory D. Black. *Hollywood Goes to War: How Politics, Profits, and Propaganda Shaped World War II.* Berkeley and Los Angeles: Univ. of California Press, 1990.

Kramer, Peter. "Post-classical Hollywood." In *The Oxford Guide to Film Studies*, edited by John Hill and Pamela Church Gibson, 289–309. New York: Oxford Univ. Press, 1998.

Landay, Lori. "The Flapper Film: Comedy, Dance, and Jazz Age Kinaesthetic." In *A Feminist Reader in Early Cinema*, edited by Jennifer Bean and Diane Negra, 221–248. Durham, N.C.: Duke Univ. Press, 2002.

Lang, Fritz. *Fritz Lang: Interviews*. Edited by Barry Keith Grant. Jackson: Univ. of Mississippi Press, 2003.

———. "Interview with Fritz Lang." By Charles Higham and Joel Greenberg. In *Fritz Lang: Interviews*, 101–126.

———. "The Viennese Night: A Fritz Lang Confession, Parts One and Two." Interview by Gretchen Berg. In *Fritz Lang: Interviews*, 50–76.

Lapidus, Gail Warshofsky. *Women in Soviet Society: Equality, Development, and Social Change*. Berkeley and Los Angeles: Univ. of California Press, 1978.

LaValley, Al. "Maintaining, Blurring, and Transcending Gender Lines in Eisenstein." In LaValley and Scherr, *Eisenstein at 100*, 52–64.

LaValley, Al, and Barry P. Scherr, eds. *Eisenstein at 100: A Reconsideration*. New Brunswick, N.J.: Rutgers Univ. Press, 2001.

Lawson, John Howard. "Banning of *Blockade* Threatens Freedom of the Screen in America." *Theatre Arts Committee*, July 1938, 5.

Leach, William. *Land of Desire: Merchants, Power, and the Rise of a New American Culture*. New York: Vintage, 1993.

Lee, Rohama. "World Cinema: The Brandon Story." *Film News* 28, no. 3 (1971): 18.

L.E.H. "Hollywood Letter: Role of the Negro in American Films." *Daily Worker*, August 14, 1933.

Lerner, Irving. "Glorified Horse Opera." *New Masses*, June 12, 1934, 29–30.

———. "The Screen." *New Masses*, January 16, 1934, 30.

Le Sueur, Meridel. "I Was Marching." *New Masses*, September 18, 1934, 16–18.

———. "Women Are Hungry." In *Ripening: Selected Work, 1927–1980*, 144–157. New York: Feminist Press, 1982.

———. "Women on the Breadlines." *New Masses*, January 1932, 5–7.

Locke, Edwin. "John Ford's *The Grapes of Wrath*." In Platt, *Celluloid Power*, 316–323.

Lorentz, Pare. "*The Grapes of Wrath*." In *Lorentz on Film: Movies 1927–1941*, 183–186. Norman: Univ. of Oklahoma Press, 1975.

———. "*Thunder over Mexico*." In *Lorentz on Film: Movies 1927–1941*, 118–120. Norman: Univ. of Oklahoma Press, 1975.

Lounsbury, Myron Osborn. *The Origins of American Film Criticism, 1909–1939*. New York: Arno, 1973.

Lövgren, Håkan. "Trauma and Ecstasy: Aesthetic Compounds in Dr. Eisenstein's Laboratory." In Kleberg and Lövgren, *Eisenstein Revisited*, 93–111.

Lugowski, David M. "Queering the (New) Deal: Lesbian and Gay Representations and the Depression-Era Cultural Politics of Hollywood's Production Code." *Cinema Journal* 38, no. 2 (Winter 1999): 3–35.

———. "'A Treatise on Decay': Liberal and Leftist Critics and Their Queer Readings of Depression-Era U.S. Film." In *Looking Past the Screen: Case Studies in American Film History,* edited by Jon Lewis and Eric Smoodin, 276–300. Durham: Duke Univ. Press, 2007.

Lukács, Georg. "The Ideology of Modernism." In *Marxism and Human Liberation,* edited by E. San Juan, Jr., 277–307. New York: Delta, 1973.

———. "The Marxism of Rosa Luxemburg." Translated by Rodney Livingstone. In *History and Class Consciousness,* 27–45. Cambridge, Mass.: MIT Press, 1971.

———. "What Is Orthodox Marxism?" Translated by Rodney Livingstone. In *History and Class Consciousness,* 1–26. Cambridge, Mass.: MIT Press, 1971.

Lumpkin, Grace. *To Make My Bread.* New York: Macaulay, 1932.

Lunn, Eugene. *Marxism and Modernism: An Historical Study of Lukács, Brecht, Benjamin, and Adorno.* Berkeley and Los Angeles: Univ. of California Press, 1984.

Macdonald, Dwight. "The Soviet Cinema: 1930–1938." *Partisan Review,* June–July 1938, 37–50.

———. "The Soviet Cinema: 1930–1938, Part II." *Partisan Review,* August–September 1938, 35–62.

———. "Soviet Society and Its Cinema." *Partisan Review,* Winter 1939, 80–95.

Macpherson, Kenneth. "As Is." *Close Up* 5, no. 2 (August 1929): 89–90.

Magil, A. B., and Henry Stevens. *The Perils of Fascism: The Crisis of American Democracy.* New York: International Publishers, 1938.

Maltz, Albert. "Four Million Dollars Worth of Wind." In Platt, *Celluloid Power,* 324–327.

Marcus, Laura. "Introduction to Part 4." In Donald, Friedberg, and Marcus, *"Close Up," 1927–1933,* 150–159.

Mast, Gerald, Marshall Cohen, and Leo Braudy, eds. *Film Theory and Criticism: Introductory Readings.* 4th ed. New York: Oxford Univ. Press, 1992.

Maxwell, William J. *New Negro, Old Left: African-American Writing and Communism between the Wars.* New York: Columbia Univ. Press, 1999.

Mayne, Judith. *Kino and the Woman Question: Feminism and Soviet Silent Film.* Columbus: Ohio State Univ. Press, 1989.

———. "Marlene Dietrich, *The Blue Angel,* and Female Performance." In *Seduction and Theory: Readings of Gender, Representation, and Rhetoric,* edited by Dianne Hunter, 28–46. Urbana: Univ. of Illinois Press, 1989.

———. *The Woman at the Keyhole: Feminism and Women's Cinema.* Bloomington: Indiana Univ. Press, 1990.

McGilligan, Patrick. *Fritz Lang: The Nature of the Beast.* New York: St. Martin's, 1997.

———. *Oscar Micheaux, the Great and Only: The Life of America's First Great Black Filmmaker.* New York: Regan Books, 2007.

Melosh, Barbara. *Engendering Culture: Manhood and Womanhood in New Deal Public Art and Theater.* Washington, D.C.: Smithsonian Institute Press, 1991.

Mennel, Barbara. "White Law and the Missing Black Body in Fritz Lang's *Fury.*" *Quarterly Review of Film and Video* 20, no. 3 (January 2003): 203–223.

Midgley, David. "Communism and the Avant-Garde: The Case of Georg Lukács." In *Visions and Blueprints: Avant-Garde Culture and Radical Politics in Early Twentieth-Century Europe,* edited by Edward Timms and Peter Collier, 52–65. Manchester: Manchester Univ. Press, 1989.

Miller, Loren. "Uncle Tom in Hollywood." *Crisis,* November 1934, 329, 336.

Millet, Martha. "Last Night." *New Masses,* June 19, 1934, 17.

Modleski, Tania. "Femininity as Mas[s]querade: A Feminist Approach to Mass Culture." In *High Theory/Low Culture: Analyzing Popular Television and Film,* edited by Colin MacCabe, 37–52. New York: St. Martin's, 1986.

Morey, Anne. *Hollywood Outsiders: The Adaptation of the Film Industry, 1913–1934.* Minneapolis: Univ. of Minnesota Press, 2003.

Muenzenberg, Willi. "Capture the Film!" *Daily Worker,* July 23, 1925.

———. "The Film Activity of the IWA." *Daily Worker,* October 10, 1925.

———. "The Picture and the Film in the Revolutionary Moment." *Daily Worker,* August 15, 1925.

———. "The Presentation of Proletarian Films." *Daily Worker,* September 26, 1925.

———. "The Role of Moving Pictures in the Labor Movement." *Daily Worker,* September 1, 1925.

Mullen, Bill, and Sherry Linkon, eds. *Radical Revisions: Rereading 1930s Culture.* Urbana: Univ. of Illinois Press, 1996.

Mulvey, Laura. "Visual Pleasure and Narrative Cinema." In Erens, *Issues in Feminist Film Criticism,* 28–40.

Murphy, James F. *The Proletarian Moment: The Controversy over Leftism in Literature.* Urbana: Univ. of Illinois Press, 1991.

Nekola, Charlotte, and Paula Rabinowitz, eds. *Writing Red: An Anthology of American Women Writers, 1930–1940.* New York: Feminist Press, 1987.

Nelson, Cary. *Repression and Recovery: Modern American Poetry and the Politics of Cultural Memory, 1910–1945.* Madison: Univ. of Wisconsin Press, 1989.

New York Amsterdam News, "All that Glitters," October 5, 1932.

———, "Soviet Seeks Negroes to Make Film of Conditions Here," March 9, 1932.

New York Times, "Group Plans Films to Aid Democracy," November 15, 1938.

Nizhny, Vladimir. *Lessons with Eisenstein.* Edited and translated by Ivor Montagu and Jay Leyda. New York: Da Capo, 1969.

North, Joseph. "The New Hollywood." *New Masses,* July 11, 1939, 14, 17–18.

———. "Renaissance in Hollywood?" *New Masses,* July 4, 1939, 3–6.

Nugent, Frank S. "*Fury,* a Dramatic Indictment of Lynch Law, Opens at Capitol." *New York Times,* June 6, 1936.

Olsen, Tillie. *Yonnondio: From the Thirties.* New York: Delacorte, 1974.

O'Malley, Alfred. "*Blockade*." *Daily Worker*, n.d.

O'Shaughnessy, Martin. *Jean Renoir*. Manchester, UK: Manchester Univ. Press, 2000.

Parker, Dorothy. "On Movie Writers and the 'Want-to-be-Alone' Spirits." *Daily Worker*, August 8, 1937.

Parker, Tyler. *Screening the Sexes: Homosexuality in the Movies*. New York: Da Capo, 1993.

Paz, Octavio. *The Labyrinth of Solitude, and Other Writings*. New York: Grove, 1985.

Peabody, Stephen. "Inquiring Reporter Learns Why Film Crowd Cheers *Confessions of a Nazi Spy*." *Daily Worker*, May 5, 1939.

Peck, David. "New Masses." In Buhle, Buhle, and Georgakas, *Encyclopedia of the American Left*, 526–527.

Peiss, Kathy. *Cheap Amusements: Working Women and Leisure in Turn-of-the-Century New York*. Philadelphia: Temple Univ. Press, 1986.

Petro, Patrice. "Mass Culture and the Feminine: The 'Place' of Television in Film Studies." In *Film and Theory: An Anthology*, edited by Robert Stam and Toby Miller, 577–593. Malden, Mass.: Blackwell, 2000.

Pickens, William. "Why the Negro Must Be Anti-Fascist." *New Masses*, May 30, 1939, 11.

Pierce, David H. "Fascism and the Negro." *Crisis*, April 1935, 107, 114.

———. "The Negro and the Jew." *Crisis*, July 1934, 107, 114.

Pitts, Rebecca. "Women and Communism." *New Masses*, February 19, 1935, 14–18.

Plant, Richard Rene. "Jean Renoir." *Theatre Arts Monthly* 23, no. 6 (1939): 429–435.

Platt, David, ed. *Celluloid Power: Social Film Criticism from "The Birth of a Nation" to "Judgment at Nuremburg."* Metuchen, N.J.: Scarecrow, 1992.

———. "Focus and Mechanism." *Experimental Cinema*, February 1930, 2–3.

———. "*Life of Emile Zola* Is Brilliant Biography and Social Document." *Daily Worker*, August 14, 1937.

———. "Progressive Films Take over Silver Screens of Hollywood." *Daily Worker*, August 29, 1937.

———. Review of *Chapayev*. *Filmfront*, January 28, 1935, 17–18.

———. "*They Won't Forget* Rivals *Fury* in Social Content." *Daily Worker*, May 21, 1937.

Polan, Dana. *Scenes of Instruction: The Beginnings of the U.S. Study of Film*. Berkeley and Los Angeles: Univ. of California Press, 2007.

Potamkin, Harry Alan. "'A' in the Art of the Movie and Kino." *New Masses*, December 1929, 14.

———. "The Aframerican Cinema." *Close Up* 5, no. 2 (August 1929): 107–117.

———. "Carl Dreyer's *The Passion of Jeanne D'Arc*." In Platt, *Celluloid Power*, 163–167.

———. *The Compound Cinema: The Film Writings of Harry Alan Potamkin*. Edited by Lewis Jacobs. New York: Teachers College Press, 1977.

———. "Eisenstein and the Theory of Cinema." In *The Compound Cinema*, 434–445.

———. "The Eyes of the Movie." In *The Compound Cinema*, 243–269.

———. "Film Novitiates, Etc." *Close Up* 7, no. 5 (November 1930): 315–324.

———. "Film Problems of Soviet Russia." In *The Compound Cinema*, 310–312.

———. "First Films." In *The Compound Cinema*, 144–146.

———. "Lost Paradise: *Tabu*." *Creative Art* 8 (June 1931): 462–463.

———. "Novel into Film: A Case Study of Current Practice." In *The Compound Cinema*, 186–196.

———. "The Ritual of the Movies." In *The Compound Cinema*, 216–222.

———. "Tendencies in the Cinema." In *The Compound Cinema*, 43–46.

———. "The Year of Eclipse." In *The Compound Cinema*, 201–207.

Preece, Harold. "Fascism and the Negro." *Crisis*, December 1934, 355, 366.

Pudovkin, V. I. *Film Technique and Film Acting: The Cinema Writings of V. I. Pudovkin*. Translated by Ivor Montagu. Sims Press, 2007.

Rabinovitz, Lauren. *For the Lover of Pleasure: Women, Movies, and Culture in Turn-of-the-Century Chicago*. New Brunswick, N.J.: Rutgers Univ. Press, 1998.

Rabinowitz, Paula. *Labor and Desire: Women's Revolutionary Fiction in Depression America*. Chapel Hill: Univ. of North Carolina Press, 1991.

———. *They Must Be Represented: The Politics of Documentary*. London: Verso, 1994.

———. "Women and U.S. Literary Radicalism." In Nekola and Rabinowitz, *Writing Red*, 1–16.

Ramsey, David. "A New Deal in Trusts." *New Masses*, January 9, 1934, 17–18.

Regester, Charlene. "The African-American Press and Race Movies, 1909–1929." In *Oscar Micheaux and His Circle*, edited by Pearl Bowser, Jane Gaines, and Charles Musser, 34–49. Bloomington: Indiana Univ. Press, 2001.

Renoir, Jean. *My Life and My Films*. Translated by Norman Denny. New York: Da Capo, 1974.

Richardson, Dorothy. "The Cinema in Arcady." In Donald, Friedberg, and Marcus, *"Close Up," 1927–1933*, 184–186.

———. "The Cinema in the Slums." In Donald, Friedberg, and Marcus, *"Close Up," 1927–1933*, 180–181.

———. "Continuous Performance." In Donald, Friedberg, and Marcus, *"Close Up," 1927–1933*, 160–161.

———. "The Film Gone Male." In Donald, Friedberg, and Marcus, *"Close Up," 1927–1933*, 205–207.

———. "Narcissus." In Donald, Friedberg, and Marcus, *"Close Up," 1927–1933*, 201–203.

———. "This Spoon-Fed Generation?" In Donald, Friedberg, and Marcus, *"Close Up," 1927–1933*, 203–205.

———. "The Thoroughly Popular Film." In Donald, Friedberg, and Marcus, *"Close Up," 1927–1933*, 177–179.

Rideout, Walter B. *The Radical Novel in the United States, 1900–1954*. New York: Hill and Wang, 1966.

R.O. "Reviewer Acclaims New Film: Calls *Fury* Worthy Indictment of Mob Violence in U.S." *New York Amsterdam News,* June 13, 1936.

Robinson, Cedric J. *Black Marxism: The Making of the Black Radical Tradition*. Chapel Hill: Univ. of North Carolina Press, 2000.

———. *Forgeries of Memory and Meaning: Blacks and the Regimes of Race in American Theater and Film before World War II*. Chapel Hill: Univ. of North Carolina Press, 2007.

Roddick, Nick. *A New Deal in Entertainment: Warner Brothers in the 1930s*. London: BFI, 1983.

Roediger, David R. *The Wages of Whiteness: Race and the Making of the American Working Class*. New York: Verso, 1991.

———. *Working toward Whiteness: How America's Immigrants Became White*. New York: Basic Books, 2005.

Rosen, Philip. "Eisenstein's Marxism, Marxism's Eisenstein." A talk given at the Society for Cinema and Media Studies, Philadelphia, Penn., March 6–9, 2008.

Rosenfelt, Deborah. "From the Thirties: Tillie Olsen and the Radical Tradition." In *The Critical Response to Tillie Olsen*, edited by Kay Hoyle Nelson and Nancy Huse, 54–89. Westport, Conn.: Greenwood, 1994.

Ross, Andrew. *No Respect: Intellectuals and Popular Culture*. New York: Routledge, 1989.

Ross, Murray. *Stars and Strikes: Unionization of Hollywood*. New York: AMS, 1941.

Rosten, Leo. C. *Hollywood: The Movie Colony, the Movie Makers*. New York: Arno, 1970.

Rubin, Martin. "The Crowd, the Collective, and the Chorus: Busby Berkeley and the New Deal." In Belton, *Movies and Mass Culture*, 59–92.

Sachs, Hanns. "Film Psychology." In Donald, Friedberg, and Marcus, *"Close Up," 1927–1933*, 250–254.

———. "Kitsch." *Close Up* 9, no. 3 (September 1932): 200–205.

Salazkina, Masha. *In Excess: Eisenstein's Mexico*. Chicago: Univ. of Chicago Press, 2009.

Sarris, Andrew. *The American Cinema: Directors and Directions, 1929–1968*. Chicago: Univ. of Chicago Press, 1986.

Schatz, Thomas. *The Genius of the System: Hollywood Filmmaking in the Studio Era*. New York: Metropolitan, 1988.

Schindler, Colin. *Hollywood in Crisis: Cinema and American Society, 1929–1939*. London: Routledge, 1996.

Schwartz, Lawrence H. *Marxism and Culture: The CPUSA and Aesthetics in the 1930s*. New York: Authors Choice Press, 2000.

Schwartz, Nancy Lynn. *The Hollywood Writers' Wars*. New York: Knopf, 1982.

Seton, Marie. *Sergei M. Eisenstein.* New York: Grove, 1960.

———. Review of *Thunder over Mexico, Film Art,* Spring 1934, 21–22.

Shohat, Ella, and Robert Stam. *Unthinking Eurocentrism: Multiculturalism and the Media.* London: Routledge, 1994.

Silverman, Kaja. "Dis-Embodying the Female Voice." In Erens, *Issues in Feminist Film Criticism,* 309–327.

———. *The Threshold of the Visible World.* New York: Routledge, 1996.

Sinclair, Upton. *"Thunder over Mexico:* Mr. Upton Sinclair Defends Himself." *Close Up* 10, no. 4 (December 1933): 361–363.

Singer, Ben. *Melodrama and Modernity: Early Sensational Cinema and Its Contexts.* New York: Columbia Univ. Press, 2001.

———. "Modernity, Hyperstimulus, and the Rise of Popular Sensationalism." In *Cinema and the Invention of Modern Life,* edited by Leo Charney and Vanessa R. Schwartz, 72–102. Berkeley and Los Angeles: Univ. of California Press, 1995.

Sklar, Robert. *Movie-Made America: A Cultural History of American Movies.* New York: Vintage, 1975.

Smedley, Agnes. *Daughter of Earth.* New York: Feminist Press, 1973.

Smedley, Nick. "Fritz Lang's Trilogy: The Rise and Fall of a European Social Commentator." *Film History* 5 (1995): 1–21.

Smith, Greg. M. "Blocking *Blockade:* Partisan Protest, Popular Debate, and Encapsulated Texts." *Cinema Journal* 36, no. 1 (Fall 1996): 18–38.

Solomon, Mark. *The Cry Was Unity: Communism and African Americans, 1917–1936.* Jackson: Univ. of Mississippi Press, 1998.

Sowinska, Suzanne. "Writing across the Color Line: White Women Writers and the 'Negro Question' in the Gastonia Novels." In *Radical Revisions: Reading 1930s Culture,* edited by Bill Mullen and Sherry Linkon, 120–143. Urbana: Univ. of Illinois Press, 1996.

Spivak, John L. "Plotting the American Pogroms." *New Masses,* October 2, 1934, 9–13; October 9, 1934, 9–13; October 16, 1934, 9–12; October 23, 1934, 10–13; October 30, 1934, 9–13; November 6, 1934, 9–12; November 13, 1934, 8–11; November 20, 1934, 9–13; November 27, 1934, 10–12.

———. "Wall Street's Conspiracy: Testimony That the Dickstein Committee Suppressed." *New Masses,* January 29, 1935, 9–15; and February 5, 1935, 10–15.

———. "Who Backs the Black Legion?" *New Masses,* June 16, 1936, 9–10.

Staiger, Janet. *Bad Women: Regulating Sexuality in Early American Cinema.* Minneapolis: Univ. of Minnesota Press, 1995.

Stamp, Shelley. *Movie-Struck Girls: Women and Motion Picture Culture after the Nickelodeon.* Princeton, N.J.: Princeton Univ. Press, 2000.

Stavis, Barbara. "Sights and Sounds: French Social Films." *New Masses,* May 2, 1939, 28.

Stebbins, Robert. "Fritz Lang and *Fury." New Theatre,* July 1936, 11.

———. "Hollywood's Imitation of Life." *New Theatre,* July 1935, 8–9.

Steedman, Carolyn Kay. *Landscape for a Good Woman: A Story of Two Lives*. New Brunswick, N.J.: Rutgers Univ. Press, 1986.

Stern, Seymour. "The Bankruptcy of Cinema as Art." In *The Movies on Trial: The Views and Opinions of Outstanding Personalities anent Screen Entertainment Past and Present,* edited by William J. Perlman, 113–140. New York: Macmillan, 1936.

———. "Cinema Notes of the Quarter." *Left* 1, no. 2 (Summer–Autumn 1931): 77–82.

———. "Eisenstein in Mexico." *Experimental Cinema,* February 1931, 22.

———. "The Greatest Thing Done on This Side of the Atlantic." *Modern Monthly* 7, no. 9 (October 1933): 525–532.

———. "Hollywood and Montage." *Experimental Cinema,* February 1933, 47–52.

———. "Introduction to *Que Viva Mexico!*" *Experimental Cinema,* February 1934, 3–4.

———. "Second Manifesto by the Editors of *Experimental Cinema.*" *Close Up,* 10, no. 2 (September 1933): 248–254.

Stites, Richard. *The Women's Liberation Movement in Russia: Feminism, Nihilism, and Bolshevism, 1860–1930.* Princeton, N.J.: Princeton Univ. Press, 1978.

Strachey, John. "Fascism in America." *New Masses,* January 2, 1934, 8, 10.

Studlar, Gaylyn. *In the Realm of Pleasure: Von Sternberg, Dietrich, and the Masochistic Aesthetic.* New York: Columbia Univ. Press, 1988.

Sylvers, Malcolm. "Popular Front." In Buhle, Buhle, and Georgakas, *Encyclopedia of the American Left,* 591–595.

Taylor, Greg. *Artists in the Audience: Cults, Camp, and American Film Criticism.* Princeton, N.J.: Princeton Univ. Press, 1999.

Taylor, John Russell. *Strangers in Paradise: The Hollywood Émigrés, 1933–1950.* New York: Holt, Rinehart and Winston, 1983.

Thompson, Louise. "The Soviet Film." *Crisis,* February 1937, 37, 46.

Thorp, Margaret Farrand. *America at the Movies.* New Haven, Conn.: Yale Univ. Press, 1939.

Tonecky, Zygmunt. "The Preliminary of Film Art." *Close Up* 8, no. 3 (September 1931): 193–200.

Trachtenberg, Alan. *The Incorporation of America: Culture and Society in the Gilded Age.* New York: Wang and Hill, 1982.

Troy, William. "Collectivism More or Less." *Nation,* October 24, 1934, 488, 490.

———. "The Eisenstein Muddle." *Nation,* July 19, 1933, 83–84.

———. "Half a Loaf." *Nation,* April 24, 1935, 491–492.

———. "The Marquis de Villa." *Nation,* May 2, 1934, 516, 518.

———. "Russia a la Mode." *Nation,* October 3, 1934, 392.

———. "Selections from Eisenstein." *Nation,* October 4, 1933, 391–392.

Tyler, Bruce M. *From Harlem to Hollywood: The Struggle for Racial and Cultural Democracy, 1920–1943.* New York: Garland, 1992.

Vasey, Ruth. *The World according to Hollywood, 1918–1939*. Madison: Univ. of Wisconsin Press, 1997.

Vertov, Dziga. *Kino-Eye: The Writings of Dziga Vertov*. Edited by Annette Michelson. Berkeley and Los Angeles: Univ. of California Press, 1984.

Vorse, Mary Heaton. "Lauren Gilfillan's Education." *New Masses*, April 10, 1934, 16.

Wald, Alan. *Exiles from a Future Time: The Forging of the Mid-Twentieth Century Literary Left*. Chapel Hill: Univ. of North Carolina Press, 2002.

———. *The New York Intellectuals: The Rise and Decline of the Anti-Stalinist Left from the 1930s to the 1980s*. Chapel Hill: Univ. of North Carolina Press, 1987.

———. *Trinity of Passion: The Literary Left and the Antifascist Crusade*. Chapel Hill: Univ. of North Carolina Press, 2007.

Waldrep, Christopher. *The Many Faces of Judge Lynch: Extralegal Violence and Punishment in America*. New York: Palgrave Macmillan, 2002.

Wasson, Haidee. *Museum Movies: The Museum of Modern Art and the Birth of Art Cinema*. Berkeley and Los Angeles: Univ. of California Press, 2005.

Watkins, T. H. *The Great Depression: America in the 1930s*. Boston: Back Bay, 1993.

Waugh, Thomas. "A Fag-Spotters Guide to Eisenstein." In *The Fruit Machine: Twenty Years of Writing on Queer Cinema*, 59–68. Durham, N.C.: Duke Univ. Press, 2000.

Weatherwax, Jack. "Hollywood Says *Confessions of a Nazi Spy* Will Be a Powerful Film." *Daily Worker*, April 14, 1939.

Weinberg, Herman G. "The 'Lesser' of Two Evils." *Modern Monthly* 7, no. 5 (June 1933): 299–301, 311.

Weinstein, Jacob J. "The Negro and the Jew." *Crisis*, July 1934, 197–198.

White, Robert. "The Screen." *New Masses*, December 1, 1936, 28.

Williams, Raymond. *Marxism and Literature*. Oxford: Oxford Univ. Press, 1977.

Winter, Ella. "Woman Freed." In Nekola and Rabinowitz, *Writing Red*, 228–235.

Wollen, Peter. "The Two Avant-Gardes." *Screen* 190, no. 978 (November–December 1975): 171–175.

Workers Film and Photo League. "The Thunder Dies." *New Masses*, January 22, 1934, 21.

Wright, Richard. *Native Son*. New York: Harper Perennial, 1940.

Youngblood, Denise J. *Movies for the Masses: Popular Cinema and Soviet Society in the 1920s*. New York: Cambridge Univ. Press, 1992.

———. *Soviet Cinema in the Silent Era, 1918–1936*. Austin: Univ. of Texas Press, 1991.

Index

Lightning Source UK Ltd.
Milton Keynes UK
UKOW03f0234140614

233414UK00001B/85/P